Lecture Notes in Computer Science   9933

Commenced Publication in 1973
Founding and Former Series Editors:
Gerhard Goos, Juris Hartmanis, and Jan van Leeuwen

Maurice H. ter Beek · Stefania Gnesi
Alexander Knapp (Eds.)

Critical Systems: Formal Methods and Automated Verification

Joint 21st International Workshop
on Formal Methods for Industrial Critical Systems and
16th International Workshop
on Automated Verification of Critical Systems, FMICS-AVoCS 2016
Pisa, Italy, September 26–28, 2016
Proceedings

 Springer

Editors
Maurice H. ter Beek
ISTI-CNR
Pisa
Italy

Stefania Gnesi
ISTI-CNR
Pisa
Italy

Alexander Knapp
Universität Augsburg
Augsburg
Germany

ISSN 0302-9743   ISSN 1611-3349 (electronic)
Lecture Notes in Computer Science
ISBN 978-3-319-45942-4   ISBN 978-3-319-45943-1 (eBook)
DOI 10.1007/978-3-319-45943-1

Library of Congress Control Number: 2016950740

LNCS Sublibrary: SL2 – Programming and Software Engineering

Printed on acid-free paper

This Springer imprint is published by Springer Nature
The registered company is Springer International Publishing AG
The registered company address is: Gewerbestrasse 11, 6330 Cham, Switzerland

Preface

This volume contains the papers presented at the International Workshop on Formal Methods for Industrial Critical Systems and Automated Verification of Critical Systems (FMICS-AVoCS), which was held in Pisa, Italy, September 26–28, 2016. FMICS-AVoCS 2016 combines the 21st International Workshop on Formal Methods for Industrial Critical Systems and the 16th International Workshop on Automated Verification of Critical Systems.

The aim of the FMICS workshop series is to provide a forum for researchers who are interested in the development and application of formal methods in industry. In particular, FMICS brings together scientists and engineers that are active in the area of formal methods and interested in exchanging their experiences in the industrial usage of these methods. The FMICS workshop series also strives to promote research and development for the improvement of formal methods and tools for industrial applications.

The aim of the AVoCS workshop series is to contribute to the interaction and exchange of ideas among members of the international research community on tools and techniques for the verification of critical systems. The subject is to be interpreted broadly and inclusively. It covers all aspects of automated verification, including model checking, theorem proving, SAT/SMT constraint solving, abstract interpretation, and refinement pertaining to various types of critical systems that need to meet stringent dependability requirements (safety-critical, business-critical, performance-critical, etc.).

The topics of interest include, but are not limited to:

- Design, specification, refinement, code generation, and testing of critical systems based on formal methods
- Methods, techniques, and tools to support automated analysis, certification, debugging, learning, optimization, and transformation of critical systems, in particular distributed, real-time systems, and embedded systems
- Automated verification (model checking, theorem proving, SAT/SMT constraint solving, abstract interpretation, etc.) of critical systems
- Verification and validation methods that address shortcomings of existing methods with respect to their industrial applicability (e.g., scalability and usability issues)
- Tools for the development of formal design descriptions
- Case studies and experience reports on industrial applications of formal methods, focusing on lessons learned or identification of new research directions
- Impact of the adoption of formal methods on the development process and associated costs
- Application of formal methods in standardization and industrial forums

This year we received 24 submissions. Each of these submissions went through a rigorous review process in which each paper was reviewed by at least three researchers from a strong Program Committee of international reputation. We selected 11 full papers and 4 short papers for presentation during the workshop and inclusion in these proceedings. The workshop also featured keynotes by Thomas Arts (QuviQ AB, Gothenburg, Sweden), Silvia Mazzini (Intecs SpA, Pisa, Italy), and Jan Peleska (Universität Bremen, Germany). We hereby thank the invited speakers for having accepted our invitation.

We are very grateful to our sponsors, the European Research Consortium for Informatics and Mathematics (ERCIM), Formal Methods Europe (FME), and Springer International Publishing AG. We thank Alfred Hofmann (Vice-President Publishing) and the Editorial staff of Springer for publishing these proceedings. We also thank Tiziana Margaria (University of Limerick & LERO, the Irish Software Research Center, Ireland), the coordinator of the ERCIM working group FMICS, and the other board members, as well as the steering committee of AVoCS, all listed below, for their continuous support during the organization of FMICS-AVoCS. We acknowledge the support of EasyChair for assisting us in managing the complete process from submission to these proceedings.

Finally, we would like to thank the Program Committee members and the external reviewers, listed below, for their accurate and timely reviewing, all authors for their submissions, and all attendees of the workshop for their participation.

July 2016

Maurice ter Beek
Stefania Gnesi
Alexander Knapp

Organization

General Chair

Maurice H. ter Beek   ISTI–CNR, Pisa, Italy

Program Committee Co-chairs

Stefania Gnesi   ISTI–CNR, Pisa, Italy
Alexander Knapp   Universität Augsburg, Germany

Program Committee

Maria Alpuente	Universitat Politècnica de Valéncia, Spain
Jiri Barnat	Masarykova Univerzita, Czech Republic
Michael Dierkes	Rockwell Collins, Blagnac, France
Cindy Eisner	IBM Research, Haifa, Israel
Alessandro Fantechi	Università di Firenze, Italy
Francesco Flammini	Ansaldo STS, Naples, Italy
María del Mar Gallardo	Universidad de Málaga, Spain
Michael Goldsmith	University of Oxford, UK
Gudmund Grov	Heriot Watt University, UK
Matthias Güdemann	Diffblue Ltd., Oxford, UK
Marieke Huisman	Universiteit Twente, The Netherlands
Gerwin Klein	NICTA and University of New South Wales, Australia
Peter Gorm Larsen	Aarhus Universitet, Denmark
Thierry Lecomte	ClearSy, Aix-en-Provence, France
Tiziana Margaria	University of Limerick and LERO, Ireland
Radu Mateescu	Inria Grenoble Rhône-Alpes, France
David Mentré	Mitsubishi Electric R&D Centre Europe, Rennes, France
Stephan Merz	Inria Nancy and LORIA, France
Manuel Núñez	Universidad Complutense de Madrid, Spain
Peter Ölveczky	Universitetet i Oslo, Norway
Charles Pecheur	Université Catholique de Louvain, Belgium
Marielle Petit-Doche	Systerel, Aix-en-Provence, France
Ralf Pinger	Siemens AG, Braunschweig, Germany
Jaco van de Pol	Universiteit Twente, The Netherlands
Markus Roggenbach	Swansea University, UK
Matteo Rossi	Politecnico di Milano, Italy
Marco Roveri	FBK-irst, Trento, Italy

Thomas Santen	Microsoft Research Advanced Technology Labs Europe, Aachen, Germany
Bernhard Steffen	Universität Dortmund, Germany
Jun Sun	University of Technology and Design, Singapore
Helen Treharne	University of Surrey, UK

Additional Reviewers

Joël Allred	Laura Panizo
Jaroslav Bendík	Enno Ruijters
Marco Bozzano	Alberto Salmerón
Ning Gee	Julia Sapiña
Stefan Hallerstede	Wendelin Serwe

FMICS WG Board Members

Álvaro Arenas	IE Business School, Madrid, Spain
Luboš Brim	Masarykova Univerzita, Czech Republic
Alessandro Fantechi	Università di Firenze, Italy
Hubert Garavel	Inria Grenoble Rhône-Alpes, France
Stefania Gnesi	ISTI–CNR, Pisa, Italy
Diego Latella	ISTI–CNR, Pisa, Italy
Tiziana Margaria	University of Limerick and LERO, Ireland
Radu Mateescu	Inria Grenoble Rhône-Alpes, France
Pedro Merino	Universidad de Málaga, Spain
Jaco van de Pol	Universiteit Twente, The Netherlands

AVoCS Steering Committee

Michael Goldsmith	University of Oxford, UK
Stephan Merz	Inria Nancy and LORIA, France
Markus Roggenbach	Swansea University, UK

Sponsors

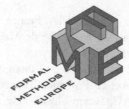

Abstracts of the Invited Talks

Lessons Learned in a Journey Toward Correct-by-Construction Model-Based Development

Laura Baracchi[1], Silvia Mazzini[1], Stefano Puri[1],
and Tullio Vardanega[2]

[1] Intecs SpA, Pisa, Italy
{laura.baracchi,silvia.mazzini,stefano.puri}@intecs.it
[2] Università di Padova, Italy
tullio.vardanega@math.unipd.it

Abstract. In our view, an effective correct-by-construction (CbyC) approach, geared to making it extremely difficult to introduce errors in the software development process, would have two main ingredients: one, the adoption of model-driven engineering (MDE) to manipulate malleable and yet powerful abstractions; the other, rigor at each development step, to enable (possibly automated) formal reasoning or analysis of the correctness of the step, and (possibly automated) derivation, whenever possible, of correct base input for the subsequent step.

We advocate that using models in most of the development steps, supported by adequate MDE techniques and tooling (far more productive today than in the early age of CbyC), makes it easier to define correct requirements, to design a system that meets the requirements, and to develop an implementation that preserves the desired correctness properties. We discuss lessons learned in the attempt to apply the long-known principles of CbyC first promoted by Dijkstra, to modern model-based development practices. We recall the intent and scrutinize the outcomes of a string of research projects that focused explicitly on the pursuit of CbyC by means of model-driven methods and technologies. The lessons learned show that when CbyC extends from the algorithmic and functional dimension to extra-functional concerns, some of the strength of original CbyC concept and its pull dilute. One of the possible causes of that phenomenon, is that — in some situation — the assertive style of algorithm refinement gives way to more tentative exploration of an unknown solution space where the known truths are insuffcient to steer the development.

Keywords: Model-based development · Model transformation · Correctness by construction · Formal methods · Contract refinement

Model-based Testing Strategies and Their (In)dependence on Syntactic Model Representations

Jan Peleska[1,2] and Wen-ling Huang[2]

[1] Verified Systems International GmbH, Bremen, Germany
[2] Department of Mathematics and Computer Science,
University of Bremen, Bremen, Germany
{jp,huang}@cs.uni-bremen.de

Abstract. Model-based testing (MBT) in its most advanced form allows for automated test case identification, test data calculation, and test procedure generation from reference models describing the expected behaviour of the system under test (SUT). If the underlying algorithms for test case identification operate only on the syntactic representation of test models, however, the resulting test strength depends on the syntactic representation as well. This observation is true, even if syntactically differing models are behaviourally equivalent. In this paper, we present a systematic approach to elaborating test case selection strategies that only depend on the behavioural semantics of test models, but are invariant under syntactic transformations preserving the semantics. The benefits of these strategies are discussed, and practical generation algorithms are presented.

Keywords: Model-based testing · Equivalence class partition testing · Kripke structures · Complete testing theories

Random Testing of Formal Properties for Industrial Critical Systems

Thomas Arts

Quviq AB, Gothenburg, Sweden
thomas.arts@quviq.com

Abstract. QuickCheck is a tool that can automatically generate test cases for software systems. These tests are generated from manually specified formal properties or models that the system is supposed to conform to. The set of possible tests for such systems is practically infinite. QuickCheck uses a random selection strategy for generating test cases. Compared to other selection strategies, QuickCheck can very quickly generate tests and more time is spent on testing than on carefully selecting tests; this works best in situations where test execution can be performed in seconds rather than days.

The result is a light-weight method for finding software faults in industrial critical systems in the domain of telecommunication, automotive, database systems, financial systems and medical devices. Compared to many formal methods, this kind of light-weight formal testing is very cost effective for finding faults.

However, if no faults are found, the obvious question is: "how well is the software tested?". We present some results based on measuring coverage. Code coverage is a poor measure for correctness, as will be confirmed for line coverage through MC/DC coverage.

As an alternative we look at requirement coverage and generate test suites that cover all requirements. This again results in very poor fault detection. Even after improving the notion of "covering requirements", we see that random testing detects more faults than carefully constructed tests that cover all requirements.

By giving the user control over defining and measuring what has been tested, we can increase the confidence in the models underlying the test generation. Nevertheless, more research is needed to find satisfactory criteria for sufficient testing.

Contents

Applications and Case Studies

Invited Talk

Model-Based Testing Strategies and Their (In)dependence on Syntactic Model Representations

Jan Peleska[1,2($\boxtimes$)] and Wen-ling Huang[2]

[1] Verified Systems International GmbH, Bremen, Germany
[2] Department of Mathematics and Computer Science,
University of Bremen, Bremen, Germany
{jp,huang}@cs.uni-bremen.de

Abstract. Model-based testing (MBT) in its most advanced form allows for automated test case identification, test data calculation, and test procedure generation from reference models describing the expected behaviour of the system under test (SUT). If the underlying algorithms for test case identification operate only on the syntactic representation of test models, however, the resulting test strength depends on the syntactic representation as well. This observation is true, even if syntactically differing models are behaviourally equivalent. In this paper, we present a systematic approach to elaborating test case selection strategies that only depend on the behavioural semantics of test models, but are invariant under syntactic transformations preserving the semantics. The benefits of these strategies are discussed, and practical generation algorithms are presented.

Keywords: Model-based testing · Equivalence class partition testing · Kripke structures · Complete testing theories

1 Introduction

Model-Based Testing. Model-based testing (MBT) can be implemented using different approaches; this is also expressed in the current definition of MBT presented in Wikipedia[1].

> *Model-based testing is an application of model-based design for designing and optionally also executing artifacts to perform software testing or system testing. Models can be used to represent the desired behavior of a System Under Test (SUT), or to represent testing strategies and a test environment.*

---

[1] https://en.wikipedia.org/wiki/Model-based_testing, 2016-07-11.

M.H. ter Beek et al. (Eds.): FMICS-AVoCS 2016, LNCS 9933, pp. 3–21, 2016.
DOI: 10.1007/978-3-319-45943-1_1

In this paper, we follow the variant where formal models represent the desired behaviour of the SUT, because this promises the maximal return of investment for the effort to be spent on test model development.

- Test cases can be automatically identified in the model.
- If the model contains links to the original requirements (this is systematically supported, for example, by the SysML modelling language [10]), test cases can be automatically traced back to the requirements they help to verify.
- Since the model is associated with a formal semantics, test cases can be represented by means of logical formulas representing reachability goals, and concrete test data can be calculated by means of constraint solvers.
- Using model-to-text transformations, executable test procedures, including test oracles, can be generated in an automated way.
- Comprehensive traceability data linking test results, procedures, test cases, and requirements can be automatically compiled.

Testing Safety-Critical Systems. In this paper, we focus on MBT for safety-critical embedded systems or cyber-physical systems. These need to be developed and verified according to certain standards, such as the documents [2,8,18] which are applicable in the avionic, railway, and automotive domains, respectively. Moreover, these systems need to be certified by independent authorities before entry into service.

Among other obligations, the completeness and the strength of the test suite needs to be demonstrated in order to obtain certification credit. This is usually performed by (1) tracing test cases back to requirements, showing that non have been left untested, (2) measuring the code coverage achieved by the test suite, so that no special cases specified in the requirements can be overlooked and superfluous or unreachable code is detected, and (3) creating mutants of the SUT or a simulation thereof and checking whether their erroneous behaviour is uncovered by the test suite.

Objectives. As of today, the standards for safety-critical systems development and verification do not yet cover all aspects of applying MBT in a safety-critical context. It is obvious, however, that MBT is very attractive for this domain, because

- due to the criticality of the systems, more time can (must) be invested into formalised modelling of the required system behaviour – so formal models already exist, and skilled personnel for modelling is available, and
- due to the higher degree of automation achieved by MBT, more test cases can be created and executed than would be possible with manual test case elaboration.

A further desirable effect of applying MBT in a safety-critical context would be if it could be guaranteed that certain types of strategies for identifying test cases in a model would come with guaranteed test strength, so that certification credit could be obtained without having to perform mutation testing. Unfortunately, this is generally not the case, because several strategies – such as model transition coverage or MC/DC coverage – create different test cases for different syntactic model representations, even if the underlying models are semantically equivalent. The obvious reason for this is that these strategies just parse the abstract syntax tree for obtaining test cases, without analysing the models' behavioural semantics.

The main topic to be investigated in this contribution is therefore to find answers to the question

Is it possible to create practically applicable test strategies, such that they
– possess guaranteed fault coverage (i.e. well-defined test strength), and
– are transformation-invariant, as long as the transformed models are semantically equivalent to the original one?

If this can be achieved, certification credit for test strength can be given without further demonstrations, because the test suites resulting from the test case generation strategies have the same strength, regardless of the concrete representation of the model from which the tests have been generated.

Main Contributions. The main contributions of this paper are as follows.

1. We present a new model-independent theory for designing equivalence class test suites. This theory is based on the *language* $L(S)$ of the reference model S alone – that is, its observable input/output behaviour. Therefore it is automatically invariant under language-preserving transformations.
2. It is shown that the theory can be practically implemented for deterministic and nondeterministic systems with potentially infinite input domains, but finite (practically enumerable) internal state variables and outputs. This is achieved by generating an initial test suite from an arbitrary reference model S and abstracting the suite to the weakest one that still possesses the guaranteed fault coverage. It is shown that this weakest suite always exists and is uniquely determined, and therefore invariant under language-preserving model transformations.
3. With respect to fault coverage, it is shown that the resulting test strategy is *complete* in relation to a given fault domain $\mathcal{D}$. This means that every SUT whose true behaviour is represented by a member $S' \in \mathcal{D}$ passes the generated test suite, if and only if it conforms to the reference model S.

Overview. In Sect. 2, the problem is described in more detail and illustrated by means of examples. The influence of representations on the test strength of standard test case identification strategies is explained. In Sect. 3, the theoretical foundations for a model-independent complete input equivalence class partition testing method are described. This theory is applied in Sect. 4 to modelling formalisms whose semantics can be expressed by so-called reactive I/O-transition systems. These are Kripke Structures over input, output, and internal variables, whose domains may be infinite for the inputs, but must be finite (and enumerable in practical applications) for internal states and outputs. It is explained how transformation-invariant input equivalence classes are calculated from an arbitrary concrete model. In Sect. 5, conclusions are presented. Throughout the exposition, we give references to related work where appropriate.

References to Complex Models and Applications. In this paper, the example models have been deliberately chosen to be as simple as possible, so that they just highlight a specific aspect of the discussion. It should be emphasised, however, that the material presented here is applied in real-world testing campaigns. Some complex models for MBT have been published on the *model-based testing benchmarks website* www.mbt-benchmarks.org and described in [1, 6, 7, 12, 13].

2   Problem Description

Syntactic Model-Based Test Case Identification. The following trivial example illustrates the problem of syntax-based test strategies. Sample SYSTEM1 has input interface x with values in range $\{0, 1, 2, 3\}$ and outputs y, z, both with domain $\{0, 1\}$, as shown in Fig. 1. It is supposed to output 1 on y if and only if $x = 1$, and 1 on z if and only if $x = 2$.

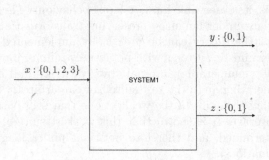

Fig. 1. Sample system SYSTEM1 – interface.

For describing the behavioural semantics of models we use state transition systems (STSs) $\mathcal{S} = (S, \underline{s}, R)$ with state space S, initial state $\underline{s}$ and transition relation $R \subseteq S \times S$. The state space S consists of valuation functions $s : V \to D$ over variables from V, to be evaluated in domain D. Finite variable set V is partitioned into disjoint sets of input variables $I = \{x_1, \ldots, x_n\}$, internal model variables $M = \{m_1, \ldots, m_p\}$, and output variables $O = \{y_1, \ldots, y_q\}$. We use tuple notation $\boldsymbol{x} = (x_1, \ldots, x_n)$, $\boldsymbol{m} = (m_1, \ldots, m_p)$, and $\boldsymbol{y} = (y_1, \ldots, y_q)$ and use shorthand $s(\boldsymbol{x})$ for $(s(x_1), \ldots, s(x_n))$, $s(\boldsymbol{m})$ for $(s(m_1), \ldots, s(m_p))$, and $s(\boldsymbol{y})$ for $(s(y_1), \ldots, s(y_q))$. By D_I, D_M, D_O we denote the crossproduct of input variable types, internal model variable types, and output variable types, respectively, so $s(\boldsymbol{x}) \in D_I$, $s(\boldsymbol{m}) \in D_M$, and $s(\boldsymbol{y}) \in D_O$.

The *language* $L(\mathcal{S})$ of $\mathcal{S}$ is the set of all I/O-traces of $\mathcal{S}$. An I/O-trace is a finite sequence $(\boldsymbol{x}_1, \boldsymbol{y}_1).(\boldsymbol{x}_2, \boldsymbol{y}_2) \ldots (\boldsymbol{x}_k, \boldsymbol{y}_k) \in (D_I \times D_O)^*$, such that there exists a sequence of states $\underline{s}.s_1.s_2 \ldots s_k$ satisfying

$$R(\underline{s}, s_1) \wedge R(s_1, s_2) \wedge \cdots \wedge R(s_{k-1}, s_k)$$

and

$$s_1(\boldsymbol{x}) = \boldsymbol{x}_1 \wedge s_1(\boldsymbol{y}) = \boldsymbol{y}_1 \wedge \cdots \wedge s_k(\boldsymbol{x}) = \boldsymbol{x}_k \wedge s_k(\boldsymbol{y}) = \boldsymbol{y}_k.$$

Its intuitive interpretation is that by changing the input valuation to $\boldsymbol{x}_i$ when residing in state s_{i-1}, system $\mathcal{S}$ transits to state s_i, such that (s_{i-1}, s_i) are connected by the transition relation, and s_i has input valuation $\boldsymbol{x}_i$ and output valuation $\boldsymbol{y}_i$.

Two state transition systems $\mathcal{S}', \mathcal{S}$ are called I/O-equivalent (written $\mathcal{S}' \sim \mathcal{S}$, if and only if $L(\mathcal{S}') = L(\mathcal{S})$. $\mathcal{S}'$ is called a *reduction* of $\mathcal{S}$ (written $\mathcal{S}' \preceq \mathcal{S}$), if and only if $L(\mathcal{S}') \subseteq L(\mathcal{S})$.

The expected behaviour of the SUT is modelled alternatively by the two SysML state machines SM-TC1 and SM-TC2 shown in Figs. 2 and 3. It is easy to see that SM-TC1 $\sim$ SM-TC2 (we will show below how the state machines can be represented by their semantic state transition system models).

Let us now determine which test cases would be generated by a typical MBT tool if the *transition coverage* strategy for test case generation were applied.

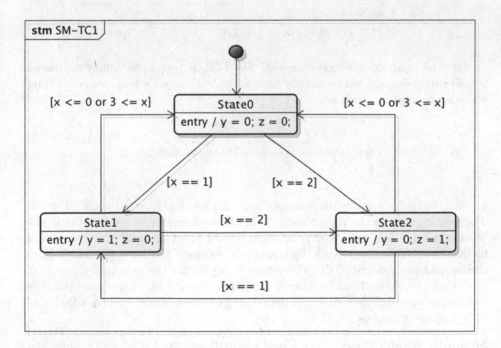

Fig. 2. Sample state machine model SM-TC1 for discussion of transition coverage.

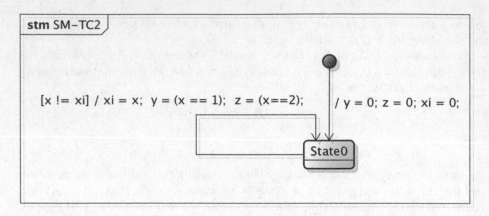

Fig. 3. Sample state machine model SM–TC2 equivalent to SM–TC1.

Recall that this strategy creates test cases such that every state machine transition is visited at least once in the model. Deriving transition coverage test cases from reference model SM–TC1, results in a test suite like the following, which performs a complete transition tour to cover all state machine transitions in a single test case.

Test suite 1	
No.	Test case $(x_1, (y_1, z_1)).(x_2, (y_2, z_2))\ldots$
1	$(1, (1, 0)).(0, (0, 0)).(2, (0, 1)).(1, (1, 0)).(2, (0, 1)).(3, (0, 0))$

For the equivalent reference model SM–TC2, a test suite achieving model transition coverage could be already be realised with a single test case containing a single stimulation, such as

Test suite 2	
No.	Test case $(x_1, (y_1, z_1)).(x_2, (y_2, z_2))\ldots$
1	$(1, (1, 0))$

Now consider a faulty implementation of SYSTEM1, as shown in Table 1. The bug injected in the right-hand side of the assignment to z would obviously be revealed by Test Suite 1 derived from model SM–TC1, while the bug would be overlooked when executing the transition coverage test suite generated from the equivalent model SM–TC2. This example highlights the well-known fact that test strategies derived from syntactic model representations alone may produce test suites with different strength, depending on the syntactic representation of I/O-equivalent models.

Semantic Model-Based Test Case Identification. Could we perhaps just perform test case selection on the semantic model, in order to solve the problem

Table 1. Faulty implementation of SYSTEM1.

```
int x,y,z; // Global I/O variables shared with the
           // environment, e.g. threads writing
           // inputs to x and reading outputs from
           // y and z.
void f() {
  while (1) {
    if ( x != xi ) {
      xi = x;
      y = ( x == 1 );
      z = ( x == 3 ); // <- Bug
}}}
```

illustrated above? From the extensive literature about test strategies with guaranteed fault coverage for finite state machines this is well-known to be possible (see [3–5,9,14,15,17] for some of the most important FSM testing strategies): given an FSM M in arbitrary syntactic representation, these test strategies calculate test cases from the so-called *prima machine of M*, which is the minimal observable FSM possessing the same language. Since the prime machine of M is uniquely determined up to isomorphism, the test suites produced by these strategies are therefore invariant under syntactic transformations preserving the language of M.

At first glance, this approach looks quite easily extensible to more general formalisms whose semantics is based on state transition systems. The STS representing the behavioural semantics of SM-TC1 is shown in Fig. 4. For SM-TC2, the STS diagram looks just like the one for SM-TC1, only with the 'state' variable replaced by the internal model variable xi. It is trivial to see that when covering every transition of the STS diagram shown in Fig. 4, the bug in the implementation from Table 1 will be uncovered, because the single test case of Test Suite 1 above is a prefix of the single test case of Test Suite 3 which results from performing a complete transition tour of the STS shown in Fig. 4.

Test suite 3	
No.	Test case $(x_1,(y_1,z_1)).(x_2,(y_2,z_2))\ldots$
1	$(1,(1,0)).(0,(0,0)).(2,(0,1)).(1,(1,0)).(2,(0,1)).(3,(0,0)).(0,(0,0)).(1,(1,0)).$ $(3,(0,0)).(0,(0,0)).(3,(0,0))$

Problems Resulting from Explicit Semantic Model Representations. It is satisfactory to see that both models SM-TC1 and SM-TC2 produce the same transition coverage suite when applying transition coverage to the semantic model. This, however, is an explicit semantic model as it had been used in the early days of global model checking. The state explosion problems associated with explicit models are well understood. Moreover, some helpful syntactic model

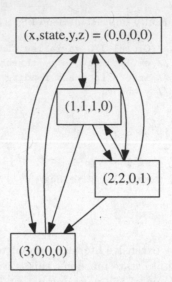

Fig. 4. State transition system representing the behavioural semantics of SM-TC1.

information may be lost when transforming the original model to its explicit semantic presentation. As an example illustrating this general problem, consider an extended domain for input variable x, which we will now assume to be of type int128_t.

While the SysML state machine models shown in Figs. 2 and 3 can remain unchanged, the explicit semantic representation would be infeasible, since a node $(x, 0, 0, 0)$ would have to be created for every int128_t-value x in range $x \leq 0 \lor 3 \leq x$. Even if we were willing to invest into that amount of storage for representing all these states, the number of resulting transition coverage test cases would be impossible to test with acceptable effort. Having reached the explicit semantic representation level, it would also be impossible to find hints in the model which transitions could be aggregated to "somehow equivalent ones", so that it would only be necessary to test one representative of a class.

Alternative Approach. With these obstacles in mind, we propose another approach which neither depends on syntactic model representations alone, nor requires explicit representations of behavioural semantics, and is still invariant under model transformations preserving the language. The theoretical foundations for this approach will be outlined in the next section, its practical application is described in Sect. 4.

3   A Model-Independent Method for Input Equivalence Class Partition Testing

Languages and Equivalence. In our application context of embedded systems testing, the fundamental notion of equivalence or refinement can be defined by means of the traces of observable interface events. Let Σ be such a set of events, which we allow to be infinite, so that also real-valued physical observables like time, speed, or temperature can be captured. For the moment, we do not distinguish between inputs and outputs, an event $e \in \Sigma$ is just the occurrence of an observable state change on some system interface. For test purposes, only finite sequences of observations are of interest, so we focus on traces $\pi \in \Sigma^*$ and abstain from arguing about liveness properties which can only be verified on infinite observation sequences.

We use the term *language of a system* for the set $\mathcal{L}$ of traces that may be observed during system execution. Since observations already made cannot be undone by consecutive observations, we require all languages under consideration to be prefix-closed.[2]

Our objective is to find a definition for "equivalent behaviour" which is based on the concept of languages alone, instead of referring to concrete models and their syntactic representations. To this end, we observe that any equivalence relation on observations, say $\sim\, \subseteq \Sigma \times \Sigma$ gives rise to an equivalence relation on traces, by defining

$$\forall \pi, \pi' \in \Sigma^* : \pi \sim \pi' \Leftrightarrow \big(|\pi| = |\pi'| \wedge (\forall i = 1, \ldots, |\pi| : \pi(i) \sim \pi'(i))\big).$$

We are only interested in equivalence relations where either all traces equivalent over Σ^* are contained in the language or none of them. More formally, given a language $\mathcal{L}$ and an equivalence relation $\sim\, \subseteq \Sigma \times \Sigma$, $\sim$ is $\mathcal{L}$-*closed* if and only if its extension to Σ^* satisfies

$$\forall \pi, \pi' \in \Sigma^* : \big(\pi \sim \pi' \Rightarrow (\pi \in \mathcal{L} \Leftrightarrow \pi' \in \mathcal{L})\big).$$

$\mathcal{L}$-closed equivalence relations are characterised by the following lemma.

Lemma 1. *Given a language $\mathcal{L}$, an equivalence relation $\sim\, \subseteq \Sigma \times \Sigma$ is $\mathcal{L}$-closed if and only if*

$$\forall \pi, \tau \in \Sigma^*, \sigma, \sigma' \in \Sigma : \big(\sigma \sim \sigma' \Rightarrow (\pi.\sigma.\tau \in \mathcal{L} \Leftrightarrow \pi.\sigma'.\tau \in \mathcal{L})\big). \tag{1}$$

$\square$

Intuitively speaking, events which are equivalent according to an $\mathcal{L}$-closed relation are *exchangeable* in the following sense: when inserted after an arbitrary trace π of observations, $\pi.\sigma$ and $\pi.\sigma'$ have exactly the same continuations τ in $\mathcal{L}$. So, regardless whether we pick σ or σ' after having run through π, the future according to $\mathcal{L}$ will always be the same.

---

[2] This is typically the first requirement for the axiomatic introduction of process algebra semantics, see, e.g. [16].

Conversely, it can be shown that any relation defined by

$$\sigma \sim \sigma' \Leftrightarrow \big(\forall \pi, \tau \in \Sigma^* : (\pi.\sigma.\tau \in \mathcal{L} \Leftrightarrow \pi.\sigma'.\tau \in \mathcal{L})\big) \tag{2}$$

is an equivalence relation. By construction, it fulfils (1) and is therefore also $\mathcal{L}$-closed. Moreover, the construction guarantees that it is the *coarsest* $\mathcal{L}$-closed equivalence relation on Σ, and every other $\mathcal{L}$-closed equivalence relation is a refinement thereof, because it must satisfy (1) as well.

Distinguishing Inputs and Outputs. Now let us set $\Sigma = D_I \times D_O$, so that every observable event consists of the pair of most recent input and most recent output. Given a language $\mathcal{L}$ over Σ, suppose that the coarsest $\mathcal{L}$-closed equivalence relation $\sim$ on Σ has been constructed according to condition (2). This induces a uniquely determined *input equivalence relation* $\sim_I$ by setting for $x, x' \in D_I$

$$x \sim_I x' \Leftrightarrow \big(\forall y \in D_O : (x, y) \sim (x', y)\big) \tag{3}$$

Here the intuition is to consider two inputs as equivalent, if and only if their combination with any output is equivalent according to the original equivalence relation $\sim$ over I/O-pairs. Obviously, $\sim_I$ is the coarsest input equivalence relation on D_I which can be extended to an $\mathcal{L}$-closed equivalence relation $\sim$ on Σ.

Example 1. As an example, consider the SysML state machine in Fig. 5, to be discussed in more detail in Sect. 4. For this example, the input x is real-valued, and the output y is in $\{0, 1\}$. The associated language $\mathcal{L}$ is therefore a subset of $\Sigma^* = (\mathbb{R} \times \{0, 1\})^*$. We "guess" an equivalence relation $\sim$ on Σ^* as follows (in Sect. 4, an algorithm for automated computation of $\sim$ and $\sim_I$ is presented).

$$\forall (c, e), (c', e') \in \mathbb{R} \times \{0, 1\} :$$
$$(c, e) \sim (c', e') \Leftrightarrow \big(e = e' \wedge (c, c' \in (-\infty, 0] \vee c, c' \in [20, \infty) \vee c, c' \in (0, 20))\big)$$

It is evident that equivalent I/O-pairs should have the same output values in this example, because the outputs are discrete values in $\{0, 1\}$, and we do not want output 0 to be equivalent to output 1. Regarding the inputs, it is easy to see that c, c' satisfying, for example, condition $c, c' \in (-\infty, 0]$ has the same effect on the system, regardless of its current state: when in STATE1, all inputs less or equal to zero do not affect the system. When in STATE2, all of these values trigger a transition to STATE1 while setting y to zero. Checking the behaviour for $c, c' \in [20, \infty)$ and $c, c' \in (0, 20)$ yields analogous results. As a consequence, the input equivalence relation

$$c \sim_I c' \Leftrightarrow \big(c, c' \in (-\infty, 0] \vee c, c' \in [20, \infty) \vee c, c' \in (0, 20)\big)$$

derived from $\sim$ conforms to our intuition of equivalent inputs to a system. It is shown in Sect. 4 that the equivalence relations $\sim, \sim_I$ are indeed the coarsest ones for the language generated by the SysML state machine from Fig. 5.   □

The following theorem formalises the intuitive understanding about equivalence relations and languages: two languages with a joint language-closed equivalence relation $\sim$ coincide or are in subset relation, if and only if their equivalence partitions resulting from $\sim$ coincide or are in subset relation.

Theorem 1. *Let $\mathcal{L}, \mathcal{L}'$ be two languages over Σ, and $\sim \subseteq \Sigma \times \Sigma$ an equivalence relation which is both $\mathcal{L}$-closed and $\mathcal{L}'$-closed. Then $\mathcal{L}' = \mathcal{L}$ if and only if $\mathcal{L}'/_\sim = \mathcal{L}/_\sim$ and $\mathcal{L}' \subseteq \mathcal{L}$ if and only if $\mathcal{L}'/_\sim \subseteq \mathcal{L}/_\sim$.* $\square$

Model-Independent Testing Theory. Given a language $\mathcal{L}$ over alphabet Σ, an abstract notion of test cases U can be introduced by defining $U = (U_{\text{pass}}, U_{\text{fail}})$ by means of sets of *pass traces* $U_{\text{pass}} \subseteq \Sigma^*$ and *fail traces* $U_{\text{fail}} \subseteq \Sigma^*$. This definition of test cases is complemented by two notions of "passing a test": an SUT with language $\mathcal{L}'$ over Σ satisfies

$$\mathcal{L}' \ \underline{\text{pass}}_1 \ U \qquad \text{if and only if} \qquad \mathcal{L}' \cap U_{\text{fail}} = \varnothing.$$

The second pass-relation is defined by

$$\mathcal{L}' \ \underline{\text{pass}}_2 \ U \qquad \text{if and only if} \qquad \mathcal{L}' \cap U_{\text{fail}} = \varnothing \wedge U_{\text{pass}} \subseteq \mathcal{L}'.$$

Relation $\underline{\text{pass}}_1$ signifies that the SUT's language does not contain any unwanted execution traces specified in U_{fail}. Relation $\underline{\text{pass}}_2$ signifies in addition that the SUT can perform all the desired execution traces specified in U_{pass}.

Since the factorisation of language $\mathcal{L}$ according to some $\mathcal{L}$-closed equivalence relation $\sim$ is again a language, the concept of test cases and the definition of the two pass-relations can be applied to $\mathcal{L}/_\sim$ as well. Pass and fail traces in $\mathcal{L}/_\sim$, however, are sequences of equivalence classes, that is, elements from $(\Sigma/_\sim)^*$. Since every $[\pi] \in (\Sigma/_\sim)^*$ is just a set of concrete traces, pass and fail traces from $(\Sigma/_\sim)^*$ can be mapped to concrete traces by selecting representatives from each class $[\pi]$.

Given a set $W \subseteq (\Sigma/_\sim)^*$, we call $\mathcal{A}(W) \subseteq \Sigma^*$ a *representative* of W, if and only if $\mathcal{A}(W)$ contains exactly one representative $\pi' \in [\pi]$ for every class $[\pi] \in W$. Given a test case $U = (U_{\text{pass}}, U_{\text{fail}})$ with $U_{\text{pass}}, U_{\text{fail}} \subseteq (\Sigma/_\sim)^*$, it can be shown that $\mathcal{L}/_\sim$ passes U in each variant 1 or 2, if and only if $\mathcal{L}$ passes the test $(\mathcal{A}(U_{\text{pass}}), \mathcal{A}(U_{\text{fail}}))$ with the same variant of the pass relation. This holds independently on the selection of representative $\mathcal{A}$.

A *fault model* $\mathcal{F} = (\mathcal{L}, \leq, \mathcal{D})$ consists of a reference language $\mathcal{L}$ representing the desired behaviour of implementations to be tested, the conformance relation $\leq \in \{=, \subseteq\}$ denoting language equivalence or language containment, and the fault domain $\mathcal{D}$ which is a set of languages conforming or nonconforming to $\mathcal{L}$, such that the true behaviour of the SUT is an element $\mathcal{L}' \in \mathcal{D}$. A test suite TS is a set of test cases. TS is called *complete*, if every implementation conforming to the reference language (i.e. $\mathcal{L}' \leq \mathcal{L}$) passes every test in TS, and every nonconforming implementation ($\mathcal{L}' \not\leq \mathcal{L}$) fails at least one test case in TS.

These considerations lead to the main theorem of the testing theory about complete test suites: any test suite that is complete on a fault model of languages factorised according to $\sim$ gives rise to a complete test suite for the unfactorised, concrete languages. To this end, a complete test suite is translated simply by selecting representatives for each pass or fail trace $[\pi] \in (\Sigma/\sim)^*$ in each test case.

Theorem 2. *Let $\mathcal{L}$ be a language over Σ and $\sim$ an $\mathcal{L}$-closed equivalence relation. Let TS be a complete test suite for some fault model $\mathcal{F}' = (\mathcal{L}/\sim, \leq, \mathcal{D}')$. Define a test suite translation by*

$$\mathcal{A}(TS) = \{(\mathcal{A}(U_{pass}), \mathcal{A}(U_{fail})) \mid (U_{pass}, U_{fail}) \in TS\},$$

where $\mathcal{A}(U_{pass}), \mathcal{A}(U_{fail})$ are suitable representatives for all sets of pass and fail traces.

Then $\mathcal{A}(TS)$ is a complete test suite for fault model $\mathcal{F} = (\mathcal{L}, \leq, \mathcal{D})$ with

$$\mathcal{D} = \{\mathcal{L}' \mid \sim \text{ is } \mathcal{L}'\text{-closed and } \mathcal{L}'/\sim \in \mathcal{D}'\}$$

When testing for equivalence ($\leq$ is '$=$') pass-relation $\underline{pass}_2$ must be used. When testing for language containment ($\leq$ is '$\subseteq$'), $\underline{pass}_1$ has to be applied.

4   Model-Based Transformation-Invariant Calculation of Input Equivalence Classes

To illustrate the practical calculation of the equivalence classes and the associated abstraction to finite state machines, consider the SysML state machine SM1 in Fig. 5, where we assume that input x has domain $\mathbb{R}$, and output y domain $\{0, 1\}$. It is easy to see that the alternative model SM2 shown in Fig. 6 looks differently on the syntactic level, but really produces the same language as SM1.

Calculation of Input Equivalence Classes and DFSM Abstraction for SM1. Following the algorithm described in [6], the IEC-generation starts with calculating the transition relation of SM1 in some arbitrary propositional form. A possible result for this is

$$
\begin{aligned}
\mathcal{R}_1 \equiv \ & (\text{state} = 1 \wedge y = 0 \wedge (x \leq 0 \vee 20 \leq x) \wedge \text{state}' = 1 \wedge y' = y \wedge (x' \leq 0 \vee 20 \leq x')) \\
& \vee (\text{state} = 1 \wedge y = 0 \wedge (x \leq 0 \vee 20 \leq x) \wedge \text{state}' = 2 \wedge y' = 1 \wedge 0 < x' < 20) \\
& \vee (\text{state} = 2 \wedge y = 1 \wedge 0 < x < 20 \wedge \text{state}' = 2 \wedge y' = y \wedge 0 < x' < 20) \\
& \vee (\text{state} = 2 \wedge y = 0 \wedge 0 < x \wedge \text{state}' = 2 \wedge y' = y \wedge 0 < x') \\
& \vee (\text{state} = 2 \wedge y = 1 \wedge 0 < x < 20 \wedge \text{state}' = 2 \wedge y' = 0 \wedge 20 \leq x') \\
& \vee (\text{state} = 2 \wedge y = 0 \wedge 0 < x \wedge \text{state}' = 1 \wedge y' = 0 \wedge x' \leq 0) \\
& \vee (\text{state} = 2 \wedge y = 1 \wedge 0 < x < 20 \wedge \text{state}' = 1 \wedge y' = 0 \wedge x' \leq 0)
\end{aligned}
$$

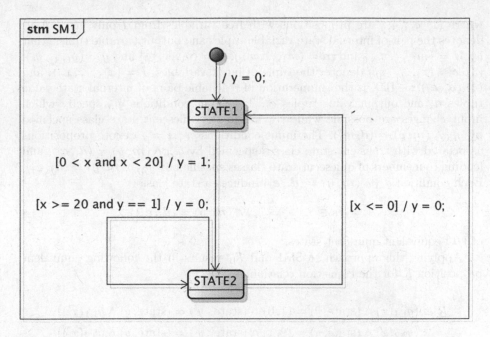

Fig. 5. Sample model SM1 for IECP calculation.

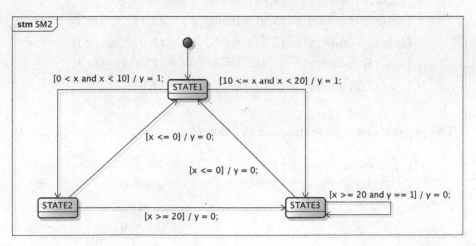

Fig. 6. Sample model SM2 – I/O-equivalent to SM1.

Next, the transition relation is transformed into a normal form with structure

$$\mathcal{R} \equiv \bigvee_{i \in \text{IDX}} \left(g_{i,i}(\boldsymbol{x}) \wedge (\boldsymbol{m}, \boldsymbol{y}) = (\boldsymbol{d}_i, \boldsymbol{e}_i) \wedge (\boldsymbol{m}', \boldsymbol{y}') = (\boldsymbol{m}, \boldsymbol{y}) \wedge g_{i,i}(\boldsymbol{x}') \right) \vee$$
$$\bigvee_{(i,j) \in J} \left(g_{i,i}(\boldsymbol{x}) \wedge (\boldsymbol{m}, \boldsymbol{y}) = (\boldsymbol{d}_i, \boldsymbol{e}_i) \wedge (\boldsymbol{m}', \boldsymbol{y}') = (\boldsymbol{d}_j, \boldsymbol{e}_j) \wedge g_{i,j}(\boldsymbol{x}') \right)$$

where (1) $g_{i,i}, g_{i,j}$ are propositions with free variables from I only, (2) $(\boldsymbol{m}, \boldsymbol{y})$ denotes the pair of internal state variable tuples and output variable tuples, that is, $M = \{m_1, \ldots m_k\}$ and $\boldsymbol{m} = (m_1, \ldots m_k)$, $O = \{y_1, \ldots y_\ell\}$ and $\boldsymbol{y} = (y_1, \ldots y_\ell)$, (3) $\boldsymbol{x} = (x_1, \ldots, x_p)$ denotes the tuple of input variables, $I = \{x_1, \ldots, x_p\}$, and (4) $(\boldsymbol{d}_i, \boldsymbol{e}_i), i \in \mathrm{IDX}$ is the enumeration of reachable pairs of internal state value tuples $\boldsymbol{d}_i$ and output value tuples $\boldsymbol{e}_i$. The input conditions $g_{i,i}$ specify which input changes are possible while staying in the quiescent state class specified by $g_{i,i} \wedge (\boldsymbol{m}, \boldsymbol{y}) = (\boldsymbol{d}_i, \boldsymbol{e}_i)$. The input conditions $g_{i,j}, i \neq j$ denote propositions associated with transient state classes specified by $g_{i,j} \wedge (\boldsymbol{m}, \boldsymbol{y}) = (\boldsymbol{d}_i, \boldsymbol{e}_i)$, and leading to members of quiescent state classes specified by $g_{j,j} \wedge (\boldsymbol{m}, \boldsymbol{y}) = (\boldsymbol{d}_j, \boldsymbol{e}_j)$. Each condition $g_{i,i} \wedge (\boldsymbol{m}, \boldsymbol{y}) = (\boldsymbol{d}_i, \boldsymbol{e}_i)$ induces a state class

$$A_i = \{s \in S \mid s \models g_{i,i} \wedge (\boldsymbol{m}, \boldsymbol{y}) = (\boldsymbol{d}_i, \boldsymbol{e}_i)\}$$

of I/O-equivalent quiescent states.

Applying this approach to SM1 and $\mathcal{R}_1$ results in the following equivalent proposition $\mathcal{R}$ for the transition relation.

$$
\begin{aligned}
\mathcal{R} \equiv{} & \big(g_{1,1}(x) \wedge (\mathrm{state}, y) = (1, 0) \wedge (\mathrm{state}', y') = (\mathrm{state}, y) \wedge g_{1,1}(x')\big) \\
\vee{} & \big(g_{2,2}(x) \wedge (\mathrm{state}, y) = (2, 1) \wedge (\mathrm{state}', y') = (\mathrm{state}, y) \wedge g_{2,2}(x')\big) \\
\vee{} & \big(g_{3,3}(x) \wedge (\mathrm{state}, y) = (2, 0) \wedge (\mathrm{state}', y') = (\mathrm{state}, y) \wedge g_{3,3}(x')\big) \\
\vee{} & \big(g_{1,1}(x) \wedge (\mathrm{state}, y) = (1, 0) \wedge (\mathrm{state}', y') = (2, 1) \wedge g_{1,2}(x')\big) \\
\vee{} & \big(g_{2,2}(x) \wedge (\mathrm{state}, y) = (2, 1) \wedge (\mathrm{state}', y') = (1, 0) \wedge g_{2,1}(x')\big) \\
\vee{} & \big(g_{2,2}(x) \wedge (\mathrm{state}, y) = (2, 1) \wedge (\mathrm{state}', y') = (2, 0) \wedge g_{2,3}(x')\big) \\
\vee{} & \big(g_{3,3}(x) \wedge (\mathrm{state}, y) = (2, 0) \wedge (\mathrm{state}', y') = (1, 0) \wedge g_{3,1}(x')\big)
\end{aligned}
$$

The propositions $g_{i,j}$ are specified as follows.

$$
\begin{array}{ll}
g_{1,1} \equiv x \leq 0 \vee 20 \leq x \qquad & g_{1,2} \equiv 0 < x < 20 \\
g_{2,2} \equiv 0 < x < 20 & g_{2,1} \equiv x \leq 0 \\
g_{3,3} \equiv 0 < x & g_{2,3} \equiv 20 \leq x \\
& g_{3,1} \equiv x \leq 0
\end{array}
$$

The state classes are calculated as follows.

$$
\begin{aligned}
A_1 &= \{s \in S \mid s \models ((x \leq 0 \vee 20 \leq x) \wedge (\mathrm{state}, y) = (1, 0))\} \\
A_2 &= \{s \in S \mid s \models ((0 < x < 20) \wedge (\mathrm{state}, y) = (2, 1))\} \\
A_3 &= \{s \in S \mid s \models ((0 < x) \wedge (\mathrm{state}, y) = (2, 0))\}
\end{aligned}
$$

The normalised representation $\mathcal{R}$ now allows us to construct an input domain partition $\mathcal{I} = \{X_1, \ldots, X_q\}$. Following [6], the X_i are identified by all conjuncts

$$\Phi_f \equiv \bigwedge_{i=1}^{3} g_{i,f(i)} \quad \text{where } f : \{1, \ldots, 3\} \rightarrow \{1, \ldots, 3\} \text{ is bijective}$$

which are satisfiable. For our example, the satisfiable Φ_f are

$$\Phi_1 \equiv g_{1,1} \wedge g_{2,1} \wedge g_{3,1} \equiv x \leq 0$$
$$\Phi_2 \equiv g_{1,1} \wedge g_{2,3} \wedge g_{3,3} \equiv 20 \leq x$$
$$\Phi_3 \equiv g_{1,2} \wedge g_{2,2} \wedge g_{3,3} \equiv 0 < x < 20$$

Each member $X_i, i = 1, 2, 3$ of the input domain partition is specified by the set of all inputs x satisfying proposition Φ_i.

Now the state classes A_i and the IECs X_j give rise to a well-defined FSM M which is deterministic, since the original SysML state machine SM1 is deterministic as well. M has states $Q = \{A_1, A_2, A_3\}$, inputs $\Sigma_I = \{X_1, X_2, X_3\}$, and its transition function and output function are given by the tables

δ	X_1	X_2	X_3
A_1	A_1	A_1	A_2
A_2	A_1	A_3	A_2
A_3	A_1	A_3	A_3

ω	X_1	X_2	X_3
A_1	$y = 0$	$y = 0$	$y = 1$
A_2	$y = 0$	$y = 0$	$y = 1$
A_3	$y = 0$	$y = 0$	$y = 0$

These tables have been created by observing that from every state in class A_i, with every input value $c \in X_j$, the system transits to a state in class $\delta(A_i, X_j)$ with accompanying output $\omega(A_i, X_j)$. In this example, the DFSM is already minimal, and its input alphabet does not contain any pair of inputs X, X' having the same effect (target state and output) in every state. It can be shown that every DFSM produced according to the steps above, minimised and free of inputs with equivalent effects induces the coarsest input equivalence class partitioning that can be constructed for SM1 and its language equivalents.

Calculation of Input Equivalence Classes and DFSM Abstraction for SM2. To illustrate the independence from the syntactic model representation, we will now perform the same construction steps as above, but using now model SM2 from Fig. 6. The construction first leads to four state classes

$$A_1' = \{s \in S \mid s \models ((x \leq 0 \vee 20 \leq x) \wedge (\text{state}, y) = (1, 0))\}$$
$$A_2' = \{s \in S \mid s \models ((0 < x < 20) \wedge (\text{state}, y) = (2, 1))\}$$
$$A_3' = \{s \in S \mid s \models ((0 < x) \wedge (\text{state}, y) = (3, 0))\}$$
$$A_4' = \{s \in S \mid s \models ((0 < x) \wedge (\text{state}, y) = (3, 1))\}$$

and to four input equivalence classes $X'_1, \ldots, X'_4$ that are specified by

$$\Phi'_1 \equiv x \leq 0$$
$$\Phi'_2 \equiv 20 \leq x$$
$$\Phi'_3 \equiv 0 < x < 10$$
$$\Phi'_4 \equiv 10 \leq x < 20$$

The associated DFSM has transition and output tables

δ	X'_1	X'_2	X'_3	X'_4
A'_1	A'_1	A'_1	A'_2	A'_4
A'_2	A'_1	A'_3	A'_2	A'_2
A'_3	A'_1	A'_3	A'_3	A'_3
A'_4	A'_1	A'_3	A'_4	A'_4

ω'	X'_1	X'_2	X'_3	X'_4
A'_1	$y = 0$	$y = 0$	$y = 1$	$y = 1$
A'_2	$y = 0$	$y = 0$	$y = 1$	$y = 1$
A'_3	$y = 0$	$y = 0$	$y = 0$	$y = 0$
A_4	$y = 0$	$y = 0$	$y = 1$	$y = 1$

This DFSM can be minimised, because state A'_2 and A'_4 are equivalent: for both states, the transition function leads for each input to equivalent target states, and the output function shows the same outputs for the associated transitions. The minimised machine has the following tables.

δ	X'_1	X'_2	X'_3	X'_4
$\rightarrow A'_1$	A'_1	A'_1	$A'_{2,4}$	$A'_{2,4}$
$A'_{2,4}$	A'_1	A'_3	$A'_{2,4}$	$A'_{2,4}$
A'_3	A'_1	A'_3	A'_3	A'_3

ω'	X'_1	X'_2	X'_3	X'_4
A'_1	$y = 0$	$y = 0$	$y = 1$	$y = 1$
$A'_{2,4}$	$y = 0$	$y = 0$	$y = 1$	$y = 1$
A'_3	$y = 0$	$y = 0$	$y = 0$	$y = 0$

Finally, we observe that IECs X'_3 and X'_4 always have the same effect (target state and output) when applied to any source state. As a consequence, these two classes can be combined to one class, and this results in the revised DFSM

δ	X'_1	X'_2	$X'_3 \cup X'_4$
A'_1	A'_1	A'_1	$A'_{2,4}$
$A'_{2,4}$	A'_1	A'_3	$A'_{2,4}$
A'_3	A'_1	A'_3	A'_3

ω'	X'_1	X'_2	$X'_3 \cup X'_4$
A'_1	$y = 0$	$y = 0$	$y = 1$
$A'_{2,4}$	$y = 0$	$y = 0$	$y = 1$
A'_3	$y = 0$	$y = 0$	$y = 0$

This machine is now isomorphic to the one generated from **SM1**, and the equivalence class partitioning is the same, because $X'_1 = X_1$, $X'_2 = X_2$, and $X'_3 \cup X'_4 = X_3$, because $\Phi'_3 \vee \Phi'_4 \Leftrightarrow \Phi_3$.

This shows that the FSM abstraction is invariant under syntactic transformations preserving the language of the reference model.

Generation of a Complete Test Suite. As described in Sect. 3, a concrete test suite for establishing I/O-equivalence, for example, is now generated by the following steps.

At first, we apply an arbitrary complete DFSM test suite which verifies I/O-equivalence between finite state machines. Applying the Wp-Method as elaborated in [9] (the algorithm described there is applicable to both deterministic and nondeterministic FSMs), results in the following test cases. They are constructed under the assumption that the SUT operates with the same IECs and has an FSM abstraction that does not exceed the number ($n = 3$) of states of the minimised FSMs above.

Test suite 4	
No.	Test case $(X_{i,1}, y_1).(X_{i,2}, y_2)\ldots$
1	$(X_3, y = 1).(X_2, y = 0).(X_3, y = 0).(X_3, y = 0)$
2	$(X_3, y = 1).(X_2, y = 0).(X_2, y = 0).(X_3, y = 0)$
3	$(X_3, y = 1).(X_2, y = 0).(X_1, y = 0).(X_2, y = 0).(X_3, y = 1)$
4	$(X_3, y = 1).(X_3, y = 1).(X_3, y = 1)$
5	$(X_3, y = 1).(X_3, y = 1).(X_2, y = 0).(X_3, y = 0)$
6	$(X_3, y = 1).(X_1, y = 0).(X_2, y = 0).(X_3, y = 1)$
7	$(X_2, y = 0).(X_3, y = 1)$
8	$(X_2, y = 0).(X_2, y = 0).(X_3, y = 1)$
9	$(X_1, y = 0).(X_2, y = 0).(X_3, y = 1)$

A concrete test suite is now created by selecting an arbitrary input value x_i satisfying Φ_i, whenever IEC X_i is referenced in Test Suite 4 above.

5   Conclusion

In this paper, the problems of purely syntactic test case generation strategies were highlighted. As an alternative, strategies that are invariant under syntactic transformations preserving the language, i.e. the behavioural semantics of the model, were advocated. To this end, a model-independent complete input equivalence class partition testing strategy has been presented. This strategy is derived from the concept of languages alone, without the need to refer to specific model representations. For reactive systems with potentially infinite input domains but finite internal state values and outputs it has been shown how the concrete calculation of test suites according to this strategy can be performed by starting with an arbitrary model and calculating the coarsest input equivalence partition by means of model abstraction to finite state machines with consecutive FSM minimisation and aggregation of inputs with identical effects. The resulting FSM is independent on the initial model representation. Complete test suites can be derived by first generating symbolic test cases from the FSM, using a complete testing theory for finite state machines. These test cases reference input equivalence classes as inputs to the SUT. By means of a mathematical constraint solver, concrete test data is determined by solving the constraints specifying each input equivalence class. While the strategy has been exemplified in this paper using deterministic models, the approach is also valid for nondeterministic systems.

The fault models guaranteeing completeness of the strategy depend on the maximum number of states in the SUT's FSM abstraction and the hypothesis that the SUT has a similar input equivalence class partition as the reference model. Extensive experiments have shown that even if this hypothesis is not fulfilled, the strategy described still has excellent test strength for SUTs outside the fault domain [7,13].

The strategy has been implemented in the model-based testing tool RT-Tester [11], and it is applied in industrial testing campaigns at Verified Systems International GmbH.

Acknowledgements. The authors would like to thank the members of the FMICS-AVOCS program committee for the invitation to present this paper. Furthermore, we thank Alexander Pretschner for stimulating discussions concerning the topic of test strategies and their potential dependencies on syntactic model representations.

The work presented in this paper has been elaborated within project *ITTCPS – Implementable Testing Theory for Cyber-physical Systems* (http://www.informatik. uni-bremen.de/agbs/projects/ittcps/index.html) which has been granted by the University of Bremen in the context of the German Universities Excellence Initiative. (http://en.wikipedia.org/wiki/German_Universities_Excellence_Initiative).

References

1. Braunstein, C., Haxthausen, A.E., Huang, W., Hübner, F., Peleska, J., Schulze, U., Vu Hong, L.: Complete model-based equivalence class testing for the ETCS ceiling speed monitor. In: Merz, S., Pang, J. (eds.) ICFEM 2014. LNCS, vol. 8829, pp. 380–395. Springer, Heidelberg (2014)
2. CENELEC: EN 50128: 2011 Railway Applications - Communication, Signalling and Processing Systems - Software for Railway Control and Protection Systems (2011)
3. Chow, T.S.: Testing software design modeled by finite-state machines. IEEE Trans. Softw. Eng. SE **4**(3), 178–186 (1978)
4. Fujiwara, S., Bochmann, G.V., Khendek, F., Amalou, M., Ghedamsi, A.: Test selection based on finite state models. IEEE Trans. Softw. Eng. **17**(6), 591–603 (1991)
5. Hierons, R.M.: Testing from a nondeterministic finite state machine using adaptive state counting. IEEE Trans. Comput. **53**(10), 1330–1342 (2004). http://doi.ieee computersociety.org/10.1109/TC.2004.85
6. Huang, W., Peleska, J.: Complete model-based equivalence class testing. STTT **18**(3), 265–283 (2016). doi:10.1007/s10009-014-0356-8
7. Hübner, F., Huang, W., Peleska, J.: Experimental evaluation of a novel equivalence class partition testing strategy. In: Blanchette, J.C., Kosmatov, N. (eds.) TAP 2015. LNCS, vol. 9154, pp. 155–172. Springer, Heidelberg (2015). doi:10.1007/978-3-319-21215-9_10
8. ISO, DIS 26262–4: Road vehicles - functional safety - part 4: product development: system level. Technical report, International Organization for Standardization (2009)
9. Luo, G., von Bochmann, G., Petrenko, A.: Test selection based on communicating nondeterministic finite-state machines using a generalized WP-method. IEEE Trans. Softw. Eng. **20**(2), 149–162 (1994). http://doi.ieeecomputer society.org/10.1109/32.265636

10. Object Management Group: OMG Systems Modeling Language (OMG SysML), Version 1.4. Technical report, Object Management Group (2015). http://www.omg.org/spec/SysML/1.4
11. Peleska, J.: Industrial-strength model-based testing - state of the art and current challenges. In: Petrenko, A.K., Schlingloff, H. (eds.) Proceedings Eighth Workshop on Model-Based Testing, Rome, Italy, 17 March 2013. Electronic Proceedings in Theoretical Computer Science, vol. 111, pp. 3–28. Open Publishing Association (2013)
12. Peleska, J., Honisch, A., Lapschies, F., Löding, H., Schmid, H., Smuda, P., Vorobev, E., Zahlten, C.: A real-world benchmark model for testing concurrent real-time systems in the automotive domain. In: Wolff, B., Zaïdi, F. (eds.) ICTSS 2011. LNCS, vol. 7019, pp. 146–161. Springer, Heidelberg (2011)
13. Peleska, J., Huang, W., Hübner, F.: A novel approach to HW/SW integration testing of route-based interlocking system controllers. In: Lecomte, T., Pinger, R., Romanovsky, A. (eds.) RSSRail 2016. LNCS, vol. 9707, pp. 32–49. Springer, Heidelberg (2016). doi:10.1007/978-3-319-33951-1_3
14. Petrenko, A., Yevtushenko, N.: Adaptive testing of deterministic implementations specified by nondeterministic FSMs. In: Wolff, B., Zaïdi, F. (eds.) ICTSS 2011. LNCS, vol. 7019, pp. 162–178. Springer, Heidelberg (2011)
15. Petrenko, A., Yevtushenko, N.: Adaptive testing of nondeterministic systems with FSM. In: 15th International IEEE Symposium on High-Assurance Systems Engineering, HASE 2014, Miami Beach, FL, USA, 9–11 January 2014, pp. 224–228. IEEE Computer Society (2014). http://dx.doi.org/10.1109/HASE.2014.39
16. Roscoe, A.W.: Understanding Concurrent Systems. Springer, Heidelberg (2010)
17. Vasilevskii, M.P.: Failure diagnosis of automata. Kibernetika (Transl.) 4, 98–108 (1973)
18. WG-71, R.S.E.: Software considerations in airborne systems and equipment certification. Technical report, RTCA/DO-178C, RTCA Inc, 1140 Connecticut Avenue, N.W., Suite 1020, Washington, D.C. 20036, December 2011

Automated Verification Techniques

Abstract Interpretation of MATLAB Code with Interval Sets

Christian Dernehl[(⊠)], Norman Hansen, and Stefan Kowalewski

Lehrstuhl Informatik 11 - Embedded Software,
RWTH Aachen University, Aachen, Germany
{dernehl,hansen,kowalewski}@embedded.rwth-aachen.de

Abstract. In this paper we present how formal methods can be applied to MATLAB programs. We apply a static analysis based on abstract interpretation to derive reachable values and identify potential programming faults fully automatically. Our verification is built on a formalization and abstraction of matrices, structures and data types, such as integers and IEEE-754 floats. Combined with previously presented static analysis for Simulink, our tool can verify block diagrams with embedded MATLAB code. We show the feasibility of our tool and compare our solutions against a commercial tool, using real world applications.

1 Introduction

Nowadays, embedded systems are used in a variety of applications, automating many processes, which have been done manually before. Due to their strong links to the environment, embedded applications bear strong safety requirements. Software failures may cause harm to humans, the surroundings and economic success. Avoiding errors is crucial when selling cutting edge technology, which is often designed using model-based approaches. The use of mathematical models for the environment allows to test and improve the behavior of systems. Different domain specific languages, such as Mathematica, Maple, MATLAB, Modelica, SCADE, SciLab, Octave and more can be used for mathematical programming. Since MATLAB is a widely used tool in the automotive domain [8] and used to develop safety critical software, we focus on the identification of potential modeling/programming flaws of MATLAB programs.

MATLAB is both a programming language and an interpreter. In this paper, we generally mean by MATLAB the language unless stated otherwise. Rapid prototyping is supported with many built-in functions for specific domains, such as controls. Similar to other programming languages, primitive data types, custom structures and objects can be designed and reused. Control flow statements include function calls, if-else and switch branches, for and while loops and exit jumps, i.e. return statements.

In previous work [3], we have presented how to apply formal methods to block diagrams, designed with Simulink. We have used abstract interpretation with interval sets to prove the absence of certain errors, such as division by zero,

© Springer International Publishing AG 2016
M.H. ter Beek et al. (Eds.): FMICS-AVoCS 2016, LNCS 9933, pp. 25–38, 2016.
DOI: 10.1007/978-3-319-45943-1_2

under-, overflows and dead paths. Thus, our proposal for code analysis intends to improve our block diagram verification, since Simulink allows the user to specify custom blocks with MATLAB code. Our technique has been implemented in the *artshop*[1] framework, which is a model repository and provides external tool adapters, different analyses and reporting capabilities.

1.1   Contribution

After the presentation of related work in Sect. 2, we formalize the syntax and concrete semantics of MATLAB programs in Sect. 3. Subsequently, Sect. 3 introduces the formal description of the abstraction and the interpretation rules. Section 4 evaluates the presented approach by comparison with an industrial tool before Sect. 5 concludes our work.

2   Related Work

Static Analysis and Abstract Interpretation. Static analysis describes procedures to analyze programs or models without execution and derive properties automatically. In this work, we focus on abstract interpretation [1] to compute reachable value ranges for variables at each program location. Over the last years, much research effort has been gone to proposing new abstractions, such as intervals [1], relational domains [13,14], congruences [9], digital filters [7] and more. In abstract interpretation, domains and corresponding operations are defined to create a mapping between concrete and abstract program states. With the abstractions, it may be easier to prove properties in the abstract domain, which can be transfered back to the concrete program. Suppose intervals as an abstraction and if there is no division by zero in the abstract domain, then there is none in the concrete domain. Finally, abstract interpretation is a formal methods, which has been applied to several large scale industry projects [2,17].

Analysis of MATLAB Code. To our knowledge, abstract interpretation with a value range analysis has not been applied to MATLAB code to perform a value range analysis so far, however several static analyses for MATLAB programs have been investigated. In 2003 Elphick et al. [6] proposed a static analysis of MATLAB code to derive types and dimensions of variables to improve computational speed. Doherty et al. [5] investigated later in 2011 the mapping of identifiers to functions and variables. Aiming at a formal verification of MATLAB programs, Lu and Mukhopadhyay [12] designed one year later an algorithm to transform MATLAB code into SAT modulo theory (SMT) for formal verification.

3   Abstract Interpretation of MATLAB

First we present briefly the syntax and semantics of MATLAB code. Afterwards, abstractions for variables and control flow are shown.

---

[1] See https://artshop.embedded.rwth-aachen.de/.

3.1   Syntax and Concrete Semantics

Similar to other programming languages, MATLAB code consists of function definitions, expression statements and control flow commands. Table 1 presents a simplified grammar, describing the syntax of MATLAB programs. Several implementation specific parts have been simplified, bitwise and postfix operators, while others have been omitted, such as sub reference expressions $expr_1(expr_2)$ for array access or function calls. Additionally, we assume for brevity that each statement is terminated with a semicolon, although statements can also be terminated with an end of line symbol. Furthermore, we have omitted that boolean, numeric and matrix expressions can be constructed by function calls. Nevertheless, all these constructs have been considered in our implementation.

Expressions can be constructed using unary ($\blacklozenge$), binary ($\lozenge$), relational ($\bowtie$) and logical (logOp) operators. Note, unlike C, MATLAB uses the () operator for both array access and function call, with array access having precedence. Additional to scalar values, MATLAB allows matrix and tensor variables. In fact, each scalar variable is treated as a 1x1 matrix. Further operators specifically for matrices, such as matrix multiplication, inversion and least square (RDIV) are available. Element wise binary operations can be specified with a dot prefix, i.e. A.*B multiplies matrices A and B element wise.

Table 1. Simplified excerpt of the MATLAB program grammar

$\langle program \rangle$	$= \langle stmts \rangle$
$\langle stmts \rangle$	$= \{ \langle stmt \rangle$ ';'$\}$
$\langle stmt \rangle$	$= \langle expr \rangle \mid \langle conditional \rangle \mid \langle assignment \rangle \mid \langle loop \rangle$
$\langle expr \rangle$	$= \langle boolExpr \rangle \mid \langle numericExpr \rangle \mid \langle matrixExpr \rangle$
$\langle boolExpr \rangle$	$= \langle primaryExpr \rangle \mid \langle numericExpr \rangle \bowtie \langle numericExpr \rangle$
	$\mid \langle boolExpr \rangle$ logOp $\langle boolExpr \rangle$
$\langle numericExpr \rangle$	$= \langle boolExpr \rangle \mid \langle numericExpr \rangle \lozenge \langle numericExpr \rangle \mid \blacklozenge \langle numericExpr \rangle$
$\langle matrixExpr \rangle$	$=$ '[' $\{ \{ \langle expr \rangle$ ',' $\}$ ';' $\{ \langle expr \rangle$ ',' $\} \}$ ']' $\mid$
	$\langle expr \rangle$ [':' $\langle expr \rangle$] ':' $\langle expr \rangle$
$\langle assignment \rangle$	$= \langle identifier \rangle$ '=' $\langle expr \rangle$, ;
$\langle varList \rangle$	$=$ '['$\{ \langle variable \rangle$ ',' $\}$ ']'
$\langle multiAssign \rangle$	$= \langle varList \rangle$ ' $=$' $\langle expr \rangle$
$\langle conditional \rangle$	$=$ '**if** ' $\langle boolExpr \rangle \langle expr \rangle$ [{ '**elseif** '$\langle boolExpr \rangle \langle expr \rangle$ }]
	['**else** ' $\langle expr \rangle$] ' **end**'
$\langle loop \rangle$	$= \langle while \rangle \mid \langle for \rangle$
$\langle while \rangle$	$=$ '**while** ' $\langle boolExpr \rangle \{ \langle stmts \rangle \}$ ' **end**'
$\langle for \rangle$	$=$ '**for** ' $\langle variable \rangle$ '=' $\langle matrixExpr \rangle \{ \langle stmts \rangle \}$ ' **end**'
$\langle primaryExpr \rangle$	$= \langle identifier \rangle \mid \langle constant \rangle$
$\langle functiondef \rangle$	$=$ '**function** ' $\langle varList \rangle$ ' $=$ '$\langle funName \rangle$ '(' $\{ \langle variable \rangle$ ',' $\}$ ')'
$\langle \bowtie \rangle$	$=$ '>' $\mid$ '>=' $\mid$ '<' $\mid$ '<=' $\mid$ '==' $\mid$ '~='
$\langle \lozenge \rangle$	$=$ '+' $\mid$ '$-$' $\mid$ '*' $\mid$ '/' $\mid$ '\' $\mid$ '^' $\mid$ ':' $\mid$ '.' $\langle \lozenge \rangle$
$\langle \blacklozenge \rangle$	$=$ '+' $\mid$ '$-$'
$\langle logOp \rangle$	$=$ '&' $\mid$ '|' $\mid$ '~' $\langle logOp \rangle$

Limitations. Our intended use of the static value range analysis for MATLAB code is the abstraction of embedded MATLAB-function blocks[2] in Simulink. Simulink constraints the use of MATLAB code within embedded MATLAB-functions to certain language constructs or restrictive use of such. These restrictions are necessary in order to be able to generate code out of and simulate the Simulink diagram. Thus, we impose limitations and assumptions about the MATLAB code to be analyzed, which are backed by the Simulink restrictions. However, we target to abstract extrinsic functions for which MATLAB code is provided and thus support some language features which Simulink does not support, too.

A first restriction of our analysis relates to the inability to analyze recursive functions or programs, which is also not supported by Simulink. Furthermore, MATLAB objects which are no structures or cell arrays are also not supported by the analysis. This includes objects such as control systems[3] and external objects, for instance from Java. As such, user defined classes with events and methods are not supported. Moreover, only integer enumerations without further functionality can be used. External code, from C/C++ and Java, either compiled or available as source code is stubbed and side effects are not considered. Error handling, using try and catch clauses is neither supported. Finally, we assume the absence of complex variables, anonymous functions and dynamic field access with the *x.(y)* operator.

Types. The MATLAB language has a dynamic type system, in which variables may change their type during execution. Primitive types for scalars are signed and unsigned integers (8,16,32 bit), 32 and 64 bit floats and fixed point numbers. Floating point numbers behave according to the IEEE-754 standard[4]. Structures and cell arrays are further non primitive data types, which are considered. Let the set of primitive data types be $\mathbb{T}$, containing all integer types and floating types, i.e. `[u]intN`, $N \in \{8, 16, 32\}$ and `float32`, `float64`. Furthermore, assume $\mathbb{S}$ to be set of strings, representing all field names of all structures, then the type set is $\mathbb{D}$.

$$\mathbb{D} := \{\mathcal{T} \times \ldots \times \mathcal{T}\}_{\mathcal{T} \in \mathbb{T}} \cup \mathbb{D} \times \ldots \times \mathbb{D} \cup \mathbb{S} \to \mathbb{D} \tag{1}$$

The left most part of the union defines matrices with a primitive type, so that all elements in the matrix must have the same primitive type. Note the recursive definition allows cell arrays ($\mathbb{D} \times \ldots \times \mathbb{D}$) to contain cell arrays or structures themselves, which also holds for structures ($\mathbb{S} \to \mathbb{D}$).

A MATLAB program consists of variables $\mathcal{V}$ and operations on these variables. A program state σ assigns a concrete value to each variable of the program. During a function call, special variable environments $\mathcal{V}_{Env}$, i.e. workspaces, are created. The set of program states are all potential variable assignments for each environment.

$$\Sigma := \{\sigma | \sigma : \mathcal{V}_{Env} \times \mathcal{V} \to \mathbb{D}\} \tag{2}$$

---

[2] See http://www.mathworks.com/help/simulink/slref/matlabfunction.html.
[3] See http://www.mathworks.com/help/control/ref/tf.html.
[4] As long as the used machine implements the IEEE-754 standard.

With concrete values for each variable, expressions can be evaluated with the val_σ function for a given state σ.

$$\text{val}_\sigma : expr \rightarrow \mathbb{D} : a \rightarrow \text{val}_\sigma(a) \tag{3}$$

For scalar expressions, the valuation function is defined below for constant c and variable $v \in \mathcal{V}$.

$$\text{val}_\sigma(c) := c \qquad\qquad \text{val}_\sigma(\blacklozenge e) := \blacklozenge \text{val}_\sigma(e) \tag{4}$$

$$\text{val}_\sigma(v) := \sigma(v) \qquad\qquad \text{val}_\sigma(e_1 \lozenge e_2) := \text{val}_\sigma(e_1) \lozenge \text{val}_\sigma(e_2) \tag{5}$$

For instance, $\text{val}_\sigma(\texttt{3*x+5})$ evaluates to $(\text{val}_\sigma(3) * \text{val}_\sigma(x)) + \text{val}_\sigma(5) = 3\sigma(x) + 5$.

Matrices. In addition to scalars, values can be grouped into matrices or tensors, leaving a single type for all values within the matrix. Compared with scalars, matrices support additional operations, such as matrix multiplication, inversion and least square optimization. For element-wise unary and binary operations, the valuation function is also applied element-wise, with $\hat{v}$ being the index vector.

$$\text{val}_\sigma(\blacklozenge A) := [\text{val}_\sigma(\blacklozenge a_{\hat{v}})]_{\hat{v}} \qquad\qquad \text{val}_\sigma(A \lozenge B) := [\text{val}_\sigma(a_{\hat{v}} \lozenge b_{\hat{v}})]_{\hat{v}} \tag{6}$$

$$\text{val}_\sigma(\blacklozenge_M A) := \blacklozenge_M \text{val}_\sigma(A) \qquad\qquad \text{val}_\sigma(A \lozenge_M B) := \text{val}_\sigma(A) \lozenge_M \text{val}_\sigma(B) \tag{7}$$

MATLAB provides a variety of functions to construct standard matrices, such as *zeros*, *ones* and *eye*, which yield matrices filled with zeros or ones and the identity matrix for given dimensions.

Structures. Since matrices cannot group values of different types, MATLAB provides structures, similar to structs in the C programming language. Each structure has several fields representing an object. A field is accessed using the dot operator(.), where the structure variable is on the left and field name is on the right hand side, i.e. *struct.fieldname*. Consider a structure s with fields x, y and z. $s.z$ would access the field z within s. Element-wise operations are not allowed on structures. Since a structure is mapped to a variable, the valuation function results also in a structure.

$$\text{val}_\sigma(s.x) := \text{val}_\sigma(\text{val}_\sigma(s).x) \tag{8}$$

The inner valuation function resolves the structure variable to a concrete structure, while the outer valuation extracts the object x within s.

Cell Arrays. Matrices compose scalars of the same type with a given dimension. Cell arrays extend matrices by allowing, similar to structures, different types and dimensions in each part. Thus, only structural operations, such as reshaping the matrix structure can be applied. In the following listing, the variable a is a cell array in which the element at position (1,1) is of type `uint8`, while the other matrices are of type `double`.

```
a = {uint8(eye(5)), ones(3,7); zeros(3,2), eye(2)};
```

A cell within a cell array can be accessed by the {,} operators, hence `a1,1` accesses the element at position (1,1). The concrete value of a cell array are all elements within the array.

$$\text{val}_\sigma(\{c_{\hat{v}}\}) = \{\text{val}_\sigma(c_{\hat{v}})\} \tag{9}$$

Although MATLAB code in Simulink and code generation do not support cell arrays, we define the correspondent abstractions. These can still be of use when extrinsic function calls from Simulink to externally defined MATLAB functions are contained within the model.

Workspaces. During the execution of programs, variables are kept in a *workspace.* Hence, the MATLAB developer interface itself has a root workspace and for each function a new empty workspace is created. For function calls, the arguments, which are passed as call by value, are stored in the workspace.

Furthermore, there are global variables, which are visible among several functions and thus are decoupled from any local workspace. Persistent variables do not loose their value after exiting a function. Hence persistent variables can be understood as static variables of a certain function.

Functions. When resolving the parenthesis operator, the value on the left hand side can either be a matrix or a function identifier. Functions can be specified in several ways. Built-in functions are shipped with the MATLAB interpreter and are resolved internally. User defined functions can either be specified by a MATLAB file (.m), containing a function definition and code. External functions may be given in other languages, such as C/C++ or Java. Generally, C/C++ functions can be compiled from MATLAB with a compiler to a mex[5] file, for which the source code must not be provided during run-time. Similarly, for functions programmed in Java, no source code is necessary for execution.

Whether functions are executed or variables are addressed, depends on an internal MATLAB algorithm. However, the following example makes it plausible, that variables have priority.

```
>>zeros = ones(5);
>>zeros(3)
ans = 1
```

In the example, a variable *zeros* is created by calling the built-in function *ones*, yielding a matrix filled with ones. When calling *zeros* in the second line, the variable *zeros* is resolved, prior to the built-in function.

Type and Dimension Inference. So far, we have assumed that constants and declared variables have a given type. However, MATLAB uses a type inference system, which has previously been investigated [6]. Regarding our implementation, consider the following example from the MATLAB console.

```
>>class(double(1.3) * uint8(3.5) * double(2.2))
ans = uint8
>> class(single(1.3) * uint8(3.5) * double(2.2))
Error using *
Integers can only be combined with integers of the same class, or scalar
    doubles.
>> uint8(5) * double(0.2)
ans = 1
```

From this behavior, we have derived the following facts. First, expressions with double are automatically casted up to double, which is also the default type for constants. This simplifies building expressions of constants with other types, including matrices. Second, after type inference, the result is casted down automatically. However, this behavior is limited to double constants. For 32 bit single floats and other primitive types, no automatic casting is performed. Thus, in our implementation, we infer double

---

[5] See http://www.mathworks.com/help/matlab/ref/mex.html.

constants by the closest defined expression. For assignments of fresh variables, we derive the type of the right hand side expression.

Deriving dimensions of matrix expressions is solved by defining additional matrix operations, such as addition or multiplication with scalars. In these cases, the scalar value is applied element-wise. Corner cases, in which a variable has multiple dimensions, but only contains a single element, such as $[1, 1, 1]$ are also considered, i.e. `ones(1,1,1)*ones(5)`.

3.2 Abstract Semantics

For our abstraction, we use an interval sets [3] domain, i.e. an ordered set of IEEE-754 intervals [10] without overlapping intervals for each concrete scalar. With this approach, we tend to increase precision, since unconnected intervals can be expressed. For instance, the interval from $[-1, 1]$ without zero can be expressed by interval sets. When applying binary operations, all resulting combinations of both sets are merged. To avoid uncontrolled growth of intervals in the set, we limit the intervals per set to a configurable number. If this number is exceeded, the intervals with the smallest distance between their bounds are merged to a single interval, as overlapping intervals are in general. Depending on the primitive data type, several interval implementations are used to capture the entire behavior of each type. Therefore, interval sets for unsigned and signed 8,16 and 32 bit integers and 32 and 64 bit floats are implemented. For floats, the user may specify an explicit IEEE-754 rounding mode to be applied when performing IEEE-754 operations. Otherwise, the result of all rounding modes is merged after each operation introducing an additional over approximation. Furthermore, special handling for operations producing and using symbols, such as NaN and $\pm\infty$ have been considered.

State Abstraction. For each abstract state ρ, there is an abstract valuation function, yielding an abstract value for expressions.

$$\mathrm{val}_\rho^\# : Expr \to \mathbb{I}_\mathbb{D} : a \to \mathrm{val}_\rho^\#(a) \tag{10}$$

In addition, abstract unary $\blacklozenge^\#$ and binary $\lozenge^\#$ operations can be carried out on the abstract domain.

$$\mathrm{val}_\rho^\#(c) := \{[c, c]\} \qquad\qquad \mathrm{val}_\rho^\#(\blacklozenge e) := \blacklozenge^\# \mathrm{val}_\rho^\#(e) \tag{11}$$

$$\mathrm{val}_\rho^\#(v) := \rho(v) \qquad\qquad \mathrm{val}_\rho^\#(e_1 \lozenge e_2) := \mathrm{val}_\rho^\#(e_1) \lozenge^\# \mathrm{val}_\rho^\#(e_2) \tag{12}$$

The $^\#$ denotes the corresponding abstraction of the operation on the abstract interval set domain. For binary operations on interval sets IS_1 and IS_2, we compute all combinations of all intervals, i.e. $IS_1 \lozenge^\# IS_2 := \cup_{I_1 \in IS_1, I_2 \in IS_2} I_1 \lozenge_I I_2$, where $\lozenge_I$ is the operation for intervals, as presented in [10].

For instance, $\mathrm{val}_\rho^\#(3*x+5)$ evaluates to $\mathrm{val}_\rho^\#(3) * \mathrm{val}_\rho^\#(x)) +^\# \mathrm{val}_\rho^\#(5) = \{[3, 3]\} *^\# \rho(x) +^\# \{[5, 5]\}$. Similarly, relational $\bowtie$ and logical operators $logOp$ are abstracted.

$$\mathrm{val}_\rho^\#(e_1 \bowtie e_2) := \mathrm{val}_\rho^\#(e_1) \bowtie^\# \mathrm{val}_\rho^\#(e_2) \tag{13}$$

$$\mathrm{val}_\rho^\#(e_1 \ logOp \ e_2) := \mathrm{val}_\rho^\#(e_1) \ logOp^\# \ \mathrm{val}_\rho^\#(e_2) \tag{14}$$

Matrix Abstraction. Similar to scalars, fixed size matrices can be abstracted.

$$\mathrm{val}_\rho^\#(\blacklozenge A) := \left[\mathrm{val}_\rho^\#(\blacklozenge a_{\hat{v}})\right]_{\hat{v}} \qquad \mathrm{val}_\rho^\#(A\lozenge B) := \left[\mathrm{val}_\rho^\#(a_{\hat{v}}\lozenge b_{\hat{v}})\right]_{\hat{v}} \qquad (15)$$

$$\mathrm{val}_\rho^\#(\blacklozenge_M A) := \blacklozenge_M^\# \mathrm{val}_\rho^\#(A) \qquad \mathrm{val}_\rho^\#(A\lozenge_M B) := \mathrm{val}_\rho^\#(A)\lozenge_M^\# \mathrm{val}_\rho^\#(B) \qquad (16)$$

Although abstract matrices have in many cases a fixed length, the dimension of matrices may depend on the run of the program. Consider Listing 1.1, where the length of x depends on a random number.

Listing 1.1. Variable Size Variables

```
if ( rand () > 0.5 )
    x = [1 2 3];
else
    x = [1 2];
end
```

In this case, the length of x is either two or three. Since the random number function **rand()** is abstracted by an interval $[0,1]$, both paths have to be taken in the abstract execution. For such cases, we use a matrix with the maximum dimension size, in this case with three elements. Additionally, the potential sizes are stored in an interval set. In case a statement yields potential access to an element of the matrix, a warning is issued. However, the abstract interpretation is continued and correct access is assumed. If our analysis can prove that an invalid access occurs, the algorithm is aborted and a message is issued.

Structures. Structures are represented by abstract structures, mapping strings to abstract values. Thus, the abstract valuation of a structure variable yields an abstract structure. In order to extract a field, we extend the abstract valuation function.

$$\mathrm{val}_\rho^\#(x.a) := \mathrm{val}_\rho^\#\left(\mathrm{val}_\rho^\#(x).a\right) \qquad (17)$$

Note, that the outer valuation function might yields an abstract object, which itself might be an abstract cell array, structure or matrix.

Cell Arrays. As with matrices, cell arrays may also have a variable size during execution, for example, **cell(uint8(rand() * 10))** yields a cell array with zero up to 10 elements. Therefore, we also store bounds on the size of a cell array. As with matrices, our implementation issues warnings for potential out of bound accesses and continues if possible, assuming a valid cell access. Our abstraction is a set of cell elements, which are abstract objects.

$$\mathrm{val}_\rho^\#(\{c_{\hat{v}}\}) := \left\{\mathrm{val}_\rho^\#(c_{\hat{v}})\right\} \qquad (18)$$

Reshaping Operations. Matrices and cell arrays provide both structural operations, which change the dimensions, while keeping elements untouched. Functions, such as **squeeze** and **reshape** perform a rearrangement of elements. Assuming variable size abstractions, we issue a warning if the reshape operation might be out of bounds and assume a correct access and continue with the analysis.

3.3   Abstract Interpretation

With data types and structures abstracted, interpretation rules for the program execution must be defined. These rules describe a transition relation, switching between two states. Formalizations for these rules have been defined, for instance for the C programming language [1,2]. Therefore, we focus in this part on differences to MATLAB code.

Built-in Functions. Since built-in functions cannot be analyzed, due to lacking MATLAB code, we have defined abstractions for a certain set of functions. These individual abstractions increase the precision of the analysis. However, we have derived the behavior from the official documentation and experiments. Hence, there is no guarantee, that our abstractions are correct. We have defined abstractions for matrix constructors, such as *zeros, ones, rand, eye, diag* and math functions, such as *sum, norm*[6], *min, max, cell* and *class*[7].

Function Stubbing. External functions, for which no MATLAB source code is available, are stubbed, i.e. over approximated by the extreme values of the corresponding type. By default, the type and dimensions are computed by type inference, however, if this yields no result, a scalar function with type `double` is assumed. Nevertheless, in practice the user could specify type and dimensions for unsupported functions.

Conditional Statements. For conditional statements, such as `if(u > f(x))`, we improve the quality of the analysis by narrowing the intervals, based on the constraint. If the expression might be true and has the form $\bigwedge \bigvee v \bowtie expr$ where $v \in \mathcal{V}$, we can improve the analysis by narrowing the interval set. With previously computed intervals for all variables, a solution can be computed using interval arithmetic with additional checks for special IEEE-754 behavior. Solutions for variables in disjunctions are unionized, while conjunctions are cut. Although, we are limited in our current implementation to these simple constraints, more advanced techniques, such as relational domains [13], interval linear programming [15] or symbolic methods [4,16] can provide solutions for complex constraints. A similar and generally better approach has been applied for different programming languages in other work [2].

In case the expression cannot be narrowed, our algorithm continues with the previously computed interval sets. We repeat the procedure for `elseif` parts, while for the `else` branch the complement of the interval set is calculated[8]. Similar to other value range analyses, we interpret both branches if necessary and merge the results.

Abstract interpretation for `switch` statements is processed in the same way, except that MATLAB has a slightly different syntax here. Instead of having multiple `case` statements without a break, MATLAB uses cell array notation. Furthermore, MATLAB does not require a `break` statement during a `switch`, so that `break` commands always refer to loop statements. For example, the following code assigns to y the value 1 if x is 1,2 or 3, so there is no fall through after the first `case` statement. In fact, a `break` statement within a `switch` would be associated to the outer `while` or `for` loop.

```
switch(x)
    case {1,2,3} y = 1;
    case 4 y = 2;
end
```

---

[6] Only p-vector norms and the $1, \infty$ norms for matrices.

[7] Only for primitive types.

[8] Which might include NaN values for floating point types.

Loops. Not only `switch` statements have a special syntax in MATLAB, but also `for` loops are more restricted, i.e. MATLAB requires loops with the `for` keyword to be of finite length. In detail, a matrix has to be supplied with a finite number of elements, since MATLAB only allows matrices to a user-defined maximum length[9]. Changes to the iterating variable within the loop are executed, but do not affect the termination condition of the `for` loop, i.e. in each iteration the next element from the vector is taken. Consequently, our abstract interpretation checks whether the supplied vector size is below a specified, but low, threshold and executes eventually all iterations.

In contrary, the condition of `while` loops is checked before each iteration. Hence there is no guarantee of termination. In both cases, i.e. large `for` and `while` loops, widening, as presented in [1] and adapted to interval sets in [3], is applied. Thus the set of reachable values is widened to $[-\infty; \infty]$ after a configured number of loop iterations, being a valid fix point for IEEE-754 values.

As for conditional statements, we narrow the interval set based on the same procedure. Especially for `for` loops the union of all elements with the given matrix can be used to shrink the interval set.

4   Evaluation

After having presented our approach to derive reachable value ranges for MATLAB code, we evaluate it against an industrial tool.

We selected three MATLAB files from external sources to be used for evaluation purpose. Those are a Kalman filter (KALMAN) implementation[10], an implementation of ℓ_1 trend filtering (L1TF)[11][11] and the MATLAB implementation of the matrix exponential function *expm()* of MATLAB R2014b (EXPM).

We intend to refine and extend our existing analysis of Simulink models (AV) by abstract interpretation of MATLAB-function blocks (MATLAB code). Since the Simulink Design Verifier (SLDV), which has been used for evaluation purpose in previous work, is able to analyze MATLAB-function blocks too, the SLDV is used for evaluation purpose. Thus, we build Simulink models containing MATLAB-function blocks implementing the examples mentioned above[12].

All constructed Simulink models are build of a MATLAB-function block containing one of the three identified examples, an outport block and either constant blocks (indicated by $modelname_{CI}$) to provide input values to the MATLAB-function block or inport blocks to provide free input (indicated by $modelname_{FI}$). Since none of the examples is intended to be used as code in embedded MATLAB-function blocks, slight modifications due to the restrictive support of the MATLAB language inside MATLAB-function blocks are necessary. These modifications are the conversion of MATLAB scripts into functions with input and output parameters, the removal of

---

[9] See   http://www.mathworks.com/help/matlab/matlab_env/set-workspace-and-vari
    able-preferences.html.

[10] http://www.mathworks.com/matlabcentral/mlc-downloads/downloads/
    submissions/37782/versions/1/previews/kalman.m/index.html.

[11] http://stanford.edu/~boyd/l1_tf/.

[12] Note that we use Simulink only to provide input to the MATLAB-function and do
    not model relevant functionality for the analysis to work or causing additional over
    approximation due to widening for loops in the Simulink model. Hence, the quality of
    the results is not affected by the MATLAB-function being integrated into Simulink.

code parts which are responsible for visual and textual output, the elimination of cell array use and the removal of variables with increasing or variable sizes by pre-allocation. We succeeded to adapt the examples accordingly, resulting in executable Simulink models. However, the modifications restrict the original functionality of the examples, e.g. with regard to the applicability to arbitrary large matrices for EXPM, which has been restricted to two dimensions. Since the KALMAN script contains two method calls `randn()` to generate noise, which will cause analyses to assume return values in the range $[-\infty; \infty]$, we construct an additional variation where `randn()` is replaced by `zeros()`. The model variants with this modification are $KALMAN_{CI}Z$ and $KALMAN_{FI}Z$ respectively.

We perform the evaluation on a 64-bit Windows 7 operating system running on an Intel i5 2.67 GHz CPU with eight gigabytes memory. The model files where constructed with MATLAB R2014b and the imports of the models for AV and the SLDV analyses performed with MATLAB 2015b. Since AV is implemented in Java, the 64 bit version of Java 8 update 77 is used.

SLDV and AV allow the user to configure the analysis in various ways. We consider two configurations ($SLDV_V$ and $SLDV_{DL}$) for SLDV analyses. $SLDV_V$ is the default configuration with additionally enabled option *Out of bound array access* for design error detection. $SLDV_{DL}$ is the same configuration as $SLDV_V$ but with enabled dead logic detection. Since the activation of dead logic detection disables the detection of other modeling flaws, such as potential divisions by zero, we analyze every evaluation model using both configurations consecutively. As for evaluations in our previous work, the default configuration of AV is used.

Besides the issued warnings, we compare the duration of the analyses AV and SLDV. Since the SLDV excludes the duration of model opening, compilation and translation to internal intermediate representation from its time measurement, we exclude the time required to start MATLAB, load the model and translate it to our intermediate abstract block diagram representation, too.

Table 2 shows the resulting time elapses and issued warnings for the computation of the different analyses and their correspondent configuration for the evaluation models and their variants. The X entries indicate that the correspondent analysis was unable to analyze the model using the given configuration due to incompatibility although the model is, due to the described adaptions, executable in Simulink. The SLDV states,

Table 2. Time elapse for analysis computation in seconds

Model	Logical lines of MATLAB code	Time elapse (s)			Warnings		
		$SLDV_V$	$SLDV_{DL}$	AV	$SLDV_V$	$SLDV_{DL}$	AV
$EXPM_{CI}$	80	X	X	2.4	X	X	1
$EXPM_{FI}$	80	X	X	1.4	X	X	50
$L1TF_{CI}$	82	X	X	0.8	X	X	10
$L1TF_{FI}$	82	X	X	0.4	X	X	20
$KALMAN_{CI}$	44	37	37	0.4	57	1	30
$KALMAN_{FI}$	44	116	44	0.7	55	1	62
$KALMAN_{CI}Z$	44	44	42	0.9	52	0	0
$KALMAN_{FI}Z$	44	111	39	0.9	51	0	57

that the reason for the incompatibility regarding the EXPM model is its inability to determine the size of the expressions

```
floor(((((j-1)*n\_m)+1)/2):floor(((((j-1)*n\_m)+n\_m)/2)
floor((((j*n\_m)+1)/2):floor(((((j*n\_m)+n\_m)/2))
```

which were introduced as modified expressions to use matrices instead of cell arrays. The L1TF model cannot be analyzed using the SLDV due to the use of logical indexing with index variables `negIdx1` and `negIndx2`, which is not supported by the SLDV inside MATLAB-function blocks.

For $EXPM_{CI}$, the AV issues a single warning regarding dead code in the MATLAB program. In particular, the `else` branch of the `if` statement is detected to be unreachable, which is true since the constant input causes the condition to be always satisfied. Allowing arbitrary two-dimensional input values ($EXPM_{FI}$), AV detects two potential divisions by zero, two potential divisions by $\pm\infty$ and 46 potential occurrences of NaN (Not-a-Number). Because $EXPM_{FI}$ considers the input to the MATLAB-function to be within the interval $[-\infty; \infty]$ and values are computed based on the input, both division operators cause each a warning about division by zero, $\pm\infty$ and the potential occurence of NaN as a result of the operation. Since NaN values are propagated along operations, e.g. $x + NaN = NaN$, further warnings about potential occurring NaN values are issued[13].

Regarding the models $L1TF_{CI}$ and $L1TF_{FI}$, AV detects two false-positive warnings, a potential overflow and a potential underflow for the statement `status = 'solved';`, which is a false positive. For both models, all other warnings are NaN warnings. For the $L1TF_{CI}$ model with constant input, the NaN warnings are introduced due to the over approximation of the contained `for` loop.

Before comparing the analysis results of AV with the results of SLDV, we take a look at the warnings issued using $SLDV_{DL}$ for $KALMAN_{CI}$ and $KALMAN_{FI}$. The SLDV output report states for both model variants, that the MATLAB-function block of the model is unsupported and thus, only partial results could be computed. Since the $SLDV_{DL}$ does not produce any other results, we will further focus only on $SLDV_V$.

Table 3 gives a detailed overview of the amount and types of warnings being produced by $SLDV_V$. It can be seen, that although there is no division by zero due to constant inputs for $KALMAN_{CI}$ and $KALMAN_{CI}Z$, both division operators in the MATLAB program cause corresponding warnings. Considering free input, one division by zero is detected and by * is indicated, that a further division by zero was undecidable. Furthermore, the mentioning of an unsupported MATLAB-function blocks originates from the over approximation of the `randn()` method call in $KALMAN_{CI}$ and $KALMAN_{FI}$. There are several warnings about array bounds for all models. However, these are false-positive warnings in all cases since the array sizes and accesses are all constant. Similar, the overflow warnings are of false-positive nature since all programs work only with the default type double. The use of `randn()` causes additional overflow warnings, too.

Table 4 presents the results using the AV analysis for the Kalman filter models. Comparing the results obtained with AV and $SLDV_V$, it can be noticed that there are no overflow warnings and considerably less array bound warnings. Because of the IEEE-754 double type, data type overflows are impossible and thus not issued. Nevertheless,

---

[13] The consecutive issuing of NaN warnings caused by NaN propagation can be disabled in order to identify only the cause of potential NaN occurrences. However, this option is disabled in the used default configuration.

Table 3. Detailed overview of warnings being issued analyzing the Kalman filter examples with $SLDV_V$

	KALMAN$_{CI}$	KALMAN$_{FI}$	KALMAN$_{CI}Z$	KALMAN$_{FI}Z$
Division by zero	2	1*	2	1*
Division by $\pm\infty$	0	0	0	0
Overflow/underflow	31	31	27	27
Array bounds	23	23	23	23
Unsupported block	1	1	0	0

Table 4. Detailed overview of warnings being issued analyzing the Kalman filter examples with AV

	KALMAN$_{CI}$	KALMAN$_{FI}$	KALMAN$_{CI}Z$	KALMAN$_{FI}Z$
Division by zero	0	1	0	1
Division by $\pm\infty$	0	2	0	2
Overflow/underflow	0	0	0	0
Array bounds	2	2	0	0
Unsupported block	0	0	0	0
Result could be NaN	28	57	0	54

the detected potential array bound violations are false-positive results. Comparing the division related warnings of both analyses, AV does not assume every division to be a division by zero. However, for arbitrary inputs (KALMAN$_{FI}Z$ and KALMAN$_{FI}Z$) potential divisions by zero and $\pm\infty$ are recognized.

As to expect, the amount of NaN related warnings increases for the models with free input and the `randn()` method due to the assumed input or return values $[-\infty; \infty]$ and correspondent operations on $\pm\infty$. Consequently, the model KALMAN$_{CI}Z$ could be proven to be safe with regard to divisions by IEEE-754 values NaN, $\pm\infty$, array access and data type overflows.

5   Conclusion

This paper provides a formal approach to derive reachable value ranges for MATLAB programs based on abstract interpretation. Combined with an existing static value range analysis for Simulink models, it enables the detection of potential modeling flaws during model-based development of embedded systems within Simulink MATLAB-function blocks. Evaluating our approach with three MATLAB programs, we were able to show the support of Simulink functionality which is not supported by the Simulink Design Verifier. Moreover, analysis time and false-positive warnings regarding divisions, overflows and array accesses are reduced. Due to the sound abstraction of IEEE-754 floating point arithmetic, IEEE-754 related warnings such as potential occurrences of NaN or divisions by $\pm\infty$ are detectable. Future work will focus on the reduction of over approximations and the extension of supported MATLAB functionality.

Acknowledgements. This project was funded within the Priority Programme "Cooperatively Interacting Automobiles" of the German Science Foundation DFG (SPP 1835). The authors acknowledge the fruitful collaboration with the project partners.

References

1. Cousot, P., Cousot, R.: Abstract interpretation: a unified lattice model forstatic analysis of programs by construction or approximation of fixpoints. In: Proceedings of the 4th ACM SIGACT-SIGPLAN Symposium on Principles of Programming Languages, POPL 1977, New York, NY, USA (1977)
2. Cousot, P., Cousot, R., Feret, J., Mauborgne, L., Miné, A., Rival, X.: Why does Astrée scale up? Formal Methods Syst. Des. **35**(3), 229–264 (2009)
3. Dernehl, C., Hansen, N., Gerlitz, T., Kowalewski, S.: Static value range analysis for MATLAB/simulink-models. In: INFORMATIK 2015 (2015)
4. Dernehl, C., Hansen, N., Kowalewski, S.: Combining abstract interpretation with symbolic execution for a static value range analysis of block diagrams. In: De Nicola, R., Kühn, E. (eds.) SEFM 2016. LNCS, vol. 9763, pp. 137–152. Springer, Heidelberg (2016). doi:10.1007/978-3-319-41591-8_10
5. Doherty, J., Hendren, L., Radpour, S.: Kind analysis for MATLAB. ACM SIGPLAN Not. **46**(10), 99–118 (2011)
6. Elphick, D., Leuschel, M., Cox, S.: Partial evaluation of MATLAB. In: Pfenning, F., Macko, M. (eds.) GPCE 2003. LNCS, vol. 2830, pp. 344–363. Springer, Heidelberg (2003)
7. Feret, J.: Static analysis of digital filters. In: Schmidt, D. (ed.) ESOP 2004. LNCS, vol. 2986, pp. 33–48. Springer, Heidelberg (2004)
8. Gerlitz, T., Minh Tran, Q., Dziobek, C.: Detection and handling of model smells for MATLAB/simulink models. In: Proceedings of the International Workshop on Modelling in Automotive Software Engineering. CEUR (2015)
9. Granger, P.: Static analysis of arithmetical congruences. Int. J. Comput. Math. **30**, 165–190 (1989)
10. Hickey, T., Ju, Q., Van Emden, M.H.: Interval arithmetic: from principles to implementation. J. ACM (JACM) **48**, 1038–1068 (2001)
11. Kim, S.J., Koh, K., Boyd, S., Gorinevsky, D.: l1 trend filtering. SIAM Rev. **51**, 339–360 (2009)
12. Lu, Z., Mukhopadhyay, S.: Model-based static code analysis for MATLAB models. In: Margaria, T., Steffen, B. (eds.) ISoLA 2012, Part I. LNCS, vol. 7609, pp. 474–487. Springer, Heidelberg (2012)
13. Miné, A.: Relational abstract domains for the detection of floating-point run-time errors. In: Schmidt, D. (ed.) ESOP 2004. LNCS, vol. 2986, pp. 3–17. Springer, Heidelberg (2004)
14. Miné, A.: The octagon abstract domain. High.-Order Symb. Comput. **19**, 31–100 (2006)
15. Rohn, J.: Interval linear programming. In: Rohn, J. (ed.) Linear Optimization Problems with Inexact Data, pp. 79–100. Springer US, Boston (2006)
16. Rümmer, P., Wahl, T.: An SMT-LIB theory of binary floating-point arithmetic. In: International Workshop on Satisfiability Modulo Theories (SMT) (2010)
17. Stattelmann, S., Biallas, S., Schlich, B., Kowalewski, S.: Applying static code analysis on industrial controller code. In: 19th IEEE International Conference on Emerging Technologies and Factory Automation (ETFA). IEEE (2014)

Workflow Nets Verification: SMT or CLP?

Hadrien Bride, Olga Kouchnarenko, Fabien Peureux, and Guillaume Voiron[(✉)]

Institut FEMTO-ST – UMR CNRS 6174, University of Franche-Comté,
16, route de Gray, 25030 Besançon, France
{hbride,okouchna,fpeureux,gvoiron}@femto-st.fr

Abstract. The design and the analysis of business processes commonly relies on workflow nets, a suited class of Petri nets. This paper evaluates and compares two resolution methods—Satisfiability Modulo Theory (SMT) and Constraint Logic Programming (CLP)—applied to the verification of modal specifications over workflow nets. Firstly, it provides a concise description of the verification methods based on constraint solving. Secondly, it presents the experimental protocol designed to evaluate and compare the scalability and efficiency of both resolution approaches. Thirdly, the paper reports on the obtained results and discusses the lessons learned from these experiments.

Keywords: Workflow nets · Modal specifications · Verification method · Experimental comparison · Satisfiability modulo theory · Constraint solving problem

1 Introduction

In recent years, the growing need by companies to improve their organizational efficiency and productivity has led to the design and the analysis of business processes. Workflows constitute a convenient way for analysts to describe the business processes in a formal and graphical manner. Intuitively, a workflow system describes the set of possible runs of a particular system/process. Furthermore, workflow analysts are required to express and to verify specific properties over the workflows they designed to make sure that no undesirable behaviour is present while performing the specified tasks.

Among existing workflow specifications, this paper focuses on modal specifications that allow the description of necessary and admissible behaviours over workflow nets, a suited class of Petri nets. As in [1], the validity of a modal specification can be inferred from the satisfiability of a corresponding constraint system, by using Constraint Logic Programming (CLP). Besides the theoretical assessment of the approach, a proof-of-concept toolchain has enabled to successfully evaluate its effectiveness and reliability. However, as advocated in [1], these first encouraging experimental results need to be confirmed by extensive experimentation, in particular to definitively assess the scalability and the efficiency of the approach. This paper precisely investigates these issues: it aims to empirically (1) assess the scalability, (2) evaluate the efficiency of the verification

M.H. ter Beek et al. (Eds.): FMICS-AVoCS 2016, LNCS 9933, pp. 39–55, 2016.
DOI: 10.1007/978-3-319-45943-1_3

approach by (3) comparing two resolution methods: Satisfiability Modulo Theory (SMT) and CLP over Finite Domains to solve the Constraint Satisfaction Problem (CSP) that represents the modal specifications to be verified.

On the one hand, using Logic Programming for solving a CSP has been investigated for many years, especially using CLP over Finite Domains, written CLP(FD). This approach basically consists in embedding consistency techniques [2] into Logic Programming by extending the concept of logical variables to the one of the domain-variables taking their values in a finite discrete set of integers. On the other hand, SMT solvers are also relevant to solve the constraint systems (a conjunction of boolean formulas expressing the constraints) since they can determine whether a first-order logic formula can be satisfied with regards to a particular theory (e.g., Linear Arithmetic, Arrays theories). Basically, SMT solvers aim to generate counter-examples [3] by combining a SAT solver, assigning a truth value to every atom composing the formula so that the truth value of the latter is true, with a theory solver determining whether the resulting interpretation can be met with regard to the theory used. The formula is satisfiable if and only if at least one interpretation from the SAT solver can be met by the theory solver.

Layout of the Paper and Contributions. Section 2 briefly recalls common concepts and standard notations concerning workflow nets as well as the key aspects of the formal method given in [1] for verifying modal specifications over workflow nets. Afterwards, Sect. 3 defines an experimental protocol designed, on the one hand, to evaluate the efficiency of each resolution approach, and, on the other hand, to compare their execution times when applied to a broad range of modal specifications and workflow nets of growing size and complexity. To achieve this goal, a mature toolchain has been developed to automatically produce, from a workflow net and its modal specification, a constraint system whose satisfiability can then be checked using either CLP or SMT. Section 4 reports on the experimental results obtained using the experimental protocol. The lessons learned as well as the reported feedback constitute the main contribution of this paper. Finally, Sect. 5 suggests directions for future work.

2   Preliminaries

This section presents workflow nets [4], modal specifications as well as the verification method proposed in [1].

2.1   Workflow Nets

Workflow nets (WF-nets) [4] are a special case of Petri nets. They allow the modelling of complex workflows exhibiting concurrencies, conflicts, as well as causal dependencies of activities. The different activities are modelled by transitions, while causal dependencies are modelled by places and arcs. For instance, the Petri net depicted in Fig. 1 is a workflow net.

Definition 1 (Workflow Net [4]). *A Petri net $N = \langle P, T, F \rangle$ is a workflow net (WF-net) if and only if P is a finite set of places, T is a finite set of transitions, $F \subseteq (P \times T) \cup (T \times P)$ is a finite set of arcs, $P \cap T = \emptyset$, and N has two special places i and o, where i has no predecessor and o has no successor.*

Let $g \in P \cup T$ and $G \subseteq P \cup T$. We use the following notations: $g^\bullet = \{g' | (g, g') \in F\}$, $^\bullet g = \{g' | (g', g) \in F\}$, $G^\bullet = \cup_{g \in G}\, g^\bullet$, and $^\bullet G = \cup_{g \in G}\, ^\bullet g$. The state of a WF-net $N = \langle P, T, F \rangle$ is given by a marking function $M : P \to \mathbb{N}$ that associates a number of tokens to places. A tran-

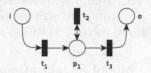

Fig. 1. An example of a WF-net

sition t is *enabled* in a marking M if and only if $\forall p \in\ ^\bullet t, M(p) \geq 1$. When an *enabled* transition t is *fired*, it *consumes* one token from each place of $^\bullet t$ and *produces* one token for each place of $t^\bullet$. Let M_a and M_b be two markings, and t a transition of N, $M_a \xrightarrow{t} M_b$ denotes that the transition t is *enabled* in marking M_a, and *firing* it results in the marking M_b. Let $\sigma = t_1, t_2, .., t_{n-1}$ be a sequence of transitions of a Petri net N, $M_1 \xrightarrow{\sigma} M_n$ denotes that $M_1 \xrightarrow{t_1} M_2 \xrightarrow{t_2} .. \xrightarrow{t_{n-1}} M_n$. We denote M_i the initial marking (i.e. $M_i(n) = 1$ if $n = i$, and 0 otherwise) and M_o the final marking (i.e. $M_o(n) = 1$ if $n = o$, and 0 otherwise). A *correct* execution of a WF-net is a transition sequence σ such that $M_i \xrightarrow{\sigma} M_o$.

The behaviour of a WF-net is defined as the set Σ of all its correct executions. Given a transition t and an execution σ, the function $O_t(\sigma)$ gives the number of occurrences of t in σ. In addition to *ordinary* WF-nets [4] (i.e. WF-nets with arcs of weight 1), this paper deals also with the following well-known and popular WF-net classes whose expressiveness is based on structural features:

- State-Machines (SM) without concurrency, but with possible conflicts among tasks (transitions): $\forall t \in T, |\, t^\bullet\, | = |\,^\bullet t\, | = 1$
- Marked-Graphs (MG) without conflict, but there can be concurrent tasks: $\forall p \in P, |\, p^\bullet\, | = |\,^\bullet p\, | = 1$
- Free-Choice nets (FC) where there can be both concurrency and conflict, but not at the same time: $\forall p \in P, (|\, p^\bullet\, | \leq 1) \vee (^\bullet(p^\bullet) = \{p\})$.

2.2 Modal Specifications

Modal specifications have been designed to allow *loose* specifications to be expressed by imposing restrictions on transitions. They allow specifiers to indicate that a transition is *necessary* or just *admissible*. In [1], modal specifications allow specifiers to express requirements on several transitions and on their causalities. The modal specifications of a workflow net $N = \langle P, T, F \rangle$ are specified using the language S of well-formed *modal* specification formulae inductively defined by: $\forall t \in T, t$ is a well-formed *modal* formula, and given $A_1, A_2 \in S$, $A_1 \wedge A_2$, $A_1 \vee A_2$, and $\neg A_1$ are well-formed *modal* formulae. These formulae allow specifiers to express modal properties about WF-nets correct executions. Any modal specification formula $m \in S$ can be interpreted as a *may*-formula or a *must*-formula. A *may*-formula describes a behaviour that has to be ensured by at least one correct execution of the WF-net whereas a *must*-formula describes a behaviour that has to be ensured by all the correct executions of the WF-net. Further, given a well-formed *may*-formula (resp. *must*-formula) $m \in S$, a WF-net N satisfies m, written $N \models_{may} m$ (resp. $N \models_{must} m$), when at least one (resp. all) correct execution(s) of N satisfies (resp. satisfy) m.

2.3   Modal Specifications Verification Method

This section provides an overall description of the verification method introduced in [1] to verify modal specifications of workflow nets. This method, based on the resolution of constraint systems, serves as a basis to compare SMT and CLP resolution approaches. Basically, a constraint system is a set of constraints (properties), which must be satisfied by the solution of the problem it models. To achieve that, each variable appearing in a constraint of the system should take its value from its domain. Such a system defines a Constraint Satisfaction Problem (CSP). Formally, a CSP is a tuple $\Omega = < X, D, C >$ where X is a set of variables $\{x_1, \ldots, x_n\}$, D is a set of domains $\{d_1, \ldots, d_n\}$, (d_i is the domain associated with the variable x_i), and C is a set of constraints $\{c_1(X_1), \ldots, c_m(X_m)\}$, where a constraint c_j involves a subset X_j of the variables of X.

A CSP thus models NP-complete problems as search problems where the corresponding search space is the Cartesian product space $d_1 \times \ldots \times d_n$. The solution of a CSP Ω is computed by a labelling function $\mathcal{L}$, which provides a set v (called valuation function) of tuples assigning each variable x_i of X to one value from its domain d_i such that all the constraints C are satisfied. More formally, v is consistent—or satisfies a constraint $c(X)$ of C—if the projection of v on X is in $c(X)$. If v satisfies all the constraints of C, then Ω is a consistent or satisfiable CSP. In the rest of the paper, the predicate $SAT(C, v)$ is true if the corresponding CSP Ω is made satisfiable by v, and the predicate $UNSAT(C)$ is true if there exists no such v.

In our context, to verify a modal specification m of a WF-net N, the constraint system is composed of a set of constraints representing the correct executions of N completed with the constraint issued from m. This constraint system can then be solved to validate or invalidate the modal specification m regarding the WF-net N. Considering a WF-net $N = (P, T, F)$, this method first models all the correct executions leading from M_a to M_b, i.e. all σ such that $M_a \xrightarrow{\sigma} M_b$. To reach that, the following constraint systems are defined:

Definition 2 (Minimum Places Potential Constraint System). *Let $N = \langle P, T, F \rangle$ be a WF-net and M_a, M_b two markings of N, the minimum places potential constraint system $\varphi(N, M_a, M_b)$ associated with it is ($\nu : P \cup T \to \mathbb{N}$ defines a valuation function):*

$$\forall p \in P. \nu(p) = \sum_{t \in p^{\bullet}} \nu(t) + M_b(p) = \sum_{t \in {}^{\bullet}p} \nu(t) + M_a(p) \tag{1}$$

The solution's space of the constraint system from Eq. (1), Definition 2, defines an over-approximation of the executions of a workflow net based on the well-known state-equation [5]: If $M_a \xrightarrow{*} M_b$ then a valuation satisfying $\varphi(N, M_a, M_b)$ exists.

Definition 3. *Let $\theta(N)$ be the following constraint system associated with a WF-net $N = \langle P, T, F \rangle$ ($\xi : P \rightarrow \{0, 1\}$ defines a valuation function):*

- $\forall p \in P, \forall t \in {}^\bullet p. \sum_{p' \in {}^\bullet t} \xi(p') \geq \xi(p)$
- $\sum_{p \in P} \xi(p) > 0$

This second constraint system from Definition 3 allows concluding on the existence of a siphon—an important structural feature describing a set of places $G \subseteq P$ such that $G \neq \emptyset$ and ${}^\bullet G \subseteq G^\bullet$—in a WF-net: N contains a siphon if and only if there is a valuation satisfying $\theta(N)$. Given a solution of the constraint system in Definition 2, it is then possible to build a subnet composed of the places (excluding places i and o) and of the transitions of the modelled execution as described in Definition 4.

Definition 4. *Let $N = \langle P, T, F \rangle$ be a WF-net, M_a, M_b two markings of N, and $\nu : P \cup T \rightarrow \mathbb{N}$ a valuation satisfying $\varphi(P, M_a, M_b)$. The subnet $sN(\nu)$ is defined as $\langle sP, sT, sF \rangle$ where:*

- $sP = \{p \in P \setminus \{i, o\} \mid \nu(p) > 0\}$
- $sT = \{t \in T \mid \nu(t) > 0\}$
- $sF = \{(a, b) \in F \mid a \in (sP \cup sT) \wedge b \in (sP \cup sT)\}$

By Theorem 1, the above constraint systems can be combined to model executions of a workflow net.

Theorem 1. *Let $N = \langle P, T, F \rangle$ be a WF-net, and M_a, M_b its two markings. If there is $\nu : P \cup T \rightarrow \mathbb{N}$ such that $SAT(\varphi(N, M_a, M_b), \nu) \wedge UNSAT(\theta(sN(\nu)))$ $\wedge \forall n \in P \cup T. \ \nu(n) \leq 1$ then $M_a \xrightarrow{\sigma} M_b$ and $\forall t \in T. \ O_t(\sigma) = \nu(t)$.*

An execution modelled by the constraint system of Theorem 1 is called a segment. Further, any execution of a workflow net can be modelled by a succession of segments as stated by Theorem 2, in which the constraint system is denoted $\phi(N, M_a, M_b, k)$, where k is the number of segments composing the execution.

Theorem 2. *Let $N = \langle P, T, F \rangle$ be a WF-net, and M_a, M_b its two markings. $M_a \xrightarrow{\sigma} M_b$ if and only if there exists $k \in \mathbb{N}$ such that $M_1 \xrightarrow{\sigma_1} M_2 \cdots M_k \xrightarrow{\sigma_{(k)}} M_{k+1}$, where $M_1 = M_a$, $M_{k+1} = M_b$ and for every i, $0 < i \leq k$, there is ν_i s.t. $SAT(\varphi(N, M_i, M_{i+1}), \nu_i) \wedge UNSAT(\theta(sN(\nu_i))) \wedge \forall n \in P \times T. \ \nu_i(n) \leq 1$.*

Our method to verify modal specifications relies on their expression by constraints. To build these constraints, for every transition $t \in T$, the corresponding terminal symbol of the modal formulae is replaced by $\nu(t) > 0$, where ν is the valuation of the constraint system. Given a modal formula $f \in S$, $C(f, \nu)$ is the constraint built from f, where ν is a valuation of the constraint system.

Theorem 3. *Let $N = \langle P, T, F \rangle$ be a WF-net and $\langle m, M \rangle$ a modal specification. The WF-net N satisfies the modal specification $\langle m, M \rangle$ if and only if:*

- *there is no $\nu, k \in \mathbb{N}$ such that $SAT(\phi(N, M_i, M_o, k) \wedge \neg C(m, \nu), \nu)$, and*
- *for every $f \in M$, there exist $\nu, k \in \mathbb{N}$ such that $SAT(\phi(N, M_i, M_o, k) \wedge C(f, \nu), \nu)$.*

By Theorem 3, using a fixed K, the *K-bounded validity of a modal formula* (i.e. validity of the modal formula over correct executions formed by at most K segments) can be inferred by evaluating the satisfiability of the corresponding constraint system. Furthermore, it has been shown that for K sufficiently large the *K-bounded validity of a modal formula* corresponds to its *unbounded validity* [1].

3   Experimental Protocol

This section introduces the experimental protocol designed to evaluate the efficiency and limitations of the compared resolution approaches, i.e. CLP and SMT, applied to the verification of modal specifications as described in Sect. 2.3.

To empirically assess the scalability and the efficiency of both resolution methods, and to be able to have convincing clues to compare them as objectively as possible, we are interested in gathering the following abilities of the methods:

1. To assign a verdict about the (in)validity of the given modal specification;
2. To return such a response as quick as possible (and in an admissible time).

Moreover, to make conclusion and feedback relevant and credible, and to be able to evaluate reliability as well as scalability of the methods, this information has to be calculated from a broad range of modal specifications and workflow nets. Indeed, the type of modal specifications shall be taken into account because, to conclude about their validity, the verification method may require the computation of the over-approximation of the workflow nets executions or a full decomposition into segments. The size of the modal formula to be verified is also important since a larger formula may constrain further the system to be solved.

The proposed experimental protocol thus considers workflow nets of realistic size by evaluating workflow nets of size up to 500 nodes. Moreover, not only the size of the workflow nets is considered but also their complexity by evaluating workflow nets of classes with a growing expressiveness (cf. Sect. 2.1). Therefore, to experimentally evaluate both resolution approaches over instances of growing size and complexity, the following parameters are taken into account:

- Class of the workflow nets:
  - State machine,
  - Marked graph,
  - Free-choice, and
  - Ordinary nets

- Size of the workflow nets:
  - $50 * i$ where $i \in \{1, .., 10\}$

- Type of modal specification:
  - Valid may-formula,
  - Invalid may-formula,
  - Valid must-formula, and
  - Invalid must-formula

- Size of the modal formula:
  - 5 and 15 literals

For each combination of the above parameters, a corresponding modal formula and a workflow net are randomly generated. This forms a data set of 320 instances of growing size and complexity. All the evaluations have been performed on three different data sets, i.e. a total of 960 workflow nets and modal specifications have thus been experimented. Moreover, in order to restrict the total time needed to perform these experiments, a time-out of 10 min (arbitrary *admissible* time) was fixed for each resolution call to the solvers. Finally, all the executions have been computed on a computer featuring an Intel(R) Xeon(R) CPU X5650 @ 2.67 GHz.

A complete and mature toolchain able to carry out this experimental protocol has been developed. To evaluate the constraint systems produced by the method in Sect. 2.3, this toolchain relies on either Z3 [6] version 4.4.0, an SMT solver, which finished first during the 2014 SMT-COMP challenge[1] for solving non-linear arithmetic problems, or SICStus Prolog [7] version 4.3.2, a CLP solver which obtained the third place during the 2014 MiniZinc challenge[2].

Figures 2 and 3 illustrate the encoding used to model the constraints seen in Sect. 2.3 respectively for the SMT-Lib and Prolog language. The constraints correspond with the workflow $N = (P, T, F)$ depicted in Fig. 1. Let $n \in P \cup T$, we use the following conventions: An stands for $M_a(n)$, Bn for $M_b(n)$, Pn for $\nu(n)$ when n is a place, Tn stands for $\nu(n)$ when n is a transition, and Xn stands for $\xi(n)$, M1n, M2n and M3n stand for $M_1(n)$, $M_2(n)$ and $M_3(n)$. For example, Tt2 and M2p1 respectively denotes $\nu(t2)$ and $M_2(p1)$.

The two next inputs allow to determine, using respectively Z3 and SICStus, whether there exists a correct execution of the workflow in Fig. 1 made of three segments such that both t1 and t2 are fired.

```
1    ; Variables declaration here
2    (define-fun initialMarking ((Ai Int)(Ao Int)(Ap1 Int)) Bool (and (= Ai 1) (= Ao 0) (= Ap1 0)))
3    (define-fun finalMarking ((Bi Int)(Bo Int)(Bp1 Int)) Bool (and (= Bi 0) (= Bo 1) (= Bp1 0)))
4    (define-fun stateEquation (
5      (Ai Int)(Ao Int)(Ap1 Int)(Bi Int)(Bo Int)(Bp1 Int)(Pi Int)(Po Int)(Pp1 Int)(Tt1 Int)(Tt2 Int)(Tt3 Int)) Bool
6      (and
7        (>= Ai 0) (>= Ao 0) (>= Ap1 0) (>= Bi 0) (>= Bo 0) (>= Bp1 0)
8        (>= Pi 0) (>= Po 0) (>= Pp1 0) (>= Tt1 0) (>= Tt2 0) (>= Tt3 0)
9        (= Pi Ai) (= Pi (+ Bi Tt1))
10       (= Po (+ Ao Tt3)) (= Po Bo)
11       (= Pp1 (+ Ap1 Tt1 Tt2)) (= Pp1 (+ Bp1 Tt2 Tt3))))
12   (define-fun formula ((Tt1 Int) (Tt2 Int)) Bool (and (> Tt1 0) (> Tt2 0)))
13   (define-fun noSiphon (
14     (Ai Int)(Ao Int)(Ap1 Int)(Bi Int)(Bo Int)(Bp1 Int)(Pi Int)(Po Int)(Pp1 Int)(Tt1 Int)(Tt2 Int)(Tt3 Int)) Bool
15     (not (exists ((Xi Int)(Xo Int)(Xp1 Int))
16       (and
17         (> (+ Xi Xo Xp1) 0)
18         (>= Xi 0) (<= Xi 1) (>= Xo 0) (<= Xo 1) (>= Xp1 0) (<= Xp1 1)
19         (=> (or (> Ai 0) (> Bi 0) (= Pi 0)) (= Xi 0))
20         (=> (or (> Ao 0) (> Bo 0) (= Po 0)) (= Xo 0))
21         (=> (or (> Ap1 0) (> Bp1 0) (= Pp1 0)) (= Xp1 0))
22         (=> (> Tt1 0) (>= (+ Xi) Xp1)) (=> (> Tt2 0) (>= (+ Xp1) Xp1)) (=> (> Tt3 0) (>= (+ Xp1) Xo))))))
23   (define-fun segment (
24     (Ai Int)(Ao Int)(Ap1 Int)(Bi Int)(Bo Int)(Bp1 Int)(Pi Int)(Po Int)(Pp1 Int)(Tt1 Int)(Tt2 Int)(Tt3 Int)) Bool
25     (and
26       (stateEquation Ai Ao Ap1 Bi Bo Bp1 Pi Po Pp1 Tt1 Tt2 Tt3)
27       (noSiphon Ai Ao Ap1 Bi Bo Bp1 Pi Po Pp1 Tt1 Tt2 Tt3)))
```

Fig. 2. SMT-Lib code of a segment of workflow

---

[1] www.smtcomp.org.

[2] www.minizinc.org/challenge.html.

```
1    initialMarking([1, 0, 0]).
2    finalMarking([0, 1, 0]).
3    stateEquation([Ai, Ao, Ap1], [Bi, Bo, Bp1], [Pi, Po, Pp1], [Tt1, Tt2, Tt3]):-
4        domain([Ai, Ao, Ap1, Bi, Bo, Bp1, Pi, Po, Pp1, Tt1, Tt2, Tt3], 0, 10),
5        Pi #= Ai, Pi #= Bi + Tt1,
6        Po #= Ao + Tt3, Po #= Bo,
7        Pp1 #= Ap1 + Tt1 + Tt2, Pp1 #= Bp1 + Tt2 + Tt3.
8    formula([Tt1, Tt2]):- Tt1 #> 0, Tt2 #> 0.
9    subnetInit([Ai, Ao, Ap1], [Bi, Bo, Bp1], [Pi, Po, Pp1], [Xi, Xo, Xp1]):-
10       domain([Xi, Xo, Xp1], 0, 1),
11       (Ai #> 0 #\/ Bi #> 0 #\/ Pi #= 0) #=> Xi #= 0,
12       (Ao #> 0 #\/ Bo #> 0 #\/ Po #= 0) #=> Xo #= 0,
13       (Ap1 #> 0 #\/ Bp1 #> 0 #\/ Pp1 #= 0) #=> Xp1 #= 0.
14   siphon([Tt1, Tt2, Tt3], [Xi, Xo, Xp1]):-
15       Xi + Xo + Xp1 #> 0,
16       Tt1 #> 0 #=> Xi #>= Xp1, Tt2 #> 0 #=> Xp1 #>= Xp1, Tt3 #> 0 #=> Xp1 #>= Xo,
17       labeling([leftmost, step, up], [Xi, Xo, Xp1]).
18   noSiphon([Ai, Ao, Ap1], [Bi, Bo, Bp1], [Pi, Po, Pp1], [Tt1, Tt2, Tt3]):-
19       subnetInit([Ai, Ao, Ap1], [Bi, Bo, Bp1], [Pi, Po, Pp1], [Xi, Xo, Xp1]),
20       labeling([leftmost, step, up], [Tt1, Tt2, Tt3]),
21       \+ siphon([Tt1, Tt2, Tt3], [Xi, Xo, Xp1]).
22   segment([Ai, Ao, Ap1], [Bi, Bo, Bp1], [Pi, Po, Pp1], [Tt1, Tt2, Tt3]):-
23       stateEquation([Ai, Ao, Ap1], [Bi, Bo, Bp1], [Pi, Po, Pp1], [Tt1, Tt2, Tt3]),
24       noSiphon([Ai, Ao, Ap1], [Bi, Bo, Bp1], [Pi, Po, Pp1], [Tt1, Tt2, Tt3]).
```

Fig. 3. Prolog code of a segment of workflow

Z3 input:

```
(assert (initialMarking M1i M1o M1p1))
(assert (finalMarking M3i M3o M3p1))
(assert (formula (+ T1t1 T2t1 T3t1) (+ T1t2 T2t2 T3t2)))
(assert (segment M1i M1o M1p1 M2i M2o M2p1 P1i P1o P1p1 T1t1 T1t2 T1t3))
(assert (segment M2i M2o M2p1 M3i M3o M3p1 P2i P2o P2p1 T2t1 T2t2 T2t3))
(assert (segment M3i M3o M3p1 M4i M4o M4p1 P3i P3o P3p1 T3t1 T3t2 T3t3))
(check-sat-using smt)
(get-model)
```

SICStus input:

```
initialMarking([M1i, M1o, M1p1]),
finalMarking([M4i, M4o, M4p1]),
segment([M1i, M1o, M1p1], [M2i, M2o, M2p1], [P1i, P1o, P1p1], [T1t1, T1t2, T1t3]),
segment([M2i, M2o, M2p1], [M3i, M3o, M3p1], [P2i, P2o, P2p1], [T2t1, T2t2, T2t3]),
segment([M3i, M3o, M3p1], [M4i, M4o, M4p1], [P3i, P3o, P3p1], [T3t1, T3t2, T3t3]),
S1 #= T1t1 + T1t2, S2 #= T2t1 + T2t2, formula([S1, S2]).
```

Both solvers give the following interpretation for the three segments:

```
1    M1i = 1, M1o = 0, M1p1 = 0, M2i = 0, M2o = 0, M2p1 = 1, M3i = 0, M3o = 0, M3p1 = 1, M4i = 0, M4o = 1, M4p1 = 0,
2    P1i = 1, P1o = 0, P1p1 = 1, P2i = 0, P2o = 0, P2p1 = 2, P3i = 0, P3o = 1, P3p1 = 1,
3    T1t1 = 1, T1t2 = 0, T1t3 = 0, T2t1 = 0, T2t2 = 1, T2t3 = 0, 3t1 = 0,
4    T3t2 = 0, T3t3 = 1
```

These segments are given in Fig. 4, starting (resp. ending) in the initial (resp. final) marking where only the input place i (resp. output place o) is marked.

Fig. 4. The three segments of execution proposed by both solvers

Finally, let us precise that multiple combinations of labelling heuristics have been experimented when using SICStus. Though some of them may marginally improve the results on specific workflows, none was found to significantly and generally improve all results. Therefore, all the experiments have been conducted with the default options (i.e. [leftmost, step, up]). However, when using Z3, since the SMT tactic improved all results, this strategy has always been used.

4   Results and Feedback from Experiments

This section presents the experimental results obtained using the dedicated tool applying the protocol introduced in the previous section. To provide relevant feedback regarding the initial challenges given in Sect. 1, the obtained results are discussed by distinguishing two different categories of modal specifications:

– May-valid and must-invalid specifications;
– May-invalid and must-valid specifications.

Note that the algorithm given in Sect. 2.3 is applied to all generated workflows and specifications, no matter what type of specification is being verified. Thus, our implementation first checks if an over-approximation is sufficient to conclude about the validity or the invalidity of a specification and, only if it is not the case, computes an under-approximation before concluding. Indeed, using the verification algorithm given in Sect. 2.3, most may-valid and must-invalid modal specifications can be verified by using only an over-approximation of correct executions of the workflow. This over-approximation is less complex than the under-approximation that must very often be computed to verify may-invalid and must-valid modal specifications.

In this context, even though may-valid and must-invalid specifications express two different behaviours (i.e. a may-valid specification is not necessarily a must-invalid specification), most of the specifications of this category may only require the computation of over-approximations of correct executions of the workflow. On the contrary, even though may-invalid and must-valid specifications express two opposite behaviours (i.e. a may-invalid specification is never a must-valid specification and vice versa), most of these specifications often require the costly computation of under-approximations of correct executions.

We also categorise the results according to the different classes of workflow nets considered in our experimental protocol. The average execution times given in the following subsections have been computed without considering time-outs. Thus, since time-outs may have occurred, similar average execution times do not always induce similar performances from both solvers. Nonetheless time-outs are stated an discussed separately. Finally, for clarity, all time-outs and singularities have been withdrawn from the plots but systematically taken into account in our feedbacks. The interested reader can also study the complete data sets and results given at https://dx.doi.org/10.6084/m9.figshare.2067156.v1.

Tables 1, 2, 3 and 4 summarize the average verification times, number of time-outs as well as the overall appreciation of the results obtained over the different studied workflow net classes. Figures 5, 6, 7, 8, 9, 10, 11 and 12 depict the plots displaying the verification times spent by SICStus and Z3 for each class of workflow nets and types of modal specifications.

The next subsections comment on these obtained results and indicate the most important feedback for each class of workflow nets.

Table 1. Metrics over State-Machine workflow nets

Type	Solver	Avg. t.(ms)	#time-outs	Overall
May-Valid	Z3	346	0	☺
	SICStus	621	28	☺
Must-Invalid	Z3	319	0	☺
	SICStus	788	31	●
May-Invalid	Z3	79	0	☺
	SICStus	77413	52	●
Must-Valid	Z3	79	0	☺
	SICStus	10194	51	●

Table 2. Metrics over Marked-Graph workflow nets

Type	Solver	Avg. t.(ms)	#time-outs	Overall
May-Valid	Z3	630	0	☺
	SICStus	776	0	☺
Must-Invalid	Z3	641	0	☺
	SICStus	758	0	☺
May-Invalid	Z3	112	0	☺
	SICStus	424	0	☺
Must-Valid	Z3	104	0	☺
	SICStus	407	0	☺

Table 3. Metrics over Free-Choice workflow nets

Type	Solver	Avg. t.(ms)	#time-outs	Overall
May-Valid	Z3	379	0	☺
	SICStus	787	16	☺
Must-Invalid	Z3	413	0	☺
	SICStus	898	14	☺
May-Invalid	Z3	91	0	☺
	SICStus	40459	38	●
Must-Valid	Z3	89	0	☺
	SICStus	50566	37	●

Table 4. Metrics over ordinary workflow nets

Type	Solver	Avg. t.(ms)	#time-outs	Overall
May-Valid	Z3	1258	22	☺
	SICStus	9010	33	●
Must-Invalid	Z3	713	17	☺
	SICStus	12258	37	●
May-Invalid	Z3	108	0	☺
	SICStus	9489	33	●
Must-Valid	Z3	106	0	☺
	SICStus	5949	37	●

☺: Reasonable time, no time-out — ☺: Reasonable time, # time-outs < 50% — ●: # time-outs > 50%

4.1 Observation from State-Machine Workflow Nets Verification

May-Valid and Must-Invalid Specifications. Both solvers were able to conclude in a comparable and reasonable time. On average, Z3 execution time was 332 ms whereas SICStus execution time was 704 ms. However, despite good results for both solvers, it should be noted that 49.2 %(59/120) of SICStus executions did not finish within 10 min, while Z3 did not suffer from any time-outs.

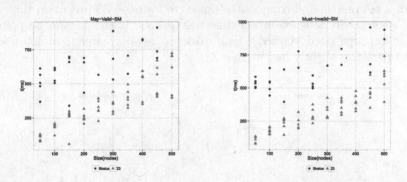

Fig. 5. State-Machine - May-Valid and Must-Invalid modal specifications

Must-Valid and May-Invalid Specifications. Both solvers were able to conclude in a reasonable time. On average, Z3 execution time was 79 ms whereas SICStus execution time was 43803 ms. These results clearly show that Z3 performs better than SICStus on this type of modal specifications. Moreover, it should be noted that 85.8 %(103/120) of SICStus executions did not finish within 10 min, whereas Z3 did not suffer from any time-outs. Indeed, SICStus was not able to conclude about workflow nets of size greater than 250.

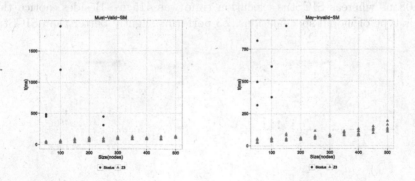

Fig. 6. State-Machine - Must-Valid and May-Invalid modal specifications

Synthesis. Over the class of State-Machines we conclude that SICStus is clearly overwhelmed due to the high number of choice points arising from the structure of state-machine workflow nets of size greater than 100 nodes. We conclude from these results that the SMT approach seems to be more suited for the modal specifications verification over State-Machine workflow nets.

4.2   Observation from Marked-Graph Workflow Nets Verification

May-Valid and Must-Invalid Specifications. Both solvers were able to conclude in a reasonable and comparable time. On average, Z3 execution time was 635 ms whereas SICStus execution time was 767 ms. It should also be pointed out that for large sized Marked-Graph workflow nets (greater than 400 nodes) SICStus performs slightly better than Z3.

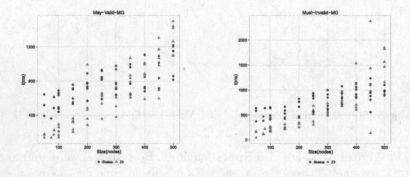

Fig. 7. Marked-Graph - May-Valid and Must-Invalid modal specifications

Must-Valid and May-Invalid Specifications. Both solvers were able to conclude in a reasonable and fairly comparable time. On average, Z3 execution time was 108 ms whereas SICStus execution time was 415 ms. Besides, notice that, for this type of modal specifications, Z3 performs slightly better than SICStus.

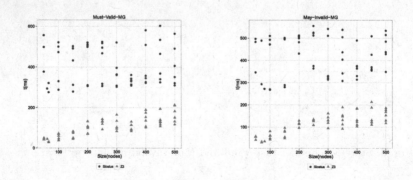

Fig. 8. Marked-Graph - Must-Valid and May-Invalid modal specifications

Synthesis. Over the class of Marked-Graph, we can conclude that SICStus and Z3 performs similarly. However SICStus seems to perform better when verifying May-Valid and Must-Invalid specifications while Z3 seems to perform better when verifying Must-valid and May-Invalid specifications. A further investigation has shown that, in general, Z3 is more effective than SICStus for the computation of the over-approximation used by the verification method, while SICStus is more effective than Z3 for the computation of the segments needed to conclude whenever the over-approximation is not sufficient.

4.3 Observation from Free-Choice Workflow Nets Verification

May-Valid and Must-Invalid Specifications. Both solvers were able to conclude in a reasonable and comparable time. On average, Z3 execution time was 396 ms whereas SICStus execution time was 842 ms. Beyond these conclusive results for both solvers, it is important to underline that 25 %(30/120) of SICStus executions did not finish within 10 min, whereas Z3 did not suffer from any time-outs.

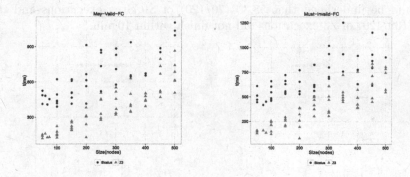

Fig. 9. Free-Choice - May-Valid and Must-Invalid modal specifications

Must-Valid and May-Invalid Specifications. Over this type of modal specifications, Z3 clearly performs better than SICStus. On average, Z3 execution time was 90 ms, while SICStus execution time was 45512 ms. We also note that 62.5 %(75/120) of SICStus executions did not finish within 10 min, whereas Z3 did not suffer from any time-outs. After investigation, these results stem from the fact that the verification of such modal specifications mostly relies on the results of an over-approximation for which Z3 performs far better off.

Synthesis. Over the class of Free-Choice workflow nets, we observe that Z3 performs better than SICStus. We thus conclude from these obtained results that the SMT approach seems to be more suited for the modal specifications verification over Free-Choice workflow nets.

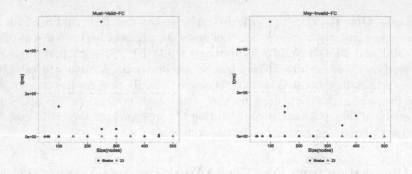

Fig. 10. Free-Choice - Must-Valid and May-Invalid modal specifications

4.4 Observation from Ordinary Workflow Nets Verification

May-Valid and Must-Invalid Specifications. Both solvers were able to conclude in a reasonable and comparable time. On average, Z3 execution time was 985 ms whereas SICStus execution time was 10634 ms. Besides these results, it should be underlined that 58.3 %(70/120) of SICStus executions and that 32.5 %(39/120) of Z3 executions did not finish within 10 min.

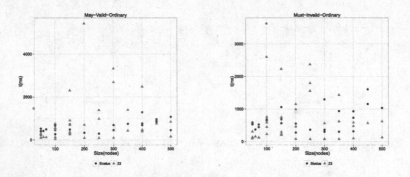

Fig. 11. Ordinary - May-Valid and Must-Invalid modal specifications

Must-Valid and May-Invalid Specifications. Both solvers were able to conclude in a reasonable time. On average, Z3 execution time was 107 ms whereas SICStus execution time was 7717 ms. Despite these conclusive results for both solvers, it is important to note that 58.3 %(70/120) of SICStus executions did not finish within 10 min, whereas Z3 did not suffer from any time-outs. As for the previous classes, Z3 indeed performs better than SICStus to compute the over-approximation constraints, which were often sufficient to conclude.

Synthesis. Over the class of ordinary workflow nets, we observe that Z3 performs better than SICStus, especially when verifying Must-valid and May-Invalid

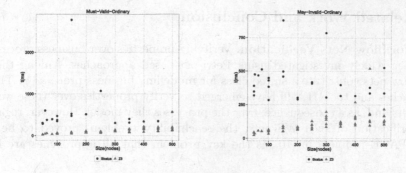

Fig. 12. Ordinary - Must-Valid and May-Invalid modal specifications

specifications. We can thus conclude from these results that the SMT approach seems to be more suited for the modal specifications verification over ordinary workflow nets. The next section summarizes the lessons learned and the benefits noticed from these experiments according to the initial challenges.

4.5 Lessons Learned from Experience

Scalability. On the basis of the results, we can confidently state that the verification method proposed in [1] is scalable in terms of modal specification and workflow net complexity, as well as regarding their size (up to at least 500 nodes).

Efficiency. The developed implementation of the method proposed in [1] and the underlying constraint solvers (i.e. Z3 and SICStus) have shown to be very efficient for the intended verification computation. Indeed, the toolchain was always able to conclude about the validity of modal specification over workflow nets of growing size and complexity within the alloted time of 10 min (for each constraint system to solve, at least one resolution method was indeed able to assign a verdict, and furthermore within only few seconds in almost all cases). Furthermore, we observed that memory usage does not seem to be a limiting factor because, for the biggest instance of workflow verification, the memory usage for SICStus and Z3 was less than 350 MB.

SMT vs CLP. According to these experiments, we can infer that the SMT approach (computed using Z3) generally performs significantly better than the CLP one (computed using SICStus). However, they also highlight that the CLP approach performs better, especially when verifying modal specifications over Marked-Graph workflow nets. We indeed observed that the CLP approach is less efficient than the SMT approach when the number of choice points increases as shown by the results over State-Machine workflow nets. It stems from the labeling done after constraints propagation by CLP solvers: an exponential number of backtracking steps may occur w.r.t. the number of pending choice points.

5　Related Work and Conclusion

On Workflow Nets Verification. Verifying properties over business processes has been widely investigated using Petri-net-based approaches. Among them, workflow nets constitute a suited class for modelling business process [4]. Thus, approaches and tools [1,8,9] have emerged to verify properties over these workflow nets and, as a consequence, over the processes they model. However, regarding verification of such WF-nets, the reachability problem, proved to be an EXPSPACE problem in [10], is the key problem that all approaches are facing.

Regarding verification methods, some research results have also been proposed to express and verify properties against a given system. Let us quote [11] where the expression of properties with modalities is investigated for automata-/transition systems, and also [12] where they are studied for Petri nets. In this context, the great expressiveness of modalities makes them popular and relevant for precisely describing a possible or necessary behavior over a system.

Using Constraint Solving for Verification. Formal verification methods based on constraints solving have been studied intensively, with most concrete implementations using the SMT or CLP approaches. On the one hand, for example, SMT has been used in [13] for checking the reachability of bounded Petri nets, as well as in [14] for verifying properties of business processes where execution paths are modelled as constraints. On the other hand, CLP has been also extensively experimented to verify business processes [15] as well as Petri nets [9]. In a very similar way, a CLP approach has been used in [16] to detect the presence of structures potentially leading to deadlocks in Petri nets. The present paper has the originality to compare SMT and CLP resolution methods.

Conclusion. This paper has compared the SMT and CLP approaches to verify modal specifications over WF-nets using constraint solving. For this purpose, an experimental protocol has been designed and a mature toolchain has been developed. Using the obtained experimental results over four classes of nets with particular features, we have empirically demonstrated that the verification method is efficient and scalable over workflow nets of size at least up to 500 nodes. In general, the SMT approach performs significantly better than the CLP approach, except when verifying modal specifications over conflict free workflow nets, i.e. Marked-Graphs. As a future work, we plan to apply our approach to real-life industrial workflows to confirm its efficiency, and to investigate innovative strategies mixing both SMT and CLP methods in order to embrace the benefits from each of them, and to take advantage of the potential synergy.

References

1. Bride, H., Kouchnarenko, O., Peureux, F.: Verifying modal workflow specifications using constraint solving. In: Albert, E., Sekerinski, E. (eds.) IFM 2014. LNCS, vol. 8739, pp. 171–186. Springer, Heidelberg (2014)

2. Tsang, E.P.K.: Foundations of Constraint Satisfaction. Computation in Cognitive Science. Academic Press, San Diego (1993)
3. De Moura, L., Bjørner, N.: Satisfiability modulo theories: Introduction and applications. Commun. ACM **54**(9), 69–77 (2011)
4. van der Aalst, W.M.P.: The application of Petri nets to workflow management. J. Circ. Syst. Comput. **08**(01), 21–66 (1998)
5. Murata, T.: Petri nets: properties, analysis and applications. IEEE **77**(4), 541–580 (1989)
6. de Moura, L., Bjørner, N.S.: Z3: an efficient SMT solver. In: Ramakrishnan, C.R., Rehof, J. (eds.) TACAS 2008. LNCS, vol. 4963, pp. 337–340. Springer, Heidelberg (2008)
7. Carlsson, M., et al.: SICStus Prolog User's Manual (Release 4.2.3). Swedish Institute of Computer Science, Kista (2012)
8. Bi, H., Zhao, J.: Applying propositional logic to workflow verification. Inf. Technol. Manag. **5**(3–4), 293–318 (2004)
9. Wimmel, H., Wolf, K.: Applying CEGAR to the Petri net state equation. Logical Methods Comput. Sci. **8**(3), 827–846 (2012)
10. Haddad, S.: Decidability and complexity of Petri net problems. In: Petri Nets: Fundamental Models, Verification and Applications, pp. 87–122 (2009)
11. Larsen, K., Thomsen, B.: A modal process logic. In: Proceedings of the Third Annual Symposium on Logic in Computer Science, LICS 1988, pp. 203–210 (1988)
12. Kouchnarenko, O., Sidorova, N., Trcka, N.: Petri nets with may/must semantics. In: Workshop on Concurrency, Specification, and Programming, CS&P 2009, Kraków-Przegorzaly, Poland, vol. 1, September 2009
13. Monakova, G., Kopp, O., Leymann, F., Moser, S., Schäfers, K.: Verifying business rules using an SMT solver for BPEL processes. In: BPSC. LNI, vol. 147, pp. 81–94. GI (2009)
14. Pólrola, A., Cybula, P., Meski, A.: Smt-based reachability checking for bounded time Petri nets. Fundam. Inform. **135**(4), 467–482 (2014)
15. Kleine, M., Göthel, T.: Specification, verification and implementation of business processes using CSP. In: TASE, pp. 145–154. IEEE Computer Society (2010)
16. Soliman, S.: Finding minimal p/t-invariants as a CSP. In: Proceedings of the 4th Workshop on Constraint Based Methods for Bioinformatics, WCB, vol. 8 (2008)

One Step Towards Automatic Inference of Formal Specifications Using Automated VeriFast

Mahmoud Mohsen[✉] and Bart Jacobs

iMinds-DistriNet, Department of Computer Science,
Katholieke Universiteit Leuven, Leuven, Belgium
{mahmoud.mohsen,bart.jacobs}@cs.kuleuven.be

Abstract. VeriFast is a sound modular formal verification tool for C and Java programs. Based on separation logic and using symbolic execution, VeriFast can verify not only memory safety of programs but also full functional correctness. Formal verification is a powerful way of analyzing code, but not yet widely used in practice. Source code has to be annotated with formal specification mostly in the form of function preconditions and postconditions. In this paper, we present Automated VeriFast which is a new extension or an automation layer that lies on top of VeriFast that, given a partially annotated program, offers to attempt to incrementally improve the annotations, e.g. by inferring a fix to the specification of a program fragment that fails to verify. Our thesis is that such small, interactive inference steps will have practical benefits over non-interactive specification inference approaches by allowing the user to guide the inference process and by being simpler and therefore more predictable and diagnosable.

Keywords: Annotations inference · Program verification · Separation logic

1   Introduction

VeriFast [1], a sound modular verifier for C and Java programs, accepts programs annotated with function preconditions and postconditions written in separation logic [2,7] and verifies the correctness of the code with respect to these annotations.

Separation logic allows VeriFast to formally prove some properties of programs that were not easy to be proven before, in particular those properties related to pointer manipulations and the heap. However, the process of writing formal annotations makes the verification of real large applications not an easy task. Time and experience in the field of formal methods are required to provide such annotations which become sometimes more complex than writing the source code itself. This motivates the idea of inferring programs' specifications and automating the process of writing the formal annotations. Of course, it is crucial that the user checks that the generated top-level specifications match the program's requirements. Internal specifications need not to be checked.

© Springer International Publishing AG 2016
M.H. ter Beek et al. (Eds.): FMICS-AVoCS 2016, LNCS 9933, pp. 56–64, 2016.
DOI: 10.1007/978-3-319-45943-1_4

The Contributions. The contribution of this paper is presenting Automated VeriFast which creates an interactive framework in which VeriFast has more automation capabilities that allow users to choose for auto-generating predicates and auto-fixing verification faults detected by VeriFast. The current approach supports some simple linked list patterns, but can be generalized in the future to include more complex data structures, such as doubly linked lists, trees, etc.

2 Architecture

Automated VeriFast is a new extension or an automation layer that lies on top of VeriFast verification layer. This new automation layer does not affect in anyway the verification core of VeriFast. This separation ensures that VeriFast's soundness is not affected.

When the user invokes the auto-fix feature after a verification failure, Automated VeriFast takes the verification error message and the symbolic path containing the symbolic states encountered in this path combined with the heap and the stack store in each state as an input. This input is the output of the VeriFast Verification layer.

VeriFast is focused on fast verification, expressive power, and the ability to diagnose errors easily rather than on automation [1]. To accomplish this, VeriFast provides an IDE that facilitates the verification process by allowing users to use the symbolic debugger in the IDE to diagnose verification errors and inspect the symbolic state at each program point.

The user interface of Automated VeriFast is the same except that there are two new buttons in the interface which trigger the new functionalities. One button is for generating the predicates; it should be pressed only once at the beginning of the verification process. The other button is for auto-fixing a verification failure.

Automated VeriFast follows the iterative incremental approach described in [5] to simulate the same manual verification process that normally users of VeriFast follow in solving verification errors. We could put the implementation of the auto-fix within a loop, so one press of auto-fix would either solve all the verification errors at once or stop in a state where an error can't be automatically solved and a manual intervention is required. We did not do that to allow the user to manually intervene at any time in the verification process.

3 An Inner Look at Automated VeriFast

In this section, we describe how Automated VeriFast works in more depth. As mentioned above, there are two new functionalities that have been added to normal VeriFast. The first is automatically generating predicates and the second is auto-fixing errors.

3.1   Auto-generating Predicates

A predicate is a named, parameterized assertion [3]. In normal manual verification cases, users define predicates based on their understanding of the different
data structures used within the code. Predicates can be considered as a kind of
data abstraction where related data can be encapsulated together in one entity
which can be decapsulated later when the data is needed. Moreover, to describe
a data structure, such as a linked list or a tree, users of VeriFast have to define
recursive predicates which can invoke themselves.

We started in Automated VeriFast by supporting only some simple linked
list patterns as a first step. Automated VeriFast generates a predicate for each
struct, not only for recursive data structures. Consider you have the following
four structs, in Fig. 1, that are part of an implementation of a banking system.

```
struct bank {                              struct user_account {
    int user_account_count;                    struct user_account *next;
    struct user_account *user_accounts;        char *user_name;
    int bank_account_count;                    char *password;
    struct bank_account *bank_accounts;        int is_teller ;
};                                             char *real_name;
struct bank_account {                      };
    struct bank_account *next;             struct transaction {
    char *id;                                  struct transaction *next;
    struct user_account *owner;                char *counterparty_bank_account_id;
    int balance;                               int amount;
    int transaction_count;                     char *comment;
    struct transaction * transactions ;    };
};
```

Fig. 1. Banking system structs

Automated VeriFast will generate a predicate for each struct that appears in
Fig. 1. For example, *user_account* is a struct representing a linked list where each
node of the list represents one account containing data fields and a pointer to
the next account. Automated VeriFast will automatically generate a predicate
for the *user_account* struct that looks like:

```
/*@ predicate user_account ( struct user_account *user_account; int count) =
    user_account == 0 ? count == 0 :
        user_account->next |-> ?next &*&
        user_account->user_name |-> ?user_name &*& string(user_name) &*&
        user_account->password |-> ?password &*& string(password) &*&
        user_account->is_teller |-> ? is_teller &*&
        user_account->real_name |-> ?real_name &*& string(real_name) &*&
        malloc_block_user_account(user_account) &*&
        user_account(next, ?count1) &*& count == count1 + 1 &*& count > 0;
@*/
```

This predicate takes two parameters. The first is a pointer to the head of
the list; the second represents the length of the linked list. The predicate's body
has a call to itself which is *user_account(next, ?count1)* that represents the tail
of the list encapsulated in a predicate of the same type. The *?count1* is a fresh
variable denoting some unknown value representing the length of the list's tail.

```
1   struct bank {
2       /*@ owns @*/ struct user_account *user_accounts;
3       int user_account_count /*@ counts user_accounts @*/;
4       /*@ owns @*/ struct bank_account *bank_accounts;
5       int bank_account_count /*@ counts bank_accounts @*/;
6   };
```

Fig. 2. Bank struct with ownership annotations

The *user_account* predicate is generated without any input from the user, but in some cases, Automated VeriFast requires some hints from users to correctly auto-generate predicates. Users may be required to define some rules of ownership between different structs. As we can see in Fig. 1, a struct *bank* instance owns the linked list of struct *user_account* instances pointed to by its field *user_accounts*. It also owns the linked list of *bank_account* instances pointed to by its field *bank_accounts*. Furthermore, it has two counters that represent the length of both linked lists it owns, namely *user_account_count* and *bank_account_count*. On the other hand, a struct *bank_account* instance doesn't own the linked list of struct *user_account* pointed to by its field *owner* of type *user_account* within its body.

The user can define the ownership relations within the *bank* struct as illustrated in Fig. 2 where *owns* and *counts* are new keywords that clarify the ownership relations between structs and allows Automated VeriFast to generate predicates automatically.

3.2   Auto-fixing

Using VeriFast, both memory safety and full functional correctness of applications can be verified. Therefore, Automated VeriFast was implemented to expect two kinds of errors. The first is memory errors, such as illegal access, buffer overflow, memory leaks, and null pointer dereference; the second is functional correctness errors.

VeriFast supports modular formal verification which means that each function is verified separately and, in case of function calls, VeriFast uses only the callee's contract not its body. To support such modularity, VeriFast implements the frame rule introduced in separation logic which states that while reasoning about a behaviour of a command, it is safe to ignore memory locations not accessed by this command. This allows VeriFast to divide the large heap into small heaplets based on functions' contracts. This concept of locality ensures that any function starts with a heap consisting of what is asserted in the function precondition, which should be taken from the global heap, and at the end of the function the resources asserted by the postcondition will be consumed and returned to the global heap.

From Automated VeriFast's point of view, this facilitates the generalization of all memory errors into two categories: something is needed from the heap, but it doesn't exist in the local heap; something exists in the local heap, but it is not needed. Taking the error message, produced by VeriFast, with other parameters, such as the state of the heap when the error occurred, the stack, the execution context, and the assumptions made out of the specification so far, Automated VeriFast tries to find a solution by generating an annotation. Automated VeriFast can only produce annotations. It doesn't make any changes in the source code. If Automated VeriFast fails to produce any more annotations and the program is not yet successfully verified, then there is either the need for a manual intervention from the user or it may be the case that there is an error in the written code and it can't be verified.

Moreover, Automated VeriFast works on detecting the changes happening to the length of the linked lists in order to infer not only memory specification but also some of the functional properties of linked lists.

4 Automated VeriFast by Examples

In this section, we present some examples of using Automated VeriFast to infer formal annotations for some programs manipulating linked lists.

4.1 Stack Example

The stack example describes how Automated VeriFast successfully infers formal annotations for some functions that are part of the stack implementation. The Implementation of the stack mentioned in this paper contains two structs. The *node* struct contains a pointer field of its own type *node* that points to the next node and it also contains an *int* value; the stack struct only contains a pointer of type node pointing to the head node. See Fig. 3.

Users just need to add the *owns* keyword before the *struct node *head* in the *stack* struct. The predicates shown in Fig. 3 will be automatically generated in the source code before the structs.

The generated predicates are precise. Precise predicates in VeriFast are similar to precise assertions in separation logic in the sense that for any heap, given a list of input arguments, there is at most one combination of a subheap and

```
1   struct node                      /*@
2   {                                predicate stack (struct stack *stack; int count) =
3       struct node *next;               stack->head |-> ?head &*&
4       int value;                       malloc_block_stack(stack) &*&
5   };                                   node(head, count) &*& count >= 0;
6   struct stack
7   {                                predicate node (struct node *node; int count) =
8       struct node *head;               node == 0 ? count == 0 :
9   };                                       node->next |-> ?next &*&
                                             node->value |-> ?value &*&
                                             malloc_block_node(node) &*&
                                             node(next, ?count1) &*&
                                             count == count1 + 1 &*& count > 0;
                                     @*/
```

Fig. 3. The node and stack structs are on the left and the auto-generated predicates are on the right

a list of output arguments that satisfies the predicate. Precise predicates are declared in VeriFast by writing a semicolon instead of a comma between input parameters and output parameters in the predicate's list of parameter.

Automated VeriFast uses precise predicates mainly for two reasons:

- In general, VeriFast requires the user to insert ghost commands to replace a predicate occurrence by its definition (which is called *opening* the predicate) or vice versa (called *closing* the predicate). If a precise predicate is included in the postcondition, VeriFast tries to automatically open and close it.
- Precise predicates cause VeriFast to infer the predicate's output parameters which helps a lot in proving the functional correctness.

Moving to the use of the auto-fix functionality, verifying the *stack_push* function, appears in Fig. 4, using VeriFast, where both precondition and postcondition have empty heaps, raises an error in line no. 7 where VeriFast tries to access the *head* field of the stack while no heap chunk representing this field exists in the heap.

```
1   void stack_push(struct stack *stack, int value)
2       //@ requires true;
3       //@ ensures true;
4   {
5       struct node *n = malloc(sizeof( struct node));
6       if (n == 0) { abort(); }
7       n−>next = stack−>head;
8       n−>value = value;
9       stack−>head = n; }
```

Fig. 4. Push functions

Automated VeriFast solves the error by adding an annotation that represents the stack and its fields encapsulated in a stack predicate in the precondition of the function. If an error is produced during the verification of a call of this function, then the responsibility will be on the caller not the callee. This preserves the compositional nature of VeriFast and hence Automated VeriFast.

With the new added annotation, VeriFast will next fail to verify the function with a memory leak error and a heap h consisting of node n and stack stack. To overcome this error, the node fields will be encapsulated into a predicate *node* and then encapsulated with the stack's fields into a stack predicate. Finally this stack predicate will be added to the postcondition of the function. The final contract of the function will be as following:

```
//@ requires true &*& stack(stack, ?count);
//@ ensures true &*& stack(stack, count + 1);
```

The *?count* is a fresh variable denoting some unknown value representing the length of the stack. Automated VeriFast was able to figure out that the length of the stack increased by one as can be seen in the postcondition.

4.2   Bank Example

The source code of the Bank example is 397 line of code. Automated VeriFast was able to provide annotations for the bank example, excluding the loop invariant annotations, with very few interventions from the user. We will show some examples of these required interventions. Look at the following function:

```
1   void  socket_write_transactions_helper2 ( struct socket *socket, int count, struct transaction
            * transactions )
2   //@ requires true &*& transaction(transactions,?count1) &*& count1 > 0 &*& socket(socket);
3   //@ ensures true &*& transaction(transactions,count) &*& socket(socket);
4   {
5          ...........
6          ...........
7   }
```

Automated VeriFast was able to generate the shown pre/post-condition. The user needs to change the *count*1 > 0 condition in line 2 in the precondition and writes instead *count1* == *count* and the function will be verified successfully.

Another example is the following function where the post-condition, auto-generated by Automated VeriFast, has to be slightly modified by the user to be successfully verified:

```
1   struct  authenticate_result  * authenticate_user ( struct  user_account *userAccounts, char *userName,
            char *password)
2   //@ requires  true &*& user_account(userAccounts,?count0) &*& string1(userName) &*&
            string1(password);
3   //@ ensures  true &*& string1(userName) &*& string1(password) &*&
            user_account(userAccounts,count0) &*& authenticate_result(result);
4   {
5          if  (userAccounts == 0) {
6                  return  0;
7              }
8          else  {
9              ...........
10             ...........
11          }
12
13  }
```

To successfully verify this function, the user has to put the last part of the post-condition *authenticate_result(result)* within a conditional statement like the following: *(result == 0 ? true : authenticate_result(result))*. Other than these kinds of possible interventions everything else is almost auto-generated except for the loop invariant which still needs to be manually provided.

5   Related Work

Infer [4, 8, 10] is a static analysis tool based on separation logic. It performs a deep heap shape analysis. Infer is able to automatically generate pre/post-conditions, but it focuses on detecting only memory errors, ignoring still a wide range of other possible functional errors. Our approach is different than the one followed by Infer. We don't claim to compete with it as we don't have a static analysis tool, but rather an automated verification tool. Static analysis tools' main goal is to find bugs, but our goal is to verify code.

Some work that was already done with VeriFast to gain some automation capabilities can be found in [5]. Automated VeriFast uses from this work the auto-open and the auto-close, but it has more functionalities, such as auto-generating predicates and inferring both the precondition and the postcondition.

Another work that shares the same aim which is inferring annotations automatically for VeriFast, but with a different way of approaching that is presented in [6]. They are using machine learning and dynamic analysis to capture some behaviours of programs that allow them to automatically generate annotations and feed it to VeriFast. Using dynamic analysis may end up giving good results regarding the shape of data structures, but it is still a headache for users to generate test suites whose quality will definitely affect the results of the dynamic analysis.

6 Conclusions and Future Work

The goal of our work is not to completely eliminate the need for user effort, but to reduce the annotation effort required as much as possible. In this paper, we presented Automated VeriFast which creates a framework in which the user can use the auto-generate predicates and the auto-fix functionality to solve verification errors, choose to write his own annotations manually, or combine both automation with his experience in writing formal annotations.

The current approach of Automated VeriFast supports some simple linked list patterns in which the linked list can be manipulated by adding or removing nodes to and from the list. We are working now on extending it to support additional patterns. We will work also on inferring the loop invariants. Furthermore, we will focus on inferring more specifications that prove functional correctness for more complex applications. The source code of Automated VeriFast is available at [9].

Acknowledgments. This work was funded by the Flemish Research Fund through grant G.0058.13.

References

1. Jacobs, B., Smans, J., Piessens, F.: A quick tour of the VeriFast program verifier. In: Ueda, K. (ed.) APLAS 2010. LNCS, vol. 6461, pp. 304–311. Springer, Heidelberg (2010)
2. O'Hearn, P.W.: A primer on separation logic (and automatic program verification and analysis). Software Safety and Security; Tools for Analysis and Verification. NATO Science for Peace and Security Series, vol. 33, pp. 286–318 (2012)
3. VeriFast tutorial. http://people.cs.kuleuven.be/~bart.jacobs/verifast/tutorial.pdf
4. Calcagno, C., Distefano, D.: Infer: an automatic program verifier for memory safety of C programs. In: Bobaru, M., Havelund, K., Holzmann, G.J., Joshi, R. (eds.) NFM 2011. LNCS, vol. 6617, pp. 459–465. Springer, Heidelberg (2011)
5. Vogels, F., Jacobs, B., Piessens, F., Smans, J.: Annotation inference for separation logic based verifiers. In: Bruni, R., Dingel, J. (eds.) FORTE 2011 and FMOODS 2011. LNCS, vol. 6722, pp. 319–333. Springer, Heidelberg (2011)

6. Mühlberg, J.T., White, D.H., Dodds, M., Lüttgen, G., Piessens, F.: Learning assertions to verify linked-list programs. In: Calinescu, R., Rumpe, B. (eds.) SEFM 2015. LNCS, vol. 9276, pp. 37–52. Springer, Heidelberg (2015)
7. Berdine, J., Calcagno, C., O'Hearn, P.W.: Smallfoot: modular automatic assertion checking with separation logic. In: de Boer, F.S., Bonsangue, M.M., Graf, S., de Roever, W.-P. (eds.) FMCO 2005. LNCS, vol. 4111, pp. 115–137. Springer, Heidelberg (2006)
8. Calcagno, C., Distefano, D., O'Hearn, P., Yang, H.: Compositional shape analysis by means of BI-abduction. In: POPL (2009)
9. https://github.com/Mahmohsen/verifast/tree/Automated-Verifast
10. Calcagno, C., et al.: Moving fast with software verification. In: Havelund, K., Holzmann, G., Joshi, R. (eds.) NFM 2015. LNCS, vol. 9058, pp. 3–11. Springer, Heidelberg (2015)

Analyzing Unsatisfiability in Bounded Model Checking Using Max-SMT and Dual Slicing

Takuro Kutsuna[✉] and Yoshinao Ishii

Toyota Central R&D Labs. Inc., Nagakute, Aichi 480-1192, Japan
kutsuna@mosk.tytlabs.co.jp

Abstract. Bounded model checking (BMC) with satisfiability modulo theories (SMT) is a powerful approach for generating test cases or finding bugs. However, it is generally difficult to determine an appropriate unrolling bound k in BMC. An SMT formula for BMC might be *unsatisfiable* because of the insufficiency of k. In this paper, we propose a novel approach for BMC using partial maximum satisfiability, in which the initial conditions of state variables are treated as soft constraints. State variables whose initial conditions are not satisfied in the solution of a maximum satisfiability solver can be regarded as bottlenecks in BMC. We can simultaneously estimate modified initial conditions for these bottleneck variables, with which the formula becomes satisfiable. Furthermore, we propose a method based on dual slicing to delineate the program path that is changed when we modify the initial conditions of the specified bottlenecks. The analysis results help us to estimate a suitable unrolling bound. We present experimental results using examples from the automotive industry to demonstrate the usefulness of the proposed method.

1 Introduction

The technique of bounded model checking (BMC) has a wide area of applications in program analysis, including formal verification, bug finding, and test-case generation. In BMC, the behavior of a program is expressed as a propositional formula under the assumption that each loop in the program is executed at most k times. We refer to k as an unrolling bound. The satisfiability of the formula is then checked using a satisfiability (SAT) or satisfiability modulo theory (SMT) solver. Large programs can be practically dealt with in the scheme of BMC by virtue of the recent progress in SAT/SMT solving techniques.

One of the major concerns in applying the BMC approach is how to determine the unrolling bound k. Satisfiability solvers return *unsatisfiable* if k is too small. On the other hand, the computation time for solving the satisfiability problem increases as k becomes larger. Moreover, there is a possibility that the formula is unsatisfiable regardless of the value of k. In other words, the formula is unsatisfiable even if k is set to an infinitely large value. A common approach for this problem is to start with a small k, and then gradually increase k until the formula becomes satisfiable, or until k reaches the predefined maximum or

© Springer International Publishing AG 2016
M.H. ter Beek et al. (Eds.): FMICS-AVoCS 2016, LNCS 9933, pp. 65–80, 2016.
DOI: 10.1007/978-3-319-45943-1_5

the computation runs into the timeout limit [15, 17]. Such a strategy works well when the required value of k is relatively small, though the computation time becomes a problem when a large k is required. Furthermore, we never reach the conclusion that the formula is unsatisfiable regardless of k.

In this paper, we propose a novel method to analyze the unsatisfiability issue in BMC. The analysis results help us to estimate an appropriate unrolling bound k, or enable us to argue that the formula is unsatisfiable regardless of the value of k for a particular class of problems. Let us consider the situation in which a formula becomes unsatisfiable in BMC. In the proposed method, we first apply a partial maximum satisfiability solver in which clauses that are related to the initial conditions of state variables are regarded as soft constraints. As a result, a set of initial conditions is specified as a potential cause of unsatisfiability. At the same time, candidate values for state variables in these initial conditions are also estimated by the maximum satisfiability solver. We then prepare a program in which the initial conditions are modified to the estimated ones. Dual slicing [19] is applied to programs with and without the modifications to investigate why the formula becomes satisfiable with the modified initial conditions.

We explain the proposed method using typical examples from embedded control software, for which selecting a proper unrolling bound is often of great concern when applying the BMC approach. There are many applications of BMC for embedded systems, such as unit testing [9], test-case generation [5, 15], and mutation testing [2]. The required unrolling bound tends to be very large when the embedded control software includes state variables that correspond to *counters*. Counter variables are often used in embedded control software, e.g., to manage shifts between different control modes. A counter can be increased, decreased, reset, or left unchanged depending on the input signals and current states of the system. The control mode is switched to another mode when the value of the counter exceeds a predefined threshold. Another example of counter usage is to capture errors based on the duration of unexpected system behavior. For example, "the system catches an error if the engine speed is less than 500 rpm for 3 seconds," in which a counter is used to represent the duration of the state whereby the engine speed is less than 500 rpm. Another factor that makes the required unrolling bound in BMC large is discrete-time integrators, which is often used in control logic, whose values might change only gradually.

The remainder of this paper is organized as follows. In Sect. 2, we present an overview of BMC for embedded control software and a motivating example. In Sect. 3, a method for analyzing unsatisfiability in BMC using maximum satisfiability is proposed. In Sect. 4, we introduce a dual slicing method for analyzing the results obtained by a maximum satisfiability solver. In Sect. 5, we present a case study based on a practical example from the automotive industry. In Sect. 6, we review existing methods related to our work in this paper. Finally, we conclude the paper in Sect. 7.

2 Background and Motivating Example

In this section, we first review BMC for embedded control software, and then present a motivating example.

2.1 Bounded Model Checking for Embedded Control Software

Embedded control systems are generally time-triggered systems in which tasks or procedures are repeatedly executed at given rates. Figure 1 illustrates an outline and the pseudo-code for embedded control systems. A salient feature of embedded control software is its limitless main loop. Generally, all other loops in the main loop have statically bounded iterations and can be fully unrolled in BMC. Therefore, the unrolling bound k in BMC for embedded control software implies an assumption on the number of main loop iterations.

Let $v^{(j)}$ be a vector of all variables in the software at the j-th iteration of the main loop, including input, output, and state variables. The following formula is used when applying BMC to embedded control software:

$$\Phi_k(v) := I\left(v^{(0)}\right) \wedge \bigwedge_{j=1,\dots,k} T\left(v^{(j-1)}, v^{(j)}\right) \wedge \neg P\left(v^{(0)}, \dots, v^{(k)}\right), \qquad (1)$$

where $v = \left(v^{(0)}, \dots, v^{(k)}\right)$. In (1), I denotes the initial condition of state variables and corresponds to the `initialize` function in Fig. 1b, T denotes the transition relation that is consistent with the procedure in the main loop, and P represents a property to be proved. The satisfiability of Φ_k is checked using a SAT or SMT solver. If Φ_k is satisfiable, a counterexample for which the property P does not hold can be found. In contrast, if Φ_k is unsatisfiable, there is no counterexample that violates P up to the k-th iteration of the main loop. Note that we use R instead of $\neg P$ in (1) for the purpose of test-case generation, where R represents a requirement that the generated test case must satisfy. The result that "Φ_k is satisfiable" then indicates that a test case that satisfies R has been successfully generated.

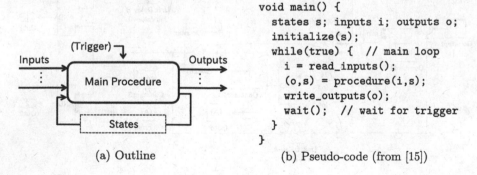

(a) Outline

```
void main() {
    states s; inputs i; outputs o;
    initialize(s);
    while(true) {  // main loop
        i = read_inputs();
        (o,s) = procedure(i,s);
        write_outputs(o);
        wait();  // wait for trigger
    }
}
```

(b) Pseudo-code (from [15])

Fig. 1. Embedded control software.

2.2   Example Model with a Counter

Simulink® [18] is a graphical programming tool that is often used to develop embedded control software in the automotive and avionics industries. Figure 2 shows an example of some embedded control software written as a Simulink® model. Although small, this model can reflect the essential difficulties in applying BMC. The model in Fig. 2 has five inputs and two outputs, all of which are of Boolean type. In executing a Simulink® model, the whole model is executed repeatedly, which corresponds to the main loop in Fig. 1b. The unit-delay block outputs the value that was input to the block in the previous execution, and therefore works as a state variable. The initial value of the unit-delay block is used as the first output. Setting the state variable of a unit-delay block to its initial value corresponds to the initialize function in Fig. 1b, and is therefore represented as I in (1).

The model in Fig. 2 includes two unit-delay blocks, Unit Delay A and Unit Delay B, both of which are initially set to 0. Hence, the model has two state variables. The state variable contained in Unit Delay A is used as a counter in the model. The counter is incremented up to 10000 if either In1 or In2 is true, and is reset to 0 if either In3 or In4 is false in each execution of the model. The model output depends on whether the counter value exceeds a threshold of 5000 (see Fig. 2). Such counters are frequently used in embedded control software, e.g., to manage shifts between control modes or to detect errors based on the duration of unexpected behavior, as mentioned in Sect. 1. The threshold value can be extremely large in practical embedded control software.

2.3   Motivation

We first consider the problem of generating a test case for the model in Fig. 2 such that Out1 will finally be true. Applying the BMC approach to this problem, Φ_k becomes unsatisfiable for $k < 5000$, and we fail to generate a test case. If we

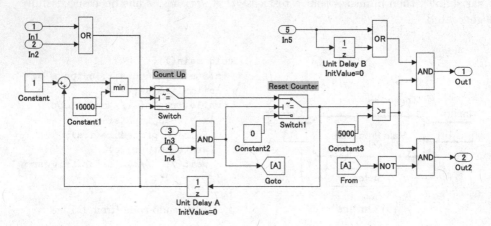

Fig. 2. Simulink® model with a counter.

use $k \geq 5000$, Φ_k becomes satisfiable and a test case is successfully generated. Next, let us consider the problem of generating a test case for the same model such that Out2 will finally be true. In fact, it is impossible to generate such a test case, and Φ_k is therefore unsatisfiable regardless of the value of k. These examples raise the following challenges in BMC, in which "test case" can be replaced with "counterexample":

1. How do we determine whether there is any possibility of finding a test case by increasing k?
2. How large should k be if there is any possibility of generating a test case?

If the model is small, as in Fig. 2, estimating an appropriate unrolling bound may not be a serious problem. However, the estimation is very hard when we deal with a practical model of embedded control software, because the model often consists of thousands of blocks and hundreds of state variables, including multiple counters. In the following sections, we propose a novel approach to address these challenges using both maximum satisfiability and dual slicing.

3 Initial Condition Analysis Using Maximum Satisfiability

We consider the situation in which Φ_k becomes unsatisfiable for a certain k in BMC. In the proposed method, we try to identify the initial conditions of state variables that might cause a bottleneck in BMC on the basis of partial maximum satisfiability. We first briefly introduce maximum satisfiability with SMT solvers, and then explain the proposed method.

3.1 Max-SMT

SMT is a decision problem for logical formulas, and SMT solvers are actively developed in many research institutions. Let us consider the SMT formula:

$$F(x) := \bigwedge_{i=1,\ldots,n} f_i(x),$$

where $f_i(x)$ $(i = 1, \ldots, n)$ are also SMT formulas. The purpose of ordinary SMT is to find an assignment of x such that $F(x)$ is satisfied. SMT solvers return the state "unsatisfiable" if $F(x)$ cannot be satisfied with any assignments of x. In contrast, maximum satisfiability modulo theories (Max-SMT) aim to find an assignment of x that satisfies as many $f_i(x)$ $(i = 1, \ldots, n)$ as possible. Max-SMT solvers therefore obtain some assignment of x for $F(x)$ that is unsatisfiable using ordinary SMT.

Partial Max-SMT (PMax-SMT) is an extension of Max-SMT in which the following form is considered:

$$G(x) := g(x) \wedge \bigwedge_{i=1,\ldots,m} g_i(x). \tag{2}$$

The goal of PMax-SMT is to find an assignment that satisfies as many $g_i(x)$ ($i = 1, \ldots, m$) as possible under the condition that $g(x)$ must be satisfied. We refer to $g(x)$ and $g_i(x)$ ($i = 1, \ldots, m$) in (2) as the hard constraint and the soft constraints, respectively. Max-SMT can be viewed as a special case of PMax-SMT in which the hard constraint $g(x) := \top$. Note that PMax-SMT solvers return "unsatisfiable" if the hard constraint itself is unsatisfiable.

Solving Max-SMT with an SMT Solver. There are few SMT solvers that can directly deal with Max-SMT problems in the present situation, though it is possible to solve Max-SMT or PMax-SMT problems with existing SMT solvers [1]. For example, we can solve PMax-SMT for $G(x)$ in (2) using an SMT solver as follows. We prepare the following formula G'_ω, in which a set of auxiliary variables $b = \{b_i \in \{0,1\} \mid i = 1, \ldots, m\}$ is introduced:

$$G'_\omega(x, b) := g(x) \wedge \bigwedge_{i=1,\ldots,m} (g_i(x) \vee (b_i = 1)) \wedge \left(\sum_{i=1,\ldots,m} b_i \leq \omega \right),$$

where ω is a non-negative integer that controls the number of formulas that are not necessarily satisfied in $\{g_i(x) \mid i = 1, \ldots, m\}$. Solving PMax-SMT for $G(x)$ then corresponds to finding the following $\tilde{\omega}$:

$$\tilde{\omega} := \underset{\omega=0,\ldots,m}{\arg\min} \left(\omega \mid G'_\omega(x, b) \text{ is satisfiable} \right). \tag{3}$$

Note that $\tilde{\omega}$ does not exist if $G'_\omega(x, b)$ is unsatisfiable for $\omega = m$, which indicates that PMax-SMT for $G(x)$ is unsatisfiable. Let $(\tilde{x}, \tilde{b})$ be an assignment that is obtained by solving $G'_{\tilde{\omega}}(x, b)$ with an SMT solver. Then, $\tilde{x}$ becomes a solution of PMax-SMT for $G(x)$. Moreover, $\{g_i(x) \mid \tilde{b}_i = 1, \tilde{b}_i \in \tilde{b}\}$ are soft constraints that are not satisfied in the solution. There are several strategies for finding $\tilde{\omega}$. The simplest one is to check the satisfiability of $G'_\omega(x, b)$ with $\omega = 0$, and then increment ω until $G'_\omega(x, b)$ becomes satisfiable or until ω reaches m. It is also possible to start with $\omega = m$, and then decrement ω as long as $G'_\omega(x, b)$ is satisfiable. Several techniques have been proposed in the literature, including those based on unsatisfiability cores [4].

3.2   Analyzing Initial Conditions with a Partial Max-SMT Solver

As mentioned in Sect. 2.2, $v^{(j)}$ denotes a vector of all variables at the j-th iteration of the main loop in Fig. 1b. Let $\mathcal{S}$ be an index set that corresponds to the state variables in $v^{(j)}$, that is, $v_i^{(j)} \left(\in v^{(j)} \right)$ represents a state variable if $i \in \mathcal{S}$. We assume that the initial condition I in (1) is given in the following form:

$$I \left(v^{(0)} \right) := \bigwedge_{i \in \mathcal{S}} \left(v_i^{(0)} = c_i \right), \tag{4}$$

where c_i denotes the initial value for the i-th state variable. For example, the initial condition for the software represented by the model in Fig. 2 is

$$I\left(v^{(0)}\right) := \left(v_A^{(0)} = 0\right) \wedge \left(v_B^{(0)} = 0\right), \tag{5}$$

where v_A and v_B represent state variables that are inherent in the Unit Delay A and Unit Delay B blocks, respectively. From (4), Φ_k in (1) can be transformed to

$$\Phi_k(v) := \bigwedge_{i \in S} \left(v_i^{(0)} = c_i\right) \wedge \bigwedge_{j=1,\ldots,k} T\left(v^{(j-1)}, v^{(j)}\right) \wedge \neg P\left(v^{(0)}, \ldots, v^{(k)}\right). \tag{6}$$

In the proposed method, we apply a PMax-SMT solver to Φ_k in which $v_i^{(0)} = c_i$ ($i \in S$) are regarded as soft constraints. Hereafter, we refer to this PMax-SMT problem as [A] for simplicity. The result of [A] can be interpreted in the following three ways.

Case 1: [A] Is Satisfiable and the Soft Constraints Are All Satisfied. This suggests that Φ_k is satisfiable in terms of the ordinary SMT. Hence, the assignment obtained by the PMax-SMT solver can be used as a counterexample in BMC.

Case 2: [A] Is Satisfiable, but Some of the Soft Constraints Are Not Satisfied. Let $S'(\subseteq S)$ be the index set of soft constraints that are not satisfied in the PMax-SMT solution. The initial conditions $v_i^{(0)} = c_i$ ($i \in S'$) are then considered to be bottlenecks in BMC. Moreover, the values assigned to $v_i^{(0)}$ ($i \in S'$) in the PMax-SMT solution can be used as estimates for these state variables. In other words, there is a possibility of finding a counterexample in BMC with k if the specified state variables reach the estimated values.

Case 3: [A] is Unsatisfiable. In this case, the hard constraint in [A], which is

$$\bigwedge_{j=1,\ldots,k} T\left(v^{(j-1)}, v^{(j)}\right) \wedge \neg P\left(v^{(0)}, \ldots, v^{(k)}\right), \tag{7}$$

is shown to be unsatisfiable. It follows from this that the following formula, which is obtained by replacing $v^{(j)}$ ($j = 0, \ldots, k$) in (7) with $v^{(L+j)}$ ($j = 0, \ldots, k$), respectively, is also unsatisfiable for any non-negative integer L:

$$\bigwedge_{j=L+1,\ldots,L+k} T\left(v^{(j-1)}, v^{(j)}\right) \wedge \neg P\left(v^{(L)}, \ldots, v^{(L+k)}\right). \tag{8}$$

It also follows from this result that the following formula is unsatisfiable:

$$I\left(v^{(0)}\right) \wedge \bigwedge_{j=1,\ldots,L} T\left(v^{(j-1)}, v^{(j)}\right) \wedge$$

$$\bigwedge_{j=L+1,\ldots,L+k} T\left(v^{(j-1)}, v^{(j)}\right) \wedge \neg P\left(v^{(L)}, \ldots, v^{(L+k)}\right). \tag{9}$$

Consequently, the result that [A] is unsatisfiable indicates that there is no coun-terexample of length $L+k$ that violates $P\left(v^{(L)}, \ldots, v^{(L+k)}\right)$ for any non-negative integer L. In particular, if P is given in the form

$$P\left(v^{(0)}, \ldots, v^{(k)}\right) := \bigwedge_{j=0, \ldots, k} q\left(v^{(j)}\right),$$

the unsatisfiability of [A] indicates that $q(v^{(j)})$ holds for any j, in which q often represents a safety property that must always be satisfied.

3.3   Example of Analyzing Initial Conditions

For the model in Fig. 2, we try to generate a test case such that "Out1 will finally be true." If we set $k = 10$ in BMC, Φ_k becomes unsatisfiable in terms of the ordinary SMT, as described in Sect. 2.3. Applying the proposed method to this problem, we obtain an assignment $\tilde{v}$ from a PMax-SMT solver in which the initial condition $v_A^{(0)} = 0$ is not satisfied. At the same time, we have an assignment of $v_A^{(0)}$ from $\tilde{v}$. In this case, a value greater than 4990 is assigned to $v_A^{(0)}$, e.g., $v_A^{(0)} = 6500$, because the counter represented by v_A can exceed the threshold 5000 within $k = 10$ steps by starting from such an initial value. These results suggest that the initial condition of state variable v_A may be a bottleneck of this problem, and test-case generation may be possible if the state variable v_A reaches 6500. Moreover, if we know that v_A is a counter, $k = 6500$ can be used as an estimate for the unrolling bound of this problem in BMC. To generate a test case for the same model such that "Out2 will finally be true," a PMax-SMT solver returns "unsatisfiable" in the proposed method. This means that there is no chance of generating a test case, regardless of the value of k, for the latter problem in BMC.

3.4   Limitations

By using the method proposed in this section, we can specify the initial condi-tions of state variables that are possible bottlenecks in BMC, and can estimate required values for these state variables. However, there is no guarantee that there exists a program path in which the state variables reach the estimated val-ues from their original initial values. Therefore, the estimated bottlenecks may not be useful in some cases. Nevertheless, it can be very informative for a class of problems. In Sect. 5, we provide a case study from the automotive industry in which the bottleneck estimation is shown to be beneficial to investigate the cause of unsatisfiability in BMC.

The proposed method is powerful in that it can directly estimate required values for state variables that are specified as bottlenecks. For example, we can easily estimate the required value for a counter in the model in Fig. 2, even if the threshold value of the counter were extremely large, which is often the case in embedded control software. However, the estimated value obtained by the proposed method can be unnecessarily large, because no restriction is placed on these variables when solving PMax-SMT. We can add some constraints to obtain better estimations, though it is generally difficult to specify such constraints.

4   Causal Path Analysis Using Dual Slicing

In this section, we propose a method to analyze the result obtained by PMax-SMT more deeply on the basis of dual slicing. This analysis helps us to understand why Φ_k becomes satisfiable when we change the initial conditions specified by a PMax-SMT solver.

4.1   Dual Slicing

Dual slicing is a variant of program slicing. Given a program and two execution traces, dual slicing aims at identifying the statements in the program that contribute to the difference between two execution traces at a given point of interest in the program. Starting from the given point, dual slicing finds a consecutive set of statements, in which two execution traces differ, according to *data* and *control* dependencies [14]. Weeratunge et al. [19] originally proposed dual slicing for analyzing concurrency bugs. They dealt with the situation in which there are two program schedules for a concurrent program, one of which causes a failure. Johnson et al. [7] proposed the similar approach of differential slicing for analyzing vulnerabilities in security software, whereby two execution traces of a program are examined to find the root cause of a vulnerability.

4.2   Causal Path Analysis

We consider the situation in which solving Problem [A] with a PMax-SMT solver results in Case 2 in Sect. 3.2. We then have a set of initial conditions $v_i^{(0)} = c_i$ ($i \in \mathcal{S}'$) that are not satisfied in the PMax-SMT solution. We also have assignments of $v_i^{(0)}$ ($i \in \mathcal{S}'$) in the solution, which we denote as $\tilde{c}_i$ ($i \in \mathcal{S}'$). Now, let $\mathcal{M}$ represent the model for the original software. We prepare a model in which $v_i^{(0)} = c_i$ ($i \in \mathcal{S}'$) are replaced with $v_i^{(0)} = \tilde{c}_i$ ($i \in \mathcal{S}'$), respectively, in $\mathcal{M}$, which we denote by $\tilde{\mathcal{M}}$. Note that $\tilde{\mathcal{M}}$ and $\mathcal{M}$ are identical except for some of the initial conditions of state variables. We denote the set of variables used in property P by v_p. We propose a method to delineate the program path that is substantially affected by modifying the initial conditions specified as bottlenecks, which involves the following steps:

Step 1: Generate an input case of length k that violates property P in $\tilde{\mathcal{M}}$. Such an input case exists because the initial conditions in $\tilde{\mathcal{M}}$ are modified so as to make $\tilde{\Phi}_k$, which represents the BMC formula for $\tilde{\mathcal{M}}$, satisfiable. Furthermore, it is possible to extract such an input case from the assignment that is obtained by solving PMax-SMT for Φ_k, because the assignment inevitably satisfies $\tilde{\Phi}_k$.

Step 2: Execute each of $\mathcal{M}$ and $\tilde{\mathcal{M}}$ with the input case generated in Step 1, and record the execution logs of all variables in each model.

Step 3: Execution logs from $\mathcal{M}$ and $\tilde{\mathcal{M}}$ must be different with respect to the variables in v_p, as property P is violated in $\tilde{\mathcal{M}}$ but is not violated in $\mathcal{M}$. As the input cases used to execute $\mathcal{M}$ and $\tilde{\mathcal{M}}$ are the same, the differences in v_p must have been caused by the differences in the modified initial conditions. We compare the execution logs in the backward direction from the variables in v_p according to data and control dependencies [14], and extract that part of the model in which the execution logs from $\mathcal{M}$ and $\tilde{\mathcal{M}}$ are inconsistent.

Figure 3 illustrates an outline of the proposed method, in which $\mathcal{S}'$ is assumed to be $\{a, b\}$. Step 3 in the above procedure corresponds to dual slicing, though this is slightly different from existing applications such as [7,19], in which dual slicing is mainly used to debug a program using two execution traces. Instead, our aim is to analyze the effect of modifying a program using a single input case. It is crucial to extract the causal path in the backward direction from v_p in Step 3, because forward analysis from the modified conditions would include parts that are different in terms of the execution logs, but are not necessarily essential. The details of comparing the execution logs from $\mathcal{M}$ and $\tilde{\mathcal{M}}$ are explained in the next section.

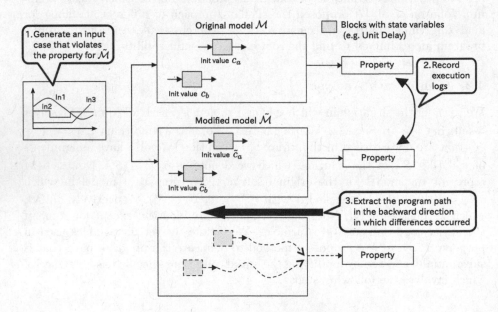

Fig. 3. Outline of the causal path analysis.

4.3   How to Compare Execution Logs

We denote the execution log of the i-th variable at the j-th iteration of the main loop in $\mathcal{M}$ and $\tilde{\mathcal{M}}$ by $w_i^{(j)}$ and $\tilde{w}_i^{(j)}$, respectively. Note that $w_i^{(j)}$ and $\tilde{w}_i^{(j)}$ correspond to one another, because $\mathcal{M}$ and $\tilde{\mathcal{M}}$ are identical other than for the initial conditions of state variables. We use the notation $w_i = (w_i^{(1)}, \ldots, w_i^{(k)})$ and $\tilde{w}_i = (\tilde{w}_i^{(1)}, \ldots, \tilde{w}_i^{(k)})$ to indicate the execution logs for the i-th variable. To apply dual slicing in Step 3 in the previous section, we need a criterion to determine whether w_i and $\tilde{w}_i$ are different. We consider there to be a significant difference between w_i and $\tilde{w}_i$ if the function:

$$d\left(w_i, \tilde{w}_i\right) := \begin{cases} 0 & \text{if } w_i^{(j)} = \tilde{w}_i^{(j)} \ (j = 1, \ldots, \lambda) \\ 1 & \text{otherwise,} \end{cases} \tag{10}$$

is equal to 1, where λ is an integer given by:

$$\lambda := \max_{i' \in I_p; j'=1,\ldots,k} \left(j' \mid w_{i'}^{(j')} \neq \tilde{w}_{i'}^{(j')} \right), \tag{11}$$

in which I_p denotes the index set of variables used in property P. It follows from (11) that λ indicates the maximum iteration step of the main loop in which the execution logs related to property P are different in $\mathcal{M}$ and $\tilde{\mathcal{M}}$. In (10), we assume that w_i and $\tilde{w}_i$ are not significantly different as long as $w_i^{(j)} = \tilde{w}_i^{(j)}$ for $j = 1, \ldots, \lambda$, because we wish to identify the difference between execution logs that leads to the difference in property P.

4.4   Example of Analyzing the Causal Path

We provide an illustrative example using the model in Fig. 4. The model includes a unit-delay block that corresponds to a counter whose initial value is 0. We consider the problem of generating a test case such that the output of the model will finally be true. The BMC formula Φ_k for this problem is unsatisfiable if we use $k \leq 1000$. The counter is then specified as a bottleneck by using the PMax-SMT-based technique proposed in Sect. 3. By applying the method proposed in this section, the bold line in Fig. 4 is specified as the causal path. The causal path delineates the relationship between the unit-delay block, which is specified as a bottleneck, and the output of the model, which is used in the definition of the property. By tracing the causal path, we can easily investigate why the test-case generation becomes possible when the initial condition of the unit-delay block is modified. From the causal path in Fig. 4, we can see that it is essential to increase the counter to a value above 1000 to generate a test case for this problem. It is worth mentioning that the counter is also compared to a threshold of 2000 in Fig. 4, though this part is not included in the causal path, because the counter does not necessarily exceed this threshold for the problem considered here.

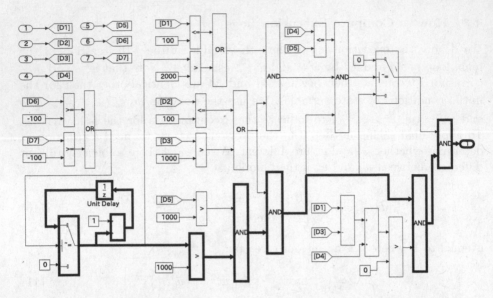

Fig. 4. Bold line indicates the causal path specified by the proposed method.

5   Case Study

We evaluated the proposed method using practical embedded control software taken from the automotive industry, which was implemented as a Simulink® model. For confidentiality reasons, we cannot give full details of this model, though we believe that the results described in this section will demonstrate the usefulness of the proposed method in practical situations. The experiment was performed on an Intel® Core™ i7 CPU (3.20 GHz) machine with 64 GB RAM, running Microsoft® Windows® 7.

5.1   Outline of the Model and Problem Setting

The model used in the experiment consists of about 17000 blocks and has 58 inputs and 51 outputs. The model includes 745 state variables that are represented by blocks such as the unit-delay block, all of which have predefined initial values. In BMC, the initial condition for this model can therefore be expressed in the form of (4). The model consists of several subsystems, each of which have a different execution period. The model has some control modes in each of which different control logic is employed. The current control mode is determined by the preceding sequence of inputs. We attempt to generate a test case for the model such that the control mode shifts from the initial mode, Mode X, to the target mode, Mode Y, using the BMC methodology.

We used STP [6] as an SMT solver. Although the original version of STP does not support maximum satisfiability, we have extended it so as to solve PMax-SMT based on the method described in Sect. 3.1. In the experiment, we also employed techniques such as program slicing [14] and function abstraction [12] to improve the scalability of test-case generation. We note that the problem considered here was provided by an automotive company as a practical example that cannot be solved with existing products on the market.

5.2 Results

We applied the BMC with $k = 17$, which was selected so that every subsystem in the model is invoked at least once, to generate a test case that induces a mode shift from Mode X to Mode Y. Formula Φ_k then turned out to be unsatisfiable. Therefore, we applied the proposed method in which Φ_k is analyzed by PMax-SMT. As a result, we detected three of the 745 state variables in the model to be bottlenecks. We denote these as $\{v_\alpha, v_\beta, v_\gamma\}$. We then applied causal path analysis to reveal the relationship between these state variables and the mode shift from Mode X to Mode Y. The computation times needed to solve PMax-SMT for Φ_k and extract the causal path were about 3 min and 1 min, respectively.

By tracing the causal path obtained by the proposed method, it was found that both v_α and v_β correspond to counters in the model, and it was necessary to increase each of these counters above a certain threshold. We also discovered that the remaining state variable v_γ is not a counter, but is used to reset v_α, that is, v_α is forced to reset to 0 unless $v_\gamma = 1$. The initial condition of v_γ, $v_\gamma^{(0)} = 0$, was therefore specified to be a bottleneck. From these observations, we found that it may be possible to generate a test case that induces a shift from Mode X to Mode Y by setting $k = 3000^1$ in BMC. However, the formula for Φ_k with $k = 3000$ was computationally intractable. Thus, we tried to generate a test case by: (1) generating an input of length 1 such that both v_α and v_β increase, (2) executing the model repeatedly using the generated input until v_α and v_β exceeded their specified thresholds, (3) from the resulting state, generating a test case that shifts the control mode from Mode X to Mode Y using an ordinary BMC with small k. As a result, we successfully generated a test case for the problem. Such an approach can be viewed as a problem reduction process.

We also attempted to generate test cases that achieve shifts between control modes other than Mode X and Mode Y. The SMT formula Φ_k became unsatisfiable with small k in each problem. A few state variables in each problem were then detected as being bottlenecks by the proposed method, and all of these included some counter variables. We succeeded in generating test cases using the problem reduction approach described above for most of these problems, although some could not be solved in this manner. Whether such problem reduction is effective depends on the characteristics of the problem. However, we think that some practical problems can be handled by such a strategy. Therefore, the proposed method is not only useful for estimating the required unrolling bound in BMC, but also for working out the problem using an approach such as problem reduction.

---

[1] This is not the actual number estimated from the real model. However, the order of the unrolling bound required for the real model was the same.

6   Related Work

As mentioned in Sect. 1, a common approach used in BMC is to start with a
small value of k, and then solve the satisfiability problem repeatedly by gradually increasing k until the formula becomes satisfiable or a timeout limit is
reached. Schrammel et al. [15] proposed a method to improve the efficiency of
such iterative solving of satisfiability problems in BMC using incremental SAT
techniques. The runtime of BMC is reduced by an order of magnitude by the
incremental approach, as reported in [15], though there still remains a difficulty
in dealing with problems for which very large k values are required. In contrast,
the method proposed in this paper does not require a satisfiability solver to be
invoked multiple times. Instead, we solve a maximum satisfiability problem once
with a fixed k, and then apply dual slicing to analyze the program.

Acceleration is a technique for summarizing loops. The effect of k iterations
of a loop is represented in a closed-form in terms of k, then the loop is replaced
or attached with its closed-form to enable model checkers to skip the loop in one
step. Kroening et al. [10] proposed an acceleration method in which a closed-
form of iterating *a path* through the loop body is estimated to skip the multiple
iterations of the path. Their method was shown to enhance the performance of
model checkers on a benchmark suite of C programs that consists of manually
sliced versions of open source programs. Acceleration methods are expected to
work well if the loop body is relatively small and not very complicated. However,
in the case of embedded control software, the most part of the program lies inside
the loop body, as mentioned in Sect. 2. The model used in our experiment, for
example, has thousands of Simulink® blocks in its loop body. The number of
possible paths through the loop body can then be extremely large. Consequently,
it is difficult even to find out a suitable path in the loop body to accelerate. There
is a possibility that the causal path, which is obtained by the method proposed
in this paper, can be informative for selecting a path to accelerate.

Clarke et al. [3] discussed the completeness threshold (CT) for BMC. CT is
an unrolling bound with which a linear temporal logic (LTL) property is proved
in an unbounded manner in the scheme of BMC. Kroening and Strichman [11]
proposed a method to calculate CT for a class of LTL properties. The calculation
of CT for a general LTL property is shown to be at least as hard as proving
the property using ordinary LTL model checking [3]. Moreover, even if CT is
obtained, it is often impractically large, as reported in [15]. The aim of the
proposed method is not to calculate CT, but to estimate an unrolling bound
that is sufficient to generate a counterexample or a test case.

Several methods that extend BMC to unbounded model checking have been
proposed, such as k-induction [16] and the Craig interpolation-based algorithm
[13]. These methods prove that the formula is unsatisfiable for $k = \infty$ based on
inductive reasoning from the fact that the formula is unsatisfiable for $k = \tilde{k}(<
\infty)$. In general, the value of $\tilde{k}$ is gradually increased until the inductive reasoning
is accepted or a counterexample is found. Such methods are very powerful if the
inductive reasoning can be completed for relatively small $\tilde{k}$. However, it will take

a long time to find a counterexample if the formula becomes satisfiable for some very large $\tilde{k}$, which is the situation considered in this paper.

7   Conclusion and Future Work

In this paper, we have proposed a method for analyzing BMC formulas that are unsatisfiable in the ordinary sense of BMC using maximum satisfiability. We also proposed a method to delineate the causal path between state variables specified as bottlenecks and the desired property in BMC on the basis of dual slicing. A case study with a practical embedded control system taken from the automotive industry was presented to demonstrate the usefulness of our approach.

It is a future challenge to examine how the proposed method works in application domains other than embedded control software. There have been several applications of maximum satisfiability in software analysis. It is worth considering applying the causal path analysis presented in this paper to other applications of maximum satisfiability. Jose and Majumdar [8], for example, proposed a method for localizing a potential cause of program bugs with a maximum satisfiability solver, in which a patch for the bug is also estimated. It would be possible to extract the causal path from the suggested patch for the bug, which would help us to investigate why the bug is fixed by the patch.

Acknowledgement. The authors are grateful for the useful comments and support provided by Tetsuya Tohdo and Hiroyuki Ihara at DENSO CORPORATION.

References

1. Ansótegui, C., Bonet, M.L., Levy, J.: Sat-based maxsat algorithms. Artif. Intell. **196**, 77–105 (2013)
2. Brillout, A., He, N., Mazzucchi, M., Kroening, D., Purandare, M., Rümmer, P., Weissenbacher, G.: Mutation-based test case generation for simulink models. In: de Boer, F.S., Bonsangue, M.M., Hallerstede, S., Leuschel, M. (eds.) FMCO 2009. LNCS, vol. 6286, pp. 208–227. Springer, Heidelberg (2010)
3. Clarke, E., Kroning, D., Ouaknine, J., Strichman, O.: Completeness and complexity of bounded model checking. In: Steffen, B., Levi, G. (eds.) VMCAI 2004. LNCS, vol. 2937, pp. 85–96. Springer, Heidelberg (2004)
4. Fu, Z., Malik, S.: On solving the partial MAX-SAT problem. In: Biere, A., Gomes, C.P. (eds.) SAT 2006. LNCS, vol. 4121, pp. 252–265. Springer, Heidelberg (2006)
5. Gadkari, A.A., Yeolekar, A., Suresh, J., Ramesh, S., Mohalik, S., Shashidhar, K.C.: AutoMOTGen: automatic model oriented test generator for embedded control systems. In: Gupta, A., Malik, S. (eds.) CAV 2008. LNCS, vol. 5123, pp. 204–208. Springer, Heidelberg (2008)
6. Ganesh, V., Dill, D.L.: A decision procedure for bit-vectors and arrays. In: Damm, W., Hermanns, H. (eds.) CAV 2007. LNCS, vol. 4590, pp. 519–531. Springer, Heidelberg (2007)

7. Johnson, N., Caballero, J., Chen, K., McCamant, S., Poosankam, P., Reynaud, D., Song, D.: Differential slicing: identifying causal execution differences for security applications. In: IEEE Symposium on Security and Privacy, pp. 347–362 (2011)
8. Jose, M., Majumdar, R.: Cause clue clauses: error localization using maximum satisfiability. In: PLDI 2011, pp. 437–446 (2011)
9. Kim, M., Kim, Y., Kim, H.: A comparative study of software model checkers as unit testing tools: an industrial case study. TSE **37**(2), 146–160 (2011)
10. Kroening, D., Lewis, M., Weissenbacher, G.: Under-approximating loops in C programs for fast counterexample detection. FMSD **47**(1), 75–92 (2015)
11. Kroning, D., Strichman, O.: Efficient computation of recurrence diameters. In: Zuck, L.D., Attie, P.C., Cortesi, A., Mukhopadhyay, S. (eds.) VMCAI 2003. LNCS, vol. 2575, pp. 298–309. Springer, Heidelberg (2002)
12. Kutsuna, T., Ishii, Y., Yamamoto, A.: Abstraction and refinement of mathematical functions toward SMT-based test-case generation. Int. J. Softw. Tools Technol. Transfer 1–12 (2015)
13. McMillan, K.L.: Interpolation and SAT-based model checking. In: Hunt Jr., W.A., Somenzi, F. (eds.) CAV 2003. LNCS, vol. 2725, pp. 1–13. Springer, Heidelberg (2003)
14. Reicherdt, R., Glesner, S.: Slicing matlab simulink models. In: ICSE 2012, pp. 551–561 (2012)
15. Schrammel, P., Kroening, D., Brain, M., Martins, R., Teige, T., Bienmüller, T.: Successful use of incremental BMC in the automotive industry. In: Núñez, M., Güdemann, M. (eds.) Formal Methods for Industrial Critical Systems. LNCS, vol. 9128, pp. 62–77. Springer, Heidelberg (2015)
16. Sheeran, M., Singh, S., Stålmarck, G.: Checking safety properties using induction and a SAT-solver. In: Johnson, S.D., Hunt Jr., W.A. (eds.) FMCAD 2000. LNCS, vol. 1954, pp. 108–125. Springer, Heidelberg (2000)
17. Shtrichman, O.: Pruning techniques for the SAT-based bounded model checking problem. In: Margaria, T., Melham, T.F. (eds.) CHARME 2001. LNCS, vol. 2144, pp. 58–70. Springer, Heidelberg (2001)
18. The MathWorks Inc. http://www.mathworks.com
19. Weeratunge, D., Zhang, X., Sumner, W.N., Jagannathan, S.: Analyzing concurrency bugs using dual slicing. In: ISSTA 2010, pp. 253–264 (2010)

Towards the Automated Verification of Weibull Distributions for System Failure Rates

Yu Lu[1,2]($\boxtimes$), Alice A. Miller[1], Ruth Hoffmann[1], and Christopher W. Johnson[1]

[1] School of Computing Science, University of Glasgow, Glasgow, UK
y.lu.3@research.gla.ac.uk,
{alice.miller,ruth.hoffmann,christopher.johnson}@glasgow.ac.uk
[2] School of Aerospace, Transport and Manufacturing, Cranfield University,
Cranfield, UK

Abstract. Weibull distributions can be used to accurately model failure behaviours of a wide range of critical systems such as on-orbit satellite subsystems. Markov chains have been used extensively to model reliability and performance of engineering systems or applications. However, the exponentially distributed sojourn time of Continuous-Time Markov Chains (CTMCs) can sometimes be unrealistic for satellite systems that exhibit Weibull failures. In this paper, we develop novel semi-Markov models that characterise failure behaviours, based on Weibull failure modes inferred from realistic data sources. We approximate and encode these new models with CTMCs and use the PRISM probabilistic model checker. The key benefit of this integration is that CTMC-based model checking tools allow us to automatically and efficiently verify reliability properties relevant to industrial critical systems.

Keywords: Satellite systems · Weibull distribution · Continuous-time markov chains · Semi-markov chains · Probabilistic model checking

1 Introduction

Satellite systems are complex due to the fact that they consist of a large number of interacting subsystems (e.g., gyro/sensor/reaction wheels; control processors (CPs); and telemetry, tracking, and command (TTC)), which ensure redundancy without an unnecessary increase in power or mass requirements. Each subsystem may itself have complex and different failure modes. The failure modes are more complex than for conventional systems because of the limited opportunities for repair except through reconfiguration. A satellite subsystem can suffer whole or partial failures, which may belong to a variety of failure classes. It has been shown that Weibull distributions are able to properly model on-orbit failure behaviours of satellite subsystems [1,2].

Y. Lu—This research was partially supported by the EC project "ETCS Advanced Testing and Smart Train Positioning System" (FP7-TRANSPORT-314219). The author Yu Lu was funded by the Scottish Informatics and Computer Science Alliance (SICSA).

M.H. ter Beek et al. (Eds.): FMICS-AVoCS 2016, LNCS 9933, pp. 81–96, 2016.
DOI: 10.1007/978-3-319-45943-1_6

Failures in satellite subsystems are conveniently modelled using Weibull distributions. Unfortunately such distributions are not amenable to continuous time model checking tools, such PRISM, that mainly support CTMCs with exponentially distributed sojourn time. It has also been shown that it is possible to approximate many common distributions using phase-type distributions such as Erlang distributions and a sum of many exponential distributions (the hyperexponential distribution), although this has proved computationally difficult [3]. Given the maturity of a CTMC solver such as PRISM, and its focus on minimising state spaces, this difficulty is less of an issue. The aim is to investigate how Weibull distributions can be approximated so that PRISM can be effectively used for model checking based reliability analysis of satellite systems.

Simulation is a commonly used and powerful analysis technique for reliability engineering. It is flexible since it supports arbitrary normal distributions (such as Pareto, Weibull, or Lognormal distributions). However, simulations may take a long time to run as the events (e.g., failure) that we are trying to model may be very rare. In addition, it involves the complex design of valid simulation models and interpretations of simulation results. Probabilistic model checking is a formal method for the specification and verification of complex systems with stochastic behaviours. It allows the additional inclusion of probabilities on transitions, and so gives us the ability to check probabilistic properties, such as, "what is the probability of a failure within 5 years?" The automation of the PRISM is essential for analysing reasonably large and non-trivial Markov models with exponential distributions. CTMC models have been used widely to model reliability and performance of engineering systems or applications. However, the exponentially distributed sojourn time of CTMCs can be unrealistic to model satellite systems that exhibit Weibull failures. PRISM is useful for analysing realistic satellite subsystems, and we can obtain results with high accuracy if good approximations of Weibull distributions can be made without resulting in a state space that is too large to yield to feasibly check.

Model checking of semi-Markov chains is more complicated than that of Markov chains. Techniques for model checking semi-Markov chains have been developed [4,5], whereas the methods are practically negative or infeasible. In recent years, applying practical probabilistic model checking tools to analyse non-Markov models has attracted a lot of attention. In [6], the authors analyse disk reliability of reasonable sized systems (such as RAID4/5/6) based on non-exponential distributions in PRISM [7]. Approximations of Weibull models are considered in [8], using an M-stage Erlang model, and in [9] where 3-state Hidden Markov Models (HMMs) are used. In both cases, results are contrasted with those obtained via simulation. In [10], a stochastic performance model is constructed and the hyper Erlang distribution of real-world data used in PRISM to analyse a public bus transportation network in Edinburgh. In [11], phase-type distributions are used to analyse a collaborative editing system in PRISM.

Our paper is organised as follows. In Sect. 2, we define semi-Markov models that specify failures of satellite subsystems based on the Weibull distributions, while in Sect. 3 we give technical background on CTMCs and PRISM. In Sect. 4, we summarise our technique to approximate the Weibull distributions. In Sect. 5, approximations of these semi-Markov models as CTMCs are developed in PRISM and their benefits are investigated. Finally, in Sect. 6 we conclude and outline directions for future research.

2   Multi-state Failure Mode in Satellite Subsystems

We propose an approach to building semi-Markov models for reliability analysis of satellite subsystems using a real-world database. The main data source consists of 1584 Earth-orbiting satellites which were launched between January 1990 and October 2008, and are provided by the SpaceTrak database[1]. The SpaceTrak launch and satellite analytical system and its database are used by most global key launch providers, satellite manufacturers, insurance companies, and satellite operators. It provides a variety of data and important information about satellite on-orbit failures and unexpected behaviour, and also launch attempts from 1957. This has enabled us to predict and analyse failure rates.

One of the problems with stochastic approaches on-orbit is the lack of prior validation given the specialised nature of many designs. Common core components e.g. NOAH and the DoD have a core platform that is then configured but many components and architectures are unique. The database used here is likely to provide a conservative base case but is not tailored to specific missions.

The database contains several satellite subsystems. In this paper, we only consider 11 subsystems (as shown in Fig. 1). These are: (1) Gyro / sensor / reaction wheel, (2) thruster / fuel, (3) beam / antenna operation / deployment (4) control processor (CP), (5) mechanisms / structures / thermal, (6) payload instrument / amplifier / on-board data / computer / transponder, (7) battery / cell, (8) electrical distribution, (9) solar array deployment (SAD), (10) solar array operating (SAO), (11) telemetry, tracking and command (TTC), and one additional category, which is (12) unknown: when the subsystem causing the failure of the satellite could not be identified.

Unlike traditional binary models of reliability analysis for which satellite subsystems are considered to be either fully operational or suffering a complete failure, additional intermediate states which characterise partial failures are introduced (as shown in Fig. 2). This multi-state modelling approach provides more insights into the failure behaviours of a satellite system and their relationship to total failure through a finer level abstraction. These states are also defined in the SpaceTrak database, and their meanings are summarised as follows:

- State 1: satellite subsystem is fully operational;
- State 2: minor, temporary, or repairable failure that does not cause a substantial and perpetual effect on the operation of the satellite subsystem;

---

[1] http://www.seradata.com/.

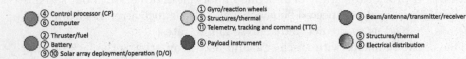

Fig. 1. An overview of key satellite subsystems

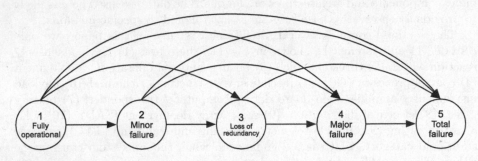

Fig. 2. Multi-state transitions for failure behaviour of satellite subsystems

- State 3: major or non-repairable failure that results in loss of redundancy[2] to the operation of the satellite subsystem on a permanent basis;
- State 4: major or non-repairable failure that influences operation of the satellite subsystems on a permanent basis;
- State 5: drastic failure results in satellite retirement, which implies total failure of the satellite.

---

[2] Redundancy: the duplication of critical components or functions of a satellite subsystem.

3   Preliminaries

3.1   Continuous-Time Markov Chains

Satellite failure events occur with a real valued rate. It is therefore natural for us to model our systems as continuous time Markov chains (CTMCs). In a CTMC, time is continuous and state changes can happen at any time. The formal definition of a CTMC is given in Definition 1. This definition is from [12].

Definition 1. *Let AP be a fixed, finite set of atomic propositions. Formally, a continuous-time Markov chain (CTMC) C is a tuple (S,s_{init},R,L) where:*

- *$S = \{s_1, s_2, ..., s_n\}$ is a finite set of states.*
- *$s_{init} \in S$ is the initial state.*
- *$R: S \times S \to \mathbb{R}_{\geq 0}$ is the transition rate matrix.*
- *$L: S \to 2^{AP}$ is a labelling function which assigns to each state $s_i \in S$ the set $L(s_i)$ of atomic propositions $a \in AP$ that are valid in s_i.*

where $R(s_i, s_j)$ specifies that the probability of moving from s_i to s_j within t time units is $1 - e^{-R(s_i,s_j)\cdot t}$, an exponential distribution with rate $R(s_i, s_j)$. We approximate the semi-Markov chains in Fig. 3 using the underlying semantics of CTMCs. A semi-Markov chain is a model in which state holding times are governed by general distributions, which is a natural extension of CTMCs.

In Fig. 3, not all transitions exist between states for most subsystems as they are not present in the database. For example, no transition from a minor failure (state 2) to a total failure (state 5) of thruster/fuel was ever recorded on orbit for this subsystem in the database. Other transitions also do not occur in the database, so the total number of transitions is reduced. For this reason, they are not subject to formal analysis.

3.2   The PRISM Model Checker

We use the model checker PRISM [7] to obtain CTMC approximations of our multi-state failure models. It supports the analysis of several types of probabilistic models: Discrete-Time Markov Chains (DTMCs), CTMCs [13], Markov Decision Processes (MDPs) [14], and Probabilistic Timed Automata (PTAs) [15], with optional extensions of costs and rewards. PRISM models are expressed using the PRISM modelling language, which is based on the Reactive Modules formalism [16]. A PRISM model consists of the parallel composition of a number of *modules*. Each module is declared in the following way:

module *name* ... **endmodule**

A module consists of a list of variable declarations and a list of commands. At any moment, the *state* associated with a PRISM model is a valuation of all of the variables in the specification. A variable declaration consists of a variable name together with a list of possible values and an initial value. E.g.:

$$x \; : \; [0..4] \; \textbf{init} \; 0;$$

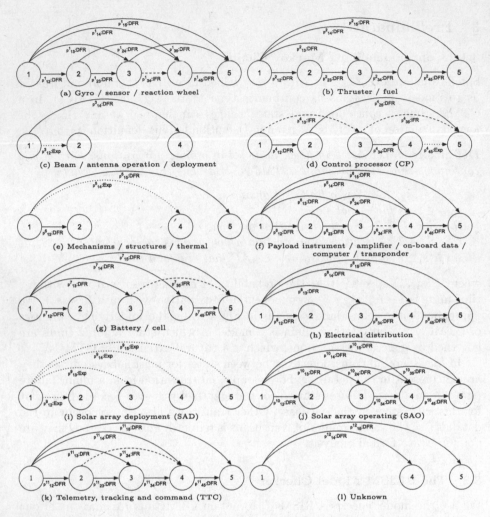

Fig. 3. Semi-Markov chains for multi-state failure mode of satellite subsystems: dotted arrows represent transitions following an exponential distribution (Exp) or Weibull distribution with increasing failure rate (IFR), and solid arrows represent transitions following a Weibull distribution with decreasing failure rate (DFR)

Every command consists of a guard and a non-deterministic choice of updates. Each update has an associated real-value rate. For example:

$$[syncLabel] \; guard \; \rightarrow \; rate_1 : update_1 + rate_2 : update_2 + \dots$$

Note that the initial label (*syncLabel* in this example) is optional, and allows for multi-module synchronisation.

3.3   Continuous Stochastic Logic

In this paper, we use Continuous Stochastic Logic (CSL) [17] to specify properties. There are two types of formulae in CSL: state formulae, which are true
or false in a specific state, and path formulae, which are true or false along a
specific path. One of the most important operators is the **P** operator, which is
used to reason about the probability of an event. The **P** operator is applicable
to all types of models supported by PRISM. It is often useful to compute the
actual probability that some behaviour of a model is observed. Thus, a variation
of the **P** operator to be used in PRISM, i.e., $\mathbf{P}_{=?}[pathprop]$, which returns a
numerical rather than a Boolean value (i.e., the probability that *pathprop* is
true). For example, we might wish to calculate the probability that $j = 1$ is true
within the first T time units. This can be specified as $\mathbf{P}_{=?}[\mathbf{F} \leq T \; j = 1]$, where
F is the "eventually" temporal operator.

4   Approximation of Weibull Failure Models

4.1   Weibull Distributions

In systems engineering, the Weibull distribution [18] is one of the most extensively used lifetime distributions for reliability analysis. It includes two parameters: (1) the shape parameter γ and (2) the scale parameter α, together with
key formulas such as cumulative density function (CDF) and probability density
function (PDF). A Weibull PDF is expressed as:

$$f(t; \gamma, \alpha) = \frac{\gamma}{\alpha}(\frac{t}{\alpha})^{\gamma-1}e^{-(\frac{t}{\alpha})^{\gamma}}, t \geq 0, \gamma, \alpha > 0 \tag{1}$$

and a Weibull CDF as:

$$F(t; \gamma, \alpha) = 1 - e^{-(\frac{t}{\alpha})^{\gamma}} \tag{2}$$

We abbreviate f(t) and F(t) as the PDF and CDF of the Weibull distribution
respectively, then the instantaneous failure rate is $\frac{f(t)}{1-F(t)}$. The failure rate is
proportional to a power of time t. The shape parameter, γ, is equal to this
power plus one.

The semantics of the Weibull distributions (also known as the bathtub curve)
with different γ can be shown in Fig. 4 and explained as follows: (1) $\gamma < 1$ means
that the failure rate decreases over time (decreasing failure rates). This occurs
whenever a clear infant mortality[3] exists, and the failure rate decreases over time
as the failure is discovered and the subsystem removed; (2) $\gamma = 1$ means that
the failure rate is constant at any time. This is the useful life of the satellite; (3)
$\gamma > 1$ means that the failure rate increases with time (increasing failure rates).
It occurs whenever a wear out exists, or a subsystem failure becomes more likely
over time.

Generally, the ways to approximate the Weibull distributions is non-trivial.
The simple technique of phase-type distributions is useful in some cases. Thus,

---

[3] Infant mortality: a subsystem fails early due to defects designed into or built into it.

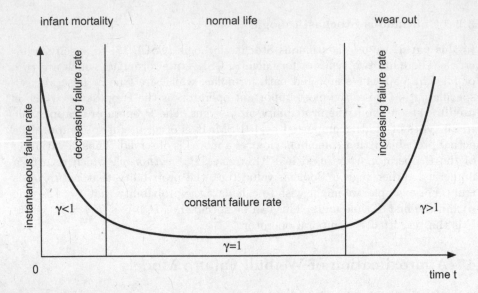

Fig. 4. Semantics of the Weibull distribution (the bathtub curve)

we follow this line of work that Weibull IFR approximated by a M-stage Erlang distribution and Weibull DFR by a hyper-exponential distribution since there are intuitive and strong justifications for the model [3,8]. Further, these general distributions provide simple mathematical structures such that the their underlying semi-Markov chains can be included in the Markov model framework.

4.2   Increasing Failure Rates (IFR)

A simple technique for the realisation of approximations to the Weibull distribution models is *matching moments*, where the mean is the first moment and the variance the second. We first consider the approximation of a Weibull distribution modelling increasing failure rates (IFR) using an M-stage Erlang distribution [19], which belongs to the class of phase-type distributions. The M-stage Erlang PDF can be expressed as:

$$f(t; M, \lambda) = \frac{\lambda^M}{\Gamma(M)} x^{M-1} e^{-\lambda x}, t \geq 0, \lambda > 0 \tag{3}$$

The Erlang CDF can be expressed as:

$$F(t; M, \lambda) = 1 - e^{-\lambda x} \sum_{n=0}^{M-1} \frac{(\lambda t)^n}{n!} \tag{4}$$

According to [8], we have the first two moments of the M-Erlang:

$$m_1 = \frac{M}{\lambda}, \ m_2 = \frac{M(M+1)}{\lambda^2} \tag{5}$$

Table 1. Difference between the Weibull distribution with IFR and its approximation as an Erlang distribution: i is the index of the semi-Markov chain for the corresponding satellite subsystem, and xy is the transition from state x to state y

P_{xy}^i	Weibull distribution with IFR		Erlang distribution	
	γ	α	k	λ
P_{34}^1	1.1593	17	2	0.1239
P_{13}^4	1.1229	664	2	0.0031
P_{35}^4	1.0366	15	2	0.1353
P_{34}^6	1.2452	16	5	0.3352
P_{35}^7	28.6487	9	20	2.2652
P_{24}^{11}	2.8232	23	3	0.1464

As a result, we have:

$$M = \frac{m_1^2}{m_2 - m_1^2}, \quad \lambda = \frac{m_1}{m_2 - m_1^2} \tag{6}$$

where m_1 and m_2 are equal to the first two moments of the Weibull distribution with IFR, and are given as follows:

$$m_1 = \alpha \Gamma(\frac{\gamma + 1}{\gamma}), \quad m_2 = \alpha^2 \Gamma(\frac{\gamma + 2}{\gamma}) \tag{7}$$

The value of M is rounded to the nearest integer and the value of λ recalculated depending on this rounded value, so that the mean is matched.

For example, we consider Weibull parameters for the control processor. The Weibull parameters for the reliability of this subsystem are given by: $\gamma = 1.4560$, $\alpha = 408$ (years). Then, according to Eqs. 6, 7 and 8, $M = 2$ and $\lambda = 0.0054$ for the M-Erlang distribution. Using the Erlang distribution, the approximation result of the Weibull distribution with increasing failure rate for the relevant satellite subsystems is given in Table 1.

4.3 Decreasing Failure Rates (DFR)

The procedure for approximating the Weibull distribution with decreasing failure rates (DFR) by hyper-exponential distributions [20] can be summarised as follows, for details see [3].

First, we choose the number k of exponential components and k arguments: $m_1 > ... > m_i > m_{i+1} > ... > m_k$, for which the ratios $\frac{m_i}{m_{i+1}}$ have to be sufficiently small (e.g., $\frac{m_i}{m_{i+1}} \geq 10$).

Second, we choose the number n such that for all i, $1 < n < \frac{m_i}{m_{i+1}}$.

Then, for the Weibull distribution CDF (see Eq. (3)), we have a complementary CDF (CCDF) given by:

$$F^c(t; \gamma, \alpha) = 1 - F(t; \gamma, \alpha) = e^{-(\frac{t}{\alpha})^\gamma} \tag{8}$$

and we choose λ and p_1 to match the CCDF $F^c(t; \gamma, \alpha)$ (we abbreviate $F^c(t; \gamma, \alpha)$ as $F^c(t)$) at the arguments m_1 and nm_1, so we solve the following equation:

$$p_1 e^{-\lambda_1 m_1} = F^c(m_1), \ p_1 e^{-\lambda_1 nm_1} = F^c(nm_1) \tag{9}$$

for p_1 and λ_1. As a result, we obtain:

$$\lambda_1 = \frac{1}{(n-1)m_1} ln\left(\frac{F^c(m_1)}{F^c(nm_1)}\right), \ p_1 = F^c(m_1)e^{\lambda_1 m_1} \tag{10}$$

Then, for $2 \le i \le k$, we have:

$$F_i^c(m_i) = F^c(m_i) - \sum_{j=1}^{i-1} p_j e^{-\lambda_j m_i}, \ F_i^c(nm_i;) = F^c(nm_i) - \sum_{j=1}^{i-1} p_j e^{-\lambda_j nm_i} \tag{11}$$

and similarly, we solve the further equation:

$$p_i e^{-\lambda_i m_i} = F_i^c(m_i), \ p_i e^{-\lambda_i nm_i} = F_i^c(nm_i) \tag{12}$$

for p_i and λ_i when $2 \le i \le k-1$. As a result, we obtain:

$$\lambda_i = \frac{1}{(n-1)m_i} ln\left(\frac{F_i^c(m_i)}{F_i^c(nm_i)}\right), \ p_i = F_i^c(m_i)e^{\lambda_i m_i} \tag{13}$$

Finally, for $i = k$, we can have:

$$p_k = 1 - \sum_{j=1}^{k-1} p_j, \ p_k e^{-\lambda_k m_k} = F_k^c(m_k), \ \lambda_k = \frac{1}{m_k} ln\left(\frac{p_k}{F_k^c(m_k)}\right) \tag{14}$$

Using the hyper-exponential distribution, the approximation result of the Weibull distribution with decreasing failure rate for the relevant satellite subsystems is given in Table 2. For clarity, we only give the distribution for the subsystem (1), which is Gyro/sensor/reaction wheel.

Table 2. Difference between the Weibull distribution with DFR and its approximation as a hyper-exponential distribution: i is the index of the semi-Markov chain for the corresponding satellite subsystem, and xy is the transition from state x to state y

P_{xy}^i	Weibull distribution with DFR		Hyper-exponential distribution							
	γ	α	p_1	λ_1	p_2	λ_2	p_3	λ_3	p_4	λ_4
P_{12}^1	0.4482	12,526	0.8149	0.000117	0.1258	0.0038	0.0384	0.0433	0.0210	0.8802
P_{13}^1	0.4334	80,050	0.9074	0.000052	0.0630	0.0037	0.0189	0.0434	0.0108	0.9015
P_{14}^1	0.3815	210,126	0.9133	0.000039	0.0548	0.0038	0.0188	0.0444	0.0131	0.9903
P_{15}^1	0.5635	65,647	0.9518	0.000045	0.0377	0.0034	0.0077	0.0408	0.0028	0.7348
P_{23}^1	0.8229	59	0.0933	0.007895	0.6383	0.0132	0.2326	0.0458	0.0359	0.5320
P_{24}^1	0.5600	4,003	0.7852	0.000218	0.1631	0.0037	0.0378	0.0411	0.0139	0.7382
P_{35}^1	0.7115	221	0.3461	0.001866	0.5000	0.0058	0.1258	0.0404	0.0281	0.6022
P_{45}^1	0.4703	135	0.2068	0.000988	0.4133	0.0058	0.2396	0.0466	0.1404	0.8653

5 Encoding the Weibull Models with CTMCs in PRISM

5.1 Encoding the Weibull Distribution with IFR

The approximation of the non-exponential sojourn time distributions can be realised via the insertion of one or more intermediate states between any existing deterioration transition. We approximate a Weibull IFR with an Erlang distribution. In Fig. 5(a), $\frac{k}{\lambda}$ is the time taken for transition from state A to state H. Thus, in order to approximate the interval, the total number of existing deterioration transitions is $k - 1 = 7$. The transition rate is proportional to k, ensuring a constant total transition time.

Consider the PRISM model in Fig. 6. Labelled action *sync* occurs with an Erlang distribution with scale μ and shape k. For the purpose of the analysis, the CSL formula used is: $\mathbf{P}_{=?}[\mathbf{F} \leq T \; j = 1]$, expressing the probability that a satellite subsystem will fail in T years. In Fig. 7, we show the probability curve of the sojourn time for various values of k, where $k = 1, 2, 5, 10, 100$.

Figure 7 shows the results of using PRISM (on our CTMC model) to approximate the probability distribution with a constant sojourn time (i.e. of $\mathbf{P}_{=?}[\mathbf{F} \leq T \; j = 1]$ for various values of k, where $k = 1, 2, 5, 10, 100$) for both 100 years and 15 years. This is useful for modelling failure rates with multiple states, while guaranteeing the Markov property. In addition, a significant trade-off exists between the accuracy and the underlying expansion in the state space of the model. For example, when $k = 100$, we can see from Fig. 7(a), that the approximation is very close to the actual distribution. However, increasing k by a factor of 100 increases the size of the underlying model by 100.

To understand the differences better, we compare the CDF of the original Weibull IFR distribution with its approximation as an Erlang distribution and its implementation as a CTMC model in PRISM. As shown in Fig. 8(a), the difference between Weibull and the other two curves apparently tends to zero, indicating the approximation and implementation both to be accurate for right long tail probabilities. In Fig. 8(b), we see that the difference is at most 0.05, this is due to the fact that we lose a little accuracy in order to reduce the size of the state space associated with our PRISM model.

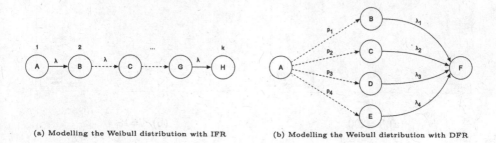

(a) Modelling the Weibull distribution with IFR   (b) Modelling the Weibull distribution with DFR

Fig. 5. Modelling the Weibull distribution with CTMCs

```
ctmc
const int k;
const double mu = 10/k;
module erlang
        i : [1..k+1];
        [] i < k -> 1/mu : (i' = i + 1);
        [sync] i = k -> 1/mu : (i' = i + 1);
endmodule
module weibull_ifr
        j : [0..1];
        [sync] j = 0 -> (j' = 1);
endmodule
```

Fig. 6. Encoding the Weibull distribution with IFR in PRISM

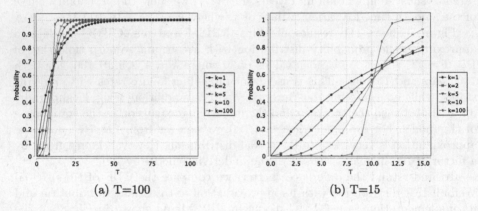

(a) T=100   (b) T=15

Fig. 7. Results of encoding the Weibull distribution with IFR in PRISM

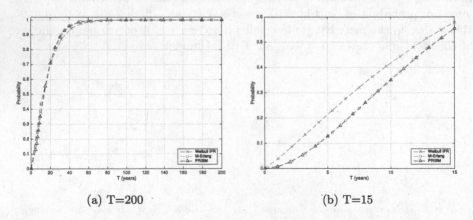

(a) T=200   (b) T=15

Fig. 8. Comparison between the Weibull distribution with IFR, its approximation, and PRISM encoding

5.2   Encoding the Weibull Distribution with DFR

We approximate a Weibull DFR with an hyper-exponential distribution, which is a mixture of exponential distributions. The hyper-Erlang distribution is also a generalisation of the hyper-exponential distribution. So, the hyper-exponential distribution also belongs to the class of phase-type distributions. In general, it can be represented with respect to the time until absorption in a CTMC. For instance, a hyper-exponential distribution having four branches $((p_1,\lambda_1), (p_2,\lambda_2), (p_3,\lambda_3),(p_4,\lambda_4))$ can be represented by a CTMC model as shown in Fig. 5(b). Dotted arrows indicate instantaneous probabilistic transitions, and solid arrows transitions with exponentially distributed durations.

In Fig. 9, we encode the behaviour of the CTMC in Fig. 5(b) using PRISM. For CTMC, updates in commands are labelled with positive-valued rates, rather than probabilities. Since there are four transitions leaving state 0 which are all instantaneous, if we make the probabilistic choice between them, the states with instantaneous transitions can be removed to construct the underlying CTMC.

Figure 10 shows the results of using PRISM (on our CTMC model – see Fig. 9) to approximate the probability distribution of a constant sojourn time (i.e. of $\mathbf{P}_{=?}[\mathbf{F} \leq T \ s = 5]$ for $k = 2, 3, 4, 5$ for both 100 years and 15 years). Although there is trade-off between the accuracy and the size of the resulting state space between $k = 2$ and $k = 4$, the difference is not so obvious between $k = 4$ and $k = 5$. Therefore, we consider $k = 4$ to be a good approximation parameter for the implementation of Weibull DFR in PRISM.

For the same purpose, we compare the CDF of the original Weibull DFR distribution with its approximation in a hyper-exponential distribution and its implementation with a CTMC in PRISM. As shown in Figs. 11(a) and (b), for a time scale ($\alpha = 5000$ years), the difference between the Weibull DFR and the other two curves in the left short head is at most 0.01, and in the right long tails apparently becomes zero, indicating the approximation and implementation both to be accurate for a short scale for both left short head and right long tail probabilities. Though for a large scale ($\alpha = 50000$ years) in Fig. 11(c), we

```
ctmc
const double p1, p2, p3, p4, lambda1, lambda2, lambda3, lambda4;
module weibull_dfr
        s : [0..5] init 0;
        [] s = 0 -> p1 : (s' = 1) + p2 : (s' = 2) + p3 : (s' = 3) +
                    p4 : (s' = 4);
        [] s = 1 -> lambda1 : (s' = 5);
        [] s = 2 -> lambda2 : (s' = 5);
        [] s = 3 -> lambda3 : (s' = 5);
        [] s = 4 -> lambda4 : (s' = 5);
endmodule
```

Fig. 9. Encoding the Weibull distribution with DFR in PRISM

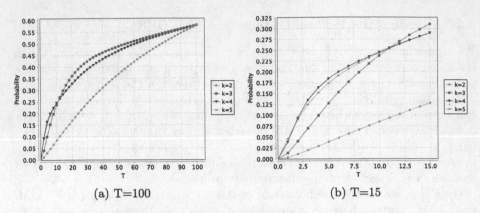

(a) T=100   (b) T=15

Fig. 10. Results of encoding the Weibull distribution with DFR in PRISM

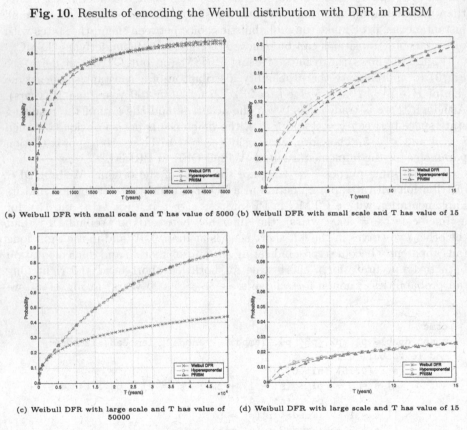

(a) Weibull DFR with small scale and T has value of 5000 (b) Weibull DFR with small scale and T has value of 15

(c) Weibull DFR with large scale and T has value of   (d) Weibull DFR with large scale and T has value of 15
50000

Fig. 11. Comparison between the Weibull distribution with DFR, its approximation, and PRISM encoding

can see that the difference can be very large in the right long tails. However, in Fig. 11(d), for $T \leq 15$ years, the approximation and implementation both appear to be accurate for large scale and left short head probabilities.

6   Conclusion and Future Work

We have shown that difficulties in modelling the Weibull distribution for satellite failures can be handled if appropriate approximations and modelling methods are considered. We have also proposed novel non-exponential models that characterise failure behaviours, based on Weibull failure modes (both increasing failure rates and decreasing failure rates) inferred from real-world datasets. We have approximated and encoded these new models with CTMCs in PRISM, and shown their approximation is accurate in matching a Weibull distribution in isolation.

The key contribution of this work is that the CTMCs-based formalisms come equipped with mature model checking tools, such as PRISM and so allow a wide range of analyses relevant to industrial critical systems to be performed automatically and efficiently. In future work, it would be interesting to see how their approximation matches the true distribution when multiple distributions are combined, e.g. when constructing a model for an entire satellite or a subset of subsystems. Another interesting direction is to use various techniques such as symmetry reduction [21, 22] for reducing the state space of the approximation.

References

1. Castet, J.F., Saleh, J.H.: Satellite and satellite subsystems reliability: statistical data analysis and modeling. Reliab. Eng. Syst. Safety **94**(11), 1718–1728 (2009)
2. Castet, J.F., Saleh, J.H.: Beyond reliability, multi-state failure analysis of satellite subsystems: a statistical approach. Reliab. Eng. Syst. Safety **95**(4), 311–322 (2010)
3. Feldmann, A., Whitt, W.: Fitting mixtures of exponentials to long-tail distributions to analyze network performance models. Perform. Eval. **31**(3–4), 245–279 (1998)
4. López, G.G.I., Hermanns, H., Katoen, J.-P.: Beyond memoryless distributions: model checking semi-Markov chains. In: de Luca, L., Gilmore, S. (eds.) PROB-MIV 2001, PAPM-PROBMIV 2001, and PAPM 2001. LNCS, vol. 2165, pp. 57–70. Springer, Heidelberg (2001)
5. Kwiatkowska, M., Norman, G., Segala, R., Sproston, J.: Verifying quantitative properties of continuous probabilistic timed automata. In: Palamidessi, C. (ed.) CONCUR 2000. LNCS, vol. 1877, pp. 123–137. Springer, Heidelberg (2000)
6. Gopinath, K., Elerath, J., Long, D.: Reliability modelling of disk subsystems with probabilistic model checking. Technical report UCSC-SSRC-09-05, University of California, Santa Cruz (2009)
7. Kwiatkowska, M., Norman, G., Parker, D.: Probabilistic symbolic model checking with PRISM: a hybrid approach. Int. J. Softw. Tools Technol. Transfer **6**(2), 128–142 (2004)
8. Malhotra, M., Reibman, A.: Selecting and implementing phase approximations for semi-Markov models. Commun. Stat.–Stochast. Models **9**(4), 473–506 (1993)
9. Xin, Q., Schwarz, Thomas J. E S.J., Miller, E.L.: Disk infant mortality in large storage systems. In: Proceedings of the 13th IEEE International Symposium on Modeling, Analysis, and Simulation of Computer and Telecommunication Systems (MASCOTS 2005), pp. 125–134. IEEE (2005)

10. Reijsbergen, D., Gilmore, S., Hillston, J.: Patch-based modelling of city-centre bus movement with phase-type distributions. Electron. Notes Theor. Comput. Sci. **310**, 157–177 (2015)

11. Ciobanu, G., Rotaru, A.: Phase-type approximations for non-Markovian systems: a case study. In: Canal, C., Idani, A. (eds.) SEFM 2014 Workshops. LNCS, vol. 8938, pp. 323–334. Springer, Heidelberg (2015)

12. Baier, C., Katoen, J.P.: Principles of Model Checking. The MIT Press, Cambridge (2008)

13. Peng, Z., Lu, Y., Miller, A.A., Johnson, C.W., Zhao, T.: Formal specification and quantitative analysis of a constellation of navigation satellites. Qual. Reliab. Eng. Int. **32**(2), 345–361 (2014)

14. Lu, Y., Peng, Z., Miller, A., Zhao, T., Johnson, C.: How reliable is satellite navigation for aviation? Checking availability properties with probabilistic verification. Reliab. Eng. Syst. Safety **144**, 95–116 (2015)

15. Peng, Z., Lu, Y., Miller, A.: Uncertainty analysis of phased mission systems with probabilistic timed automata. In: Proceedings of the 7th IEEE International Conference on Prognostics and Health Management (PHM 2016). IEEE (2016)

16. Alur, R., Henzinger, T.A.: Reactive modules. Formal Methods Syst. Des. **15**(1), 7–48 (1999)

17. Aziz, A., Sanwal, K., Singhal, V., Brayton, R.: Model-checking continuous-time Markov chains. ACM Trans. Comput. Logic **1**(1), 162–170 (2000)

18. Weibull, W.: A statistical distribution function of wide applicability. J. Appl. Mech. **18**, 293–297 (1951)

19. Evans, M., Hastings, N., Peacock, B.: Erlang Distribution. In: Distributions, Statistical (ed.) 3rd edn., pp. 71–73. Wiley, New York (2000)

20. Bolch, G., Greiner, S., de Meer, H., Trivedi, K.S.: Introduction. In: Queueing networks and markov chains: modeling and performance evaluation with computer science applications. Wiley, New York (1998)

21. Miller, A., Donaldson, A., Calder, M.: Symmetry in temporal logic model checking. ACM Computing Surveys 38(3) (2006)

22. Kwiatkowska, M., Norman, G., Parker, D.: Symmetry reduction for probabilistic model checking. In: Ball, T., Jones, R.B. (eds.) CAV 2006. LNCS, vol. 4144, pp. 234–248. Springer, Heidelberg (2006)

Fault-Aware Modeling and Specification for Efficient Formal Safety Analysis

Axel Habermaier[(✉)], Alexander Knapp, Johannes Leupolz, and Wolfgang Reif

Institute for Software and Systems Engineering,
University of Augsburg, Augsburg, Germany
{habermaier,knapp,leupolz,reif}@isse.de

Abstract. Deductive Cause Consequence Analysis (DCCA) is a model checking-based safety analysis technique that determines all combinations of faults potentially causing a hazard. This paper introduces a new fault modeling and specification approach for safety-critical systems based on the concept of fault activations that decreases explicit-state model checking and safety analysis times by up to three orders of magnitude. We augment Kripke structures and LTL with fault activations and show how standard model checkers can be used for analysis. Additionally, we present conceptual changes to DCCA that improve efficiency and usability. We evaluate our work using our safety analysis tool S# ("safety sharp").

1 Introduction

Safety-critical systems have the potential to cause hazards, i.e., situations resulting in economical or environmental damage, injuries, or loss of lives [17]. *Deductive Cause Consequence Analysis* (DCCA) is a model-based safety analysis technique [7,12] that uses model checking to compute how faults such as component failures or environmental disturbances (the causes) can cause such hazards (the consequences): From a model of a safety-critical system that describes the system's nominal behavior as well as the relevant faults, DCCA determines all *minimal critical fault sets*, i.e., the smallest possible combinations of faults that can cause hazards, allowing the evaluation of the system's overall safety. DCCAs are conducted automatically by tools like S# [13] or VECS [20]; the FSAP/COMPASS toolsets [6,7], ALTARICA [4], and *BT Analyser* [19] perform similar safety analyses. Alternatively, compositional safety analysis approaches and tools such as HiP-HOPS or *Component Fault Trees* [10,26] allow for faster analyses at the expense of requiring explicitly modeled fault propagations between components. Model checking-based techniques, by contrast, deduce these propagations automatically, albeit requiring additional states and transitions for each fault which reduce model checking efficiency exponentially [7,12].

This paper's first contribution is a fault-aware modeling and specification approach for safety-critical systems that decreases explicit-state analysis times by up to three orders of magnitude. We augment Kripke structures and *Linear*

© Springer International Publishing AG 2016
M.H. ter Beek et al. (Eds.): FMICS-AVoCS 2016, LNCS 9933, pp. 97–114, 2016.
DOI: 10.1007/978-3-319-45943-1_7

Temporal Logic (LTL), making them aware of *fault activations* [2] within the analyzed systems: Faults are activated when they can in fact influence the system's behavior, preventing model checkers from considering possibly many situations with irrelevant active faults during analyses. We show how the extended formalisms can be mapped back to the classical ones for analysis with standard model checkers such as LTSMIN [18]. We demonstrate the efficiency improvements over the traditional fault modeling approach, showing that explicit-state model checking becomes feasible for safety-critical systems that incorporate faults.

The second contribution is a conceptual change of DCCA formalized using LTL instead of *Computation Tree Logic* (CTL). It improves the model checking workflow as witnesses are generated to explain how critical fault sets *can* cause a hazard, which is more useful in practice than witnesses showing how non-critical fault sets *cannot* do so. We also formalize another DCCA variant that reduces analysis times in many cases.

2   Model-Based Safety Analysis

Throughout this section, we assume models of safety-critical systems to be given as Kripke structures $K = (P, S, R, L, I)$ consisting of a set of atomic propositions P, a set of states S, a left-total transition relation $R \subseteq S \times S$, a labeling function $L \colon S \to 2^P$, and a non-empty set of initial states $I \subseteq S$ [9]. Kripke structures are a well-known modeling formalism that established model checkers such as LTSMIN, SPIN, or NUSMV [8,14,18] are based on. Consequently, tools built for formal safety analyses [6,7,13,19,20] either implicitly or explicitly transform their models to Kripke structures for model checking, while their actual modeling formalisms are higher-level.

Figure 1 gives a description of the running example used throughout the paper that is based on the fault tree handbook's pressure tank case study [28]. The system is safety-critical because of the hazard of tank ruptures that might injure nearby people. Ruptures only happen when *both* suppression faults ¬is full and ¬timeout occur; consequently, there is only one minimal critical fault set for the hazard that consists of these two faults. For more complex systems with more faults, however, minimal critical fault sets are not as easily deduced. Instead, model-based safety analysis techniques such as DCCA are required to compute these critical sets automatically and rigorously.

2.1   Fault Terminology

Safety analyses consider situations in which faults cause system behavior that would not have occurred otherwise. In accordance with common terminology [2], these situations represent *fault activations*; that is, a fault is *activated* when it influences the system, affecting its behavior or state in a concealed or observable way. Faults are *dormant* until they are *activated* and become *active*, turning dormant again when they are *deactivated*. A fault's *persistence* constrains the

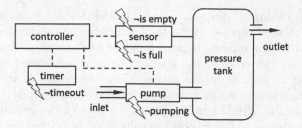

Fig. 1. A schematic overview of the running example: the fluid contained in the pressure tank is refilled by the pump that is activated and deactivated by a controller. The pressure sensor signals the controller when the pressure limit is reached or the tank is empty, causing the controller to deactivate or activate the pump, respectively; once the tank is empty, a new refill cycle begins. To tolerate pressure sensor faults, the controller disables the pump after 60 s of continuous operation as it would risk a tank rupture otherwise. For time measurements, the controller uses the timer. The pressure sensor has two suppression faults: It might not report that the pressure limit is reached (¬is full) or that the tank is empty (¬is empty). The timer might not signal a timeout (¬timeout) and a fault of the pump (¬pumping) prevents it from filling the tank.

transitions between its active and dormant states. *Transient* faults, for instance, are activated and deactivated completely nondeterministically, whereas *permanent* faults, while also activated nondeterministically, never become dormant again. Fault activations result in *effects* that change the internal state of affected components, thereby causing *errors*. Errors are deviations of the components' states from what they should have been. Errors *propagate* through the components, causing other errors. Eventually, errors might result in *failures* where the errors manifest themselves in a way that is externally observable. Failures either provoke faults in other components or they represent system *hazards*; safety analyses are conducted for the latter to determine all faults causing them.

2.2 State-Based Fault Modeling

VECS, COMPASS, FSAP, and other safety analysis tools [6,7,19,20] share a common, state-based fault modeling approach: For each modeled fault, the tools' high-level modeling formalisms require at least one additional Boolean variable where changes of the variable's value represent fault activations and deactivations. These variables increase both the number of reachable states as well as the number of transitions of the Kripke structures generated from the high-level models [6,12]. Transient faults represent the worst case as they occur completely nondeterministically: n additional transient faults increase the generated Kripke structure's reachable state space by a factor of 2^n and each state has an additional 2^n successor states. Permanent faults, by contrast, have an overall lower number of possible successor states compared to transient faults, so the amount of reachable states and transitions might not increase as noticeably; model checking and safety analysis efficiency is reduced significantly with each additional fault in both cases.

The running example's pressure sensor modeled with S# in Listing 1, for instance, is a high-level representation that can either be checked using the classical state-based fault modeling approach or the fault-aware one introduced in this paper. In the former case, the Kripke structure generated for the model would be similar to the one shown in Fig. 2(a), whereas fault-aware modeling would eventually result in a significantly smaller classical Kripke structure similar to the one in Fig. 2(b). Figure 2(a) shows a part of the running example's Kripke structure shortly before the tank is fully filled and either the pump is shut off or the tank ruptures. After 56 s of pumping, neither fault has any observable effect on the system. During the next step, only the activation of ¬is full has an observable effect, namely that pumping continues even though it should have stopped. If pumping is not stopped by the sensor, the pump is shut off only if ¬timeout is not activated, otherwise the tank ruptures. The Kripke structure shown in Fig. 2(b) can be seen as an abstraction of the one in Fig. 2(a). It unifies states that are equivalent modulo active faults, thereby reducing both the state and the transition counts significantly; the states where ¬is full is active cannot be unified due to the cyclic nature of the model. The Kripke structure is *minimal* in the sense that irrelevant active faults are omitted while all *system* states remain reachable, including, in particular, the hazard. The notion of minimality is based on the observation that the exact points in time in which faults become active are irrelevant as long as they do so before or when they can affect the system. Inspired by partial order reduction [3], fault-aware modeling and specification is a fundamental change of model-based safety analysis that inherently considers only minimized Kripke structures similar to the one in Fig. 2(b).

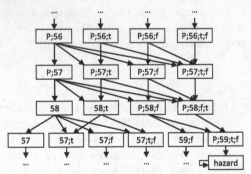

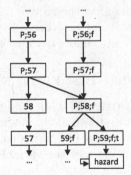

(a) The Kripke structure resulting from state-based fault modeling has redundant states and transitions where faults are active without any observable effects.

(b) The activation-minimal Kripke structure has no state or transition redundancy by considering relevant active faults only.

Fig. 2. Partial view of the running example's Kripke structures resulting from state-based fault modeling (a) or fault-aware modeling (b). States are labeled with P when the pump is running; the number represents both the tank's pressure level and the timer's counter. The faults ¬is full and ¬timeout are active in states that show their respective labels f and t. For reasons of brevity, the other two faults are omitted and ¬is full and ¬timeout are assumed to be permanent.

3   Fault-Aware Modeling and Specification

Instead of the commonly used state-based fault modeling approach, we focus on fault activations, making them central to the models and specifications of safety-critical systems as well as the safety analysis techniques. Our approach is *event*-based where events are fault activations and deactivations; we exclusively consider the former only, as we have not yet found a use case that requires the latter. The significant state and transition count reductions demonstrated by Fig. 2(b) make the potential advantages for model checking efficiency evident. We augment the classical notion of Kripke structures and LTL to incorporate fault activations explicitly, allowing us to more conveniently formalize DCCA, fault injection, and fault removal in the remainder.

3.1   Fault-Aware Kripke Structures

Fault-aware Kripke structures explicitly denote the faults that can affect the system they represent. They highlight states in which faults can be activated by labeling their outgoing transitions with sets of activated faults as can be seen in Fig. 3(a): The transition relation of the running example's fault-aware Kripke structure is *activation-minimal* in the sense that no transitions can be removed without affecting the Kripke structure's behavior or losing system states; in particular, there are no transitions labeled with ¬is full or ¬timeout between the two shown states as these two faults obviously cannot be activated when the tank is empty. The Kripke structure in Fig. 2(a), on the other hand, has many superfluous states and transitions that can safely be removed without losing any system states or behavior. The actual state and transition count reductions made possible by activation minimality depend on how often a fault can be activated: ¬timeout, for instance, is only activatable right before the hazard occurs, resulting in a significant state space reduction; ¬pumping, by contrast, is activatable in roughly 50 % of all states and therefore does not profit as much from fault-aware modeling and specification.

Definition 1 (Fault-Aware Kripke Structures). *A* fault-aware Kripke structure $K = (P, F, S, R, L, I)$ *consists of a set of* atomic propositions P; *a set of* faults F; *a set of* states S; *a transition* relation $R \subseteq S \times 2^F \times S$ *labeled with fault activations that is*

– left-total, *i.e.,* $\forall s \in S . \exists s' \in S, \Gamma \subseteq F . (s, \Gamma, s') \in R$ *and*
– activation-minimal, *i.e.,* $(s_1, \Gamma, s_2) \in R \wedge (s_1, \Gamma', s_2') \in R \wedge \Gamma \subsetneq \Gamma' \rightarrow s_2 \neq s_2'$;

a labeling function $L : S \rightarrow 2^P$ *indicating the set of atomic propositions holding in a state; and a non-empty set of* initial fault activations and states $\emptyset \neq I \subseteq 2^F \times S$ *that is also* activation-minimal, *i.e.,* $(\Gamma_1, s_1) \in I \wedge (\Gamma_2, s_2) \in I \wedge \Gamma_1 \subsetneq \Gamma_2 \rightarrow s_1 \neq s_2$. *We also write $P(K)$ for P, $F(K)$ for F, etc. A fault-aware Kripke structure K is* finite *if $P(K)$, $F(K)$, and $S(K)$ are finite.*

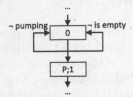

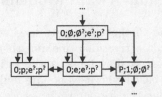

(a) A fault-aware Kripke structure explicitly labels its transitions with the minimal amount of possible fault activations to avoid any state or transition redundancy.

(b) The classical Kripke structure generated from the fault-aware one to the left requiring additional states labeled with actual and potential fault activations.

Fig. 3. Part of the running example's fault-aware Kripke structure where the tank is empty, which the sensor should report to start the pump. Activations of either ¬pumping or ¬is empty prevent the system from doing so. State label P indicates that the pump is running; the number represents the pressure level. Labels e and p indicate activations of ¬is empty and ¬pumping, respectively, whereas e? and p? denote potential activations of these faults when leaving the state.

For a fault-aware Kripke structure K, a *path fragment* $\varsigma = \Gamma_0 s_0 \Gamma_1 s_1 \ldots$ of K is an infinite, alternating sequence of fault activations $\Gamma_i \subseteq F(K)$ and states $s_i \in S(K)$ such that $(s_i, \Gamma_{i+1}, s_{i+1}) \in R(K)$ for all $i \geq 0$. We write $\varsigma[i]$, $\varsigma_F[i]$, and $\varsigma_S[i]$ for (Γ_i, s_i), Γ_i, and s_i, respectively. A *path* of K is a path fragment ς of K with $\varsigma[0] \in I(K)$; the set of all paths of K is denoted by $paths(K)$. The *reachable* states $\mathcal{R}(K)$ are given by $\{\varsigma_S[i] \mid \varsigma \in paths(K) \wedge i \geq 0\}$. The following notion of path equivalence *modulo* faults Γ allows us to compare the paths of two fault-aware Kripke structures, ignoring activations of faults $f \in \Gamma$:

Definition 2 (Path Equivalence). *Two fault-aware Kripke structures K_1 and K_2 are path equivalent modulo faults F, denoted as $K_1 \equiv_F K_2$, if for all $\varsigma = \Gamma_0 s_0 \Gamma_1 s_1 \ldots$ with $s_i \in S(K_1) \cup S(K_2)$, $\Gamma_i \subseteq F(K_1) \cup F(K_2)$, and $\Gamma_i \cap F = \emptyset$ for all $i \geq 0$, $\varsigma \in paths(K_1)$ if and only if $\varsigma \in paths(K_2)$. $K_1 \equiv_\emptyset K_2$ is abbreviated as $K_1 \equiv K_2$.*

In order to use standard model checkers such as LTSMIN, a fault-aware Kripke structure $K = (P, F, S, R, L, I)$ can be converted to a classical Kripke structure $K' = (P', S', R', L', I)$: We encode *actual* and *potential* fault activations into atomic propositions Γ and $\Gamma^?$, respectively; the latter indicates that the faults Γ are activated by at least one outgoing transition of a state. We have $P' = P \cup 2^F \cup \{\Gamma^? \mid \Gamma \subseteq F\}$; $S' = 2^F \times S$; $R' = \{((\Gamma, s), (\Gamma', s')) \mid (s, \Gamma', s') \in R\}$; and $L'(\Gamma, s) = \Gamma \cup L(s) \cup \{\Gamma'^? \mid \exists s' \in S . (s, \Gamma', s') \in R\}$. While S' is much larger than S, most additional states are not reachable due to activation minimality and are thus irrelevant for explicit-state model checkers such as LTSMIN; with state-based fault modeling, even more additional and often superfluous states would be introduced, most of which would be reachable and thus slow down model checking unnecessarily. Figure 3(b) shows the classical Kripke structure generated from the fault-aware one in Fig. 3(a). The additional states are required to support fault-aware LTL; they are unavoidable without fault-aware model checkers.

3.2   Fault-Aware Linear Temporal Logic

Fault-aware Kripke structures only model fault activations, disregarding any persistence constraints. Instead, we assume the constraints to be encoded into the checked LTL formulas to filter out paths violating any of them. The following definition of fault-aware LTL is based on the classical variant with both future- and past-time operators [3,21]. The past modalities do not increase the expressiveness of the logic, but make some formulas exponentially more succinct [21] while in many practical cases still allowing for efficient model checking [27]. Compared to classical LTL, fault-aware LTL provides two additional operators related to fault activations: Formula Γ requires that at least the faults in Γ were activated to reach a state, that is, it checks whether a state was reached because of the activations of all $f \in \Gamma$, and potentially more, during the last transition. Formula Γ therefore allows a glimpse into the immediate past, whereas the other new operator supported by fault-aware LTL conceptually looks into the immediate future: Formula $\Gamma^?$ checks whether exactly the fault set Γ might potentially be activated when leaving a state, i.e., it allows to check whether precisely the faults $f \in \Gamma$ can be activated to reach the next state. The $\Gamma^?$ operator therefore considers multiple distinct futures that are possible instead of one single future as is usually the case with LTL; the operator is conceptually similar to **EX** in CTL. Fault-aware LTL is unable to directly express that a fault is active or dormant, which we found of little practical use.

Definition 3 (Fault-Aware LTL). *Fault-aware LTL formulas Φ over a set P of atomic propositions and a set F of faults are formed according to the following grammar, where φ, φ_1, and φ_2 are fault-aware LTL formulas over P and $F, p \in P$, and $\Gamma \subseteq F$:*

$$\Phi ::= \text{true} \mid p \mid \Gamma \mid \Gamma^? \mid \neg\varphi \mid \varphi_1 \wedge \varphi_2 \mid \mathbf{X}\,\varphi \mid \varphi_1 \mathbf{U} \varphi_2 \mid \mathbf{P}\,\varphi \mid \varphi_1 \mathbf{S}\,\varphi_2$$

Propositional connectives are defined as usual; we write $\mathbf{F}\,\varphi$ for $\text{true}\mathbf{U}\varphi$, $\mathbf{G}\,\varphi$ for $\neg\mathbf{F}\neg\varphi$, $\mathbf{O}\,\varphi$ for $\text{true}\mathbf{S}\,\varphi$, and $\mathbf{H}\,\varphi$ for $\neg\mathbf{O}\neg\varphi$. Additionally, $\varphi_1\mathbf{U}^=\varphi_2$ abbreviates $\varphi_1\mathbf{U}(\varphi_1 \wedge \varphi_2)$. A fault-aware LTL formula $\varphi \in \Phi$ is valid at a position $i \geq 0$ of a path fragment ς of a fault-aware Kripke structure K, written as $\varsigma, i \models \varphi$, if:

$\varsigma, i \models \text{true}$ $\varsigma, i \models p$ *iff* $p \in L(K)(\varsigma_S[i])$

$\varsigma, i \models \Gamma$ *iff* $\Gamma \subseteq \varsigma_F[i]$

$\varsigma, i \models \Gamma^?$ *iff* $(\varsigma_S[i], \Gamma, s) \in R(K)$ *for some* $s \in S(K)$

$\varsigma, i \models \neg\varphi$ *iff* $\varsigma, i \not\models \varphi$ $\varsigma, i \models \varphi_1 \wedge \varphi_2$ *iff* $\varsigma, i \models \varphi_1$ *and* $\varsigma, i \models \varphi_2$

$\varsigma, i \models \mathbf{X}\,\varphi$ *iff* $\varsigma, i+1 \models \varphi$

$\varsigma, i \models \varphi_1\mathbf{U}\varphi_2$ *iff there is a* $k \geq i$ *with* $\varsigma, k \models \varphi_2$ *and* $\varsigma, j \models \varphi_1$ *for all* $i \leq j < k$

$\varsigma, i \models \mathbf{P}\,\varphi$ *iff* $i > 0$ *and* $\varsigma, i-1 \models \varphi$

$\varsigma, i \models \varphi_1\mathbf{S}\varphi_2$ *iff there is a* $k \leq i$ *with* $\varsigma, k \models \varphi_2$ *and* $\varsigma, j \models \varphi_1$ *for all* $k < j \leq i$

$\varsigma \models \varphi$ *abbreviates* $\varsigma, 0 \models \varphi$. φ *is valid in* K, *written as* $K \models \varphi$, *if* $\varsigma \models \varphi$ *for all* $\varsigma \in paths(K)$.

For all faults $f \in F$, we generally require that they do not have to be activated in an initial state, i.e., $K \not\models f$ with f abbreviating $\{f\}$. Fault-aware Kripke structures violating this assumption always start with at least one activated fault, making their adequacy questionable. Additionally, a transient fault $f \in F$ must be activated completely nondeterministically. The corresponding persistence constraint is $\mathbf{G} \bigvee_{\Gamma' \subseteq F \setminus f} \Gamma'^?$: There always is a transition where f is not activated; otherwise, f's activation would be deterministically enforced. Permanent faults $\Gamma \subseteq F$ behave like transient ones until the first time they are activated: $\bigwedge_{\Gamma' \subseteq \Gamma} \mathbf{G}((\Gamma'^? \wedge \bigwedge_{f \in \Gamma'} \mathbf{O} f) \to \mathbf{X} \Gamma')$ ensures that all subsets $\Gamma' \subseteq \Gamma$ of the faults are indeed activated whenever they are activatable and all faults $f \in \Gamma'$ have already been activated at least once.

To determine whether a formula $\varphi \in \Phi$ holds for a fault-aware Kripke structure K with $K \not\models f$ for all $f \in F(K)$, we check $K \models (\bigwedge_{\psi \in \Psi} \psi) \to \varphi$ for a set of persistence constraints Ψ; such formulas are similar to fairness conditions in that they can only be expressed in LTL but not in CTL [3]. The extended formula might result in a more complex Büchi automaton; however, constraints for transient faults are both the common and the general case with a simple single-state Büchi representation. Therefore, transient faults no longer represent the worst case as with state-based fault modeling, but the best case instead. The transformation of fault-aware LTL to classical LTL is straightforward by making formulas Γ and $\Gamma'^?$ propositions; the Kripke structures generated from fault-aware ones contain the required state labels for Γ and $\Gamma'^?$.

3.3 Fault Injection

The intended behavior of a safety-critical system is commonly modeled first with the faulty behavior injected later in a separate step [6]. State-based fault modeling requires additional states, labels, and transitions for injected faults just to distinguish the faults' active and dormant states. For fault-aware Kripke structures, however, injecting a fault can only add new transitions when the fault is actually activated; additional states, labels, and transitions are only required to model a fault's effects on the system. Formally:

Definition 4 (Fault Injection). Injecting *the faults* F' *into* $K = (P, F, S, R, L, I)$ *yields the set of* extended *fault-aware Kripke structures* $K \triangleleft F'$, *where for all* $K' = (P', F \cup F', S', R', L', I') \in K \triangleleft F'$, $P \subseteq P'$, $S \subseteq S'$, $L(s) \subseteq L'(s)$ *for all* $s \in S$, $R \subseteq R'$ *such that for all* $(s, \Gamma, s') \in R' \setminus R$, $s \in S \to \Gamma \cap F' \neq \emptyset$, *and* $I \subseteq I'$ *such that for all* $(\Gamma, s) \in I' \setminus I$, $\Gamma \cap F' \neq \emptyset$.

The definition reflects the fact that there are many possible ways of injecting faults F' into a model by yielding a *set* of extended fault-aware Kripke structures incorporating F'. For reasons of adequacy, the model including the faults is required to be an *extension* of the model without these faults; that is, fault injection may add but can never remove behavior. We can formally show that the original Kripke structure and all possible extensions are path equivalent as long as the injected faults are never activated:

Proposition 1 (Conservative Extension). *For a fault set F and fault-aware Kripke structures K and $K_F \in K \triangleleft F$, $K \equiv_F K_F$.*

Fault injection is purely additive, as new behavior can only be reached by activations of injected faults; until then, the system behaves as before. The high-level models of the safety analysis tools typically guarantee conservative extension syntactically [6,13].

4   Deductive Cause Consequence Analysis

By model checking a series of formulas, DCCA uncovers cause consequence relationships between faults (the causes) and hazards (the consequences): For each hazard, DCCA computes all *minimal critical* fault sets Γ that can cause the occurrence of the hazard. We assume a finite fault-aware Kripke structure K representing the system to be analyzed with a hazard H given as a propositional logic formula over K not referencing any faults $f \in F = F(K)$. A fault set Γ is *critical* for a hazard H if and only if there is the possibility that H occurs and before that, at most the faults in Γ have been activated. The following *original* definition [12] of the criticality property uses CTL, which could be extended to fault-aware Kripke structures similar to fault-aware LTL. The usage of CTL, however, limits DCCA's applicability to Kripke structures with a *single* initial state, since a CTL formula is only valid on a Kripke structure if it holds in *all* initial states.

Definition 5 (Minimal Critical Fault Sets). *Let $|I(K)| = 1$. A fault set $\Gamma \subseteq F$ is critical for hazard H if $K \models (only_\Gamma \mathbf{EU}^= H)$, where $only_\Gamma :\Leftrightarrow \bigwedge_{f \in F \setminus \Gamma} \neg f$. A critical fault set Γ is minimal if no proper subset $\Gamma' \subsetneq \Gamma$ is critical.*

The CTL formula checks whether there is a path $\varsigma \in paths(K)$ on which the hazard H occurs and before that, none of the faults $f \notin \Gamma$ are activated; conversely, at most the faults $f \in \Gamma$ are activated. The use of the $\mathbf{EU}^=$ operator guarantees that the transition leading to the state where the hazard occurs still enables at most the faults $f \in \Gamma$; if $\mathbf{EU}$ was used instead, there could be activations of faults $f \in F \setminus \Gamma$ right before the hazard occurs, which is obviously unintended. Activation is only (implicitly) required for minimal criticality, but not for criticality: Any superset $\Gamma' \supseteq \Gamma$ of a critical fault set Γ is also critical as additional fault activations cannot be expected to fix other faults and thus to improve safety. In practice, the criticality's *monotonicity* with respect to set inclusion [12] often allows for significant reductions in the number of checks required to find all minimal critical fault sets; otherwise, *all* subsets of F would have to be checked for criticality. DCCA's worst-case complexity, however, is in fact exponential.

DCCA determines all minimal critical fault sets for a hazard; it is a *complete* safety analysis technique [12] in the sense that the hazard cannot occur as long as at least one fault of each minimal critical fault set is never activated. Formally, $K \models (\bigwedge_{\Gamma \in \Lambda} \neg \bigwedge_{f \in \Gamma} \mathbf{F} f) \to \mathbf{G} \neg H$ always holds where Λ is the set of all minimal critical fault sets for H determined by conducting a DCCA for H over K. DCCA is always complete, regardless of whether faults were injected into the Kripke structure in accordance with Definition 4 or added in some other, arbitrary way. Adequacy, however, is only guaranteed for fault-aware Kripke structures with injected faults. Only then is the check for criticality of the empty fault set equivalent to a check of functional correctness, namely whether the hazard can already occur even without any fault activations.

4.1   Conceptual Improvement: Safe Fault Sets

Similar to fairness conditions, persistence constraints cannot be enforced while checking the criticality of a fault set due to the use of CTL [3]. We therefore base DCCA on the dual of critical fault sets instead, which can indeed be formalized using fault-aware LTL:

Definition 6 (Safe Fault Sets). *A fault set $\Gamma \subseteq F$ is* safe *for hazard H if and only if $K \models \neg(only_\Gamma \mathbf{U}^= H)$ with $only_\Gamma$ as in Definition 5.*

A fault set Γ is considered safe for a hazard H if it is impossible that at most the activations of faults $f \in \Gamma$ result in an occurrence of H. Intuitively, a fault set should be critical if and only if it is not safe. This correlation, however, does *not* hold as criticality assumes Kripke structures to have a single initial state only, whereas for safe fault sets, we do not make this assumption. For multiple initial states, the original definition would classify critical sets as safe in certain cases. To establish the correlation, we from now on consider a fault set $\Gamma \subseteq F$ to be critical for H if and only if there is some path $\varsigma \in paths(K)$ with $\varsigma \models only_\Gamma \mathbf{U}^= H$. The monotonicity property and DCCA's completeness guarantee continue to hold for the new definition of criticality; the proofs are similar to the original ones [12]. Additionally, for any safe fault set Γ, any subsets $\Gamma' \subseteq \Gamma$ are safe as well: Under no circumstances is it possible that less fault activations make a system less safe.

DCCA is model checker-independent, whereas other techniques similar to DCCA are tied to certain model checkers such as NuSMV or *BT Analyser* [5, 7, 19]. In contrast to DCCA, some of these techniques [5, 7] are only able to assume monotonicity or require permanent persistence [19]; with DCCA, monotonicity is guaranteed regardless of the analyzed model and all kinds of persistence constraints are supported. Using safe fault sets to conduct DCCAs results in three notable usability improvements: Firstly, DCCA now supports multiple initial states, avoiding workarounds that construct a unique pseudo initial state by changing both the model and the analyzed formula. Ironically, LTSMIN only supports a unique initial state, forcing us to work around this limitation nevertheless. Secondly, both LTL and CTL can be used to conduct DCCAs, enabling broader model checker support; with CTL, a fault set is safe if and only if $K \models \neg(only_\Gamma \mathbf{EU}^= H)$. Thirdly, the model checker now generates a counter example when a fault set Γ is not safe, i.e., it constructs a witness that explains why Γ is critical and how it causes the hazard. Consequently, the model checking

$$K \xrightarrow{\quad K \triangleleft F_1 \uplus F_2 \quad} K_{F_1 \uplus F_2}$$

$$K \triangleleft F_1 \Downarrow \qquad\qquad\qquad \Downarrow K_{F_1 \uplus F_2} \setminus F_2$$

$$K_{F_1} \xrightarrow{\qquad\qquad \equiv \qquad\qquad} (K_{F_1 \uplus F_2}) \setminus F_2$$

Fig. 4. Illustration of the relation of fault injection and fault removal that enables fault removal DCCA: starting with a fault-aware Kripke structure K and two disjoint fault sets F_1 and F_2, path equivalent fault-aware Kripke structures can be obtained by either injecting the relevant faults F_1 only or by first injecting all faults $F_1 \uplus F_2$ and subsequently removing the irrelevant faults F_2.

workflow is improved as witnesses for safe fault sets showing how a hazard is *not* caused are typically of no interest in practice.

4.2 Efficiency Improvement: Fault Removal

Formal safety analysis tools can automatically conduct complete DCCAs. Instead of using a series of LTL formulas to check for safe faults sets within a model, the tools could alternatively change the model to make the checks more efficient: Faults $F \setminus \Gamma$ are not allowed to be activated during a check of Γ due to $only_\Gamma$, so they could just as well be *removed* from the model entirely as outlined by Fig. 4, reducing the model's state space. Thus, instead of checking multiple formulas on the same model, the same simplified formula can be checked for multiple reduced models. We formalize a fault removal variant of DCCA based on this idea, which generalizes an ad hoc approach to conduct DCCAs within the SCADE tool [11]. We first define the notion of *activation independence* that is required to show that DCCA always computes the same minimal critical fault sets, regardless of whether the multiple formulas or multiple models approach is used. We consider a fault set to be activation independent if activations are never forced, that is, there is always an alternative future or initial state in which none of the faults are activated; trivially, transient and permanent faults are activation independent.

Definition 7 (Activation Independence). *A fault set $\Gamma \subseteq F(K)$ of a fault-aware Kripke structure K is* activation independent *in K if $K \not\models \Gamma \neq \emptyset \wedge \Gamma$ and $K \models \mathbf{G} \bigvee_{\Gamma' \subseteq F(K) \setminus \Gamma} \Gamma'$?.*

In particular, the following set of *reduced* fault-aware Kripke structures is non-empty if and only if an activation independent fault set is removed, as activation independence preserves left-totality for all reachable states $\mathcal{R}(K)$ during fault removal:

Definition 8 (Fault Removal). *Removing the fault set $F' \subseteq F$ from a fault-aware Kripke structure $K = (P, F, S, R, L, I)$ yields the set of reduced fault-aware Kripke structures $K \setminus\!\!\setminus F'$, where for all $K' = (P', F \setminus F', S', R', L', I') \in K \setminus\!\!\setminus F'$, $P' \subseteq P$, $\mathcal{R}(K) \subseteq S' \subseteq S$, $R' = \{(s, \Gamma, s') \in R \mid s, s' \in S' \wedge \Gamma \cap F' = \emptyset\}$, $L'(s) = L(s)$ for all $s \in S'$, and $I' = \{(\Gamma, s) \in I \mid s \in S' \wedge \Gamma \cap F' = \emptyset\}$.*

In contrast to fault injection which is a creative activity, fault removal is mechanic and can therefore be done automatically by a tool. All $K' \in K \setminus\!\setminus F$ have identical sets of paths as they can only differ in irrelevant details such as unreachable states or transitions. Similar to fault injection, fault-aware Kripke structures are path equivalent before and after fault removal as long as the removed faults are never activated:

Proposition 2. *For fault set $F \subseteq F(K)$ and fault-aware Kripke structures K and $K_{\setminus F} \in K \setminus\!\setminus F$, $K \equiv_F K_{\setminus F}$.*

In general, we can only infer that $K \setminus\!\setminus \Gamma \neq \emptyset$ when removing an activation independent fault set $\Gamma \subseteq F(K)$ from a fault-aware Kripke structure K. When removing previously injected faults, we trivially obtain a fault-aware Kripke structure that is path equivalent to the original one. Fault-aware LTL can also be used to effectively remove an activation independent fault set $\Gamma' \subseteq F(K)$ from a fault-aware Kripke structure K, similar to how persistence constraints suppress undesirable fault activations or deactivations: For $K_{\setminus \Gamma'} \in K \setminus\!\setminus \Gamma'$ and $\varphi \in \Phi$ expressible over both K and $K_{\setminus \Gamma'}$, $K \models (\mathbf{G} \bigwedge_{f \in \Gamma'} \neg f) \to \varphi$ if and only if $K_{\setminus \Gamma'} \models \varphi$ by Proposition 2. In particular, while conducting a DCCA, all faults whose activations are suppressed by the $only_\Gamma$ part of the safe fault sets formula can be removed from the checked model, thereby replacing checks of multiple LTL formulas on a model with all faults by a series of reachability checks of multiple reduced models:

Theorem 1 (Fault Removal DCCA). *Let K be a fault-aware Kripke structure with faults $F = F(K)$, $\Gamma \subseteq F$ be a fault set, and $K_{\setminus (F \setminus \Gamma)} \in K \setminus\!\setminus (F \setminus \Gamma)$. Γ is safe for hazard H if and only if $K_{\setminus (F \setminus \Gamma)} \models \mathbf{G} \neg H$.*

The proof of Theorem 1 generalizes and completes the one given for SCADE-DCCA [11]. Overall potential analysis time reductions depend on the model adaptation overhead and the size of the minimal critical fault sets; as the latter are usually rather small, efficiency can improve significantly. The following proposition establishes the adequacy of the fault removal optimization for injected, activation-independent faults $\Gamma' \subseteq F(K)$, i.e., the criticality of $\Gamma = F(K) \setminus \Gamma'$ can be determined by either removing Γ' or by injecting only Γ in the first place. That is, it is not even necessary to construct the complete fault-aware Kripke structure containing all analyzed faults and subsequently to remove the faults that the analyzed DCCA formula would suppress anyway; instead, only the analyzed faults can be injected into the model, avoiding any potential analysis tool overhead when carrying out the fault removals. More generally, the following proposition summarizes the formal justification for the equivalence at the bottom of Fig. 4, allowing only the smaller fault set to be injected in the first place; a similar result can be obtained for the reverse direction.

Proposition 3. *For fault sets F and $F' \subseteq F$ and all fault-aware Kripke structures K, $K_F \in K \lhd F$, and $(K_F)_{\setminus F'} \in K_F \setminus\!\!\setminus F'$, there is a $K_{F \setminus F'} \in K \lhd (F \setminus F')$ such that $K_{F \setminus F'} \equiv (K_F)_{\setminus F'}$.*

5   Tool Support and Evaluation

Fault-aware modeling and specification is implemented in the S# modeling and analysis framework for safety-critical systems [13]. The following gives a brief overview of S#'s high-level modeling language, its fault modeling capabilities, and its integration with the explicit-state model checker LTSMIN [18]. S#'s efficiency is contrasted with the explicit-state and symbolic model checkers SPIN and NuSMV [8,14] as well as the safety analysis tools VECS and COMPASS [20,23]. In particular, we highlight S#'s analysis efficiency improvements over previous versions of S# for three case studies which result from the use of fault removal DCCA as well as fault-aware Kripke structures. The latest version of S# as well as documentation about its installation and usage are available at http://safetysharp.isse.de. Detailed descriptions of the case studies as well as the S# case study models are also available there, including interactive, S#-based visualizations that support visual replays of model checking counter examples.

5.1   The S# Modeling and Analysis Framework for Safety-Critical Systems

The S# modeling and analysis framework conducts DCCAs fully automatically for system models authored in the ISO-standardized C# programming language and .NET runtime environment [15,16]. Its modeling language and the underlying model of computation put particular emphasis on flexible system design variant modeling and composition capabilities as well as support for fault modeling and automated fault injection which guarantees conservative extension. While S# models are *represented* as C# programs, they are still models of the safety-critical systems to be analyzed; the running example's tank, for instance, is part of the model even though it is not software-based in the real world. Even the software parts of S# models are not intended to be used as the actual implementations; these are typically done in C or C++ for reasons of efficiency. Thus, S# is best regarded as an executable, text-based extended subset of SysML [24] even though no automated transformations between the two exist. The underlying model of computation is a series of discrete system steps, where each step takes a clock tick. As shown by Listing 1, S# components are represented by C# classes, instances of which correspond to S# component instances. Methods are considered to be either required or provided ports; inheritance, interfaces, generics, lambda functions, etc. are fully supported by S#. To instantiate a model, the appropriate component instances must be created, their initial states and subcomponents must be set, and their required and provided ports must be connected.

```
class PressureSensor : Component { // incomplete due to space restrictions
    int Max;
    public PressureSensor(int max) { Max = max; }

    public extern int GetPhysicalPressure();
    public virtual bool MaxReached() { return GetPhysicalPressure() >= Max; }

    PermanentFault NotIsFull = new PermanentFault();

    [FaultEffect(Fault = nameof(NotIsFull))]
    class NotIsFullEffect : PressureSensor {
        public override bool MaxReached() { return false; }
    }
}
```

Listing 1. A partial S# model of the running example's pressure sensor. The provided port MaxReached checks the required port GetPhysicalPressure against the Max value set via the constructor to determine whether the maximum pressure level is reached. The permanent fault ¬is full is represented by NotIsFull; its effect is modeled by the nested class NotIsFullEffect marked with the FaultEffect attribute that links the effect to the fault. The effect overrides the original behavior of MaxReached such that it always returns false when the fault is activated, regardless of the actual pressure level; the port's original implementation is invoked only when the fault is dormant.

S#'s unified model execution approach [13] integrates the explicit-state model checker LTSMIN [18]: Instead of model transformations typically employed by safety analysis tools such as VECS, COMPASS, and ALTARICA [4,20,23], S# unifies simulations, visualizations, and fully exhaustive model checking by executing the models with consistent semantics regardless of whether a simulation is run or some formula is model checked. During model checking, all combinations of nondeterministic choices and fault activations within a model are exhaustively enumerated, the generated transitions are minimized with regard to the faults they activate, and a fault-aware Kripke structure is generated on-the-fly and subsequently transformed into a classical one for LTSMIN. However, S# is not a software model checker such as Java Pathfinder or Zing [1,29] as it does not analyze states after every instruction; only state changes between individual, more coarse-grained system steps are considered. Additionally, heap allocations or threads are unsupported during model checking.

5.2   Evaluated Case Studies

S#'s analysis efficiency with fault removal DCCA and fault-aware Kripke structures is evaluated with three case studies. The first two case studies were previously analyzed using hand-written NUSMV models [12,25]; the safety analysis results obtained with S# match those from previous analyses, the main improvements over them lie in S#'s modular, high-level modeling language and flexible model composition capabilities based on C# that, for instance, no longer require manual work for composing system design variants. Additionally, S#'s unified model execution approach not only generates and checks the required DCCA formulas fully automatically, but also allows for interactive visualizations and visual replays of model checking counter examples based on the same underlying S# model without sacrificing analysis efficiency unacceptably.

Radio-Controlled Railroad Crossing. The radio-controlled railroad crossing replaces sensors on the track by onboard computations of the train position and radio-based communication between the train and the crossing [12]. The hazard is a train passing an unsecured crossing, potentially resulting from faults such as lost communication messages or the crossing's barrier getting stuck. Being model checking-based, DCCA is automatically able to cope with temporal dependencies inherent to the case study: Simultaneous occurrences of multiple faults might be safe, while consecutive occurrences might not due to the communication interplay between the train and the crossing.

Height Control System. The height control system [25] of the Elbe Tunnel in Hamburg, Germany, tries to prevent overheight vehicles from entering the tunnel at unsuitable locations to avoid collisions with the tunnel's ceiling. The antagonistic hazards of collisions and false alarms must be balanced, taking failures of various sensors into account. The system's design space is restricted by the physical properties of the sensors as well as the road layout; the "best" designs strike a balance between the two aforementioned hazards. S# supports modular modeling of different design variants and their composition in order to analyze the safety of all modeled design variants.

Hemodialysis Machine. The third case study is a hemodialysis machine [22], consisting of several physical components such as tubing valves, pumps, drip chambers, and the dialyzer itself. To adequately express the causal dependencies between these components, it is necessary to model the fluid flows that interconnect them. The analyzed hazard is that of contaminated blood entering the patient's vein.

5.3 Evaluation Results

S#'s latest version makes use of fault removal DCCA and automatically generates fault-aware Kripke structures for explicit-state model checking with LTSMIN. Compared to previous versions of S# that employed explicit-state model checking with state-based fault modeling, analysis efficiency improves by up to almost four orders of magnitude depending on the case study as outlined by Table 1. S# is generally faster than the established explicit-state model checker SPIN: In the worst case of valid formulas where the model's entire state space must be enumerated, S# and LTSMIN take 68.8 s for the height control model. SPIN, by contrast, takes 553 s to check a hand-optimized, non-modular version of the model that semantically corresponds to the S# version. On a quad-core CPU, LTSMIN achieves a speedup of 3.7x, bringing the analysis time down to 18.6 s whereas SPIN scales by a factor of 1.5x only. Fault awareness makes S# more efficient than SPIN, causing it to compute less transitions while still finding all reachable states. For the height control case study, activation minimality is partially encoded into the SPIN model; general and automated support would require changes to SPIN's model checking algorithms, however.

For the height control case study, BDD-based symbolic analysis with NUSMV is faster than using S#: For a hand-written, very low-level and

Table 1. The results of the S#-based evaluation of the explicit-state efficiency improvements, comparing fault-aware modeling and specification with state-based fault modeling in (a). A comparison of both DCCA variants is shown in (b). Three S# case studies were evaluated on a 3.4 GHz quad-core CPU: The height control system (T), the radio-controlled railroad crossing (R), and the hemodialysis machine (H), checking the hazards of tunnel collisions, trains on unsecured crossings, and contaminated blood entering the patient's vein, respectively.

	State-Based			Fault-Aware			
	States	Trans	Time	States	Trans	Time	
T	249	1219724	1.5d	1.3	57	14.2s	9127x
R	116	10564	12m	2.5	8.5	1.9s	379x
H	0.6	152	3m	0.05	0.9	10.1s	18x

	Fault-Aware				
	Faults	MCS	Std Time	FR Time	
T	11	3	3010s	33.1s	91x
R	7	6	23s	1.4s	16x
H	8	4	1040s	15.9s	65x

(a) Comparison of both fault modeling approaches. The "States" columns show the models' approximate amount of reachable states in millions, "Trans" the approximate amount of reachable transitions in millions, and "Time" the time to enumerate all states. The last column shows the analysis speed-up.

(b) Comparison of both DCCA variants. "Faults" lists the number of faults, "MCS" the amount of minimal critical sets. The time columns show the times of standard and fault removal DCCA; the speed-up is shown on the right.

non-modular NuSMV model that is approximately equivalent to the S# model, the entire state space is generated almost instantly, despite state-based fault modeling. By contrast, the railroad crossing case study is more efficiently checked by S# or SPIN than by NuSMV, so the relative efficiency of explicit-state and symbolic model checking is case study-specific and independent from S#. In general, highly nondeterministic models seem to profit more from symbolic techniques. Fault awareness can partially be encoded into NuSMV models using input variables [5], slowing down analysis noticeably in some cases, however.

6   Conclusion and Future Work

Fault-aware modeling and specification of safety-critical systems has two main advantages over the commonly used state-based fault modeling approach: Explicitly denoting faults and their activations simplifies the descriptions and formal definitions of safety analysis techniques like DCCA and of safety-related concepts such as fault injection and fault removal. Moreover, model checking efficiency in general and safety analysis times in particular are improved significantly such that explicit-state model checking becomes competitive with symbolic techniques when analyzing safety-critical systems. Some case studies still have higher analysis times with S# compared to NuSMV; this tradeoff seems acceptable, however, when considering the step-up in modeling flexibility and expressiveness as well as the guarantees of semantic consistency and conservative fault injection that S# provides over SPIN, NuSMV, or, in parts, VECS. Compared to other approaches for safety modeling and analysis like COMPASS, VECS, ALTARICA, or HiP-HOPS, S# has a competitive edge by tightly integrating the development, debugging, and simulation of models with their formal analysis with no or only minor sacrifices in analysis efficiency. In general, however, fair comparisons between these tools and S# are hard to achieve due to their different models of computation. For instance, it took us about 740 lines to create a scaled down COMPASS version of the railroad crossing model that is semantically similar to the S# version written in 400 lines of C# code. COMPASS performs a safety analysis that is equivalent to DCCA in 21 min using NuSMV instead of the 1.4 s it takes S# to do the same. Of course, the comparison is unfair as forcing COMPASS semantics onto S# might likewise slow down analyses.

While S# and DCCA only compute the minimal critical fault sets for a hazard, the actual hazard probability is also of interest. We are therefore working on fault-aware probabilistic model checking; preliminary results are promising, bringing the achieved analysis time reductions for non-probabilistic analyses to probabilistic ones. Additionally, we plan to explore (semi-)automatic abstractions from irrelevant environment states to decrease analysis times similar to partial order reduction [3]: S# models always contain parts of the system's physical environment for reasons of adequacy [13], for which the system's sensors might readily serve as abstraction functions.

References

1. Andrews, T., Qadeer, S., Rajamani, S.K., Rehof, J., Xie, Y.: Zing: a model checker for concurrent software. In: Alur, R., Peled, D.A. (eds.) CAV 2004. LNCS, vol. 3114, pp. 484–487. Springer, Heidelberg (2004)
2. Avižienis, A., Laprie, J.C., Randell, B., Landwehr, C.: Basic concepts and taxonomy of dependable and secure computing. Dependable Secure Comput. 1(1), 11–33 (2004)
3. Baier, C., Katoen, J.P.: Principles of Model Checking. MIT Press, Cambridge (2008)
4. Batteux, M., Prosvirnova, T., Rauzy, A., Kloul, L.: The AltaRica 3.0 project for model-based safety assessment. In: Industrial Informatics, pp. 741–746. IEEE (2013)
5. Bozzano, M., Cimatti, A., Griggio, A., Mattarei, C.: Efficient anytime techniques for model-based safety analysis. In: Kroening, D., Păsăreanu, C.S. (eds.) CAV 2015. LNCS, vol. 9206, pp. 603–621. Springer, Heidelberg (2015)
6. Bozzano, M., Cimatti, A., Katoen, J.-P., Nguyen, V.Y., Noll, T., Roveri, M.: The COMPASS approach: correctness, modelling and performability of aerospace systems. In: Buth, B., Rabe, G., Seyfarth, T. (eds.) SAFECOMP 2009. LNCS, vol. 5775, pp. 173–186. Springer, Heidelberg (2009)
7. Bozzano, M., Cimatti, A., Tapparo, F.: Symbolic fault tree analysis for reactive systems. In: Namjoshi, K.S., Yoneda, T., Higashino, T., Okamura, Y. (eds.) ATVA 2007. LNCS, vol. 4762, pp. 162–176. Springer, Heidelberg (2007)
8. Cimatti, A., Clarke, E., Giunchiglia, E., Giunchiglia, F., Pistore, M., Roveri, M., Sebastiani, R., Tacchella, A.: NuSMV 2: an opensource tool for symbolic model checking. In: Brinksma, E., Larsen, K.G. (eds.) CAV 2002. LNCS, vol. 2404, pp. 359–364. Springer, Heidelberg (2002)
9. Clarke, E.M.: The birth of model checking. In: Grumberg, O., Veith, H. (eds.) 25 Years of Model Checking. LNCS, vol. 5000, pp. 1–26. Springer, Heidelberg (2008)

10. Grunske, L., Kaiser, B.: An automated dependability analysis method for COTS-based systems. In: Franch, X., Port, D. (eds.) ICCBSS 2005. LNCS, vol. 3412, pp. 178–190. Springer, Heidelberg (2005)
11. Güdemann, M., Ortmeier, F., Reif, W.: Using deductive cause-consequence analysis (DCCA) with SCADE. In: Saglietti, F., Oster, N. (eds.) SAFECOMP 2007. LNCS, vol. 4680, pp. 465–478. Springer, Heidelberg (2007)
12. Habermaier, A., Güdemann, M., Ortmeier, F., Reif, W., Schellhorn, G.: The For-MoSA approach to qualitative and quantitative model-based safety analysis. In: Railway Safety, Reliability, and Security, pp. 65–114. IGI Global (2012)
13. Habermaier, A., Knapp, A., Leupolz, J., Reif, W.: Unified simulation, visualization, and formal analysis of safety-critical systems with S#. In: ter Beek, M., Gnesi, S., Knapp, A. (eds.) FMICS-AVoCS 2016. LNCS, vol. 9933, pp. 150–167. Springer, Heidelberg (2016)
14. Holzmann, G.: The SPIN Model Checker. Addison-Wesley, Reading (2004)
15. ISO: ISO/IEC 23270: Information technology - Programming languages – C# (2006)
16. ISO: ISO/IEC 23271: Information technology – Common Language Infrastructure (2012)
17. ISO/IEC/IEEE: ISO 24765: Systems and software engineering – Vocabulary (2010)
18. Kant, G., Laarman, A., Meijer, J., van de Pol, J., Blom, S., van Dijk, T.: LTSmin: high-performance language-independent model checking. In: Baier, C., Tinelli, C. (eds.) TACAS 2015. LNCS, vol. 9035, pp. 692–707. Springer, Heidelberg (2015)
19. Kromodimoeljo, S., Lindsay, P.A.: Automatic Generation of Minimal Cut Sets. In: Engineering Safety and Security Systems, pp. 33–47 (2015)
20. Lipaczewski, M., Struck, S., Ortmeier, F.: Using tool-supported model based safety analysis – progress and experiences in SAML development. In: High-Assurance Systems Engineering, pp. 159–166. IEEE (2012)
21. Markey, N.: Temporal logic with past is exponentially more succinct. In: EATCS Bulletin, vol. 79, pp. 122–128. European Association for Theoretical Computer Science (2003)
22. Mashkoor, A.: The hemodialysis machine case study. In: Butler, M., Schewe, K.-D., Mashkoor, A., Biro, M. (eds.) ABZ 2016. LNCS, vol. 9675, pp. 329–343. Springer, Heidelberg (2016). doi:10.1007/978-3-319-33600-8_29
23. Noll, T.: Safety, dependability and performance analysis of aerospace systems. In: Artho, C., Ölveczky, P.C. (eds.) FTSCS 2014. CCIS, vol. 476, pp. 17–31. Springer, Heidelberg (2015)
24. Object Management Group: OMG Systems Modeling Language (OMG SysML), Version 1.4 (2015)
25. Ortmeier, F., Schellhorn, G., Thums, A., Reif, W., Hering, B., Trappschuh, H.: Safety analysis of the height control system for the Elbtunnel. In: Anderson, S., Bologna, S., Felici, M. (eds.) SAFECOMP 2002. LNCS, vol. 2434, pp. 296–308. Springer, Heidelberg (2002)
26. Papadopoulos, Y., Walker, M., Parker, D., Rüde, E., Hamann, R., Uhlig, A., Grätz, U., Lien, R.: Engineering failure analysis and design optimisation with HiP-HOPS. Eng. Fail. Anal. 18(2), 590–608 (2011)
27. Pradella, M., San Pietro, P., Spoletini, P., Morzenti, A.: Practical model checking of LTL with past. In: Automated Technology for Verification and Analysis (2003)
28. Vesely, W., Dugan, J., Fragola, J., Minarick, J., Railsback, J.: Fault tree handbook with aerospace applications. Technical report, NASA, Washington, DC (2002)
29. Visser, W., Havelund, K., Brat, G., Park, S., Lerda, F.: Model checking programs. Autom. Softw. Eng. 10(2), 203–232 (2003)

Model-Based System Analysis

Block Library Driven Translation Validation for Dataflow Models in Safety Critical Systems

Arnaud Dieumegard[1], Andres Toom[2,3,4], and Marc Pantel[2(✉)]

[1] Institut de Recherche Technologique Antoine de Saint Exupéry,
118 route de Narbonne, CS 44248, 31432 Toulouse Cedex 4, France
arnaud.dieumegard@irt-saintexupery.com
[2] Institut de Recherche en Informatique de Toulouse, Université de Toulouse,
ENSEEIHT, 2 rue Charles Camichel, 31071 Toulouse Cedex, France
Marc.Pantel@enseeiht.fr
[3] Institute of Cybernetics at Tallinn University of Technology,
Akadeemia tee 21, 12618 Tallinn, Estonia
toom@cs.ioc.ee
[4] IB Krates OÜ, Mäealuse 4, 12618 Tallinn, Estonia

Abstract. Model driven engineering is widely used in the development of complex and safety critical systems. Systems' designs are specified and validated in domain specific modeling languages and software code is often produced by autocoding. Thus the correctness of the final systems depend on the correctness of those tools. We propose an approach for the formal verification of code generation from dataflow languages, such as SIMULINK, based on translation validation. It relies on the BLOCKLIBRARY DSL for the formal specification and verification of the structure, semantics and variability of the complex block libraries found in these languages. These specifications are then used here for deriving model and block-specific semantic contracts that will be woven into the generated C code. We present two different approaches for performing the block matching and weaving step. Finally, we rely on the FRAMA-C toolset and state-of-the-art SMT solvers for verifying the annotated code.

Keywords: Translation validation · Deductive verification · Data flow languages · Block libraries · Why3 toolset · Frama-C toolset

1 Introduction

Automatic code generators (ACG) are nowadays used for the development of most safety-critical systems in order to avoid human-related programming errors, and ensure both quality standards conformance and efficient maintenance cycles. As these tools replace humans in a key software production step, their design or implementation flaws usually result in errors in the generated software. Safety critical software development must usually satisfy certification/qualification standards like the *DO-178C* for avionics which is one of the best known and most stringent one. One key requirement in its Model Based Software Engineering (MBSE) and Formal Methods (FM) supplements (*DO-331* & *DO-333*)

© Springer International Publishing AG 2016
M.H. ter Beek et al. (Eds.): FMICS-AVoCS 2016, LNCS 9933, pp. 117–132, 2016.
DOI: 10.1007/978-3-319-45943-1_8

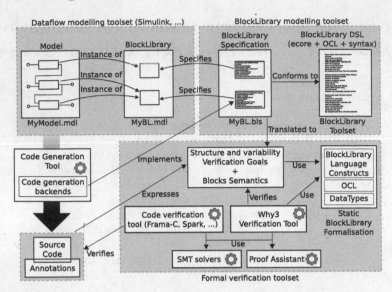

Fig. 1. The process for the formal specification of block libraries and the use of these specifications for the verification of automatically generated code

is to provide a precise, complete and unambiguous specification of the input and output languages for ACG.

Overview of the Approach. Figure 1 gives an overview of the elements in our specification and verification process. In [3,4] we proposed a Domain Specific Language (DSL) for writing and formally analyzing specifications for configurable function blocks in dataflow languages. We refer to this as the BLOCK-LIBRARY specification language. In the current contribution it is used for the formal verification of automatically generated code from dataflow models. The WHY3 toolset [2] is first used for the formal verification of the well-formedness and semantic consistency of the specification. Then these specifications are used for the verification of generated source code from dataflow models by weaving model-specific formal annotations into the generated source code. The annotated code is then verified using the FRAMA-C toolset[1]. Both verification steps are in turn relying on SMT solvers and proof assistants as a formal backbone.

Dataflow Languages. Dataflow languages are widely used for specifying control and command algorithms. SIMULINK[2] is the most used in the industry but there exist other similar graphical formalisms, such as SCADE, SCICOS, XCOS and textual languages such as LUSTRE and SIGNAL. The main constructs in dataflow models are *blocks* (computation nodes) and *signals* (data connections). The concrete execution of dataflow models is divided into three phases: an *initialization* phase, where the memories of all the blocks in the model are initialized; followed

---

[1] http://frama-c.com.
[2] http://www.mathworks.com/simulink.

by a recurring cycle alternating the *compute* and *update* phases. During the former each enabled block produces data to its outputs according to data at its inputs, previous state(s) and configuration parameters. The computed data is immediately available for the following blocks. The order of these computations is defined statically by a sequencing algorithm such as [9], formalized in [7]. The *update* phase updates the memories of all sequential blocks according to the data at their inputs, previous values in memory and configuration parameters.

Use Case. Our final goal is the verification of the generated code for a complete dataflow model with respect to requirements for the system expressed as top level software contracts that are either manually written or generated from a specification model (e.g. dataflow system observer). This part is not directly addressed in the current work. However, the semantics of the model that implements this top level specification is given by the semantics and configuration of the blocks it relies on. We propose to weave the generated code with semantic contracts derived from the BLOCKLIBRARY specifications for two purposes: (a) verify that the generated code for each block matches its specification and (b) help the deductive verification tools in proving the top level contracts. We illustrate our proposal with the specification of the *IntegerDelay* block and the verification of its code as generated by the GENEAUTO ACG [17].

Organization of the Paper. This paper is organized as follows: Sect. 2 provides an overview of the BLOCKLIBRARY language and associated verification technique. Section 3 focuses on the verification of the low-level requirements for an ACG relying on a translation validation approach. Section 4 applies this approach on a use case. Section 5 compares our approach to related works. Planned future extensions and a conclusion are given in Sect. 6.

2 Formal Specification of Blocks in Dataflow Languages

Besides the core principles of data flowing through signals from output ports to input ports, the semantics of dataflow languages is mainly determined by the semantics of elementary blocks that compute data on their outputs depending on data on their inputs, memories and parameters. Tools such as SIMULINK have large block libraries with highly configurable blocks. The BLOCKLIBRARY DSL proposed in [3,4] relies on the core concepts of Software Product Line Engineering (SPLE) adapted to the domain of block libraries to handle this variability. This DSL is expressed as a metamodel in MOF (OMG Meta Object Facility standard) capturing the concepts required for the specification of both the structure (ports, parameters and memories) and the semantic phases (initialization, computation and memory update) of dataflow blocks. Each structural element is parameterized by data types and constraints expressed in the OMG standard Object Constraint Language (OCL) describing the set of allowed values for valid instances of each structural elements. A semantic specification element contains the specification of the behavior of one specific configuration of the block expressed either in an axiomatic style using pre/post-conditions or operationally by giving the function's definition. One can also provide both, since the two styles offer different possibilities for automatic verification. The pre/post-conditions are specified using OCL. Operational specifications are specified using the BLOCKLIBRARY Action Language (BAL).

The next section illustrates the specification for a block family with an emphasis on the variability management relying on the SIMULINK *IntegerDelay* block. The verification technique for the block specification is then summarized (the interested reader can find more detailed information in [3,4] and on the project's website http://block-library.enseeiht.fr/html). Finally, we will elaborate on the verification of loop constructs.

2.1   Example of Block Specification: IntegerDelay

Listing 1.1 provides a partial specification of the *IntegerDelay* block that delays data flow by a given number N of clock cycles. Such blocks are often used in control and command algorithms for writing recurrent equations (the discrete equivalent of difference equations). This block is one of the simplest, but its Simulink version is nevertheless highly variable with multiple semantics variations. The number of delayed clock cycles is specified statically as a parameter. As the block delays its input values by N clock cycles, it is mandatory to provide the first N values to be used for the block's output. These initial values IV are either provided by a static parameter or via an input of the block. The block has other parameters and inputs making this block representative of the typical variability of SIMULINK blocks. In the complete specification also N can be provided via the block's input and there can be yet another input to dynamically reset the block's state (according to 4 different activation algorithm variants – rising edge, falling edge, zero crossing and level). Finally, the specification provided here only handles scalar and vector values of the double data type for the input and output ports, whereas the full specification also allows integer (signed, unsigned, 8, 16 or 32 bits) and boolean data types, as well as matrices of all of those types. The full specification of this block family has 144 distinct configurations.

```
1   library BlockLibrary {
        type signed realInt TInt32 of 32 bits
        type realDouble TDouble
        type array TArrayDouble of TDouble [-1]
        blocktype IntegerDelay {
6           variant DelayParameter {
                parameter N : TInt32 { invariant ocl { N.value > 0 } } }
            variant IOScalar {
                in data Input : TDouble
                out data Output : TDouble}
11          variant IVScalarParam extends IOScalar {
                parameter IV isMandatory : TDouble}
            variant IVScalarInput extends IOScalar {
                in data IV : TDouble    }
            variant IOVector {
16              in data Input : TArrayDouble
                out data Output : TArrayDouble}
            variant IVVectorParam extends IOVector {
                parameter IV isMandatory : TArrayDouble }
            variant IVVectorInput extends IOVector {
21              in data IV : TArrayDouble}
            variant ScalarValues extends ALT(IVScalarParam , IVScalarInput)
```

```
       variant VectorValues extends ALT(IVVectorParam, IVVectorInput)
       variant ScalarOrVectorValues extends ALT(ScalarValues,
           VectorValues)
       variant Mem extends AND(ScalarOrVectorValues, DelayParameter) {
26         invariant ocl { Input.size = Output.size }
           invariant ocl { IV.size = N.value }
           memory Mem {
               datatype auto ocl { Input.value }
               length auto ocl { N.value }}}
31     mode DelaySemantics implements Mem {
           definition bal = init_Delay {
               postcondition ocl { Mem.value = IV.value }
               Mem.value := IV.value;}
           definition bal = compute_Delay {
36             postcondition ocl { Output.value = Mem.value }
               Output.value := Mem.value[0];}
           definition bal = update_Delay {
               postcondition ocl { Mem.value->last() = Input.value }
               postcondition ocl {
41                 Mem.value := (Mem.value@pre)->subList(2,N.value)
                                               ->append(Input.value)}
               Vector_Shift_Left(Mem.value, 1, Input.value);}
           init init_Delay
           compute compute_Delay
46         update update_Delay}}
    }
```

Listing 1.1. Partial specification of the *IntegerDelay* block

2.2   Specifying a Block Family

A block family is a set of possible configurations for a given block (a product line of blocks in the "feature modeling" or FODA methodology and terminology from Kang et al. in [8]). A block family specification in the BLOCKLIBRARY language starts with the definition of block's structure. The structure can be decomposed using *BlockVariant*s and *BlockMode*s. *BlockVariant* is a basic specification unit that defines a subset of structural or semantic elements. *BlockVariant*s can be reused in the specifications of different block types. They can be extended and combined into larger units by using inheritance. A *BlockMode*, on the other hand, is associated to a particular subset of the complete block configurations whose behavior can be captured with a similar algorithm. Each *BlockMode* implements one or more *BlockVariant*s and inherits the elements defined in those. The specification of a block type thus consists of a structural variation graph (DAG) whose roots and inner nodes are *BlockVariant*s and leafs are *BlockMode*s.

Two kinds of inheritance: AND and ALT, both *n*-ary operators, are available. For AND, respectively ALT, the inheriting node inherits the definitions and contracts from *all*, respectively exactly *one*, of the inherited nodes. AND is similar to multiple inheritance as found in many object-oriented languages. In our case, we require that all the inherited elements are distinct (i.e., no overloading or overlap is allowed). This relation is thus unambiguous and commutative. Line 25 of Listing 1.1 is an example of AND, and line 22 an example of ALT. This last one specifies that, in one configuration of the Delay block, the initial value is provided as a static parameter and, in the other, it is provided via an input.

From a BLOCKLIBRARY specification we can extract the set of all valid block configurations. Each configuration has exactly one *BlockMode* and one or more

*BlockVariant*s. Figure 2 displays the block configurations extracted from the specification in Listing 1.1. In a well-formed dataflow model, all block instances must match to exactly one configuration in the respective block family.

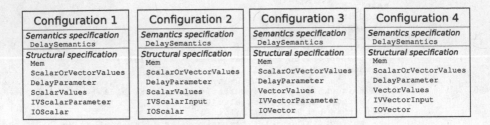

Configuration 1	Configuration 2	Configuration 3	Configuration 4
Semantics specification DelaySemantics	*Semantics specification* DelaySemantics	*Semantics specification* DelaySemantics	*Semantics specification* DelaySemantics
Structural specification Mem	*Structural specification* Mem	*Structural specification* Mem	*Structural specification* Mem
ScalarOrVectorValues	ScalarOrVectorValues	ScalarOrVectorValues	ScalarOrVectorValues
DelayParameter	DelayParameter	DelayParameter	DelayParameter
ScalarValues	ScalarValues	VectorValues	VectorValues
IVScalarParameter	IVScalarInput	IVVectorParameter	IVVectorInput
IOScalar	IOScalar	IOVector	IOVector

Fig. 2. Configurations extracted from the specification of the *IntegerDelay* block

2.3   Verification and Validation of Block Specifications

The block specifications written in the BLOCKLIBRARY language are formally assessed using a translation into the WHY property and WHYML behavior specification languages [2]. These generated specifications can be verified using the dedicated WHY3 toolset relying either on automated proofs by SMT solvers or manual ones using proof assistants such as COQ. The structural part of the BLOCKLIBRARY specifications, including the variability aspects are translated to WHY. The blocks' semantics are translated to WHYML. This translation is currently written in Java and relies on the modeling support in EMF[3]. BLOCKLIBRARY models are translated to WHY and WHYML models that are serialized using the XTEXT toolset[4]. It is not the aim of this paper to assess the correctness of this translation. On the one hand, it defines the semantics of the BLOCKLIBRARY language. On the other hand, it enables writing accurate specifications for the blocks in the chosen languages (e.g., SIMULINK). This translation is being validated using various testing strategies.

Verification of Structure and Variability. For each block configuration extracted from a BLOCKLIBRARY specification, we generate a WHY theory containing the definitions for each structural element contained in its structural specification altogether with a set of predicates expressing the: (a) explicit constraints defined as invariants of the structural elements; (b) implicit constraints related to the structural elements' data types; and (c) global invariants constraining the *BlockVariant* and *BlockMode* elements.

Two properties, *completeness* and *disjointness*, are used to assess the well-formedness of the structure and variability of the specification. The first one states that for all the well-formed instantiations of the block there exists at least

---

[3] https://eclipse.org/modeling/emf/.
[4] https://eclipse.org/Xtext/.

one suitable configuration in the specification. This covers both the fact that, all *BlockVariant*s are used and that no contradictions are present in the set of associated constraints. The second one ensures the unambiguous interpretation of any configuration of a block. Both properties are automatically converted to goals relying on the previously generated predicates.

The verification is performed using the WHY3 platform and SMT solvers. In our experiments it was performed in a few seconds for most of the blocks on a common modern laptop. Some block specifications with more variability require more time (with a time factor of up to 100 in our experiments) for fully automated verification. This cost is generally not an issue as this verification must be done only once for each block specification.

Verification of Semantics. If the block's semantics is specified both axiomatically and operationally, then the consistency of these definitions can be verified. The specification of the three execution phases (in Listing 1.1 the resp. sections are following: initialization lines 32–34, computation lines 35–37 and update lines 38–43) are translated to distinct WHYML functions. The body of each function is a direct translation of the respective semantic function of the block in this mode. This function is given a contract consisting of the pre/post conditions specified in the axiomatic semantics and an additional pre-condition computed based on the structural properties that hold in this particular mode.

The verification of the WHYML functions is done as previously by relying on the WHY3 platform and SMT solvers. While this verification can be straightforward for the specifications of simple blocks, it can require additional annotations for code with more complex data types (vectors, matrices) or algorithmically more complex blocks. In practice, fully automatic proofs are often only possible, when additional annotations are given in the form loop invariants, variants and even ghost code. The BAL language allows one to write such annotations and our transformation tool translates them into annotations in the generated WHYML function body. If a consistent specification is provided, the verification is usually handled automatically in a short time (a few tenths of a second) by the SMT solvers. As the number of configurations can grow exponentially, the verification of a complete block library specification can still take some time but, as previously stated, this verification is only done once for a given library.

Validation of Specifications. While it is important to verify the specifications for well-formedness and consistency, it is also necessary to validate that they adequately capture the intended semantics of the corresponding blocks, e.g., that is in the existing reference library implementations. The validation strategy that we have planned and are currently implementing for the specifications of SIMULINK blocks relies on the translation of all configurations of all blocks to corresponding MATLAB code. That code is executed and the execution result is compared to the result of the simulation of a correspondingly configured SIMULINK block. Test vectors for block inputs and parameters can be automatically generated based on the block specifications. This work is currently ongoing and the results will be reported in the future.

2.4   Handling Loop Constructs

Programs containing loops are the main difficulty in the automated deductive verification. Loops usually must be annotated with complex invariants and variants. Loops are very common programming constructs that occur especially often in mathematical computations, including the ones done in dataflow blocks. However, in this context, loops have often a very regular structure with similar annotations. Thus, the specification designer should be relieved from the writing of these annotations. This topic has been addressed by many authors and various solutions have been proposed. For example, Furia and Meyer [6] propose a technique to generate invariants for certain loop patterns automatically, when larger program units such as routines have explicit post-conditions which is also the case in our context. The technique in [6] was partly implemented in the Boogie tool. Unfortunately, in the general case such methods are also limited due to undecidability. Recent work by Wiik and Boström [19] targets contract-based verification of MATLAB-style matrix programs making this work very relevant to ours. The authors propose a solution for efficient encoding of a subset of MATLAB's built-in matrix functions for deductive verification. However, the specification of loop invariants is still required. According to the authors' experiments, k-induction can be used to remove some, but still not all of these invariants. The work currently addresses partial correctness only. Filliâtre and Pereira [5] have presented an approach that can be applied to different iteration paradigms including non-deterministic and infinite iterations as well as iterations with side-effects. It does not completely remove the need to specify loop invariants, but it allows encapsulating and hiding the implementation aspects of iterators. Thus, simplifying considerably the specification left to the "users".

In our context loop specifications occur in two places: specifications of the blocks operational semantics and annotations of generated code. Given the state of the art, we have chosen the following strategy to deal with them. As explained earlier, the operational specification of blocks semantics is optional and is not needed for the translation validation. However, it can be beneficial otherwise. The BAL language contains *for* and *while*-style loop statements with both *invariant* and *variant* annotations that the user can explicitly specify. However, explicit loop constructs can be in many cases avoided by using polymorphic operators with implicit support for non-scalars and/or using higher order iterators. For instance, element-wise operations on non-scalars can be specified in terms of an elementary operation and a higher-order *map* operator and collapsing operations using a *fold* operator (i.e., catamorphism). Other operations, such as matrix product, require more specific encoding. The *Vector_Shift_Left* binary operator used in line 43 of Listing 1.1 is another example. It is applied on a vector or a matrix. In case of a vector, it shifts all the values in the vector by one position downwards, starting from the second element, and inserts a specified new value as the very last element. If the first argument is a matrix, it applies the same operation to each row of the matrix. The last argument should be a vector in this case. Line 43 of Listing 1.1 is automatically expanded to Listing 1.2. The specification of these operators in BAL and their translation to WHY

```
    var iter = 0;
    ghost { var i = 0; }
    while (iter < (N.value - 1)){
       invariant ocl { 0 <= iter < N.value }
5      invariant ocl { 0 <= i and i < iter and
          Mem.value->subList(1,i) = (Mem.value@pre)->subList(2,i+1) }
       variant ocl { N.value - iter }
       Mem.value[iter] := Mem.value[iter + 1];
       iter := iter + 1;}
10  Mem.value[N.value - 1] := Input.value;
```

Listing 1.2. Expanded version of the Vector_Shift_Left operation

and WHYML are currently in progress. This work relies largely on earlier work performed in GENEAUTO [17] and its successor project QGEN[5] on specifying the semantics of the embeddable subsets of MATLAB and SIMULINK and can benefit also from the formalization presented in [19]. The difference in our work is that the invariants and variants for such operators will be generated based on the static parameters of concrete block instances.

The same loop annotations are required in the translation validation context for verifying the correctness of the generated code. The BAL language supports such annotations and it would be thus possible to specify them manually. However, this is rather laborious. We could try to weave these annotations into the generated code just like the pre- and post-conditions. However, this can be significantly more complex. First, it would make the existence of the operational specification mandatory for semantic functions containing loops. Secondly, it would require the generated low-level code to be structurally very close to the operational specification and prohibit the usage of more abstract operators in the specifications or the generation of optimized code. One solution is to let the ACG itself generate annotations for primitive operators involving loops. This might seem to jeopardize the intent of translation validation. However, if applied with care, it does not. It is a similar situation to the Assertion Inference Paradox stated in [6]. The pre- and post-conditions of the larger program units (here code sections generated from block instances) are not generated by the untrusted ACG whose output is under verification. The intent of the intermediate annotations derived from the primitive operators is to help the verification tool in proving the satisfaction of the main contracts. If these annotations do not introduce any axioms to the axiom base used by the deductive verification toolset, then they cannot contribute to a false claim of correctness. In our case no axioms would be generated. However, generally, it must be separately ensured.

The generated C code for the *Vector_Shift_Left* operator corresponding to Listing 1.1, together with the generated annotations, can be seen in lines 32–42 of Listing 1.3. Note that in case the block's semantics is not implemented using operators supporting automatic annotation generation and uses general loop constructs instead, the current deductive verification tools might not be able to

---

[5] http://www.adacore.com/qgen.

automatically prove the correctness of the code. Thus, it would be necessary to use a proof assistant for proving these parts or add some annotations manually in the generated code.

3   Verification of the Correctness of Generated Code

Automatic code generation is one of the key benefits of MBSE for critical systems. The correctness of the code can be assessed by verifying the correctness of the ACG or by verifying that the code has the expected properties. For both approaches there are many techniques available. The assurance gained by classical methods like testing or code reviewing has well-known limits. Formal methods can provide a much higher level of confidence but they have a higher entry barrier that requires good tool support and well integrated development processes.

We will detail below our approach for the formal verification of automatically generated code relying on the Translation Validation (TV) methodology proposed by Pnueli et al. in [15]. In TV the transformation (code generation) workflow is complemented by an independent verification workflow. The latter relies on the common formalization of the input and output languages and must establish whether the input and output data of a given transformation run conform to the expected equivalence relation or not. In our case we rely on the formalization of dataflow blocks in the BLOCKLIBRARY language and use that to derive formal contracts for code generated from block instances in a given input model. In particular ACSL [1] annotations for C code. The same principle can also be applied for other languages providing Design By Contract or annotation facilities like SPARK/ADA 2012, Spec#, JML, B method, Eiffel, etc.

The annotated code is passed to the FRAMA-C toolset and its weakest precondition plugin generating proof obligations that are then verified using SMT solvers. This can be done either directly through FRAMA-C or through the WHY3 toolset. In many cases the verification can be performed fully automatically. When this cannot be achieved, one can use proof assistants to complete the verification manually. Yet another option is to manually add additional annotations such as loop invariants and ghost code into the generated code to assist the verification tools. This option is, however, undesirable, since it is rather laborious and requires modifying the generated code, which impairs the whole process.

3.1   Semantic Annotation of the Generated Code

In order to derive appropriate semantic contracts for the block instances in the input model the model must be first analyzed and the block instances and their configurations must be identified. Secondly, the concrete (ACSL) contracts must be generated and woven into the (C) code generated by the ACG. This involves a number of technical steps. We have considered two alternatives for that.

White Box Approach. If the ACG source code is available, then a light-weight option is to encode the annotation generation directly into the ACG, e.g., by hand-writing the annotation generation functions for each block type. This is rather laborious. Alternatively, these functions could be automatically generated from the BLOCKLIBRARY specifications and integrated with the ACG source code. However, this approach still isn't true translation validation as it relies a lot on the ACG internals. Also, according to *DO-330*, this extra verification-oriented code must be qualified with the same stringency as the rest of the tool as it may introduce errors into the code generation. We have considered this option as a compromise allowing one to concentrate on the BLOCKLIBRARY specific aspects and paving the way for the more complete approach explained next.

Black Box Approach. In this case an external tool must parse the input model, generate the annotations and weave them into the generated code. Regarding *DO-330*, such a separate verification tool must be also qualified in order to gain certification credit for using it. However, the qualification process is much lighter as the tool cannot have any direct impact on the generated code.

3.2   Verification Using the Frama-C Toolset

We decided to target C code annotated with ACSL as: (a) this language is widely used in the safety-critical systems industry, (b) the GENEAUTO ACG has mainly been used and evaluated in this context, and (c) the ACSL annotation language is supported by formal analysis tools such as the FRAMA-C framework. Similar work could have also been done based on most of the other alternatives mentioned earlier.

The FRAMA-C framework targets the analysis of C code in order to extract information provided by various plugins. These plugins allow for the static analysis of the source code to extract information like variables' ranges and scope, code metrics, detect dead code, and many others[6]. Verification of ACSL annotations expressed on the source code is done through the WP plugin implementing a weakest precondition calculus generating proof obligations to be verified. Those are directly assessed using SMT solvers or sent to the previously presented WHY3 platform to rely both on a wider range of SMT solvers or, when needed, on proof assistants. Proof assistants are used in order to manually tackle difficult proofs when the automatic SMT solvers fail to achieve the proof.

White Box Experiment Using the Open Source GENEAUTO ACG. We have extended GENEAUTO with the support for annotation manipulation[7]. For this purpose, we developed a metamodel based on a subset of the ACSL specification including annotations, ghost code and function contracts. We relied on the EMF

---

[6] Visit the FRAMA-C framework website for detailed information: http://frama-c.org.

[7] This work has been performed in partnership with Timothy Wang from the Georgia Institute of Technology and has been partly used in the context of the verification of automatically generated code presented in [18].

framework to generate the corresponding JAVA classes that we integrated into the GENEAUTO source code. We also implemented printing facilities for ACSL annotations. Finally, we implemented the annotation generation functions. As a possible future alternative, the current version of FRAMA-C also accepts annotations written directly in WHY3 instead of ACSL.

Black Box Proposal Through FRAMA-C. For the full translation validation we are considering a following approach. The FRAMA-C toolset provides C code manipulation facilities and is extensible using plugins. It is thus possible to define a new FRAMA-C plugin to conduct automated annotation of the generated code. This plugin must extract data from both the dataflow (SIMULINK) model, as well as from BLOCKLIBRARY specifications. Developing a parser for these two formalisms directly in the plugin would be very time-consuming. Instead, we plan to develop or reuse a separate parser for dataflow models and provide within the BLOCKLIBRARY toolbox a transformation exporting the derived contracts as a data structure that would be easier to use within the FRAMA-C plugin. The plugin must then weave the contracts into the generated code. It is reasonable to simplify that part by relying on minimal traceability information provided by the ACG relating blocks and corresponding code sections. ACGs used for the development of critical software must anyhow provide such links for traceability.

For instance, GENEAUTO provides them in the form of code annotations.

4   Translation Validation of IntegerDelay

As example, an instance of the *IntegerDelay* block is embedded in a small model containing an *Inport* block In1 and an *Outport* block Out1. Such models can also be generated automatically from BLOCKLIBRARY specifications. In this example, the block's input and initial conditions are scalars, and the delay length N is 2. Listing 1.3 shows the code and annotations generated for this example.

The code for the initialization phase is defined in the system_init function while the computation and update phases are together in the system_compute function. While the initialization code is straightforward, the code for the two other phases requires some explanation. The compute function starts with the assignment of the Delay2 block's output, since it only depends on the value of the block's memory (lines 14–17). Then the output of the In1 block is computed based on the current input to the system (lines 18–21), and the output of Out1 is computed (lines 22–25) based on the output of Delay2 computed earlier. Finally, the memory of Delay2 is updated (lines 32–42).

Each code section generated for a block needs to be annotated with pre/post-conditions (in the example, only post-conditions are used) derived from its BLOCKLIBRARY specification. These are the *ensures* annotations surrounding each block code. These annotations are currently generated and inserted into the code using the ACG and the white box approach. Whereas in the black box approach they would be generated directly from the BLOCKLIBRARY toolset and woven into the code using the weaver plugin that relies just on the traceability annotations provided by the ACG.

While these annotations make the core for the semantic verification of the generated code, some additional annotations are required in order to ensure that the generated code is embedded in a suitable environment: these annotations specify properties like memory independence of the data structures (the **separated** annotations) and correct instantiation of the previously described data structures (the **valid** annotations). These annotations make explicit the implementation choices made by the ACG for the generated code. The annotated code in Listing 1.3 is verified automatically using the FRAMA-C toolset and the ALT-ERGO[8] and SPASS[9] SMT solvers in a few seconds.

```
     /*@ requires \valid(_state_->Delay2_memory+(0..1)); */
     void system_init(t_system_state *_state_) {
        /*   START Block: <SequentialBlock: name=Delay2>  */
        /*@ ensures _state_->Delay2_memory[0] == 2;
 5          ensures _state_->Delay2_memory[1] == 3;*/
        { _state_->Delay2_memory[0] = 2;
          _state_->Delay2_memory[1] = 3;}
        /*   END Block: <SequentialBlock: name=Delay2>  */
     }
10   /*@ requires \separated(_state_->Delay2_memory , _io_);
          requires \valid(_io_);
          requires \valid(_state_->Delay2_memory+(0..1)); */
     void system_compute(t_system_io *_io_, t_system_state *_state_) {
        /*   START Block: <SequentialBlock: name=Delay2>  */
15      /*@  ensures system_Delay2 == _state_->Delay2_memory[0]; */
        system_Delay2 = _state_->Delay2_memory[0];
        /*   END Block: <SequentialBlock: name=Delay2>  */
        /*   START Block: <SourceBlock: name=In1>  */
        /*@  ensures system_In1 == _io_->In1; */
20      system_In1 = _io_->In1;
        /*   END Block: <SourceBlock: name=In1>  */
        /*   START Block: <SinkBlock: name=Out1>  */
        /*@  ensures _io_->Out1 == system_Delay2; */
        _io_->Out1 = system_Delay2;
25      /*   END Block: <SinkBlock: name=Out1>  *//
        /*   START Block memory write: <SequentialBlock: name=Delay2>  */
        /*@ ensures append: _state_->Delay2_memory[1] == system_In1;
          ensures sublist: \forall integer i; 0 <= i < 1 ==>
             _state_->Delay2_memory[i] ==
30           \old(_state_->Delay2_memory[i+1]);
        */
        {/*@ loop invariant \forall integer i; 0 <= i < iter ==>
              _state_->Delay2_memory[i] ==
              \at(_state_->Delay2_memory[i+1],LoopEntry);
35        loop invariant 0 <= iter < 2;
          loop assigns iter, _state_->Delay2_memory[0];
          loop variant 1 - iter; */
        for (int iter = 0; iter < 1; iter++){
          _state_->Delay2_memory[iter] = _state_->Delay2_memory[iter+1];
40      }
        _state_->Delay2_memory[1] = system_In1;}
        /*   END Block memory write: <SequentialBlock: name=Delay2>  */
     }
```

Listing 1.3. Annotated code for a small subsystem containing the *IntegerDelay* block

[8] http://alt-ergo.ocamlpro.com/.
[9] http://www.spass-prover.org/.

5   Related Work

Our work relies on translation validation as introduced by Pnueli [15]. This technique has suffered in its early years from scalability issues as the verification was mostly done using model checking. This has improved with the use of modern automated provers (SMT) and proof assistants. However, for complex blocks handling complex data types, it still seems mandatory to rely on intermediate annotations to avoid relying on proof assistants too often.

Recent examples of translation validation are found in the work of Ryabtsev et al. [16] for the verification of the code generated from SIMULINK models and [12] for the proof of preservation of clock related properties on generated code. The BLOCKLIBRARY language allows for a simple specification of the blocks semantics and its formal verification that was a missing point in Ryabtsev approach. Our approach differs as we do not interpret the generated code in order to compare its semantics to the one of the input model, but we rather rely on code verification tools to check that the generated code complies with the input model semantics specified as code annotations.

O'Halloran [13] reports on the successful use of the CLAWZ system for translation validation from a subset of SIMULINK to ADA independently from any concrete ACG. This work relies on a SIMULINK formalization effort using the Z notation performed over many years. The author reports that, in the last versions, the translation validation can be performed fully automatically using the PROOFPOWER toolset which is a significant achievement. The Z notation is a very general formalism that requires a sophisticated methodology to reach fully automated proofs. Our BLOCKLIBRARY DSL is designed to model only block families. Thus, it permits meta-level analysis such as the completeness and consistency of specifications or automated generation of validation tests. Inspection and testing techniques for the verification of implementations could have been preformed also using a formal specification language such as SOFL CDFD [10], but the specification of the blocks variability would suffer from the same limitations.

Our proposal can also be related to proof-carrying code by Necula and Lee [11] as the generated code contains annotations required to verify safety properties. But, in their setting the purpose of the carried proof was to ensure the correctness of the executed code dynamically and to replay the proof during execution. We do not have such need in our work as the correctness proof can be performed once and for all prior to the compilation of the generated C code.

A similar approach was proposed by Pires et al. in [14] for the verification of hand-written code. The system specification is written using the UML and OCL languages. The implementation is hand written as the models are not low level enough to generate the whole software. The generated annotations are not sufficiently low level either to ensure the automatic verification of the user code and the user may need to provide intermediate annotations and conduct the proof. We believe and partly experimented that relying on formally verified specification such as provided by the BLOCKLIBRARY language is providing a higher level of automation and thus eases the verification task.

6   Conclusion and Future Work

To summarize, we have advocted the advantages brought by the formal specification of an existing complex language such as SIMULINK. We designed the BLOCK-LIBRARY DSL for capturing the specific complex features of block libraries and have shown how to use that for verifying the correctness of generated code in a formal translation validation style approach. The verification technique has been demonstrated here on a simple block, but the *white box* strategy has been experimented on a representative subset of the SIMULINK blocks selected by the industrial partners of the GENEAUTO project.

In the close future, we plan to prototype the *black box* annotation generation process including the generation of loop annotations to simplify writing specifications of complex blocks. The BLOCKLIBRARY specification language will be used as a source for the automatic generation of a reliable set of test cases for the verification of the ACG implementation. The test cases will be used for both simulation and code generation. The results will then be compared for the verification and validation of the ACG. Another application direction is using the block-level annotations in conjunction with top-level formal contracts expressed for the entire system to aid proving the functional correctness of the latter. Our current experiments have been performed mainly using the GENEAUTO ACG. We are currently extending the whole work and, among other things, are adapting it for the industrial *DO-330* conformant qualification process of the QGEN ACG that is a successor of GENEAUTO.

Acknowledgements. This work has been funded by the French and Estonian Ministries of Research, Industry and Defense through the PROJET-P (http://www.open-do.org/projects/p/), HI-MOCO (http://www.adacore.com/press/project-p-and-hi-moco/) and VORACE (http://projects.laas.fr/vorace/) projects and through the Estonian Ministry of Education and Research institutional research grant no. IUT33-13. The authors wish to thank the members of these, the QGEN project and the anonymous reviewers of this paper for providing valuable feedback for improving the work.

References

1. ANSI/ISO C Specification Language (ACSL). http://frama-c.com/acsl.html
2. Bobot, F., Filliâtre, J.C., Marché, C., Paskevich, A.: Why3: shepherd your herd of provers. In: Boogie 2011: First International Workshop on Intermediate Verification Languages, Wrocław, Poland, pp. 53–64, August 2011
3. Dieumegard, A., Toom, A., Pantel, M.: Model-based formal specification of a DSL library for a qualified code generator. In: Proceedings of the 12th Workshop on OCL and Textual Modelling, pp. 61–62. ACM, New York (2012)
4. Dieumegard, A., Toom, A., Pantel, M.: A software product line approach for semantic specification of block libraries in dataflow languages. In: Gnesi, S., Fantechi, A., Heymans, P., Rubin, J., Czarnecki, K. (eds.) 18th International Software Product Line Conference, SPLC 2014, Florence, Italy, 15–19 September 2014, pp. 217–226. ACM (2014). http://doi.acm.org/10.1145/2648511.2648534

5. Filliâtre, J.C., Pereira, M.: A modular way to reason about iteration. In: 8th NASA Formal Methods Symposium, Minneapolis, United States, June 2016. https://hal.inria.fr/hal-01281759

6. Furia, C.A., Meyer, B.: Inferring loop invariants using postconditions. In: Blass, A., Dershowitz, N., Reisig, W. (eds.) Fields of Logic and Computation. LNCS, vol. 6300, pp. 277–300. Springer, Heidelberg (2010)

7. Izerrouken, N., Pantel, M., Thirioux, X.: Machine-checked sequencer for critical embedded code generator. In: Breitman, K., Cavalcanti, A. (eds.) ICFEM 2009. LNCS, vol. 5885, pp. 521–540. Springer, Heidelberg (2009)

8. Kang, K.C., Cohen, S.G., Hess, J.A., Novak, W.E., Peterson, A.S.: Feature-oriented domain analysis (FODA) feasibility study. Technical report, Carnegie-Mellon University Software Engineering Institute, November 1990

9. Lee, E., Messerschmitt, D.: Static scheduling of synchronous data flow programs for digital signal processing. IEEE Trans. Comput. $C-36$(1), 24–35 (1987)

10. Liu, S., Offutt, A.J., Ho-Stuart, C., Sun, Y., Ohba, M.: SOFL: a formal engineering methodology for industrial applications. IEEE Trans. Softw. Eng. 24(1), 24–45 (1998)

11. Necula, G.C., Lee, P.: Safe kernel extensions without run-time checking. SIGOPS Oper. Syst. Rev. 30, 229–244 (1996)

12. Ngo, V., Talpin, J.P., Gautier, T., Le Guernic, P., Besnard, L.: Formal verification of synchronous data-flow program transformations toward certified compilers. Front. Comput. Sci. 7(5), 598–616 (2013). doi:10.1007/s11704-013-3910-8

13. O'Halloran, C.: Automated verification of code automatically generated from Simulink. Autom. Softw. Eng. 20(2), 237–264 (2013). doi:10.1007/s10515-012-0116-5

14. Pires, A.F., Polacsek, T., Wiels, V., Duprat, S.: Behavioural verification in embedded software, from model to source code. In: Moreira, A., Schätz, B., Gray, J., Vallecillo, A., Clarke, P. (eds.) MODELS 2013. LNCS, vol. 8107, pp. 320–335. Springer, Heidelberg (2013)

15. Pnueli, A., Siegel, M.D., Singerman, E.: Translation validation. In: Steffen, B. (ed.) TACAS 1998. LNCS, vol. 1384, pp. 151–166. Springer, Heidelberg (1998)

16. Ryabtsev, M., Strichman, O.: Translation validation: from simulink to C. In: Bouajjani, A., Maler, O. (eds.) CAV 2009. LNCS, vol. 5643, pp. 696–701. Springer, Heidelberg (2009)

17. Toom, A., Naks, T., Pantel, M., Gandriau, M., Wati, I.: Gene-Auto - an automatic code generator for a safe subset of Simulink-stateflow and scicos. In: ERTS, p. (electronic medium). Société des Ingénieurs de l'Automobile (2008). http://www.sia.fr

18. Wang, T.E., Ashari, A.E., Jobredeaux, R.J., Feron, E.M.: Credible autocoding of fault detection observers. In: 2014 American Control Conference, pp. 672–677, June 2014

19. Wiik, J., Boström, P.: Contract-based verification of MATLAB-style matrix programs. Formal Aspects Comput. 28(1), 79–107 (2016). doi:10.1007/s00165-015-0353-z

A Model-Based Framework for the Specification and Analysis of Hierarchical Scheduling Systems

Mounir Chadli[1], Jin Hyun Kim[1], Axel Legay[1], Louis-Marie Traonouez[1(✉)],
Stefan Naujokat[2], Bernhard Steffen[2], and Kim Guldstrand Larsen[3]

[1] Inria Rennes, Rennes, France
{mounir.chadli,jin-hyun.kim,axel.legay,louis-marie.traonouez}@inria.fr
[2] Technische Universität Dortmund, Dortmund, Germany
{stefan.naujokat,steffen}@cs.tu-dortmund.de
[3] Aalborg University, Aalborg, Denmark
kgl@cs.aau.dk

Abstract. Over the years, schedulability of Cyber-Physical Systems (CPS) has mainly been performed by analytical methods. Those techniques are known to be effective but limited to a few classes of scheduling policies. In a series of recent work, we have shown that schedulability analysis of CPS could be performed with a model-based approach and extensions of verification tools such as UPPAAL. One of our main contribution has been to show that such models are flexible enough to embed various types of scheduling policies that go beyond those in the scope of analytical tools. In this paper, we go one step further and show how our formalism can be extended to account for stochastic information, such as sporadic tasks whose attributes depend on the hardware domain.

1 Introduction

Cyber-Physical Systems (CPS) are software-implemented control systems that control physical objects in the real world. These systems are being increasingly used in many critical systems, such as avionics and automotive systems. They are now integrated into high performance platforms, with shared resources. This motivates the development of efficient design and verification methodologies to assess the correctness of CPS. Among the panoply of existing techniques to respond to these challenges, one distinguishes between those that rely on an analytic approach, using tools like CARTS [10], from those that rely on formal models and tools such as UPPAAL [2], or SpaceEx [8].

In this paper, we mainly focus on schedulability for CPS. Over the years, schedulability has mostly been performed by analytical methods [12]. Those techniques are known to be effective but limited to specific classes of scheduling policies and systems. In a series of recent work, we have shown that schedulability analysis of CPS could be performed with a model-based approach and extension of verification tools such as UPPAAL. One of our main contribution has been to show that such models are flexible enough to embed various types of scheduling policies that go beyond those in the scope of analytical tools. In addition, we

© Springer International Publishing AG 2016
M.H. ter Beek et al. (Eds.): FMICS-AVoCS 2016, LNCS 9933, pp. 133–141, 2016.
DOI: 10.1007/978-3-319-45943-1_9

proposed a hierarchical approach that allows us to reduce the complexity of this computation [3,4]. This approach is well-suited to perform worst-case analysis of scheduling systems, and even average performance analysis via a stochastic extension of timed automata. This extension allows us to make hypothesis about time at which tasks are scheduled. However, high-performance hardware architectures, as well as advanced software architectures, have more unpredictable behaviors. This makes the verification of these real-time systems much harder, in particular the schedulability analysis, that is essential to evaluate the safety and reliability of mission-critical systems. For this reason, designers are still reluctant to use lower-price hardware components with higher capabilities, such as multi-core processors, for these mission-critical systems.

In this paper, we propose a stochastic extension of our scheduling framework that allows us to capture tasks whose real-time attributes, such as deadline, execution time or period, are also characterized by probability distributions. This is particularly useful to describe mixed-critical systems and make assumptions on the hardware domain. These systems combine hard real-time periodic tasks, with soft real-time sporadic tasks. Classical scheduling techniques can only reason about worst-case analysis of these systems, and therefore always return pessimistic results. Using tasks with stochastic period we can better quantify the occurrence of theses tasks. Similarly, using stochastic deadlines we can relax timing requirements. Finally stochastic execution times model the variation of the computation time needed by the tasks. These distributions can be sampled from executions or simulations of the system, or set as requirements from the specifications. For instance in avionics, display components will have lower criticality. They can include sporadic tasks generated by users requests. Average user demand will be efficiently modelled with a probability distribution. Timing executions may vary due to the content being display and can be measured from the system. This formal verification framework is embedded in a graphical high-level modeling tool developed with the CINCO meta tooling suite [9]. It is available at http://cinco.scce.info/applications/.

2   Background

Given a set of clocks C, a function $v : C \to \mathbb{R}_{\geq 0}$ is called a *clock valuation*. A stopwatch is a vector $s : C \to \{0,1\}$ that distinguishes between a set of running clocks and a set of frozen clocks. For a delay $d \in \mathbb{R}_{\geq 0}$ and a stopwatch s, let $v + s \cdot d$ denotes the clock valuation assignment that maps all $x \in C$ to $v(x) + s(x) \cdot d$. A *clock constraint* on C is a finite conjunction of expressions of the form $x \sim k$ where $x \in C$, $\sim \in \{<, \leq, >, \geq\}$, and $k \in \mathbb{N}$. Let B(C) denote the set of all clock constraints on C. A clock valuation v satisfies the clock constraint $g \in \mathcal{B}(C)$, written $v \vDash g$, *iff* g holds after all the clocks in g have been replaced by their value $v(c)$.

A **Stopwatch Automata (SWA)** [6] is a tuple $(L, l_0, \Sigma, C, \to, I, S)$, where L is a finite set of locations, $l_0 \in L$ is the initial location, Σ is an alphabet of actions, C is a finite set of real-time clocks, $\to \subseteq L \times \mathcal{B}(C) \times \Sigma \times 2^C \times L$ is the set of discrete transitions, $I : L \rightarrow \mathcal{B}(C)$ associates an invariant constraint to each location, $S : L \rightarrow \{0,1\}^C$ is the location stopwatch. A state $s = (l, v)$ of a SWA consists in a location l and a clock valuation v.

An execution of the SWA is an alternating sequence of discrete and continuous transitions. Continuous transitions update the clock valuation in a location by the same value $d \in \mathbb{R}_{\geq 0}$ for all running clocks in $S(l)$, provided that $v + S(l) \cdot d \models I(l)$. Discrete transitions switche from one location to another, if there exists a transition $(l, a, g, r, l') \in E$ with $v \models g$, and it resets the clocks in r to 0. We distinguish between internal and communication transitions. There are two types of communication transitions, the input ones (noted with ?) to receive a message and the output ones (noted with !) to send a message. As classical transition systems can do, SWA can be combined in networks of SWA by synchronizing inputs and outputs in a broadcast manner. This means that when a SWA executes one output, all those SWA that can receive it must be synchronized.

In Fig. 1a, we illustrate the concept with an abstract real-time task modeled via SWA. The task execution time is measured by a clock x, that can progress in location Executing (we denote $x' = 1$ the fact that the stopwatch is running) but is stopped in location Ready (denoted $x' = 0$). It starts its execution when receiving the event schedule?. It sends an event done! as soon as the clock x has reached the best case execution time (bcet) and before reaching the worst case execution time (wcet), or goes to location MissingDeadline if the clock exceeds the deadline. Finally it returns to location JobDone for the next execution round. The running task at location Executing can be preempted when receiving the event not_schedule?, in which case it returns to the location Ready.

Probabilistic Timed Automata (PTA) [1] is an extension of SWA that adds discrete probabilities to the transitions. Thus the transition relation is replaced by $\rightarrow \subseteq L \times \mathcal{B}(C) \times \Sigma \times Dist(2^C \times L)$, where $Dist(2^C \times L)$ is a discrete probability distribution over clock reset and next location.

This extension is useful to initialize the parameters of a model with random values e.g., to specify that the period or the deadline of a task depends on some random information. The simple PTA in Fig. 1b allows to select two values for the period of the task: 10 with probability 1/3 and 15 with probability 2/3. In

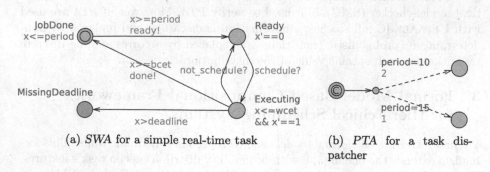

(a) SWA for a simple real-time task

(b) PTA for a task dispatcher

Fig. 1. (Probabilistic) stopwatch automata

what follows, we will call this automaton a *dispatcher*. It is worth mentioning that UPPAAL, the tool we use to model *SWA* and *PTA*, can also model global variables and parameters. Such parameters can be modified either via internal transitions, or via output transitions. In that example the period is a shared variable, initialized by the dispatcher and read by the task. This semantics of *PTA* still exhibits nondeterministic behaviors, because several probabilistic transitions may be enabled at the same time, and the time at which transitions can happen is not randomized. Therefore it can only be used to analyze best case or worst case scenario.

It is however of great interest to analyze scheduling systems with average scenario generated by a fully stochastic semantics. This will allow us to quantify performance analysis. In our early works [5,7], we have proposed a stochastic semantics for networks of priced timed automata, an extension of *SWA*. The stochastic semantics associates probability distributions on both the delays one can spend in a given state, as well as on the transitions between states. In UPPAAL uniform distributions are applied for bounded delays and exponential distributions in the case a component can remain indefinitely in a state. In a network of *PTA* the components repeatedly race against each other, i.e. they independently and stochastically decide on their own how much to delay before outputting, the "winner" being the component that chooses the minimum delay.

Model-checking queries are represented via a subset of the Computational Tree Logic (*CTL*) as defined by the model-checker UPPAAL. More precisely, we consider $\varphi :: = A[]P \mid A<>P \mid E[]P \mid E<>P$. A and E are path operators, meaning respectively "for all paths" and "there exists a path". [] and <> are state operators, meaning respectively "all states of the path" and "there exists a state in the path". P is an atomic proposition that is valid in some state. For example the formula "A[] not error" specifies that in all the paths and all the states on these paths we will never reach a state labelled as an error. For schedulability analysis, an error state is one where a task has missed a deadline.

Statistical model-checking queries require a time bound. The following query for instance "Pr[<=maxTime](<> error)" asks to compute the probability of reaching an error state before maxTime.

UPPAAL model-checker (MC) [2] is used to verify *SWA* and UPPAAL statistical model-checker (SMC) [5] is used to verify *PTA*. Moreover, if *PTA* are used with UPPAAL MC, all stochastic information is discarded and replaced by non-determinism (probabilistic transitions are replaced by a corresponding discrete transition for each specific value of the distribution).

3   Formal Model-Based Compositional Framework for Hierarchical Scheduling Systems

We first introduce the formal model used to represent scheduling units. This formalism extends the one in [3,4] with probability distributions on task's features. Then, we show how formal tools such as UPPAAL MC and UPPAAL SMC can be used to solve queries such as deadlock or schedulability.

3.1   Automata-Based Models for a Scheduling Unit

In our framework, a scheduling unit is composed of a set of real-time tasks, a scheduler, that implements a scheduling algorithm, and a queue, that manages jobs instantiated by tasks. Additionally we provide each scheduling unit with a resource supplier that allocates the resource (CPU time) for a given amount of time. As explained in [11] and illustrated in Sect. 3.2 such a resource supplier can be used to perform scheduling of complex systems in a hierarchical manner.

Tasks and Stochastic Dispatcher: We use two types of tasks: 1. a classical task model as presented in [4], implemented with *SWA*; 2. a new stochastic task model whose real-time attributes (period, delay, execution time) depend on a probability distributions, and are dynamically chosen by a stochastic dispatcher. This stochastic feature is of interest to model the variation of execution time with respect to the computation logics and the capability of the execution environments (CPU, memory, I/O and caches, etc.). Such real values can be obtained by sampling the execution times from the real world system (and this objective is out of scope of this paper). Observe that other task's parameters, such as deadline and period, are determined according to the timing requirements of the functionality implemented by a set of tasks. For instance, some video decoder/encoder would update the deadline and period of tasks according to the frequency of input streams. For those reasons, they can also be represented by probability distributions.

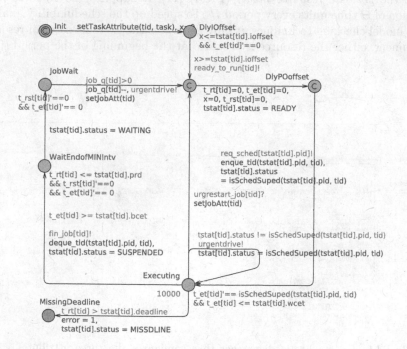

Fig. 2. *SWA* model of a stochastic task

Figure 2 shows the *SWA* for the stochastic task model. From the Init location, a job is initialized with real-time attributes obtained by setTaskAttribute (and assigned by the dispatcher as explained below). This job is queued for execution at location DlyPOoffset. There it requests the scheduler to assign a CPU, which is granted by the synchronisation on the channel req_sched(pid), and reaches location Executing. Its execution can be stopped and resumed according to the availability of the CPU resource. This is implemented by a stopwatch clock t_et[tid]. The clock progresses only when the CPU is available, that is when the function isSchedSuped returns 1. Finally, the job exits from location Executing when it has completed its execution time. This releases the CPU resource using function deque_tid(tstat[tid].pid, tid). The *SWA* waits the end of the minimal inter-arrival time (WaitEndofMINIntv) and then waits for a new job instantiated by the stochastic dispatcher (JobWait).

The stochastic dispatcher, presented in Fig. 3, configures the real-time attributes of the tasks at each individual execution round.

Scheduler: The scheduler *SWA* (Fig. 4) implements the scheduling policy of the scheduling unit. We use two types of scheduling policy: *earliest deadline first* (EDF) and *fixed priority* (FP). These schedulers synchronize with the task model on the channel req_sched.

Resource Supplier: The resource supplier is responsible for supplying a scheduling unit with the resource allocated from another scheduling unit. We adopt the *periodic resource model* (PRM) [11]. It supplies the resource for a duration of Θ time units every period Π. To speed up the schedulability analysis using model checking techniques, it only generates the extreme cases of resource assignment: either the resource is provided at the beginning of the period (from

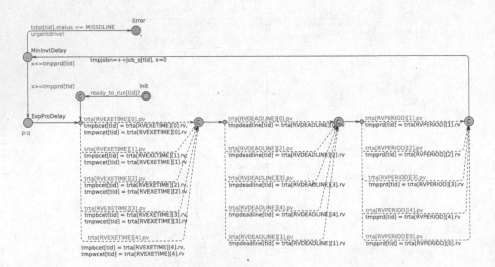

Fig. 3. *PTA* of a stochastic dispatcher that configures the three attributes with a probabilistic choice between five values.

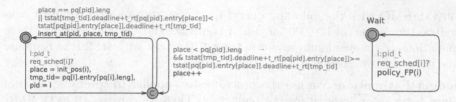

Fig. 4. EDF (left) and FP (right) schedulers

0 to Θ) or at the very end (from $\Pi - \Theta$ to Π). The choice between the two assignments is non-deterministic. The PRM automata communicates with the task model through a shared variable isSupply that is set to true during the supply period. We also use the probabilistic supplier model presented in [4]. Instead of using a fixed budget Θ, it uses a range of values specified between an interval. This will allow to perform a parameter sweep with SMC by selecting uniformly a value of the budget and help determining the optimal budget.

3.2   Formal Analysis of Hierarchical Scheduling Systems

A **hierarchical scheduling system (HSS)** is a set of scheduling units organized in a tree structure. It allows to dispatch a common CPU resource to different scheduling units with the help of resource suppliers. As presented in [11], HSSs can be analyzed in a compositional manner by analyzing each scheduling units individually. Below, we present different types of real-time properties in the format of the tool UPPAAL MC and UPPAAL SMC.

Absence of Deadlock: We check that the formal models have been correctly designed, because they cannot reach a deadlock state in which time is blocked and no action is available. We use UPPAAL MC to analyze this query with the following CTL formula A[] not deadlock.

Schedulability: The main objective of analyzing a scheduling unit and an HSS is to determine whether the tasks are schedulable. In our formal models we analyze this property by searching for error states in tasks, that correspond to the tasks missing their deadline. All these error states are identified by a single Boolean variable error, set to true when a task misses a deadline.

The schedulability can be analyzed by UPPAAL SMC using the following probabilistic query: Pr[<=runTime](<> not error). It computes the probability that not error state is found within runTime t.u. This probability must be 1 to assert that the scheduling unit is schedulable. We can also performed the exhaustive analysis of the SWA model with UPPAAL MC. In that case, we use the CTL formula A[] not error.

Maximum Response Time: Performances of the HSS are measured by analyzing the maximum response time of tasks, that is to say the maximum time between a job instantiation and its completion. We measure this property using

UPPAAL SMC with the following query: E[<=100000;1000](max:t_rst[2]). It asks for 1000 simulations of 100'000 t.u. and it computes the average value over these simulations of the maximum response time of the task with ID 2 (the response time of task 2 is measured in the variable t_rst[2]).

Budget Estimation: We use the probabilistic supplier to specify a range of values between an interval for the budget Θ. Then we can use UPPAAL SMC to randomly select a value within this range and check whether the scheduling unit it schedulable with this value. We use the following probabilistic query: Pr[estBudget[1]<=runTime](<>globalTime>=runTime and error). It computes the probability distribution of all the possible budget values that are not schedulable. By looking at the support of this distribution we can determine the minimum budget whose probability is zero, that is the minimum budget necessary to schedule all the tasks of the scheduling unit.

Simulate Queries: Additional parameters of the model can be observe during random simulations with UPPAAL SMC. Results can be displayed in a graph.

References

1. Beauquier, D.: On probabilistic timed automata. Theort. Comput. Sci. **292**(1), 65–84 (2003)
2. Behrmann, G., David, A., Larsen, K.G., Håkansson, J., Pettersson, P., Yi, W., Hendriks, M.: UPPAAL 4.0. In: QEST, pp. 125–126 (2006)
3. Boudjadar, A., David, A., Kim, J.H., Larsen, K.G., Mikučionis, M., Nyman, U., Skou, A.: Hierarchical scheduling framework based on compositional analysis using uppaal. In: Fiadeiro, J.L., Liu, Z., Xue, J. (eds.) FACS 2013. LNCS, vol. 8348, pp. 61–78. Springer, Heidelberg (2014)
4. Boudjadar, A., David, A., Kim, J.H., Larsen, K.G., Mikučionis, M., Nyman, U., Skou, A.: Widening the schedulability of hierarchical scheduling systems. In: Lanese, I., Madelaine, E. (eds.) FACS 2014. LNCS, vol. 8997, pp. 209–227. Springer, Heidelberg (2015)
5. Bulychev, P.E., David, A., Larsen, K.G., Mikucionis, M., Poulsen, D.B., Legay, A., Wang, Z.: UPPAAL-SMC: statistical model checking for priced timed automata. In: QAPL, EPTCS, vol. 85, pp. 1–16 (2012)
6. Cassez, F., Larsen, K.G.: The impressive power of stopwatches. In: Palamidessi, C. (ed.) CONCUR 2000. LNCS, vol. 1877, p. 138. Springer, Heidelberg (2000)
7. David, A., Larsen, K.G., Legay, A., Mikučionis, M., Poulsen, D.B., van Vliet, J., Wang, Z.: Statistical model checking for networks of priced timed automata. In: Fahrenberg, U., Tripakis, S. (eds.) FORMATS 2011. LNCS, vol. 6919, pp. 80–96. Springer, Heidelberg (2011)
8. Frehse, G.: SpaceEx: scalable verification of hybrid systems. In: Gopalakrishnan, G., Qadeer, S. (eds.) CAV 2011. LNCS, vol. 6806, pp. 379–395. Springer, Heidelberg (2011)
9. Naujokat, S., Lybecait, M., Kopetzki, D., Steffen, B.: CINCO: A Simplicity-Driven Approach to Full Generation of Domain-Specific Graphical Modeling Tools (2016, to appear)
10. Phan, L.T.X., Lee, J., Easwaran, A., Ramaswamy, V., Chen, S., Lee, I., Sokolsky, O.: CARTS: a tool for compositional analysis of real-time systems. SIGBED Rev. **8**(1), 62–63 (2011)

11. Shin, I., Lee, I.: Periodic resource model for compositional real-time guarantees. In: RTSS, pp. 2–13. IEEE Computer Society (2003)
12. Shin, I., Lee, I.: Compositional real-time scheduling framework with periodic model. ACM Trans. Embed. Comput. Syst. **7**(3), 1–39 (2008)

Utilising $\mathbb{K}$ Semantics for Collusion Detection in Android Applications

Irina Măriuca Asăvoae[1], Hoang Nga Nguyen[2], Markus Roggenbach[1(✉)], and Siraj Shaikh[2]

[1] Swansea University, Swansea, UK
{I.M.Asavoae,M.Roggenbach}@swansea.ac.uk
[2] Coventry University, Coventry, UK
{Hoang.Nguyen,Siraj.Shaikh}@coventry.ac.uk

Abstract. The Android OS supports multiple communication methods between apps. This opens the possibility to carry out threats in a collaborative fashion, c.f. the Soundcomber example from 2011. In this paper we demonstrate an effective attempt to detect collusion via model-checking a set of apps utilising the $\mathbb{K}$ framework.

1 Introduction

Malware has been a major problem in desktop computing for decades. With the recent trend towards mobile computing, malware is moving rapidly to smart-phone platforms. Smart-phones pose a particular security risk because they hold personal details (accounts, locations, contacts, photos) and have potential capabilities for eavesdropping (with cameras/microphone, wireless connections).

Android is an open source software stack for a wide range of mobile devices. The Android operation system supports multiple communication methods between apps. This opens the possibility to carry out threats in a collaborative fashion, c.f. the Soundcomber example from 2011. Potential threats include information theft, money theft, or service misuse, to name just a few. In recent work, we have discovered app collusion in more than 5000 mobile app installation packages [4].

In this paper we discuss our approach to detect colluding Android apps by model checking based on the $\mathbb{K}$ framework [13] – c.f. Fig. 1. We start with a set of apps in the form of an Application Package File (APK) which accommodates all application code in the Dalvik Executable format DEX, resources, assets and a manifest file. The DEX code in each APK file is disassembled into the Smali format with open source tools. The Smali code of the apps is parsed by the $\mathbb{K}$ tool. Compilation in the $\mathbb{K}$ tool translates the $\mathbb{K}$ representation of the Android apps into a rewrite theory in Maude [7]. Finally, the Maude model checker searches the transition system compiled by the $\mathbb{K}$ tool to provide an answer if the input set of Android apps colludes or not. In the case when collusion is detected, the tool provides a readable counter example trace.

This research has been partially supported by the ACID project.

M.H. ter Beek et al. (Eds.): FMICS-AVoCS 2016, LNCS 9933, pp. 142–149, 2016.
DOI: 10.1007/978-3-319-45943-1_10

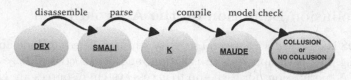

Fig. 1. Work-flow for the Android formal semantics in the $\mathbb{K}$ framework.

Formalising Dalvik Byte-code in $\mathbb{K}$ poses a number of challenges: there are about 220 instructions to be formalised, the codes object oriented, it is register based (in contrast to stack based, as Java Byte-code), it utilises callbacks and intent based communication, see [2]. We provide two different semantics for DEX code, namely a concrete and an abstract one. While the concrete semantics has the benefit to be intuitive and thus easy to be validated, it is the abstract semantics that we employ for app model checking. We see the step from the descriptive level provided by [2] to the concrete, formal semantics as a 'controllable' one, where human intuition is able to bridge the gap. In future work, we intend to justify the step from the concrete semantics to the abstract one by a formal proof. Our implementation of both Android semantics in $\mathbb{K}$ is freely available[1]. The code of the colluding apps discussed in this paper is accessible via an encrypted web-page. The password is available on request[2].

1.1   Related Work

A frontal attack on detecting collusion of pairs, triplets, and larger sets of Android apps is not practical given the search space. Filters to isolate potential app sets which require further examination are discussed in [3].

As detecting malware in single apps is well developed, it suggests itself to tackle collusion by merging apps into a single one [9]. There are also dynamic approaches. For instance, TrustDroid [6] classifies apps into logical domains and forbids app communication between different domains. In contrast, we analyse sets of apps by unfolding their executions while looking for colluding patterns.

Static approaches to detecting collusion are closest to our work. The tool Epicc [11] reduces the collusion detection to an inter procedural data flow problem, where communication is analysed by a subsequent tool, IC3 [10]. The FUSE tool [12] builds a multi-app information flow graph on which collusion can be detected. We propose a similar approach, namely to track (sensitive) information flow and to detect app communication via model checking.

The $\mathbb{K}$ framework was proposed in [13] as a rewrite-based formalism to facilitate design and analysis of programming languages. A number of languages have already been defined in $\mathbb{K}$, including C [8] and Java [5], facilitating their program analysis, e.g., using a Maude back-end. We contribute to the pool of $\mathbb{K}$ defined real languages by giving formal semantics to Android byte code.

---

[1] http://www.cs.swan.ac.uk/~csmarkus/ProcessesAndData/androidsmali-semantics-k.

[2] http://www.cs.swansea.ac.uk/~csmarkus/ProcessesAndData/sites/default/files/uploads/resources/code.zip.

2   A Collusion Definition on the Android Level

Android OS is designed with several security features. These include application sand-boxing, i.e., each app runs in isolation, and access control based on permissions, i.e., permissions for each app to access system resources are granted at installation time. However, Android also offers horizontal app interaction providing inter-app communication via *intents*, and vertical ones by using API calls to access suitable system resources. Such inter-app communication mechanisms can be exploited by app coalitions to carry out attacks which they could not perform on their own which can be seen as a camouflage mechanism. We call this form of security breach *collusion*.

Collusion refers to the ability of a set of apps to produce malware in a collaborative fashion via inter-app communication, c.f. [3]. Such malicious behaviour can be described by a number of actions executed in a certain order where (A) actions are operations provided by Android API such as record audio, access file, write file, send data, etc. (let *Act* denote the set of all actions); (M) a malicious behaviour $m = (A, \leq)$ is a partially ordered set with $A \subseteq Act$ and $\leq$ specifying the execution order; and (C) $Com \subseteq Act$ is a set of actions producing interactions such as intent based communication, e.g., a broadcast intent). Let μ denote the set of all possibly malicious behaviours[3], $Ex((A, \leq))$ denote the set of all possible ways of realising the malicious behaviour $(A, \leq)$, i.e., all possible total extensions of $(A, \leq)$.

Definition 1. *A set S of at least two apps is colluding if there exists some $m \in \mu$ such that the apps in S together execute a sequence $A \in Act^*$ with: (i) there exists a sub-sequence A' of A such that $A' \in Ex(m)$, i.e., together the apps in S realise m; (ii) each app in S executes at least one action in A', i.e., A' is collectively executed involving all apps in S; and (iii) there exists a non-empty sub-sequence C' of A such that $C' \in Com^*$, i.e., some communication is involved (Fig. 2).*

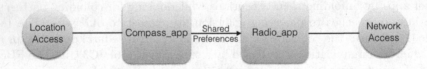

Fig. 2. An example of colluding apps

Example: Consider the two apps `Compass_app` (with only a permission to access the device location) and `Radio_app` (with only a permission to access the network). Obviously, individually none of these two apps poses a threat of publishing location information. However, by forming a coalition using inter-app

---

[3] We refrain to define what malicious behaviour might be and assume that the security community already has classified (sets of) apps to be malware. For example, our industrial partner Intel Security does so on a daily a basis for single apps.

communication, they may produce malware: the Compass_app reads the device location and passes (parts of) this data to the Radio_app, which sends the (part of) this data to a remote, unauthorised server via the internet. Using our collusion definition we can describe the actions performed by these two apps as: $Act_{\text{Compass\_app}} = \{a_{read\_location}\}$ and $Act_{\text{Radio\_app}} = \{a_{send\_file}\}$. The malicious behaviour m is given by $A = \{a_{read\_location}, a_{send\_file}\}$ and by defining $a_{read\_location} \leq a_{send\_file}$. The set of inter-app communications includes $Com = \{send_{shared\_prefs}, recv_{shared\_prefs}\}$.

3   The $\mathbb{K}$ Framework

The $\mathbb{K}$ framework [13] proposes a methodology for the design and analysis of programming languages; the framework comes with a rewriting-based specification language and tool support for parsing, interpreting, model-checking and deductive formal verification. The ideal work-flow in the $\mathbb{K}$ framework starts with a formal and executable language syntax and semantics, given as a $\mathbb{K}$ specification, which then is tested on program examples in order to gain confidence in the language definition. Here, the $\mathbb{K}$ framework offers model checking via compilation into Maude programs (i.e., using the existing reachability tool and LTL Maude model checker).

A $\mathbb{K}$ specification consists of *configurations*, *computations*, and *rules*, using a specialised notation to write semantic entities, i.e., $\mathbb{K}$-cells. For example, the $\mathbb{K}$-cell representing the set of program variables as a mapping from identifiers Id to values Val is given by $\langle Id \mapsto Val \rangle_{\text{vars}}$. Configurations in $\mathbb{K}$ are labelled and nested $\mathbb{K}$-cells, used to represent the structure of the program state. Rules in $\mathbb{K}$ are of two types: computational and structural. Computational rules represent transitions in a program execution and are specified as configuration updates. Structural rules provide internal changes of the program state such that the configuration form can enable the application of computational rules.

4   Concrete Android Semantics

The concrete semantics specifies system configurations, Smali instructions, and a number of Android API calls in $\mathbb{K}$ closely following their explanation as given at [1]. Configurations are defined in $\mathbb{K}$ style as cells which might contains subcells. Top of a concrete configuration is a "sandboxes" cell, containing a "broadcasts" sub-cell abstracting the Android intent broadcast service and possibly multiple "sandbox" cells capturing the states of the installed apps, c.f. Fig. 3. Each sandbox cell simulates the environment in which an application is isolated. It contains the classes of the application, the current instructions left to be run in a "k" cell, the content of the current registers in a "regs" cell and the memory storing the objects that have been instantiated so far. Classes and Method cells can be defined similarly. We categorise Smali instructions into four groups: *invoke/return* includes instructions that call methods and return method results, *control* consists of instructions that might change the value of a program counter

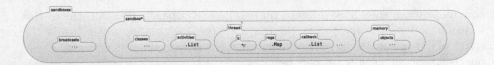

Fig. 3. Android configuration.

non-trivially (such as goto or if-then), *read/write* includes instructions that allow
access and modify objects in memory, and, finally, *arithmetic* is for instructions
that handle arithmetic operations. The semantics of each group is defined in a
separate $\mathbb{K}$ module. Additionally, there are two $\mathbb{K}$ modules, namely *loading* and
starting. The former defines the semantics for constructing the initial configuration. The later specifies the initialisation and running of component objects as
described in the app manifest.

Android API classes and methods come together with Android OS on an
Android device. Hence, they are not included in an app's DEX code. On possibility to deal with APIs would be to obtain their Smali code. However, this
would significantly increase the size of the Smali code to be analysed in $\mathbb{K}$ and,
consequently, increase the state space of the obtained models. Therefore, based
on their description [1], we directly implement the semantics of some of these
classes and methods in $\mathbb{K}$ rules. In particular, we have implemented a number
of APIs, including the modules Location, Intent, Broadcast, and Apache-Http.
Other API classes and methods can be implemented similarly. For those modules
that are not (yet) implemented in $\mathbb{K}$, we provide a mechanism that a call to any
of them returns an unknown result, i.e., the "$\cdot K$" value.

We detect information theft via collusion by annotating any "object" cell
with two additional values: "sensitive" and "created". *Sensitive* is a Boolean
value indicating if the object is sensitive (e.g., device locations, contacts, private
data, etc.). *Created* is a set of app ids that initialise the object. Information theft
collusion is detected when an API method is called that semantically exports
some sensitive object out of the device.

5   Abstract Android Semantics

The abstract semantics takes a far less detailed view on configuration and transitions in order to gain efficiency for model checking whilst maintaining enough
information to detect collusion. The abstract configuration has a cell structure
similar to the concrete configuration except for the memory cell: instead of creating actual objects, in the abstract semantics we just record their information
flow by propagating object types and constants. Structurally, the $\mathbb{K}$ specification
for the abstract semantics is organised in the same way as the concrete one. In
the following we describe the differences that render the abstraction.

In the "read/write" module the abstract semantics neglects the memory-
related details as follows: The abstract semantics for instructions that create
new object instances (e.g., "new-instance *Register*, *Type*") sets the register to

the type of the newly created object (rather than to the reference to the new object as it is done in the concrete semantics). The arithmetic instructions define only a data dependency between the source registers and the destination register. The move instruction, that copies one register into another, sets the contents of the source register into the destination. Similarly, instructions that copy from or into the memory are abstracted into data-dependencies. We exemplify this latest class of instructions with the abstract semantics of the `iget` instruction that, in Smali, copies the value of field F from the object indicated by register $R2$ into register $R1$:

$$\frac{\langle \mathtt{iget}\, R_1{:}Register, R_2{:}Register, F{:}FieldId \ \cdots\rangle_k \ \langle \cdots \ R_1 \mapsto \underset{L}{\_} \quad R_2 \mapsto L{:}K \ \cdots\rangle_{\mathsf{regs}}}{\bullet}$$

As our abstract semantics is field insensitive, the `iget` instruction only stores the information L of type K as present in the register R_2 in register R_1.

The module "invoke/return" contains the most significant differences between abstract and concrete semantics. All "invoke" instructions add information to the data-flow as follows: the object for which the method is invoked is made dependent on the parameters of the invoked method. Similarly, the "move-result" instruction defines data-dependence between the parameters of the latest invoked method and the register to which the result is written. The data-flow abstraction allows us to see an API call just as an instruction that produces a data dependency. Hence, there is no need to treat APIs individually – as it is the case in the concrete semantics.

In the abstract semantics, the rules for branching, i.e., "if-then" instructions, are always considered non-deterministic. The rules for the "goto" instruction check if the goto destination was already traversed in the current execution. If this is the case, the jump to the destination is replaced by a fall through. Consequently, loops are traversed at most once since the data-flow collection only requires one loop traversal.

Detecting collusion with the abstract semantics works as follows: When an API accessing sensitive data is invoked, the data-flow is augmented with a special label *"secret"*. If the "secret" flows into the parameters of a publish invocation of a different app than the one that produces the "secret", we discover a collusion pattern for information theft.

The price paid for the abstract view taken by our abstract semantics that we consider an over-approximation of an app's behaviour. In principle, this could lead to false positives in collusion analysis.

6 Model Checking for Collusion

We demonstrate how collusion is detected using our concrete and our abstract semantics on two Android applications, called `LocSender` and `LocReceiver`. Together, these two apps jointly carry out an "information theft". They consist of about 100 lines of Java code/3000 lines of Smali code each. Originally written to explore if collusion was actually possible (there is no APK of the Soundcomber example), here they serve as a test for our model checking approach.

LocSender obtains the location of the Android device and communicates it using a broadcast intent. LocReceiver constantly waits for such a broadcast. On receiving such message, it extracts the location information and finally sends it to the Internet as an HTTP request. We have two variants of LocReceiver: one contains a while loop pre-processing the HTTP request while the other does not. Additionally, we create two further versions of each LocReceiver variant where collusion is broken by (1) not sending the HTTP request at the end, (2) altering the name of the intent that it waits for – named LocReceiver1 and LocReceiver2, respectively. Furthermore, we (3) create a LocSender1 which sends a non-sensitive piece of information rather than the location. In total, we will have eight experiments where the two firsts have a collusion while the six lasts do not[4]. Figure 4 summarises the experimental results.

App1	App2	Loop	Collusion	Concrete		Abstract	
				Runtime	Detected	Runtime	Detected
LocSender	LocReceiver		✓	55s	✓	30s	✓
LocSender	LocReceiver	✓	✓	time-out		33s	✓
LocSender	LocReceiver1			1m13s		31.984s	
LocSender	LocReceiver1	✓		time-out		34s	
LocSender	LocReceiver2			53s		32s	
LocSender	LocReceiver2	✓		time-out		33s	
LocSender1	LocReceiver			1m11s		32s	
LocSender1	LocReceiver	✓		time-out		34s	

Fig. 4. Experimental result.

Our experiments indicate that our approach works correctly: if there is collusion it is either detected or has a timeout, if there is no collusion then none is detected. In case of detection, we obtain a trace providing evidence of a run leading to information theft. The experiments further demonstrate the need for an abstract semantics, beyond the obvious argument of speed: e.g. in case of a loop where the number of iterations depends on an environmental parameter that can't be determined, the concrete semantics yields a time out, while the abstract semantics still is able to produce a result. Model checking with the abstract semantics is about twice as fast as with the concrete semantics. At least for such small examples, our approach appears to be feasible.

7   Concluding Remarks and Future Work

We have presented two implementations of Android Byte-code semantics within the $\mathbb{K}$ framework, namely a concrete and an abstract one. We demonstrated that

---

[4] All experiments are carried out on a Macbook Pro with an Intel i7 2.2 GHz quad-core processor and 16 GB of memory.

both semantic approaches are – in principle – able to successfully model check for app collusion realising the threat of information theft. Here, naturally the abstract semantics outperforms the concrete one. Though it is still early days, we dare to express the following expectation: we believe that our approach will scale thanks to its powerful built-in abstraction mechanisms.

In future work, we aim to establish a formal simulation relation between the two semantics. By establishing a simulation relation, we can be sure that our abstraction design does not go astray and stays sound. Furthermore, we would like to address further collusion properties, such as money theft or service misuse.

Acknowledgement. The authors would like to thank our colleagues in ACID for the good cooperation in the project, and Erwin R. Catesbeiana Jr. for excellent guidance through the Android ecosystem.

References

1. Android Package Index (2016). http://developer.android.com/reference/packages.html
2. Android Open Source Project. Dalvik Bytecode (2016). https://source.android.com/devices/tech/dalvik/dalvik-bytecode.html
3. Asavoae, I.M., Blasco, J., Chen, T.M., Kalutarage, H.K., Muttik, I., Nguyen, H.N., Roggenbach, M., Shaikh, S.A.: Towards automated Android app collusion detection (2016). CoRR, abs/1603.02308
4. Blasco, J., Chen, T.M., Muttik, I., Roggenbach, M.: Wild android collusions. In: Virus Bulletin (2016, to appear)
5. Bogdănaş, D., Roşu, G.: K-Java: a complete semantics of Java. In: POPL 2015. ACM (2015)
6. Bugiel, S., Davi, L., Dmitrienko, A., Heuser, S., Sadeghi, A.-R., Shastry, B.: Practical and lightweight domain isolation on Android. In: SPSM 2011. ACM (2011)
7. Clavel, M., Durán, F., Eker, S., Lincoln, P., Martí-Oliet, N., Meseguer, J., Talcott, C. (eds.): All About Maude - A High-Performance Logical Framework. LNCS, vol. 4350. Springer, Heidelberg (2007)
8. Hathhorn, C., Ellison, C., Roşu, G.: Defining the undefinedness of c. In: PLDI 2015. ACM (2015)
9. Li, L., Bartel, A., Bissyandé, T.F., Klein, J., Traon, Y.L.: ApkCombiner: combining multiple android apps to support inter-app analysis. In: Federrath, H., Gollmann, D., Chakravarthy, S.R. (eds.) SEC 2015. IFIP AICT, vol. 455, pp. 513–527. Springer, Heidelberg (2015). doi:10.1007/978-3-319-18467-8_34
10. Octeau, D., Luchaup, D., Dering, M., Jha, S., McDaniel, P.: Composite constant propagation: application to android inter-component communication analysis. In: ICSE 2015. IEEE Computer Society (2015)
11. Octeau, D., McDaniel, P., Jha, S., Bartel, A., Bodden, E., Klein, J., Traon, Y.L.: Effective inter-component communication mapping in android: an essential step towards holistic security analysis. In: Security Symposium. USENIX Association (2013)
12. Ravitch, T., Creswick, E.R., Tomb, A., Foltzer, A., Elliott, T., Casburn, L.: Multi-app security analysis with FUSE: statically detecting Android app collusion. In: ACSAC 2014. ACM (2014)
13. Roşu, G., Şerbănuţă, T.F.: An overview of the K semantic framework. J. Log. Algebr. Program. **79**(6), 397–434 (2010)

Unified Simulation, Visualization, and Formal Analysis of Safety-Critical Systems with S#

Axel Habermaier[⊠], Johannes Leupolz, and Wolfgang Reif

Institute for Software and Systems Engineering,
University of Augsburg, Augsburg, Germany
{habermaier,leupolz,reif}@isse.de

Abstract. We give an overview of the S# (pronounced "safety sharp") framework for rigorous, model-based analysis of safety-critical systems. We introduce S#'s expressive modeling language based on the C# programming language, showing how S#'s fault modeling and flexible model composition capabilities can be used to model a case study from the transportation sector with multiple design variants. Fully automated formal safety analyses are conducted for the case study using the explicit-state model checker LTSmin. Analysis efficiency is evaluated in comparison with other safety analysis tools and model checkers.

1 Introduction

Safety-critical systems have the potential to cause hazards, i.e., situations resulting in economical or environmental damage, injuries, or loss of lives [11]. Deductive Cause Consequence Analysis (DCCA) is a model-based safety analysis technique that uses model checking to compute how faults such as component failures or environmental disturbances (the causes) can cause such hazards (the consequences) [7]: From a model of a safety-critical system that not only describes the system's nominal behavior but also the relevant faults, DCCA determines all minimal critical fault sets, that is, combinations of faults that can cause hazards, allowing the evaluation of the system's overall safety.

The S# modeling and analysis framework [6] conducts DCCAs fully automatically for system models authored in the ISO-standardized C# programming language and .NET runtime environment [10,12]. This paper provides an overview of modeling and analyzing safety-critical systems with S#, using a well-known case study from the transportation sector [20]. It discusses the core concepts of S#'s modeling language and the underlying model of computation; particular emphasis is placed on S#'s flexible system-design variant modeling and composition capabilities as well as its support for fault modeling. Additionally, this paper introduces S#'s unified model execution approach based on an integration of the explicit-state model checker LTSmin [13] into S#: Instead of model transformations typically employed by safety analysis tools such as VECS, Compass, and AltaRica [3,17,18], S# unifies simulations, model-based tests, visualizations, and fully exhaustive model checking by executing the models with consistent semantics regardless of whether a simulation is run or some formula is model

© Springer International Publishing AG 2016
M.H. ter Beek et al. (Eds.): FMICS-AVoCS 2016, LNCS 9933, pp. 150–167, 2016.
DOI: 10.1007/978-3-319-45943-1_11

checked. S#'s explicit-state model checking and safety analysis efficiency is evaluated using the case study, comparing it with the analysis times of hand-written models for the explicit-state model checker SPIN as well as the symbolic model checker NuSMV [5,9]. The safety analysis tools VECS and Compass [17,18] are also briefly compared with S#.

S# and its usage documentation are available at http://safetysharp.isse.de. The S#, SPIN, and NuSMV models of the case study are also available there, including an interactive, S#-based visualization for replays of model checking counter examples.

2 Case Study: Height Control System

Figure 1 shows a schematic overview of the height control system of the Elbe Tunnel in Hamburg which raises alarms and closes the tunnel when it detects overheight vehicles trying to enter the old tube, risking collisions with the tunnel's ceiling. Overall, the height control consists of five sensors: Two light barriers lb_1 and lb_2 as well as three overhead detectors od_r, od_l, and od_f; the sensors are grouped into the pre, main, and end control. The light barriers span the entire width of both lanes, whereas each overhead detector is positioned hovering above only one of the lanes. Consequently, the light barriers can only report that an overheight vehicle passes by, but cannot determine the lane they drive on; it is physically impossible to install the light barriers in a way that would allow this distinction. The overhead detectors, on the other hand, can in fact distinguish between the lanes, but they cannot differentiate between overheight vehicles and regular, non-overheight ones; they are, however, not triggered by passenger cars. By contrast, the light barriers are positioned high enough to ensure that they are only triggered by passing overheight vehicles. The height control therefore has to combine the data of both types of sensors to determine the positions of overheight vehicles in the observed area.

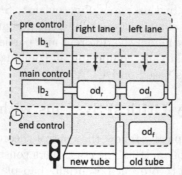

Fig. 1. A schematic overview of the case study: there are two lanes entering and exiting the two tunnel tubes at the bottom, with the arrows indicating the driving direction; overheight vehicles are only allowed to enter the new tube on the right lane. The height control consists of a pre, main, and end control that use light barriers and overhead detectors to monitor approaching vehicles.

Height Control Mechanism. When no overheight vehicles approach the tunnel, only the pre control is active, that is, the sensors of the main and end controls are deactivated. When lb_1 detects an overheight vehicle, the main control is activated, enabling its sensors and starting its timer. Additionally, a counter is increased that counts the number of overheight vehicles assumed to be between the pre and main control. The main control is deactivated when a vehicle is reported by lb_2 and od_r or od_l and the counter reaches zero, or the main control's timer times out. If the main control discovers an overheight vehicle driving on the left lane, the tunnel is closed immediately. Otherwise, the end control is activated, enabling its sensor and starting its timer. When the end control does not detect a high or overheight vehicle before its timer runs out, it is deactivated; otherwise, the tunnel is closed. Due to the road layout, vehicles cannot switch lanes after passing od_f.

Faults & Hazards. Two failure modes are considered for each sensor: Misdetections and false detections. Misdetections are false negatives, that is, omission faults preventing a sensor from reporting a vehicle passing by that it should detect. False detections, by contrast, are false positives, i.e., a sensor detects something that is not a vehicle, but, say, a bird. There are two antagonistic hazards: On the one hand, the height control system is designed to prevent collisions by closing the tunnel whenever an overheight vehicle is about to enter the wrong tube. On the other hand, false alarms should be prevented, as unnecessary closures cause traffic jams and economical losses. The system design is intended to strike an acceptable balance that minimizes both hazards as far as reasonable.

Design Variants. Previous analyses revealed that collisions and false alarms can happen without any sensor fault occurrences [20]. Design alternatives that add additional sensors or remove the main control's counter to reduce false alarms were proposed to fix the problem, necessitating additional safety analyses to check for newly introduced safety issues. Prior work [20] discusses the design variants in greater detail, with each analyzed variant requiring manual changes to a copy of the model. In this paper, by contrast, S#'s support for variant modeling and automated composition of different design variants can be leveraged to more conveniently model the different and partially orthogonal variants in a modular way, automatically composing all combinations together for fully automated safety analyses based on DCCA.

3   Modeling Safety-Critical Systems with S#

Safety-critical systems typically follow the control-theoretical system partitioning into plants and controllers [16]: The controllers constantly and continuously interact with their plants to prevent potentially bad plant behavior that might result in hazards. A controller internally has an implicit or explicit model of its plant, using sensors to predict and actuators to affect the plant's state and future behavior. Discrepancies can emerge between the controller's perceived plant state and the plant's actual state: Due to faults such as component failures or environmental disturbances, sensors can provide incorrect data or actuators can have unintended effects on the plant. Subsequently, the controller is likely to mispredict the plant's future behavior, omitting control actions or unknowingly issuing destructive actions that potentially result in hazards. Models of safety-critical systems must contain both plants and controllers in order to adequately represent such control failures for formal safety analyses. In the case study, for instance, the vehicles constitute the plants with the hazards of collisions and false alarms specified over the vehicles' positions as well as tunnel closures; false alarms are control failures that the height control is unaware of, making it necessary to model the vehicles: The hazard of false alarms can only be adequately expressed over the state of the vehicles as the height control is completely unaware of its control failure; had it known that no overheight vehicles are on the left lane, it would not have closed the tunnel in the first place.

The case study model is iteratively decomposed into less complex subcomponents to increase modularity and composability, also enabling variant modeling; Fig. 2(a) gives an overview using SysML block definition diagrams [19].

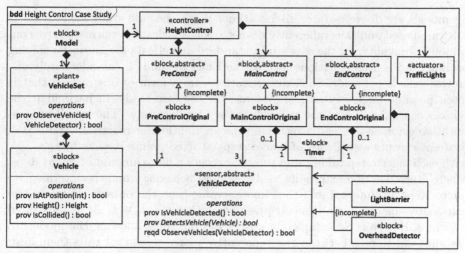

(a) A partial block definition diagram of the case study showing some of the blocks' ports and operations. The model consists of the plant, i.e., a set of vehicles, and the actual height control system. The latter is subdivided into three subcontrollers which are abstract to support variant modeling. Only the blocks for the original controller designs are shown for reasons of brevity.

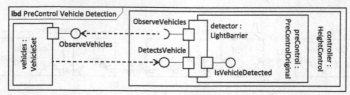

(b) A partial internal block diagram showing the connection of the preControl's detector to the vehicles. While the ObserveVehicles ports are connected, the VehicleSet directly calls the DetectsVehicle port on the VehicleDetector instance passed to ObserveVehicles as shown in Listing 1.

Fig. 2. A partial overview of the case study's structure and composition using SysML notation.

The leaves of the hierarchy represent components for which further decomposition is not required: Either the components are modeled in sufficient detail for implementation in hardware or software, or they are standard off-the-shelf components such as light barriers that can be bought from third-party vendors and incorporated into the final system. Dependencies between a component and its parent, siblings, or subcomponents are broken up with behavioral encapsulation: Components expose provided and required ports that allow component interactions but hide actual component implementations. For the case study, the vehicle detectors are abstracted away behind a common VehicleDetector block to increase modularity and the PreControl, MainControl, and EndControl abstract blocks are introduced in order to facilitate variant modeling. The SysML internal block diagram in Fig. 2(b) illustrates the interdependencies between the vehicles and the preControl.

3.1 Model of Computation

S# models are discrete-state, discrete-time. While the case study's controller is software-based and thus inherently discrete, the vehicles, by contrast, move continuously in reality; for the case study, standard numerical procedures for solving ordinary differential equations such as the Euler method [4] can adequately discretize vehicle behavior. Such discretizations are a form of abstraction that is often possible for safety-critical systems; for the case study, in particular, the sensors can only observe the vehicles at very few locations. The model of computation embraces the zero execution time assumption for reactive systems [15]: Systems execute a sequence of macro steps at fixed points in time $t_0, t_1, t_2, \ldots$, with each macro step taking zero time to execute a finite amount of micro steps. Macro steps describe externally visible system behavior while the intermediate micro steps are internal and thus unobservable from the outside. Between two consecutive macro steps, time Δt passes such that $t_i = t_0 + i \cdot \Delta t$ as illustrated by Fig. 3. However, S# completely abstracts from time, allowing the models to assume a Δt to pass between two consecutive marco steps that suits them best.

S#'s model of computation implicitly considers two separate components synchronously concurrent when their actions have no effect on each other within the same macro step, like the vehicles in the case study; as asynchronous concurrency can be modeled explicitly, neither modeling flexibility nor adequacy is limited.

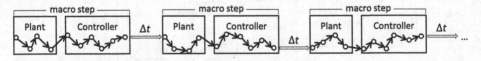

Fig. 3. Each macro step is not only subdivided into a finite sequence of micro steps, it also separates plant behavior from controller behavior, with the plant behavior always executed first. The controller's last micro step ends the macro step, causing time to pass and a new macro step to begin; no time passes between the plant and controller parts of a macro step.

Algorithm 1. Macro Step Execution in Two Phases

---

function MACROSTEP(plants : Component[*], controllers : Component[*])
    for p **in** plants **do** SIGNAL(p, Update) **end for**
    for c **in** controllers **do** SIGNAL(c, Update) **end for**
end function

As illustrated by Fig. 3, however, macro steps linearize plant and controller execution, conceptually allowing the controllers to immediately react to changes in their plants' states: During a macro step at time t_n, the plants change their state in zero time through a sequence of micro steps. Within the same macro step, the controllers observe these changes through their sensors, compute the appropriate control actions, and update their actuators, all in zero time as well through multiple micro steps. Subsequently, the macro step ends and a new macro step begins at time t_{n+1} in which the plants are influenced by the control actions from the previous step. Sensors therefore observe the most recent plant states within a macro step, whereas actuator effects are delayed to the next step. Algorithm 1 conceptually illustrates macro step execution, sending Update signals to all components; Update signals trigger a component's autonomous macro step behavior, if it has any.

3.2   The S# Modeling Language

S# provides a domain specific modeling language embedded into the C# programming language and the .NET runtime environment [10,12]. While S# models are *represented* as C# programs, they are still models of the safety-critical systems to be analyzed; for the case study, for instance, the vehicles are part of the model even though they are not software-based in the real world. Even the software parts of S# models such as the preControl of Fig. 2(b) are not intended to be used as the actual implementations; these are typically done in C or C++ for reasons of efficiency. Additionally, the S# models are typically abstractions of the real controller software to make model checking-based safety analysis feasible. Thus, S# is best regarded as an executable, text-based extended subset of SysML, though there currently is not automatic conversion between the two.

S# inherits C#'s language features and expressiveness and can use third-party .NET libraries and tools, in particular during model composition and initialization. However, some restrictions apply during simulations and model checking: No heap allocations are allowed, for instance, and the only source of nondeterminism can be S#'s own Choose function; threads, in particular, are unsupported. S# components are represented by C# classes, instances of which correspond to S# component instances. Listing 1 declares the abstract VehicleDetector component from Fig. 2(a) as a class derived from S#'s Component base class. All of its methods are considered to be either required or provided ports; required ports are marked as extern and have no implementation. Class inheritance, interfaces, generics, lambda functions, etc. are fully supported; for example, `LightBarrier` derives from `VehicleDetector`, overriding the abstract provided port `DetectsVehicle` as necessary using C#'s shorthand syntax `=>` for simple expression-returning methods. The hierarchical system structure is established by defining fields that are of a `Component`-derived type; in Listing 1, for instance, the `VehicleSet` component has multiple subcomponents of type `Vehicle` because of the `_vs` array field.

```
enum Lane { Left, Right }     enum Height { Regular, High, Over }
abstract class VehicleDetector : Component {
    public Fault Misdetection = new TransientFault();
    public Fault FalseDetection = new TransientFault();

    public virtual bool IsVehicleDetected() => ObserveVehicles(this);
    public abstract bool DetectsVehicle(Vehicle vehicle);
    public extern bool ObserveVehicles(VehicleDetector detector);

    [FaultEffect(Fault = nameof(Misdetection))]
    abstract class MisdetectionEffect : VehicleDetector {
        public override bool IsVehicleDetected() => false;
    }

    [FaultEffect(Fault = nameof(FalseDetection))]
    abstract class FalseDetectionEffect : VehicleDetector {
        public override bool IsVehicleDetected() => true;
    }
}
class LightBarrier : VehicleDetector {
    int _pos;
    public LightBarrier(int pos) { _pos = pos; }
    public override bool DetectsVehicle(Vehicle v) =>
        v.Height == Height.Over && v.IsAtPosition(_pos);
}
class VehicleSet : Component { // other members omitted due to space
        restrictions
    Vehicle[] _vs;
    public bool ObserveVehicles(VehicleDetector d) =>
        _vs.Any(d.DetectsVehicle);
}
class Vehicle : Component { // other members omitted due to space
        restrictions
    int _pos; int _speed; Lane _lane; const int StepTime = 1;

    public extern bool IsTunnelClosed();
    public bool IsAtPosition(int pos)
        => _pos - _speed * StepTime <= pos && _pos > pos;
    public bool IsCollided() => Height() == Height.Over && _pos >=
        Model.TunnelPosition && _lane == Lane.Left;
    protected virtual Lane ChooseLane() => Lane.Right;
    protected virtual int ChooseSpeed() => MaxSpeed;

    public override void Update() {
        if (IsTunnelClosed()) return;
        if (_pos < Model.EndControlPosition) _lane = ChooseLane();
        _speed = ChooseSpeed(); _pos += _speed * StepTime;
    }

    [FaultEffect] public class DriveLeft : Vehicle {
        protected override Lane ChooseLane() => Choose(Lane.Right, Lane.Left);
    }

    [FaultEffect] public class SlowTraffic : Vehicle {
        protected override int ChooseSpeed() => ChooseFromRange(MinSpeed,
            MaxSpeed);
    }
}
```

Listing 1. Parts of the S# model for Fig. 2(a); the remaining parts of the model are omitted for reasons of brevity but are available online. The abstract `VehicleDetector` base type declares two provided ports **IsVehicleDetected** and **DetectsVehicle**. The former simply passes the detector instance to the required port **ObserveVehicles** that is connected to the **ObserveVehicles** provided port of a **VehicleSet** instance (cf. Listing 2 and Fig. 2(b)). The **VehicleSet** uses .NET's standard **Any** function to invoke the given detector's DetectsVehicle port for each Vehicle instance in _vs.LightBarriers, for instance, detect such a Vehicle if it is overheight and passes the light barrier's position; the position the detector is installed at is specified via the component's constructor. The Vehicle's IsAtPosition provided port hides the effects of positional discretization, because of which the vehicles might never reach a detector's exact position. Vehicles, by default, drive on the right lane with their maximum speed (see also Listing 2); different Vehicle instances conceptually execute their discretized movement behavior concurrently as they have no interdependencies. The IsCollided port is used to check for collision hazards.

To instantiate a S# model, the appropriate component instances must be created, their initial states and subcomponents must be set, and their required and provided ports must be connected. All C# language features and .NET libraries can be used to compose model instances; S#'s limitations for heap allocations, etc. only apply during simulations and model checking. The case study uses reflection to automatically instantiate all design variants of the model as shown in Listing 2; alternatively, valid model configurations could also be read from a database, for instance. A total of 16 different design alternatives result from the four main control variants and the two variants of the pre and end controls each; of these 16 variants, four are not analyzed in detail as their main controls ignore the improved detection capabilities of their pre controls, which makes them unrealistic. While the model supports an arbitrary amount of vehicles, their number has to remain constant during model checking, i.e., a model instance cannot create or remove vehicles while it is analyzed. Therefore, a fixed amount of Vehicle instances must be created and initialized during model composition. By default, model instances contain two overheight vehicles and one high vehicle which turned out to be sufficient to find all minimal critical fault sets for the analyzed hazards.

```
IEnumerable<Model> CreateVariants() {
    var preControls = GetVariants<PreControl>();
    var mainControls = GetVariants<MainControl>();
    var endControls = GetVariants<EndControl>();
    return from preControl in preControls
           from mainControl in mainControls
           from endControl in endControls
           where IsRealisticCombination(preControl, mainControl, endControl)
           select new Model(preControl, mainControl, endControl);
}

IEnumerable<Type> GetVariants<T>() => from type in
        typeof(T).Assembly.GetTypes()
    where type.IsSubclassOf(typeof(T)) && !type.IsAbstract select type;

void BindDetectors(VehicleSet s, VehicleDetector[] ds) {
    foreach(var d in ds) Bind(nameof(s.ObserveVehicles),
        nameof(d.ObserveVehicles));
}

void VehicleFaults(VehicleSet s, Fault leftOHV, Fault leftHV, Fault
        slowTraffic) {
    leftOHV.AddEffects<Vehicle.DriveLeft>(s.Where(v => v.Height() ==
        Height.Over));
    leftHV.AddEffects<Vehicle.DriveLeft>(s.Where(v => v.Height() ==
        Height.High));
    slowTraffic.AddEffects<Vehicle.SlowTraffic>(s);
}
```

Listing 2. Partial overview of model initialization; the full code is available online: The CreateVariants method instantiates all 12 realistic design variants of the case study using reflection and C#'s language integrated query functionality, filtering out unrealistic variants using the `IsRealisticCombination` method (not shown). `BindDetectors` sets up the connections between the vehicles and the detectors as illustrated by Fig. 2(b). `VehicleFaults` programmatically adds the two `Vehicle` fault effects for slow-moving and left-driving vehicles to three faults using S#'s `AddEffects` method and .NET's array filter method `Where` in combination with some C# lambda functions: When either `leftOHV` or `leftHV` is activated, overheight or high vehicles are allowed to drive on the left lane, respectively. `slowTraffic` allows all vehicles to drive slower than assumed during system design.

3.3   Fault Modeling

Safety analyses consider situations in which faults cause system behavior that would not occur otherwise. Fault behavior must therefore be part of the analyzed models as illustrated by the `Misdetection` and `FalseDetection` faults in Listing 1, for example. In accordance with common terminology [2], faults are activated when they somehow affect and influence actual system behavior. They are dormant until they are activated and become active, turning dormant again when they are deactivated. A fault's persistence constrains the transitions between its active and dormant states. Transient faults, for instance, are activated and deactivated completely nondeterministically, whereas permanent faults, while also activated nondeterministically, never become dormant again. In the case study, all faults are modeled with transient persistency.

Fault activations trigger effects, represented by the nested classes `MisdetectionEffect`, `FalseDetectionEffect`, `DriveLeft`, and `SlowTraffic` in Listing 1, which cause errors or failures, i.e., internal or externally observable deviations of the components' behaviors from what they should have been, respectively. Faults therefore affect the internal state of a component or the behavior of one or more of its ports. The two fault effects of the `VehicleDetector` component, for instance, immediately result in component failures whenever their corresponding faults are activated. Failures either provoke faults in other components or they represent system hazards; S# deduces such propagations automatically using DCCA.

False detections of the `VehicleDetector` component in Listing 1 cause the detector to incorrectly report the presence of a `Vehicle`: The field `FalseDetection` of type `Fault` is initialized with a `TransientFault` instance, activating and deactivating the fault completely nondeterministically. The fault's local effect on the component is modeled by adding the nested class `FalseDetectionEffect` that is marked with the `FaultEffect` attribute to link the effect to the fault. The effect overrides the original behavior of the `IsVehicleDetected` provided port; when the fault is activated, the port always returns `true`, regardless of the actual `Vehicle` positions. The port's original implementation is invoked only when the fault is dormant; if both the false detection and misdetection faults of a detector are activated simultaneously, S# chooses one of the fault effects nondeterministically.

As high or overheight vehicles on the left lane violate traffic laws and slow-moving vehicles violate basic design assumptions about traffic flow that influences the choice for the durations of the timers, left- and slow-driving vehicles are modeled using faults. To demonstrate S#'s flexibility in fault modeling, these faults affect multiple `Vehicle` instances: It is generally irrelevant which over-height vehicles drives on the left, hence there is only one single fault, `leftOHV` in Listing 2, whose activation allows all overheight vehicles to switch lanes. For false alarms, it is important to differentiate between high and overheight vehicles on the left lane, however, hence there is also a `leftHV` fault; `slowTraffic`, by contrast, can affect all kinds of vehicles. Due to the use of S#'s nondeterministic `Choose` function in `DriveLeft` and `SlowTraffic`, each `Vehicle` instance decides independently whether it is actually affected by a fault activation.

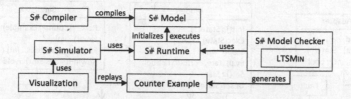

Fig. 4. Illustration of S#'s execution-centric architecture: The runtime initializes S# models compiled by a slightly extended version of the C# compiler to ensure the desired S# semantics of required ports and faults. Both the simulator and the model checker use the runtime to execute a model. The only difference between simulation and model checking is that the latter is exhaustive, checking all combinations of nondeterministic choices within a model whereas the former considers a single combination only. Counter examples generated by the model checker can be replayed by the simulator for debugging purposes. Model visualizations build upon the simulator.

4 Analyzing Safety-Critical Systems with S#

S# unifies LTSmin-based, fully exhaustive, explicit-state model checking and non-exhaustive simulations as shown in Fig. 4: In both cases, the S# runtime executes a model compiled with the S# compiler, ensuring the correct execution semantics of faults and required ports. During model checking, all combinations of nondeterministic choices and fault activations within a model are exhaustively enumerated. S# is not a software model checker such as Java Pathfinder or Zing [1,22], however, as it does not analyze states after every instruction; only state changes between macro steps are considered.

4.1 Execution Semantics of S# Models

The `Model` class shown in Fig. 5 captures S#'s model execution semantics. It consists of a hierarchy of `Component` instances, each having fields that form the component's state. Fields are allowed to be of most .NET types, including arrays, delegates, object references, and classes comprised of any of these like `List<T>`; e.g., the state of a `Vehicle` instance from Listing 1 consists of `_pos`, `_speed`, and `_lane`. For efficient storage and comparison, `Component` states are serialized and deserialized to and from fixed-sized byte arrays, represented by the State class. The set of State instances has to be finite, therefore object creation and other forms of heap allocations during model checking and simulation are unsupported; during model initialization, on the other hand, no such restrictions exist. The method Model::Ser stores Component states in a State instance, whereas Model::Deser does exactly the opposite. S# generates these two methods dynamically at runtime via reflection, tailoring them to a specific Model instance to guarantee maximum efficiency with respect to serialization time and state storage size.

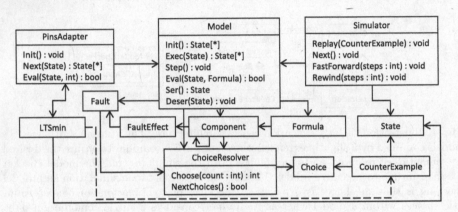

Fig. 5. A UML class diagram showing the classes required to simulate and model check S# models. The Model class is responsible for Formula evaluation and model execution with the intended S# semantics; in particular, it uses a ChoiceResolver instance to determine all combinations of nondeterministic choices and fault activations. Therefore, the Simulator class and LTSmin are decoupled from Model execution semantics, only requiring them to take care of State management.

The method Model::Init generates all initial states of a Model instance while Model::Exec computes all successors of a state as shown by Algorithm 2: For all combinations of nondeterministic choices and fault activations determined by ChoiceResolver::NextChoices, the given state is deserialized using Model::Deser so that Model::Step can allow all Component instances to compute their successor states, which are subsequently serialized using Model::Ser and then returned. Model::Step is conceptually equivalent to Algorithm 1. The Formula class represents state formulas that evaluate arbitrary Boolean C# expressions over Component instances. The evaluation is expected to be terminating, deterministic, and side effect free; otherwise the exact behavior is unspecified. Model::Eval evaluates a Formula instance for a given serialized state.

The only allowed source of nondeterminism within a Model are Fault instances and invocations of ChoiceResolver::Choose; the latter records the number of choices that can be made at a specific point during the execution of Model::Step and returns the index of the chosen value. Other sources of nondeterminism,

Algorithm 2. Model::Exec (s : State) : State[*]

---

var successors : State[*] = []
while choiceResolver.NextChoices() **do** Deser(s); Step(); successors += Ser() **end**
while
return successors

---

such as race conditions of threads, are not captured by S#; S# does not analyze the code it executes for illegal nondeterminism. There are two reasons why a state might not have any successors at all: Either Model::Step does not terminate or its execution is aborted abnormally due to an unhandled exception, for example. Both cases indicate bugs in the model or in the S# runtime that are readily discoverable.

4.2 Model Checking S# Models

LTSmin allows S# to execute a Model using Model::Exec during model checking. In order to enable the integration of various modeling languages into LTSmin, the so-called PINS interface written in C [13] is provided that S# makes use of. S#'s integration of LTSmin takes about 250 lines of C++/CLI code, a Microsoft-specific variant of C++ that integrates into the .NET framework, allowing for easy interoperability between C/C++ and C#. The PinsAdapter class maps LTSmin's C-based PINS interface to the C# interface of the Model class: PinsAdapter::Init initializes and sets up LtsMin, which in turn repeatedly calls PinsAdapter::Next to compute all successors of a serialized state using Model::Exec. PinsAdapter::Eval prompts S# to evaluate a Formula instance identified by its index for some serialized state by calling Model::Eval.

For a S# model m : Model, a Kripke structure K is generated on-the-fly such that $K = (\text{m.Formula}, \text{State}, R, L, \text{m.Init}())$ where $R = \{(\sigma, \sigma') \mid \sigma' \in \text{m.Exec}(\sigma)\}$ and $L(\sigma) = \{f \in \text{m.Formula} \mid \text{m.Eval}(\sigma, f)\}$. If there are no bugs that cause the S# model to get stuck in an infinite loop or to throw an unhandled exception, exploration of the Kripke structure terminates as soon as all reachable states are encountered. S# models always generate Kripke structures without any deadlock states, consequently all paths through the Kripke structure are of infinite length. It is the responsibility of LTSmin to do the actual model checking, that is, to check whether an LTL formula or an invariant is satisfied by an induced Kripke structure. In the case study, for example, the LTL formula checking whether there either is no tunnel closure or no collisions occur before the tunnel is closed is specified as

```
G(!model.TunnelClosed()) ||
    U(model.Vehicles.All(v => !v.IsCollided()), model.TunnelClosed())
```

in S#; the formula obviously does not hold as faults are indeed able to cause situations in which collisions occur before any tunnel closures. The two operands of the LTL until operator used above are two C# expressions that are represented by two Formula instances and evaluated during model checking; similarly, the operand of the globally operator is also such a Formula instance. Both LTL operators and their disjunction are also converted into Formula instances that are subsequently transformed for interpretation by LTSmin which in turn invokes the contained C# expressions at the appropriate times. If LTSmin detects a violation of the Formula instance that is checked, it generates a CounterExample that consists of a sequence of State instances, which are trivial to deserialize back into sequences of Component states using Model::Deser. For later replay, a CounterExample also captures the nondeterministic choices that the ChoiceResolver made during the generation of the CounterExample, which also include fault activations.

4.3   Simulating S# Models

Simulations of S# models work similar to model checking except that only a single path of the induced Kripke structure is explored. Simulator instances are either guided or unguided: Unguided simulations do not follow a predetermined path through the Kripke structure, whereas guided ones are used to replay the CounterExample instance passed to Simulator::Replay by forcing the nondeterministic choices made by the model checker upon the simulator. Consequently, counter examples cannot only be stepped through state by state, but also allow debugging each transition, giving insights into why and how some possibly undesired successor state is reached from some source state. A simulation stores all computed states, allowing it to be fast forwarded or rewound by some number of steps using Simulator::FastForward and Simulator::Rewind. In contrast to Algorithm 2, Simulator::Next computes only one successor of the current state using the sequence of method calls Model::Deser, Model::Step, and Model::Ser based on a set of predetermined choices. Both simulation-based model tests as shown in Listing 3 as well as visualizations can be implemented on top of the Simulator class. In the interactive visualization of the case study, for instance, the user can spawn high and overheight vehicles and change their speed and lanes using the mouse or touch; visual replays of counter examples help to understand the situations in which hazards occur.

```
var model = new Model(new PreControlOriginal(), new MainControlOriginal(),
    new EndControlOriginal());
SuppressAllFaultActivations(model);
new Simulator(model).FastForward(steps: 20);
foreach (var vehicle in model.Vehicles)
    Assert.IsFalse(vehicle.IsCollided());
```

Listing 3. A model test based on a S# simulation of the case study's original design with all faults suppressed by the helper method `SuppressAllFaultActivations` (not shown), i.e., dormant the entire time. The test asserts that after the first 20 simulated steps, no vehicles collide with the tunnel, as all vehicles drive on the right lane without any fault activations.

4.4   Evaluation of S# Model Checking Efficiency

Many safety analysis tools such as VECS, the Compass toolset, or AltaRica [3,17,18] rely on the standard approach of model transformations to use model checkers like SPIN or NuSMV [5,9]. By contrast, S# unifies simulations, visualizations, and fully exhaustive model checking by executing the C# models with consistent semantics regardless of whether a simulation is run or some formula is model checked with LTSmin. Consequently, no model transformations are necessary, avoiding significant implementation complexity while retaining competitive model checking efficiency. S# only has to execute C# code instead of understanding and transforming it, supporting most C# language features without any additional work; transformations, by contrast, would require large parts of the .NET virtual machine to be encoded for model checking or to forgo many higher level C# features such as virtual dispatch or lambda functions.

The two main challenges of S#'s LTSmin integration were efficient state serialization and efficient handling of nondeterminism. The algorithm that allows ChoiceResolver to handle and track all combinations of nondeterministic choices, however, turned out to require only around 40 lines of C# code. Generating low overhead serialization methods, by contrast, is more involved, taking about 700 lines of C# code to generate the appropriate serialization methods at runtime. For the case study, serialization causes only around 5 % of overhead during entire model checking. The serialized states are smaller than the state vectors of a hand-optimized SPIN model of the height control, taking only 12 instead of 24 bytes per state. Another S# case study, the hemodialysis machine, has 71 variables but only requires 112 bytes per state.

In the worst case of valid formulas, S# and LTSmin have to enumerate the model's entire state space, taking 68.8 seconds for the case study's 950,249 states and 40,197,857 transitions. SPIN, by contrast, takes 553 seconds to check a hand-optimized, non-modular version of the model that semantically corresponds to the S# version. On a quad-core CPU, LTSmin achieves a speedup of 3.7x, bringing the analysis time down to 18.6 seconds whereas SPIN scales by a factor of 1.5x only. One reason for S#'s superior performance are automatic symmetry reductions [8] that allow S# to ignore irrelevant fault activations more efficiently than SPIN, causing it to compute less transitions while still finding all reachable states. These symmetry reductions enable S# to provide smaller models to LTSmin for model checking, increasing model checking efficiency noticeably; however, they can only be partially encoded into SPIN models, for full support, changes to SPIN would be required. For the case study, symbolic analysis with NuSMV, on the other hand, is faster than using S#: For a hand-written, very low-level and non-modular NuSMV model that is approximately equivalent to the S# model, the entire state space is generated almost instantly. However, some other S# case studies are more efficiently checked by S# or SPIN than by NuSMV, so the relative efficiency of explicit-state and symbolic model checking is case study-specific and independent from S#; in general, highly nondeterministic models seem to profit more from symbolic techniques.

S# models have a much higher level of expressiveness than either SPIN or NuSMV models, allowing variant modeling and analysis in a way that is not supported by either model checker directly. Additionally, S#'s explicit support for fault modeling guarantees conservative extension [7], i.e., faults only add or suppress system behavior when they are activated but cannot do so while they are dormant, which is important for adequate modeling and safety analyses. SPIN, NuSMV, or Zing, by contrast, cannot give this guarantee at a language level. While S# is more efficient than SPIN due to its fault optimizations, the increase in analysis time compared to NuSMV seems acceptable given the step-up in modeling flexibility, expressiveness, and fault modeling adequacy.

4.5 Safety Analysis of the Height Control Case Study

S# automatically conducts DCCAs to compute all minimal critical fault sets for a hazard H given as a Formula instance, i.e., an arbitrary C# expression that is interpreted as a propositional logic formula over the induced Kripke structure K: For faults F contained in K, S# individually checks all combinations of faults $\Gamma \subseteq F$, determining whether Γ does or does not have the potential to cause an occurrence of H [7]. Γ is a critical fault set for H if and only if there is the possibility that H occurs and before that, at most the faults in Γ have occurred. More formally, using LTL: $\Gamma \subseteq F$ is safe for H if and only if $K \models \neg(only_F(\Gamma)\mathbf{U}H)$, where $only_F(\Gamma) :\Leftrightarrow \bigwedge_{f \in F \setminus \Gamma} \neg f$. A fault set is critical if and only if it is not safe. A critical fault set Γ is minimal if no proper subset $\Gamma' \subsetneq \Gamma$ is critical; a complete DCCA computes all such minimal critical fault sets. For any critical fault set Γ, any superset $\Gamma' \supseteq \Gamma$ is also critical because, in general, additional fault activations cannot be expected to improve safety. The criticality property's monotonicity with respect to set inclusion [7] trivially holds regardless of the actual model as the LTL formula above does not require any critical faults $f \in \Gamma$ to be activated; instead, it only suppresses the activations all other faults $f \in F \setminus \Gamma$. In practice, monotonicity often allows for significant reductions in the number of checks required to find all minimal critical fault sets; otherwise, all subsets of F would have to be checked for criticality. As seen in Listing 4, S# automatically takes advantage of monotonicity, significantly reducing the amount of fault sets that have to be checked for criticality; in particular for the hazard of false alarms, only 3 % of all possible sets have to be analyzed for criticality. In the worst case, however, DCCA does indeed have exponential complexity.

```
DCCA Results: Collisions (866 seconds)
Minimal Critical Sets (4453 fault sets had to be checked; 54
    (1) { leftOHV, slowTraffic }
    (2) { leftOHV, misdetectionLB2 }
    (3) { leftOHV, misdetectionLB1 }
    (4) { leftOHV, misdetectionODF, misdetectionODL }
    (5) { leftOHV, falseDetectionLB2, falseDetectionODR, misdetectionODF }

DCCA Results: False Alarms (44.5 seconds)
Minimal Critical Sets (261 fault sets had to be checked; 3
    (1) { leftHV }
    (2) { falseDetectionODF }
    (3) { falseDetectionODL }
    (4) { falseDetectionLB2 }
    (5) { misdetectionODR }
```

Listing 4. Overview of the DCCA results for both hazards using the case study's original design. S# automatically analyzes a total of 13 faults; exploiting the monotonicity of the criticality property is especially effective for the hazard of false alarms, significantly reducing analysis times.

Listing 4 shows the DCCA results for the original case study design; for collisions, specified in S# as `m.Vehicles.Any(v => v.IsCollided())` for a Model instance `m`, at least one overheight vehicle must drive on the left lane, hence the `leftOHV` fault of Listing 2 is contained in all minimal critical fault sets. For instance, the fault set {`leftOHV`, `slowTraffic`} is critical for collisions because two overheight vehicles can pass the pre control's light barrier simultaneously while one is faster than the other: The faster vehicle deactivates the main control, and the slower vehicle can pass the end control when it is already deactivated again. {`leftHV`} is minimal critical for false alarms, specified as `m.HeightControl.IsTunnelClosed() && m.Vehicles.All(v => v.DrivesRight())`, because of a high vehicle passing the main control's left overhead detector when an overheight vehicle passes the main control's light barrier at the same time. Safety analysis times for some design variants are significantly higher than the ones in Listing 4 due to the larger number of faults that have to be checked. S# therefore allows incomplete analyses up to a maximum fault set cardinality; for fault sets containing at most three faults, safety analyses of all 12 valid design variants take around 400 seconds for false alarms and 852 seconds for collisions.

5   Conclusion and Future Work

S# provides an expressive C#-based modeling language for safety-critical systems and conducts fully automated DCCAs over these models to determine the minimal critical fault sets for all hazards. S#'s model execution approach not only has competitive analysis efficiency but also unifies model simulation and model checking to guarantee semantic consistency. The safety analysis results of the case study match those from previous analyses [20]; the main improvements over them lie in S#'s modular modeling language and flexible model composition capabilities based on C# and .NET that no longer require manual work for composing multiple modeled design variants. Additionally, S#'s unified model execution approach not only generates and checks the required DCCA formulas fully automatically, but also allows for interactive visualizations and visual replays of model checking counter examples based on the same underlying S# model.

S# has a competitive edge over other approaches for safety modeling and analysis like Compass or VECS [17, 18] by tightly integrating the development, debugging, and simulation of models with their formal analysis. Our findings, however, are solely based on our own experience with other modeling languages and other case studies analyzed with S#. For example, the railroad crossing case study available online in the S# repository is faster to check with S# than with NuSMV or VECS, the latter of which is a small abstraction over NuSMV. In general, however, fair comparisons between these tools and S# are hard to achieve due to their different models of computation. For instance, it took us about 740 lines to create a scaled down Compass version of the railroad crossing model that is semantically similar to the S# version written in 400 lines of C#

code. Compass performs a safety analysis that is equivalent to DCCA in 21 min using NuSMV instead of the 1.9 seconds it takes S# to do the same. Of course, the comparison is unfair as forcing Compass semantics onto S# might likewise slow down analyses.

S#'s model execution approach opens up new possibilities in the context of runtime safety analysis of self-organizing systems [6] that are simply not possible or at least harder to achieve with transformation-based or symbolic analysis approaches: We plan to use the systems' actual reconfiguration mechanisms based on constraint solving during safety analyses, requiring the integration of constraint solvers into the model checking process [6]. Additional ideas for future work include analysis efficiency improvements based on automated abstraction of plant behavior by using the controller's sensors as abstraction functions as well as combined analysis of entire families of design variants [21]. Moreover, we are already working on supporting probabilistic hazard analysis, allowing S# to compute the occurrence probabilities of hazards with the help of the MRMC model checker [14]. Preliminary results are promising, benefiting from S#'s and LTSmin's efficient state space enumeration capabilities.

References

1. Andrews, T., Qadeer, S., Rajamani, S.K., Rehof, J., Xie, Y.: Zing: a model checker for concurrent software. In: Alur, R., Peled, D.A. (eds.) CAV 2004. LNCS, vol. 3114, pp. 484–487. Springer, Heidelberg (2004)
2. Avižienis, A., Laprie, J.C., Randell, B., Landwehr, C.: Basic concepts and taxonomy of dependable and secure computing. Dependable Secure Comput. 1(1), 11–33 (2004)
3. Batteux, M., Prosvirnova, T., Rauzy, A., Kloul, L.: The AltaRica 3.0 project for model-based safety assessment. In: Industrial Informatics, pp. 741–746. IEEE (2013)
4. Butcher, J.: The Numerical Analysis of Ordinary Differential Equations: Runge-Kutta and General Linear Methods, 2nd edn. Wiley, Hoboken (2003)
5. Cimatti, A., Clarke, E., Giunchiglia, E., Giunchiglia, F., Pistore, M., Roveri, M., Sebastiani, R., Tacchella, A.: NuSMV 2: an opensource tool for symbolic model checking. In: Brinksma, E., Larsen, K.G. (eds.) CAV 2002. LNCS, vol. 2404, pp. 359–364. Springer, Heidelberg (2002)
6. Habermaier, A., Eberhardinger, B., Seebach, H., Leupolz, J., Reif, W.: Runtime model-based safety analysis of self-organizing systems with S#. In: Self-Adaptive and Self-Organizing Systems Workshops, pp. 128–133 (2015)
7. Habermaier, A., Güdemann, M., Ortmeier, F., Reif, W., Schellhorn, G.: The ForMoSA approach to qualitative and quantitative model-based safety analysis. In: Railway Safety, Reliability, and Security, pp. 65–114. IGI Global (2012)
8. Habermaier, A., Knapp, A., Leupolz, J., Reif, W.: Fault-aware modeling and specification for efficient formal safety analysis. In: ter Beek, M., Gnesi, S., Knapp, A. (eds.) FMICS-AVoCS 2016. LNCS, vol. 9933, pp. 97–114. Springer, Heidelberg (2016)
9. Holzmann, G.: The SPIN Model Checker. Addison-Wesley, Boston (2004)
10. ISO: ISO/IEC 23270: Information technology– Programming languages–C# (2006)
11. ISO: ISO 24765: Systems and software engineering - Vocabulary (2010)

12. ISO: ISO/IEC 23271: Information technology - Common Language Infrastructure (2012)

13. Kant, G., Laarman, A., Meijer, J., van de Pol, J., Blom, S., van Dijk, T.: LTSmin: high-performance language-independent model checking. In: Baier, C., Tinelli, C. (eds.) TACAS 2015. LNCS, vol. 9035, pp. 692–707. Springer, Heidelberg (2015)

14. Katoen, J.P., Zapreev, I., Hahn, E., Hermanns, H., Jansen, D.: The Ins and outs of the probabilistic model checker MRMC. Perform. Eval. **68**(2), 90–104 (2011)

15. Kirsch, C., Sengupta, R.: The evolution of real-time programming. In: Kirsch, C., Sengupta, R. (eds.) Handbook of Real-Time and Embedded Systems. CRC Press (2007)

16. Leveson, N.: Engineering a Safer World. MIT Press, Cambridge (2011)

17. Lipaczewski, M., Struck, S., Ortmeier, F.: Using tool-supported model based safety analysis - progress and experiences in SAML development. In: High-Assurance Systems Engineering, pp. 159–166. IEEE (2012)

18. Noll, T.: Safety, dependability and performance analysis of aerospace systems. In: Artho, C., Ölveczky, P.C. (eds.) FTSCS 2014. CCIS, vol. 476, pp. 17–31. Springer, Heidelberg (2015)

19. Object Management Group: OMG Systems Modeling Language, Version 1.4 (2015)

20. Ortmeier, F., Schellhorn, G., Thums, A., Reif, W., Hering, B., Trappschuh, H.: Safety analysis of the height control system for the Elbtunnel. In: Anderson, S., Bologna, S., Felici, M. (eds.) SAFECOMP 2002. LNCS, vol. 2434, pp. 296–308. Springer, Heidelberg (2002)

21. Thüm, T., Apel, S., Kästner, C., Schaefer, I., Saake, G.: A classification and survey of analysis strategies for software product lines. ACM Comput. Surv. **47**(1), 6: 1–6: 45 (2014)

22. Visser, W., Havelund, K., Brat, G., Park, S., Lerda, F.: Model checking programs. Autom. Softw. Eng. **10**(2), 203–232 (2003)

Applications and Case Studies

Formal Verification of a Rover
Anti-collision System

Ning Ge[1]([⊠]), Eric Jenn[1], Nicolas Breton[2], and Yoann Fonteneau[2]

[1] IRT Saint-Exupéry, Toulouse, France
{ning.ge,eric.jenn}@irt-saintexupery.com
[2] Systerel, Toulouse, France
{nicolas.breton,yoann.fonteneau}@systerel.fr

Abstract. In this paper, we integrate inductive proof, bounded model checking, test case generation and equivalence proof techniques to verify an embedded system. This approach is implemented using the Systerel Smart Solver (S3) toolset. It is applied to verify properties at system, software, and code levels. The verification process is illustrated on an anti-collision system (ARP for Automatic Rover Protection) implemented on-board a rover. Focus is placed on the verification of safety and functional properties and the proof of equivalence between the design model and the generated code.

Keywords: SAT · Safety critical system · S3 · Bounded model checking · Inductive proof · Equivalence proof · Test case generation

1 Introduction

Even though significant progress has been made towards the integration of formal methods in the industry of safety critical systems, their usability is still impaired by their cost. Nevertheless, the hope is that once the initial integration is done, subsequent verifications can be achieved at significantly lower costs. In this paper, we show how this could be achieved using a formal verification toolset, Systerel Smart Solver (S3)[1], and draw some lessons from our experience.

S3 [8] is built around a synchronous language and a model checker (S3-core) based on SAT [4] techniques. As the proof engine, S3-core relies on Bounded Model Checking (BMC) [3] and k-induction [6,16] techniques. S3 supports different activities of a software development process: property proof, equivalence proof, automatic test case generation, simulation, and provides necessary elements to comply with the software certification processes. It can be applied on designs expressed in SCADE [7]/Lustre [11] (including floating-point arithmetic) and implementations coded in C and Ada, and has been used for the formal verification of railway signaling systems for years by various industrial companies in this field.

N. Ge — Seconded from Systerel, Toulouse, France
E. Jenn — Seconded from Thales Avionics, Toulouse, France.
[1] S3 is maintained, developed and distributed by Systerel (http://www.systerel.fr/).

M.H. ter Beek et al. (Eds.): FMICS-AVoCS 2016, LNCS 9933, pp. 171–188, 2016.
DOI: 10.1007/978-3-319-45943-1_12

In this work, we apply S3 on an anti-collision system (ARP for Automatic Rover Protection) that is deployed on a three-wheeled rover. Focus is placed on three main activities: (1) Formal specification of the critical functional and safety requirements, (2) Verification of expected properties using appropriate formal techniques, (3) Proof of the equivalence between the design model and the generated code. An additional purpose is to make the ARP use case publicly available to the research community.

This paper is organized as follows: Sect. 2 presents the S3 toolset; Sect. 3 describes the ARP use case; Sect. 4 exposes the verification of safety and functional properties using inductive proof, BMC, and test cases generation techniques; Sect. 5 illustrates the process of equivalence proof for the verification of the generated code; Sect. 6 draws some lessons from the verification activities, and Sect. 7 gives some concluding remarks and discusses perspectives.

2   The S3 Toolset

S3 is composed of the following main elements:

– A synchronous declarative language similar to the Lustre language [11], called HLL (High Level Language) that is used to model the system, its environment constraints as well as its properties. As an example, Fig. 1 presents an HLL model that calculates the population count (popcount) of an input boolean table of size N. The boolean elements of the input table are constrained to be conjunctively true. The function counter() is defined as the algorithm of popcount. Finally, the proof obligation clause expresses one expected property on the result.

```
Constants:    int N := 10;
Inputs:       bool in[N];
Constraints: SOME i: [0, N-1] (in[i]);
Declarations:
 int unsigned 10 counter(int);
 int unsigned 10 cnt_num;
Definitions:
 counter(i)   := if i == -1 then 0
                 else if in[i] then counter(i-1)+1 else counter(i-1);
 cnt_num      := counter(N-1);
Outputs:      cnt_num;
Proof Obligations: cnt_num <= N & cnt_num >= 1;
```

Fig. 1. Example of HLL Model

– Several translators to convert models or code (Scade, Lustre, C and Ada) to HLL models.
– An expander to translate HLL models into a bit level language, called LLL (Low Level Language) that only contains boolean streams and is restricted to three bitwise operators: negation, implication and equivalence.

- A SAT-based proof engine, named S3-core, to check LLL models.
- Tools to build equivalence proof between models, or between models and code.
- Tools to animate and debug models.

S3 supports the following activities of a typical development process:

- **Static detection of runtime errors and standard conformance check**, including array bounds check, range check, division by zero check, over and underflow check, output and constraint initialization check, etc. Proof obligations are also generated to ensure that the generated HLL models show no undefined behavior with respect to the semantics of the source language.
- **Property Proof:** Figure 2 presents the workflow of property proof. The design model, e.g. Lustre, is translated into an HLL model. Combined with properties expressed in HLL as well, it is then expanded to a LLL model that is fed to the S3-core. If a property is falsifiable, a generated counterexample can be simulated at the HLL level. This activity will be detailed in Sect. 4.

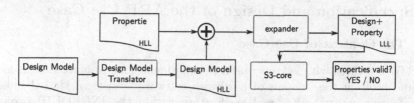

Fig. 2. Process of Property Proof

- **Equivalence Proof:** Figure 3 presents the process of proving the equivalence between the design model, e.g. Lustre, and the generated/implemented code, e.g. C code. Models and code are translated into HLL models. The HLL models are then expanded to LLL models using diversified expanders[2]. Equivalence models are respectively constructed at the HLL level and the LLL level. Equivalence proof is performed on one of the equivalence models or both. This activity will be detailed in Sect. 5.
- **Test Case Generation:** Test scenarios are generated from properties expressed as test goals using BMC. This activity will be detailed in Sect. 4.3.

The architecture of S3 facilitates the construction of formal verification solutions compliant with certification standards, e.g. DO178C [10]. Towards this goal, S3 is organized in a set of small, independent components, from which the most critical ones - an equivalence model constructor, and a tool to verify the validity of the proof - are developed according to the highest integrity levels. The performance of the proof engine allows users to manage the proof of industrial size problems: the size of those models routinely attains ten millions variables

---

[2] The diversified expanders are designed and implemented by different teams using different programming languages.

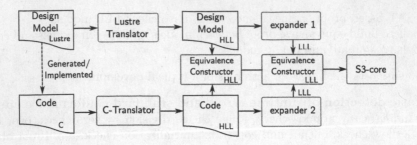

Fig. 3. Process of Equivalence Proof

and several hundred millions clauses. Verification of designs using floating-point arithmetic (FPA) compliant with IEEE Standard for FPA (IEEE 754) [1] are addressed by means of bit-blasting[3] [8].

3   Specification and Design of the ARP Use Case

3.1   The Context of Use Case

TwIRTee is a three-wheeled rover used to experiment and evaluate various methods and tools in the domain of hardware/software co-design, virtual integration of equipments, and formal verification within the INGEQUIP project[4]. TwIRTee's architecture and its software and hardware components are representative of typical aeronautical, spatial and automotive systems [9]. The overall system is composed of a unique stationary supervision station and a set of TwIRTee rovers moving in a controlled environment (Fig. 4). The architecture of rover is composed of a mission and a power control subsystems. The power control subsystem is in charge of power supply, motor control and sensor acquisition. The mission subsystem is composed of a pair of redundant channels A and B. Each channel contains a monitoring unit (MON) in charge of monitoring the data and a command unit (COM) in charge of calculating commands for the rovers. The mission and power control systems communicate via CAN bus.

In the nominal case, each rover moves autonomously on a set of predefined tracks so as to perform its missions, i.e., moving from a start waypoint to a target waypoint under speed and positioning constraints. In this system, the ARP function is aimed at preventing collisions between the rovers. It generates the maximal accelerations and minimal decelerations that are taken into account by the rover trajectory management function. The communication between rovers are carried out via WIFI.

Here, we introduce several terms used in the paper. A **mission** is defined by a list of **waypoints** to be "passed-by"? by the rover. A **segment**, defined by a

---

[3] Bit-blasting is a classic method that translates bit-vector formulas into propositional logic expressions.

[4] The INGEQUIP project is conducted at the IRT Saint-Exupéry.

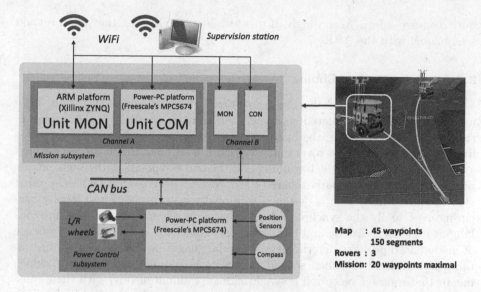

Fig. 4. Overview of the TwIRTee System

couple of waypoints on the track, corresponds to a straight path. Segments only intersect at waypoints. The set of all waypoints and segments constitutes a **map**. Dedicated monitoring mechanisms ensure that if the rover gets out of the track, it is placed in a stopped safe mode and the supervisor is alerted. Accordingly, we consider that all displacements of rovers comply with the map. In the use case, we consider 3 rovers moving on a map of 45 segments and 150 waypoints. A mission contains at most 20 waypoints.

3.2   System-Level Safety and Functional Requirements

The requirements of ARP use case comes from the industrial partners of the INGEQUIP project. The ARP is expected to ensure system-level safety requirement.(REQ-SAF-1) stated in Table 2 in the Appendix. REQ-SAF-1 states that at any time, the minimal distance between the centers of two rovers shall be greater or equal to 0.4 m. It is split in two subsets of requirements: one about the exclusive access to segments (REQ-SAF-1-1) and several others about the design of a map (IR-F1, IR-F2 and IR-F3). Compliance with the requirements of map data is under the map supplier's responsibility.

Table 3 in the Appendix presents other system-level requirements. The functional ones (REQ-F1 and REQ-F2) are mainly about excluding trivial implementations that would prevent collisions by, e.g., freezing all rovers. In the same manner, REQ-QoS-1 is introduced to guarantee the performance of the design, and to prevent trivial solutions of anti-collision, e.g., by performing missions sequentially. Note that the ARP is not to schedule the movement of the rovers but to ensure safety. Accordingly, if missions are schedulable, they shall remain schedulable with the ARP.

3.3 System Design Choice

Missions are elaborated off-line and transmitted via the supervision station. They are considered to be validated on-board (according to the REQ-F1 in Table 3 in the Appendix). To ensure the main safety requirements, separation of rovers is implemented as follows: a rover may only enter a segment if it has been granted exclusive access to both the beginning and the end waypoints of the segment. As waypoints are global resources shared by all rovers, their reservation is ensured at system-level. Our system is designed as globally asynchronous and locally synchronous. Usually the synchronous programming schema used in synchronous languages, such as Lustre and HLL, supposes that time is defined as a sequence of instants. To preserve determinism, these languages use the concept of instantaneous broadcast [2] when several processes in parallel communicate, which means that message reception is synchronous (or simultaneous) with their emission. To comply with this execution semantics, we consider the PALS approach proposed in [13] where system-level clock synchronization is used to provide a global logical synchronicity.

3.4 High-Level Software Requirements and Software Design

During the software design process, the system-level requirements are refined into High-Level software Requirements (HLRs), given in Table 4 in the Appendix. The HLRs represent "what" to be implemented, while the Low-Level Requirements (LLRs) represent "how" to implement it. In this work, the LLRs are expressed by a Lustre model[5]. Some figures about the size of the design are provided. For an ARP system containing 3 rovers and missions of at most 20 waypoints performed on a map of 45 waypoints and 150 segments, there are about 50 variables and 1700 lines of code in the Lustre model. For space reasons, the Lustre model is not presented in the paper[6]. We briefly describe some of its key points.

The ARP is split in two parts: one that manages segments reservation and one that calculates the speed and position of the rover with respect to the reservation decision. As mentioned in Sect. 3.3, the problem of reserving a track segment can be reduced to the problem of managing access to critical sections in a distributed system. In our design, this problem is solved by decomposing time into "time-slots" and allocating a dedicated reservation slot to each rover: so that only one rover at a time can perform a reservation. Each time slot is split in four sub-slots

---

[5] With respect to the DO178, the Lustre model is considered to express LLRs, since the source code is directly generated from the model with no other interpretation/refinement.

[6] Contact the authors for the specification document, design model and formal properties.

respectively for request, reply, reservation and empty tasks. For example, if there are two rovers (R_1 and R_2) in the system, the first time slot (sub-slots t0 - t3) is assigned to R_1, while the second time slot (sub-slots t4 - t7) is assigned to R_2.

4   Property Verification

We have specified the system and produced a candidate Lustre design model in Sect. 3. Before generating C code from the Lustre model, one needs to check whether the model actually complies with its specification. With S3, this property verification process combines inductive proof, BMC, test case generation and equivalence proof techniques. The first three techniques are used to verify properties of the design model. The equivalence proof technique is used to verify that the generated code is equivalent to the model, which implies that the properties verified in the design model are also satisfied in the code. We illustrate the property verification in this section and present the equivalence proof in Sect. 5.

4.1   The Workflow of Property Verification

Figure 5 presents the property verification workflow. The Lustre model is translated into an HLL model, to which properties and environment constraints expressed in HLL are concatenated[7]. The full HLL model is then expanded to the LLL model used as the input of the S3-core. This verification workflow can be split in two phases: first, the properties are checked for a certain time length n. If no property is violated, n is increased until either a counterexample (cex) is found, or some pre-known upper bound of n is reached. In case a safety property[8] fails, a cex in the form of a sequence of states is generated, where the last state contradicts the property. The cex trace is then directly exploited to debug the property or the design model.

The BMC represents a partial decision procedure for a model checking problem, which is not complete. The completeness of a safety property can be achieved with k-inductive proof based on strengthening inductive invariants (also referred to as lemmas hereafter) if needed[9]. The k-induction relies on an iterative process to search for lemmas by analyzing the repeatedly produced step counterexamples, until the proof is complete. Examples of k-induction proofs and BMC verification are given in Sects. 4.2 and 4.3 respectively.

4.2   K-Inductive Proof of Safety Property

Recent works have shown that k-induction often gives good results in practice when implemented by SAT or SMT based model checking [6,16]. Mathematical

---

[7] It's the verifier's duty to translate the natural language properties to HLL.

[8] Usually, the safety referred by requirements means the system is safe, while the safety referred by properties is related to the deterministic process. Here is the latter case.

[9] Lemma searching is not a must. It is possible that a property is k-inductive.

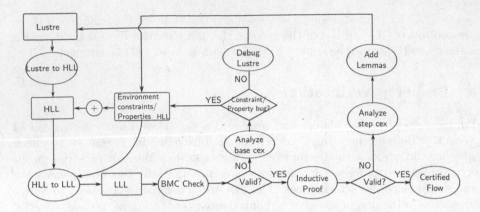

Fig. 5. The Workflow of Property Verification

induction is the classical proof technique that consists of proving a base case (Eq. 1) and an inductive step case (Eq. 2). Let a transition system S be specified by an initial state condition $I(x)$ and a transition relation $T(x, x')$ where x, x' are vectors of state variables. A state property $P(x)$ is invariant for S, i.e., satisfied by every reachable state of S, if the entailments in Eq. 1 and 2 hold for some $k \geq 0$.

$$I(x_0) \wedge T(x_0, x_1) \wedge \cdots \wedge T(x_{k-1}, x_k) \models P(x_0) \wedge \cdots \wedge P(x_k) \tag{1}$$

$$T(x_0, x_1) \wedge \cdots \wedge T(x_k, x_{k+1}) \wedge P(x_0) \wedge \cdots \wedge P(x_k) \models P(x_{k+1}) \tag{2}$$

A counterexample trace for the base entailment indicates that the property P is falsifiable in a reachable state of S. This is similar to the counterexamples produced by BMC, but a counterexample trace for the induction step entailment may start from an unreachable state or an over-approximated reachable state of S. In Fig. 6, we distinguish the reachable part of the state space and the over-approximated reachable state space. The transition $T(x_n, x_{n+1})$ starts from an over-approximated reachable state in step n, and ends in a unreachable state in step $n + 1$. One way to rule out such step counterexamples is to increase the depth k of the induction. However, some invariant properties are not inductive for any k. So, instead of increasing k, the method to enhance k-induction of a property is to strengthen the induction hypothesis using new lemmas to reduce the over-approximation of the reachable state space.

Many recent efforts are dedicated to the automatic generation of invariants (used as lemmas in this work): automatic invariant checking based on BDDs [15]; unbounded model checking using interpolation [12]; property-directed reachability (PDR) [5]; quadratic invariant generation using templates based on abstract interpretation [14]. S3 provides a lemma generation tool based on a speculation strategy that searches for equivalent variables at bit-level. According to our experience, it is still very difficult for those tools to generate all necessary lemmas for an arbitrary system, and manual elaboration of lemmas to complete

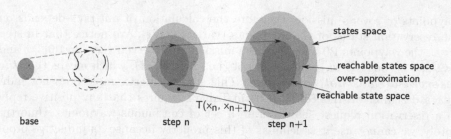

Fig. 6. Step Counterexample in Inductive Proof

the proof remains important. So, to keep the approach as generic as possible, we do not apply invariant generation methods. Instead, we show how lemmas can be found "manually" on the basis of the step-counterexamples. We pick the property HLR-06-1 in Table 4 as an example to illustrate the process of inductive proof.

Example 1. HLR-06-1 states that *the rover position shall be in front of or at the initial position of the reserved area.* It is formally expressed in Eq. 3, where, at time t, $pos_r(t)$ is the position of the rover r, and $pos_r(init_{rsv}, t)$ is the initial position of the reserved area of rover r. The corresponding property expressed in HLL is given in Eq. 4, where i is the id of rover r, and the $FLT\_ge()$ is the floating point greater-or-equal operator. The notion of time cycle does not appear in Eq. 4, because it is implicit in the HLL model. To simplify the explanation, we suppose that the mission of each rover contains at most 5 waypoints.

$$\forall r \in Rovers, t \in Time \left(pos_r(t) \geq pos_r(init_{rsv}, t)\right) \tag{3}$$

$$FLT\_ge(pos_i, init\_rsv_i) == true; \tag{4}$$

Following the workflow defined in Fig. 5, BMC is executed first, with no counterexample found within a time length of 20 cycles. Then k-induction is executed. With k = 1, a step counterexample is found in the next inductive depth (depth = 2), shown in Fig. 7. The FPA-lib of S3 follows the IEEE 754 FPA standard, thus a variable of float type (here variables pos1 and init_rsv1) is composed of a sign, an exponent, and a mantissa. To facilitate the explanation, the converted decimal values of floating numbers are given in Fig. 7. The boolean variable rsv1[i] represents the reservation status (by the local rover) of waypoint i of a rover's mission. Values of variables pos1, init_rsv1 and rsv1 are given for steps 0–3, where a step-counterexample is produced in step 2.

This step-counterexample contradicts the property HLR-06-1 because of pos1 (=0.75) < init_rsv1 (=1.20) in step k=2. This means that the rover locates outside the reserved area. The reserved area is in fact a set of continuous[10] reserved

---

[10] As explained by the REQ-01-4 in Table 4 in the Appendix, we use *continuous (continuity)* hereafter for the fact that each waypoint has a unique precedent waypoint in a mission or in a reserved area, except that it is the initial one.

waypoints of rover's mission, therefore the calculation of init_rsv1 depends on the reservation status of the waypoints (variable rsv1). We notice that in step $k = 1$, the waypoints P0 and P2 in the mission are reserved (i.e., rsv1[0] = t and rsv1[2] = t), but the waypoint P1 is not (i.e., rsv1[1] = f), which means that *the reserved area is not continuous*. This step-counterexample does not indicate a design error. Indeed, HLR-09 in Table 4 requires that any positive reply to a reservation request shall contain a set of continuous waypoints. Unfortunately, we cannot use it as lemmas of this property because its inductive proof also produces step-counterexamples and needs to be analyzed. We thus have two solutions: (1) express and prove a property about the continuity of the reserved area, if valid, use it as a lemma to prove HLR-06-01; (2) investigate the step-counterexamples of HLR-09 to make it proved, and then use HLR-09 as a new lemma to prove HLR-06-1.

For the first solution, the added lemma is expressed in HLL as Eq. 5, where N is the number of waypoints in a mission. Using this additional lemma, HLR-06-1 as well as all other indeterminate[11] properties are proved by 1-induction. Although this step-counterexample is not due to any missing or wrong property in the specification, we still suggest to report it to the designer. Then s/he might decide to add the new lemma as a complementary requirement about the continuity of reserved areas in the specification. This may reduce the re-verification effort. In this case, as the designer thinks this implicit property is important, and he decides to add it in the specification as a derived requirement from the development process.

$$\text{ALL } i : [0, N-3], j : [2, N-1] \ (rsv1[i] \wedge rsv1[i+1] \wedge i + j \leq N - 1 \rightarrow rsv1[i+j]); \quad (5)$$

```
[depth 2] > pos1
$1: pos1 is 0.45 0.55 [0.75] 1.05
```

```
[depth 2] > init_rsv1
$2: init_rsv1 is 0  0  [1.20]  0.60
```

```
[depth 2] > rsv1
rsv1 is a composite
$28*: rsv1[0] is t t [f] f
$29:  rsv1[1] is f f [f] t
$30:  rsv1[2] is t t [t] t
$31:  rsv1[3] is f f [f] f
$32:  rsv1[4] is f f [f] f
```

Fig. 7. Step-counterexample of Property HLR-06-1

For the second solution, we can first consider HLR-09 as an axiom. Inductive proof demonstrates that even if HLR-09 were proved, HLR-06-1 would remain indeterminate and a step-counterexample similar to the one in Fig. 7 would be produced again. Following the same idea, we assume all indeterminate properties except HLR-06-1 are valid, all the step-counterexamples indicate that the step $k + 1$ contains non-continuous reserved areas. This leads the verifier to add the same lemma as the one in the first solution.

---

[11] Indeterminate means neither valid nor violated.

4.3 BMC and Test Case Generation

In general, properties are classified as *safety* or *liveness* properties. The former declares what should not happen (or should always happen), while the latter declares what should eventually happen. The vast majority of properties in the ARP system are safety ones, except the system-level functional property REQ-F2 in Table 3 and the software-level functional property HLR-13 in Table 4 in the Appendix.

Example 2. REQ-F2 states that *at any time, if the definition of schedulable missions are free of deadlock, a deadlock shall not occur due to the ARP.* HLR-13 states that *the ARP shall ensure that the schedulable mission is completed within worst case mission time (WCMT).*

HLR-13 is a bounded liveness property because an over-approximated WCMT can be used as the upper bound of checking. Hence it is a good candidate for BMC. If no counterexample[12] is found before the time bound, the property is valid. In the case of HLR-13, a counterexample is easily produced using BMC. A precondition of HLR-13 is REQ-F2, because a rover may not complete its mission when deadlocks occur. The validation of REQ-F2 requires that missions are schedulable, otherwise it is possible that deadlocks occur, and HLR-13 fails. As we cannot check these two properties considering the actual mission schedules, we use BMC to generate test case scenarios containing deadlocks due to unschedulable missions. These test cases can be used later to check the verification tool of mission schedules.

To explain the generation of deadlock scenarios, we consider a system with two rovers. REQ-F2 is satisfied if the property expressed in Eq. 6 is false, where rovers r_i and r_j are stopped, r_i (r_j) requests waypoint p_j (p_i), but p_i (p_j) is reserved by r_i (r_j). Both rovers wait for a locked resource.

$$\forall p_i \in Mis_i, p_j \in Mis_j, r_i, r_j \in Rovers, t \in Time \ (i \neq j \land state(r_i, t) = STOP \land$$
$$state(r_j, t) = STOP \land req(r_i, p_j, t) \land req(r_j, p_i, t) \land rsvd(r_i, p_i, t) \land rsvd(r_j, p_j, t)) \ (6)$$

We launch BMC for this property for some time length, and test case scenarios are extracted from the generated counterexamples.

4.4 Safety Property and Map Data Validation

Once the design is delivered to the verifier, it is the verifier's duty to express and verify the properties. S/He might have several ways to express one property. Some safety properties can hardly be verified by induction or BMC. In that case, we may take benefit of divide and conquer strategy by decomposing the property into a set of simpler ones, even static ones. Take the REQ-SAF-1 in Table 2 as an example.

---

[12] The counterexample of liveness property is a path to a loop that does not contain the desired state. This implies that with an infinite loop path, the system never reaches the specified state.

Example 3. REQ-SAF-1 states that *at any time, the minimal distance between the centers of two rovers shall be greater or equal to 0.4* m.

This property can be verified by calculating the distance between two rovers at any time and then checking its value, unfortunately this solution is expensive due to the nonlinear floating-point arithmetic. To alleviate this problem, REQ-SAF-1 is split in another safety property about the reservation of waypoints (REQ-SAF-1-1) and a set of properties about the map data (IR-F1, IR-F2 and IR-F3), see Table 2. REQ-SAF-1-1 is proved by k-induction using similar process as described in the Sect. 4.2. IR-F1, IR-F2 and IR-F3 are requirements about the length of segment, the distance between a waypoint and a segment, and the absence of intersection between segments. In this work, the map data are modeled in Lustre, as same as the software. Beside the advantage of using a unique toolchain, this approach allows to reuse directly the properties expressed on the map data in the verification process of the software. In fact, these static map data could be easily checked using a dedicated verification program. However, when these map properties are used as sub-properties of the safety property REQ-SAF-1, they need in any case to be re-verified in the Lustre model.

4.5 Property Verification Results

The safety, functional and performance properties of ARP are formally expressed. As shown in Table 1, some safety properties can be directly proved by 0 or 1-induction, while some others need additional lemmas. REQ-QoS-1 is a system-level performance property. It is difficult to verify it at system-level without having software design, it is thus expressed as HLR-12 and verified at software-level by inductive proof.

Table 1. ARP property verification results

Verification techniques	REQ-ID	Verification results
Inductive Proof	IR-F1, IR-F2, IR-F3, REQ-F1, HLR-01, HLR-03, HLR-04, HLR-05, HLR-07, HLR-08, HLR-11	Valid by 0-induction
	REQ-SAF-1-1, HLR-10	Valid by 1-induction
	HLR-02, HLR-06-1, HLR-06-2, HLR-06-3, HLR-06-4, HLR-09, HLR-12 (REQ-QoS-1)	Valid by 1-induction using additional lemmas
Data Validation	REQ-SAF-1 (IR-F1, IR-F2, IR-F3)	Valid
BMC and Test Case Generation	HLR-13, REQ-F2	Test cases generated

5   Equivalence Proof Between Design and Generated Code

The property verification activities depicted in Sect. 4 demonstrate that the design model complies with its specification. However, there is still a gap between the design model and the code embedded in the system. The code can be either implemented by the developer or be generated automatically from the Lustre model. In our case, we use the lus2c translator[13] to generate the C code from the Lustre model. However, as this translator is not qualified[14], it is still unknown whether this C code satisfies the specification.

To prove the code is correct, two approaches are applicable. The first one follows the strategies presented in Sect. 4. We first translate the C code into the HLL model using a C2HLL translator, and verify that this HLL model satisfies all requirements defined in Sect. 3. The second approach demonstrates that the code is equivalent to the design model, i.e., the same inputs generate the same outputs. This guarantees that the properties (related to inputs and outputs) satisfied by the design model will be satisfied by the code.

Figure 8 presents several verification activities (A) in the process of equivalence proof: A1 generates C code from Lustre model with a qualified translator; A2 translates Lustre models into HLL models, where properties are combined and verified; A3 translates C code into HLL models, where properties are combined and verified; A4 proves that the HLL models generated from the Lustre model and the C code are equivalent; A5 proves that the LLL models generated from the Lustre model and the C code (through the HLL model) are equivalent.

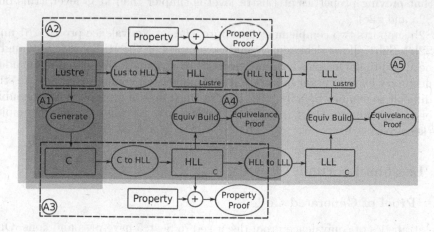

Fig. 8. Activities in the Process of Equivalence Proof

Based on different development contexts and the activities in Fig. 8, we summarize a set of strategies (S) for the verification of the C code, as follows:

---

[13] The translator lus2c is provided by Lustre v4 toolset.

[14] Qualification is a requirement in getting a system certified.

- S1: The code generator is qualified as a development tool at the same level as the application. Properties are verified on the Lustre model (A2). Thanks to the qualified translation (A1), properties are preserved in the generated C code.
- S2: The code generator is not qualified at the same level as the application.
  - S2a: Properties are directly verified on the C code (A3).
  - S2b: Properties are verified on the Lustre model (A2). The C code is proved to be equivalent to the Lustre model (A4 or A5). Thanks to the equivalence proof, properties are preserved by the C code.
    - * S2b1: The equivalence is proved at HLL level (A4).
    - * S2b2: The equivalence is proved at LLL level (A5).
  - S2c: Properties are verified at both Lustre and C code level (A2 and A3).

In our case study, we have proved the equivalence between the Lustre model (including the map data) and the generated C code. The strategy S2b has been applied for the following reasons:

1. The C code generator lus2c is non-qualified. (rule out S1)
2. It is reasonable to assume that only a subset of the requirements will be formally expressed and verified. One will probably use other more classical approaches, such as testing. The cost of test increases as the abstraction level decreases, thus test is less expensive at Lustre level than at C level. (rule out S2a and S2c)
3. Specific formal verification techniques can be applied on Lustre thanks to its abstract semantics, which is lost once the C code is generated. This implies that proving properties at Lustre level is simpler than at C level. (rule out S2a and S2c)
4. S2b supports two complementary approaches of equivalence proof S2b1 and S2b2. S2b1 allows debugging counterexamples at the HLL level, but might need additional lemmas for some cases. S2b2 automatically searches and adds necessary lemmas using speculation techniques, but counterexamples are still difficult to exploit. Usually S2b2 is performed first; if a property is falsifiable or indeterminate, the S2b1 is used to analyze the (step-)counterexample. (keep S2b)

6   Lessons Learned

6.1   Proof of Generated Code

The strategies of equivalence proof discussed in Sect. 5 have pros and cons. One can select appropriate strategies under the development contexts and the available resources.

- S1 requires a qualified code generator. This was not an option in our case, but this is the usual strategy in the domain of safety critical applications where the cost of a failure largely exceeds the cost of qualification. A qualified code generator saves a lot of effort, but is very expensive.

- S2a and S2c require to express and verify properties and lemmas at code level. As the code is less abstract and more complex than the Lustre model, property verification requires more effort.
- S2c seems redundant as property proofs are performed at both Lustre and C level. However, it might be useful to determine the origin of an error: a property satisfied in Lustre but falsifiable in C reveals probably an error during translation.
- S2b is "S1 without qualified generator". The equivalence proof between Lustre model and C code ensures that the generated C code implements exactly the properties expressed in Lustre. S2b does not need expensive qualified generator, but needs more effort to carry out equivalence proof. Each time the Lustre model is modified and the new code is generated, the equivalence needs to be re-proved.

6.2 Proof-Driven Design Guidance

The formal verification of a system could fail because of the complexity of the system, the lacking of complete requirements to support formal verification, etc. For instance, in Sect. 4.2, the HLR-06-1 is proved by k-induction after searching and adding a lemma. If we consider that the verifier has not a complete or deep knowledge about the design, s/he reports a scenario that contains the step-counterexample to the designer. If necessary, the designer may then decide to add a complementary requirement derived from this lemma in the initial specification, in order to reduce the cost of subsequent verification. The other way round, the verifier may ask the designer to state as many detailed requirements as possible about the system. These properties may be written as comment and/or assertions to be checked at runtime.

Sometimes, a lemma may not be provable from the initial hypotheses. This might be the case that some environment hypotheses have been considered as granted by the designer without ever being explicitly expressed. This case could be handled either by a modification of the requirements to make the hypothesis explicit or by a modification of the design to make it independent from these hypotheses.

7 Conclusion and Perspective

This paper shows how multiple formal verification techniques (inductive proof, BMC, test case generation, and equivalence proof) can be integrated to verify an actual system with an industrial grade toolset. Some significant activities of a typical verification process have been addressed, from the specification and design to the formal verification. Focus has been placed on the verification of safety and functional properties and on the equivalence proof between the design model and the generated code. We have drawn some lessons about the equivalence proof and the proof-driven design guidance from this experiment. This verification process is classic when the proof of property is based on SAT/SMT solvers. The main effort lies in searching for lemmas for the property proof using k-induction. This needs good understanding of the proof techniques. As our verification tool provides step-counterexamples feedback, the debug process can be seen as an engineer work. This case study is built on the Lustre modelling language and S3 toolset. Similar property proof process can be applied to other modelling languages and SAT/SMT tools.

Appendix

Table 2. System-level safety requirements

REQ-ID	REQ
REQ-SAF-1	**Minimal separation:** At any time, the minimal distance between the centers of two rovers shall be greater or equal to 0.4 m
REQ-SAF-1-1	**Exclusive access to segment:** The ARP shall consider that it has been granted exclusive access to a segment
IR-F1	**Length of segment:** The length of a segment shall be greater or equal to 0.4 m
IR-F2	**Distance between waypoint and segment:** The distance between a segment and a waypoint on a non-continuous segment shall be greater or equal to 0.4 m
IR-F3	**No intersection:** There shall not be any intersection between two segments

Table 3. System-level functional and performance requirements

REQ-ID	REQ
REQ-F1	**Missions shall be structurally deadlock free**
REQ-F1-1	The initial waypoints of missions shall not be the same
REQ-F1-2	The end waypoints of missions shall not be the same
REQ-F1-3	The end waypoint of a rover's mission shall not exist in the missions of other rovers
REQ-F2	**No deadlock:** At any time, if the definitions of scheduled missions are free of deadlocks, a deadlock shall not occur due to the ARP
REQ-QoS-1	**Fairness:** At any time, any rover shall be given the opportunity to move

Table 4. High-level software requirements

REQ-ID	REQ
HLR-01	**Mission validation:** The ARP shall validate the missions to be executed. A mission is an ordered set of waypoint indexes. (HLR-01-1) The mission shall have a starting waypoint. (HLR-01-2) The mission shall refer to existing waypoints in the map. (HLR-01-3) The mission shall not successively refer to the same waypoint. (HLR-01-4) Each waypoint in a mission shall have unique precedent waypoint except the starting waypoint (referred to as continuity in this document)
HLR-02	**Motor Request:** The ARP shall control the motor using one command out of emergency braking, acceleration, and deceleration
HLR-03	**Emergency braking:** The ARP function shall send a non-null emergency brake request to the motor control if the distance to the end of the reserved area is less than or equal to [D_BRK] and the reserved end is not the mission end, or if the rover is at the reserved end
HLR-04	**Deceleration:** The ARP function shall send a non-null deceleration request to the motor control subsystem if the distance to the end of the reserved area is less than or equal to [D_DEC] and greater than [D_BRK], and the reserved end is not the mission end
HLR-05	**Acceleration:** The ARP function shall send a non-null acceleration request to the motor control if the distance to the end of the reserved area is greater than [D_DEC], or if the distance to the end of the reserved area is less than or equal to [D_DEC] and the reserved end is the mission end
HLR-06	**Inside Reserved Area:** The ARP shall only allow a rover to enter an area that has been previously reserved. (HLR-06-1) The rover position shall be in front of or at the initial position of the reserved area. (HRL-06-2) The rover position shall be behind or at the final position of the reserved area. (HLR-06-3) The initial waypoint of the reserved area shall be reserved. (HLR-06-4) The final waypoint of the reserved area shall be reserved
HLR-07	**Desired Reservation Zone:** At any time, the ARP shall require segments that enclose a zone of length [D_RSV] in front of the rover
HLR-08	**Request of waypoints:** The ARP shall send reservation request for all the waypoints in the desired reservation area
HLR-09	**Reply to requests:** The ARP shall reply to reservation requests sent by other rovers. It shall acknowledge positively (accept) a reservation for a waypoint if and only if the waypoint it not currently reserved by the local rover. The acknowledgement shall contain a continuous set of waypoints
HLR-10	**Reservation of waypoints:** The ARP shall reserve a waypoint once it has received positive reservation acknowledgement from all other rovers
HLR-11	**Release of waypoints:** The ARP shall release the waypoints of a segment as soon as the segment is on longer in its reserved area
HLR-12	**Fairness of reservation:** The ARP shall send waypoint reservation requests when its reservation slot is activated. The APR shall have the possibility to perform a reservation if the required waypoint is not reserved by other rovers
HLR-13	**End of mission:** The ARP shall ensure that the scheduled mission is completed within worst case mission time (WCMT)

References

1. IEEE Standards Association. IEEE standard for floating-point arithmetic (2008)
2. Benveniste, A., Berry, G.: The synchronous approach to reactive and real-time systems. Proc. IEEE **79**(9), 1270–1282 (1991)
3. Kern, C., Ono-Tesfaye, T., Greenstreet, M.R.: Symbolic model checking without BDDs. In: Cleaveland, W.R. (ed.) TACAS 1999. LNCS, vol. 1579, pp. 193–207. Springer, Heidelberg (1999)
4. Biere, A., Heule, M., van Maaren, H.: Handbook of Satisfiability, vol. 185. IOS Press, Amsterdam (2009)
5. Birgmeier, J., Bradley, A.R., Weissenbacher, G.: Counterexample to induction-guided abstraction-refinement (CTIGAR). In: Biere, A., Bloem, R. (eds.) CAV 2014. LNCS, vol. 8559, pp. 831–848. Springer, Heidelberg (2014)
6. Bjesse, P., Claessen, K.: SAT-based verification without state space traversal. In: Johnson, S.D., Hunt Jr., W.A. (eds.) FMCAD 2000. LNCS, vol. 1954, pp. 372–389. Springer, Heidelberg (2000)
7. Caspi, P., Curic, A., Maignan, A., Sofronis, C., Tripakis, S., Niebert, P.: From simulink to scade, lustre to TTA: a layered approach for distributed embedded applications. In: ACM Sigplan Notices, vol. 38, pp. 153–162. ACM (2003)
8. Clabaut, M., Ge, N., Breton, N., Jenn, E., Delmas, R., Fonteneau, Y.: Industrial grade model checking - use cases, constraints, tools and applications. In: International Conference on Embedded Real Time Software and Systems (2016)
9. Cuenot, P., Jenn, E., Faure, E., Broueilh, N., Rouland, E.: An experiment on exploiting virtual platforms for the development of embedded equipments. In: International Conference on Embedded Real Time Software and Systems (2016)
10. RTCA DO. 178c. Software considerations in airborne systems and equipment certification (2011)
11. Halbwachs, N., Caspi, P., Raymond, P., Pilaud, D.: The synchronous data flow programming language LUSTRE. Proc. IEEE **79**(9), 1305–1320 (1991)
12. Dransfield, M.R., Marek, V.W., Truszczyński, M.: Satisfiability and computing van der Waerden numbers. In: Giunchiglia, E., Tacchella, A. (eds.) SAT 2003. LNCS, vol. 2919, pp. 1–13. Springer, Heidelberg (2004)
13. Meseguer, J., Ölveczky, P.C.: Formalization and correctness of the PALS architectural pattern for distributed real-time systems. In: Dong, J.S., Zhu, H. (eds.) ICFEM 2010. LNCS, vol. 6447, pp. 303–320. Springer, Heidelberg (2010)
14. Roux, P., Jobredeaux, R., Garoche, P.-L.: Closed loop analysis of control command software. In: Proceedings of the 18th International Conference on Hybrid Systems: Computation and Control, pp. 108–117. ACM (2015)
15. Rushby, J.: Integrated formal verification: using model checking with automated abstraction, invariant generation, and theorem proving. In: Dams, D.R., Gerth, R., Leue, S., Massink, M. (eds.) SPIN 1999. LNCS, vol. 1680, p. 1. Springer, Heidelberg (1999)
16. Sheeran, M., Singh, S., Stålmarck, G.: Checking safety properties using induction and a SAT-solver. In: Johnson, S.D., Hunt, W.A. (eds.) FMCAD 2000. LNCS, vol. 1954, pp. 127–144. Springer, Heidelberg (2000)

Verification of AUTOSAR Software Architectures with Timed Automata

Steffen Beringer[1]([☒]) and Heike Wehrheim[2]

[1] dSPACE GmbH, Paderborn, Germany
sberinger@dspace.de
[2] Paderborn University, Paderborn, Germany

Abstract. Today, automotive software is getting increasingly complex while at the same time development cycles are shortened due to time and cost constraints. For the validation of electronic control unit software, this results in a major challenge. Especially for safety critical software, like automotive software, high quality must be guaranteed. Formal verification of automotive software architecture *models* enables early verification of safety constraints, before the complete system is assembled and ready for simulation. One option for formal verification of safety critical software is modeling and verification using timed automata. In this paper, we present a method for the verification of AUTOSAR software models by transforming the software architecture as well as the corresponding AUTOSAR timing constraints into timed automata.

1 Introduction

Complexity of electronic control units (ECUs) and controller algorithms in cars increases, for example due to more comfort functionalities and more complex controllers for electric vehicles. Therefore development and test of these types of systems becomes time consuming. Late availability of prototype ECUs hinders the early validation of the overall system. One necessary condition for the integration of various controller functionalities from different vendors into a combined system is to have a standardized description of the software architecture and integration methodology. In this regard, AUTOSAR [1] has become the de facto standard in the automotive domain as it provides a common infrastructure for automotive systems of all vehicle domains based on standardized interfaces.

The company dSPACE[1], in which this work has been carried out, is the world's leading provider of solutions for developing ECU software and mechatronic controls. The dSPACE product area *Virtual Validation* comprises tools for using virtual (i.e. software-based) ECUs for testing and validating ECU software throughout the whole development process by a PC-based simulation. By using virtual validation, development, verification and validation tasks can be performed much earlier and also reduce the number of additional tests, prototype systems and ECU prototypes needed. Virtual Validation needs a virtual ECU

---

[1] http://www.dspace.de.

© Springer International Publishing AG 2016
M.H. ter Beek et al. (Eds.): FMICS-AVoCS 2016, LNCS 9933, pp. 189–204, 2016.
DOI: 10.1007/978-3-319-45943-1_13

(V-ECU) for the PC-based simulation. Therefore in a first step, the V-ECU has to be configured, generated and compiled out of an existing AUTOSAR software architecture. However, this step takes some time to execute. Furthermore, when errors in the simulation are detected, it is necessary to repeat this step. Another point is that all controller algorithms have to be fully implemented, but in early validation phases this case is rather rare.

Therefore for the early validation of an AUTOSAR architecture, analysis methods have to be investigated, which exclusively rely on the existing software architecture, because controller software is not available. Furthermore model properties exist which even cannot be validated by elaborated simulation scenarios. This applies for example for timing requirements which have to be met under all possible circumstances. The validation of timing requirements therefore needs special analysis methods, which cover all possible corner cases. An established method for verification of timed systems is modeling and verification of the system as a network of timed automata and the specification of properties with the help of temporal logic.

This work presents an approach for the transformation of AUTOSAR architecture models into a network of timed automata. Furthermore, AUTOSAR timing constraints as part of the AUTOSAR model are transformed. By exclusively considering the architecture model and not the controller functionalities, analysis can be performed early in the development process. Model checking of timed automata in addition can prove correctness of the architecture with respect to the timing requirements.

Related Work. There are different methods for the analysis of timing requirements. Besides the modeling and verification of timed systems via timed automata, methods exists that are based on scheduling analysis methods. In the works presented in [2,3] a compositional scheduling approach based on traditional scheduling theory in real-time systems is presented. The approach assumes that signals can arrive at components only in a restricted fashion, e.g. with fixed frequency and maximum jitter. The arrivals are specified in event functions. If signal arrivals do not match the predefined models, timing analysis becomes imprecise [4]. *Real-Time Calculus* is a framework for performance analysis of real-time systems, which is based on the network calculus [4]. By specification of an *Event Stream Model* a signal flow through a system can be analyzed. This is a more generic framework than the one in [2]. Both methods apply a different sort of abstraction on analysis level than our method. Furthermore, we directly apply our method to AUTOSAR timing extensions, while other methods only partly describe the application onto the AUTOSAR standard. A similar approach described in the work presented in [5] also utilizes timed automata for the analysis of AUTOSAR architectures. In contrast to this approach, the transformations enable general timing error detections, but do not apply transformations to the AUTOSAR Timing Constraints, which is nessessary for the analysis of timing requirements. Further approaches for timed automata suggest the method of constructing test automata (or *Scenario-Automata*) for the specification of requirements [6], but also do not consider AUTOSAR Timing Extensions.

In the work presented in [7] tool support for the verification of AUTOSAR timing requirements is presented. The requirements are verified by comparing them against specified *timing guarantees*. For this approach, timing guarantees have to be specified, which is not necessary in our approach. Besides methods for timing analysis of software architectures there is a lot of work dealing with timing based on single program tasks available as code snippets or binary artifacts [8]. These methods can determine upper bounds for the Worst-Case Execution Time and thus are a necessary prerequisite for the analysis on architecture level, where the artifacts are assembled.

2 Background

This chapter discusses the foundations of AUTOSAR and the integrated timing extensions, because most of the software in automotive contexts is currently AUTOSAR-based. Furthermore, foundations of timed automata are treated. Timed automata are used for the verification of the AUTOSAR architecture.

2.1 Introduction to AUTOSAR

AUTOSAR[2] is short for **AUT**omotive **O**pen **S**ystem **AR**chitecture and is the established standard for the development of automotive software. AUTOSAR defines the architecture and interfaces of the software as meta-model as well as the file format for data exchange. Furthermore, the standard defines its own development methodology. The concepts of this paper are based on the current AUTOSAR version 4.2.

On the outer level AUTOSAR software is structured as layered architecture (see Fig. 1). There are three different layers:

- The *application layer* is the upper software layer. It contains the actual controller software, which includes mostly controller algorithm implementations in the automotive domain. Inside of this layer software is structured in a component-based architecture. Therefore software components are modeled, which can communicate via ports and connections.
- The *Runtime Environment layer* (RTE) administrates the communication between software components, and furthermore the communication between software components and basic software parts (see below). It realizes a standardized interface for the software on application level.
- The *basic software layer* incudes modules for basic functions of ECUs. The basic software layer is subdivided into a *Service Layer* (purple), an *ECU abstraction layer* (green) and a *Microcontroller Abstraction Layer, MCAL* (red) (see Fig. 1). The service layer contains the main ECU services like operating system, ECU state management, services for diagnosis, memory services and communication services. The ECU abstraction layer realizes an abstraction between ECU hardware for the upper layers and contains modules for the

---

[2] http://www.autosar.org.

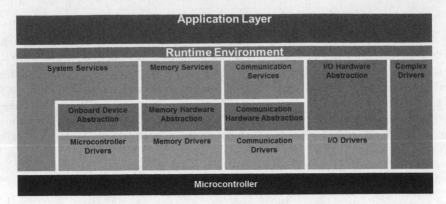

Fig. 1. AUTOSAR layered architecture taken from [9] (Color figure online)

access of hardware peripherials. The MCAL provides low level driver modules and acesses the hardware directly. A detailed description of all modules can be found in [9].

The AUTOSAR Authoring Tool SystemDesk®. SystemDesk®[3] is the tooling environment for AUTOSAR models from dSPACE. It supports sophisticated and extensive modeling of AUTOSAR architectures by providing a rich graphical user interface as well as code generation for virtual ECUs. Graphical model representations are available for important elements. For example software components, ports and connections within a software composition can be visualized in a *Composition Diagram.* Furthermore, single software components with their ports, interfaces and data types can be visualized in a *Component Diagram.* Other model elements are ordered hierarchically in a tree structure.

Example 1. In the following we will consider a simple example AUTOSAR software architecture, which manages the left and right direction indicators of a vehicle. The application layer consists of several software components, which comprise several so-called runnable entities, which contain executable software. The example architecture is shown in Fig. 2. The two software components on the left read in sensor data and check for errors before forwarding the signal data to the next software component. The *IndicatorComposition* software component receives the raw sensor values and encapsulates several runnable entities for pre-processing of the signal values as well as the logic of the system. The actuator software components on the right are responsible for activating the left respectively right bulb of the direction indicator. Furthermore, the example contains a configuration of the RTE, and on the *basic software layer* the configuration for the Operating System. Other basic software modules are not considered in this example.

---

[3] http://www.dspace.com/en/pub/home/products/sw/system_architecture_software/systemdesk.cfm.

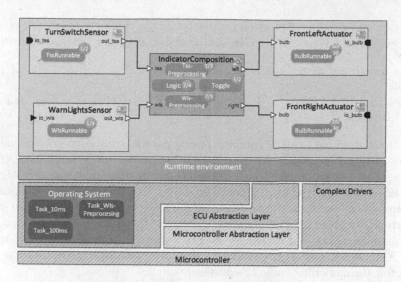

Fig. 2. Example software architecture

2.2   Timed Automata

While AUTOSAR specifies a formal syntax defined as an OMG meta model, its semantics is only described in a textual manner. To formally verify timing requirements on AUTOSAR, we need to define a formal semantics for the timing relevant meta model elements. Here, we employ timed automata as they are capable of formally describing timing behavior. Timed Automata were first introduced 1994 by Alur and Dill [10]; in the following, we follow the notation of [11].

Definition 1 (Timed Automata). *A* timed automaton *is a tuple* $\mathcal{A} = (L, B, B^* X, I, U, E, I_{ini})$ *with a finite set of locations* L, *a set of signals communicating via handshake* B, *a set of signals communicating via broadcast channels* B^*, *a set of clocks* X, *an assignment of invariants to locations:* $I : L \to \Phi(X)$, *a mapping for the locations whether they are urgent (so that time is not allowed to increase)* $: U : L \to \{true, false\}$, *a set of edges labeled with an action, a guard and a set of clocks, which need to be reset:* $E \subseteq L \times B \cup B^* \times \Phi(X) \times \mathcal{P}(X) \times L$, *and an initial location* $I_{ini} \in L$.

Here, $\Phi(X)$ specifies a set of clock constraints (like $x < 3$, see [11]). A *configuration* of a timed automaton is a pair of a location and a *clock valuation* $\nu : X \to Time$, where $Time \in \mathbb{R}^{(\geq 0)}$ are the real numbers. We use $\nu \models \phi$ for a clock constraint $\phi \in \Phi(X)$ if the constraint is true for the clock valuation. In Fig. 4 an example automaton is shown.

Definition 2 (Semantics of Timed Automata). *The* operational semantics of a timed automaton $\mathcal{A}$ *is defined as a labelled transition system* $T(\mathcal{A}) = (Conf(\mathcal{A}), \to, C_{ini})$, *where* $Conf(\mathcal{A}) = \{\langle l, \nu \rangle \mid l \in L, \nu : X \to Time,$

$\nu \models I(l)\}$, an initial configuration $C_{ini} = \{\langle l_{ini}, \nu_{ini}\rangle\}$ and a transition relation $\rightarrow \subseteq Conf(\mathcal{A}) \times (Time \cup B) \times Conf(\mathcal{A})$ with two different types of transitions:

- delay-transition: $\langle l, \nu\rangle \xrightarrow{t} \langle l, v + t\rangle$ if $\nu + t' \models I(l) \forall t' \in [0, t] \wedge \forall l \in L : U(l) = false$
- action-transition: $\langle l, v\rangle \xrightarrow{\alpha} \langle l', v'\rangle$ iff $(l, \alpha, \phi, Y, l') \in E$ with $v \models \phi$ and $\nu' = \nu[Y := 0]$ and $\nu' \models I(l')$

Single timed automata can be combined using parallel composition resulting in a network of timed automata. In the network, automata can communicate in two ways: *synchronously* via handshake communication (like in the process algebra *CCS* [12]) or in a broadcast manner. The sender in a broadcast communication can communicate with an abitrary number of receivers, namely all of those which are currently enabled for a communication. In the following, we will use synchronous communication as a means of synchronising the behaviour of components in the AUTOSAR architecture while we use broadcast for synchronisation with test automata modelling timing requirements.

To express properties on Timed Automata the query language *Timed Computation Tree Logic (TCTL)* is used. It allows specifying real-time constraints on Timed Automata, which can be checked in tools like *UPPAAL*[4] [13]. In TCTL, different types of formulas can be expressed: In *state formulas* properties on states can be specified, while *path formulas* quantify over paths or traces of the model [13,14].

3   Transformation of AUTOSAR Models

In this section we describe the transformation of AUTOSAR meta-model elements into timed automata. The AUTOSAR meta-model is very large. However, many model elements do not influence the dynamic behavior of the system. Furthermore, many specialized classes exist, but only for some of them the specified transformations are performed. Therefore we only give an introduction for timing relevant meta model elements and afterwards give a simplified formalization of the meta model. In this work we focus on the timing of ECUs and abstract from bus communication. As there is no formal semantics defined for AUTOSAR, we cannot prove the correctness of the transformations.

Timing on Application Layer. The AUTOSAR application layer consists of application software. Software is encapsulated in so-called *RunnableEntities* (abbreviated: *runnable*). For modeling timing behavior on application layer it is necessary to represent the runnables, variable accesses and their interconnections by appropriate timed automata. We abstract from the concept of software components and ports as it is not relevant for the timing whether two runnables in different software components are connected via ports or directly in a single software component as we assume that all software components are mapped onto a single ECU.

---

[4] http://www.uppaal.org.

Timing on RTE Layer. The RTE-Layer is a standardized interface for the software on application layer and is responsible for triggering runnables as specified in the operating systen, which is located on the basic software layer. The operating system has a scheduler and maintains the execution of resources by OSTasks. For this reason runnables have to be mapped onto OSTasks to specify the execution order of runnables. This is done in the RTE configuration using the so-called *RTEEventToTaskMapping*, which maps events, representing the triggering of a runnable, onto tasks.

Timing on Basic Software Layer. On the basic software layer AUTOSAR specifies many modules, which can be specified for every ECU. Most important for the runtime behavior are the modules which have influence on the execution order of the runnable entities. This is mainly the AUTOSAR operating system, which is based on the OSEK standard[5].

We consider the following parts of an AUTOSAR architecture during transformation.

Definition 3 (AUTOSAR Architecture). *The simplified formal* AUTOSAR *architecture* $AR = (R, C, VA, T, TRM)$ *consists of*

1. *a set of VariableAccess elements VA,*
2. *a set of RunnableEntities*

$$R \subseteq \{(VA_{read}, VA_{write}, wcet, bcet) \mid VA_{read} \subseteq VA, VA_{write} \subseteq VA, bcet \leq wcet\}$$

with VA_{read} a set of variable read accesses, VA_{write} a set of variable write accesses with $VA_{read} \cap VA_{write} = \emptyset$, $wcet \in \mathbb{N}$ the worst case and $bcet \in \mathbb{N}$ the best case execution time,
3. *a set of AssemblyConnections $C \subseteq \{(left, right) \mid left \in VA, right \in VA\}$, which connect two variable access elements,*
4. *a set of periodically triggered tasks T with period p and*
5. *a Task-Runnable-Mapping $TRM : R \rightarrow T$ mapping runnables to operating system tasks.*

3.1   Transformation

For the verification of timing requirements in AUTOSAR, a mapping from AUTOSAR models onto timed automata was modelled, where the AUTOSAR model contains the software architecture and timing requirements, which are formulated as AUTOSAR timing extensions. The AUTOSAR software architecture is transformed into a network of timed automata, while each timing requirement is transformed into a test automaton and a TCTL-query (see Fig. 3). In the resulting overall network test automata and architecture automata communicate via broadcast channels.

For a given AUTOSAR model $AR = (R, AC, VA, T, TRM)$ a network of timed automata $\mathcal{N} = (A_1 \parallel .. \parallel A_n)$ is constructed. Below the transformations are described in a bit more detail, where we – due to lack of space – however cannot formally define all parts.

---

[5] http://osek-vdx.org/.

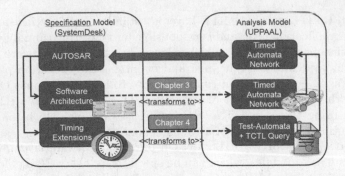

Fig. 3. Transformation of AUTOSAR models into a set of timed automata and TCTL queries

RunnableEntities. RunnableEntities represent the code fragments which are integrated into the architecture. Triggering is controlled by the RTE. Furthermore, runnables have access to a defined set of variables. Variables with reading access are read directly when a runnable is started, while write accesses are executed before termination[6]. Execution of runnable code requires time.

For every RunnableEntity in the analysis model a timed automaton is generated, which considers the variable accesses as well as the runtime behavior. In the case that all software components are executed on the same ECU, it is negligible whether the runnable entities communicate via interrunnable variables in a single software component or via ports. The generation of locations and transitions is therefore identical for ports and interrunnable variables.

For every RunnableEntity $r \in R$ with $r = (VA_{read}, VA_{write}, wcet, bcet)$ a timed automaton $\mathcal{A} = (L, B, B^*, X, I, U, E, I_{ini})$ is generated. Let $VA_{read} = \{r\_VA_{read_1}, \ldots, r\_VA_{read_n}\}$ be the set of read accesses (VA_{write} analogously). In the following, we use an arbitrary ordering 1 to n of these sets.

- Locations: $L = \{r\_ready\_loc, r\_running\_loc\} \cup \{r\_VA_{read}\_loc \mid VA_{read} \in VA_{read}\}$
  $\cup \{r\_VA_{write}\_loc \mid VA_{write} \in VA_{write}\}$,
- Handshake Communication: $B = \{r\_start, r\_finished\}$,
- Broadcast Communication: $B^* = \{r\_va_{read} \mid VA_{read} \in VA_{read}\}$
  $\cup \{r\_va_{write} \mid VA_{write} \in VA_{write}\}$
- Clocks: $X = \{x\}$, Invariants: $I(r\_running\_locc) = \{x <= wcet\}$,
- Urgency: $\forall Va \in VA_{read} \cup VA_{write} : U(r\_Va) = true$,
  $U(r\_ready) = false, U(r\_running) = false$,
- Edges: $E = \{(r\_ready, r\_start?, \emptyset, \{x\}, r\_VA_{read_1}),$
  $(r\_VA_{read_n}, r\_va_{read_n}!, \emptyset, \emptyset, r\_running)\} \cup$
  $\{(r\_VA_{read_j}, r\_va_{read_j}!, \emptyset, \emptyset, r\_VA_{read_{j+1}}) \mid 1 \le j \le |VA_{read}| - 1\} \cup$
  $\{(r\_VA_{write_j}, r\_va_{write_j}!, \emptyset, \emptyset, r\_VA_{write_{j+1}}) \mid 1 \le j \le |VA_{write}| - 1\} \cup$

---

[6] This is called implicit variable access and in this work only implicit access will be considered, while there is also an explicit access method where the access is not controlled by the RTE.

$\{(r\_running, r\_va_{write_1}!, \{x \geq bcet\}, r\_Va_{write_1})\} \cup$
$\{(r\_Va_{write_n}, r\_finished!, \emptyset, \emptyset, r\_ready)\},$
– Initial location: $I_{ini} = r\_ready.$

The generated timed automaton consists of at least the locations *ready* and *running* (prefixed by the name of the runnable). The automaton is in location *ready* when the RunnableEntity is currently not running and in location *running* otherwise. Initially, the RunnableEntity is in location *ready*. Every implicit variable access of a RunnableEntity is also represented as a location. Identification of the access is done by signals on the transitions. These signals are not only used for synchronization, but also, if available, for existing test automata, which need to detect the data flow in the architecture. Therefore channels (for communication) are defined as *broadcast* channels.

Figure 4 exemplifies a transformed runnable with one incoming and two outgoing variable accesses. It shows the runnable *TssPreprocessing* located in the software component *IndicatorLogic* (see Fig. 2), which reads the raw turn switch sensor value *tss_value*, preprocesses it and writes its results in *tss_status*. Furthermore *wcet* and *bcet* are assumed to be 5 ms and 2 ms respectively.

AssemblyConnections. AssemblyConnections $C = (left, right)$ connect write and read accesses of variable access elements. For every AssemblyConnection a timed automaton is generated which describes the data flow between runnables. There is one location, and for the variable accesses *left* and *right*, there is a transition to track the connections in the software architecture. Thus, for each AssemblyConnection $C = (left, right)$ we get a timed automaton $\mathcal{A} = (L, B, B^*, X, I, U, E, I_{ini})$ with:

– Locations: $L = \{ac\_start\}$, Signals: $B = \{left, right\}, B^* = \{\}$,
– Clocks: $X = \emptyset$, Invariants $I : \emptyset$, Urgency: $U(ac\_start) = false$,
– Edges: $E = \{(ac\_start, left?, \emptyset, \emptyset, ac\_start), (ac\_start, right?, \emptyset, \emptyset, ac\_start)\}$,
– Initial location: $I_{ini} = ac\_start.$

TaskRunnableMapping. For the correct execution order of runnables in the analysis model, a timed automaton A is generated for every OsTask. This automaton triggers the contained runnables in an OsTask in the defined order.

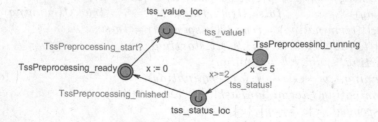

Fig. 4. Timed automata for the runnable preprocessing turn switch sensor values

The automata sends *Start*-signals to the receiving runnable automata. Afterwards the runnable is set to *running*-location and it leaves the *running*-location when the runnable automaton sends the *finish*-signal back to the runnable mapping automaton. Since no time passes between starting and stopping, the corresponding locations are marked as *urgent* locations.

Let T be the set of all OsTasks and for every OsTask $t \in T$, let $R_t = \{r \in R \mid TRM(r) = t\}$ be the set of all *RunnableEntities*, which are triggered by the OsTask t. Again we impose an arbitrary ordering on the set R_t, using indexes 1 to n. Then for every OsTask $t \in T$, a timed automaton A in the analysis model exists with

- $L = \{t\_ready, t\_running\} \cup \{t\_r\_start, t\_r\_stopped \mid r \in R_t\}$
- $B = \{t\_run, t\_processed\} \cup \{t\_r\_start, t\_r\_finished \mid r \in R_t\}, B^* = \{\},$
- Clocks: $X = \{x\}$, Invariants: $I(t\_running) = \{x == 0\}$,
- Urgency: $\forall r \in R_t : U(t\_r\_finished) = true, U(t\_running) = true,$
- $E = \{(t\_ready, t\_run?, \emptyset, \emptyset, t\_running),$
  $(t\_running, t\_r_1\_start!, \emptyset, \emptyset, t\_r_1\_running),$
  $(t\_r_n\_stopped, t\_processed!, \emptyset, \emptyset, t\_processed),$
  $\cup\{(t\_r\_stopped, t\_r\_start!, \emptyset, \emptyset, t\_r\_running),$
  $(t\_r\_running, t\_r\_finished?, \emptyset, \emptyset, t\_r\_stopped) \mid r \in R_t\},$
- Initial location: $I_{ini} = t\_ready.$

OS Tasks. Every AUTOSAR-based ECU includes an AUTOSAR-compliant OSEK operating system, which maintains the execution of *OsTasks* on the ECU. OSEK differentiates between *Basic-Tasks*, which can only be interrupted by the operating system itself, and *Extended-Tasks*. Extended tasks can be interrupted and set into *waiting* state. For this work we focus on basic tasks. Basic tasks have states *suspended, ready* and *running*. A task is in state *ready*, if it can be scheduled by the scheduler. If the scheduler selects the task for running, it is set in *running* state. After termination, but before the timing period is passed, the task is set to state *suspended*.

For every OsTask $t \in T$ a timed automaton A is generated:

- $L = \{t\_ready, t\_starting, t\_running, t\_terminating, t\_suspended\},$
- $B = \{t\_startTask, t\_run, t\_processed, t\_terminateTask, t\_isNotReady\},$
- $B^* = \{\}, X = \{x\},$
- $I(t\_running) = \{x <= p\}, I(t\_suspended) = \{x <= p\},$
- $U(ready) \quad = \quad false, U(starting) \quad = \quad true, U(running) \quad =$ $false, U(terminating) = true, U(suspended) = false,$
- $E = \{(t\_ready, t\_startTask?, \emptyset, \emptyset, t\_starting),$
  $(t\_starting, t\_run!, \emptyset, \emptyset, t\_running),$
  $(t\_running, t\_processed?, \emptyset, \emptyset, t\_terminating),$
  $(t\_terminating, t\_terminateTask!, \emptyset, \emptyset, t\_suspended),$
  $(t\_suspended, \phi, \{x == p\}, \{x\}, t\_ready),$
  $(t\_suspended, t\_isNotReady!, \emptyset, t\_suspended)\},$
- $I_{ini} = t\_ready.$

The behavior of an OsTask is modeled by generation of locations for *ready, running* and *suspended* and additional (urgent)-locations for sending and receiving multiple signals for synchronization with the *RunnableToTask-Mapping-automaton*. The OsTask starts in the *ready*-location and can be triggered by the Task Scheduler. By receiving the signal *startTask* the *EventToTaskMapping* is signaled and the OsTask is set to *running*. Afterwards the EventToTaskMapping is executed, i.e. all RunnableEntities have been executed, the signal *processed* is received and the signal *terminateTask* is sent to the *Scheduler*. The OsTask then stays in *suspended* until the period of the OsTask is due. In between the automaton only synchronizes via the signal *isNotReady* to the scheduler. Afterwards the OsTask is set back to *ready* and can again be executed by the *scheduler*.

4   AUTOSAR Timing Extensions

The transformations described before cover the behavior of the AUTOSAR system. To verify timing constraints on the system, the requirements also need to be formalized. To this end, for each timing requirement specified as AUTOSAR timing constraint, a test automaton as well as a TCTL-query for checking the requirement are created.

We start with explaining timing requirements. AUTOSAR Timing Extensions extends the AUTOSAR meta model with timing annotations for different model elements [15]. A *TimingExtension* contains a set of *TimingDescriptions* and *TimingConstraints*. *TimingDescriptions* are elements that describe events and event chains within a system, whereas *TimingConstraints* formulate timing requirements and timing guarantees for these events.

4.1   Timing Events

Formally, the set of Timing Events $E \subseteq (R \cup VA \cup T)$ is a subset of the AUTOSAR model elements, for which the dynamic behavior needs to be observed. Thus, runnables, variable accesses and tasks can be observed.

Requirements for Data Latency on Events. A *LatencyTimingConstraint* describes the latency requirement from the start to the event of a sequence of events. Formally, a LatencyTimingConstraint is defined as $lc = (chain, maximum)$ where

– $chain = (e_1, \ldots, e_n)$ is an ordered sequence of events,
– $maximum \in \mathbb{N}$ is the maximum time for the constraint.

In the transformation of the *TimingExtension* with *LatencyTimingConstraint* the event chain is transformed to a test automaton, which models the event chain as chain of locations. In between every location a transition is generated which receives the corresponding signal defined in the event chain. Verification of the required latency is achieved by a clock which measures the time spent in the event chain and which is reset when the event chain is due. Maximum latency is checked by a TCTL-query which checks the maximum clock value in the test automaton. Hence for every *LatencyTimingConstraint lc*, a timed automaton A is generated as follows:

- Locations: $L = \{lc\_e | e \in chain\}$, Signals: $B^* = \{e | e \in chain\}$, Clocks: $X = \{x\}$,
- Invariants $I(lc\_e_1) = \{x \leq 1\}$,
- $E = \{(lc\_e_j, e_j?, \emptyset, \emptyset, lc\_e_{j+1}) | 1 \leq j < n - 1\}$
  $\cup \{lc\_e_n, e_n, \emptyset, \{x\}, lc\_e_1 \cup \{(lc\_e_1, e_1?, \emptyset, \{x\}, lc\_e_1)\}$,
- Initial location: $I_{ini} = lc\_e_1$.

In the first location lc_e_1 (i.e. *before* the first event is received) the automaton cyclically resets its clock (implemented by a self-transition and invariant on lc_1) so that the clock value only exeeds 1, when the first event is received. Note that according to the definition of B^*, the generated signals are using broadcast communication. Additionally the TCTL-query $\varphi = AG(x < maximum)$ is generated. Here, AG requires the property to hold always on all paths.

Figure 5 shows a latency timing constraint automaton measuring the time from the start event when the turn switch sensor receives the raw signal to the bulb actuator which switches the indicator bulbs.

Requirements for Ordered Execution of Runnables. Requirements on the ordered execution of runnables are captured by the *ExecutionOrderConstraint*. An *ExecutionOrderConstraint eoc* $= (r_1, \ldots, r_n), r_i \subseteq R$, is defined by an ordered sequence of a subset of the available runnable entities for which the execution order is specified.

For every *ExecutionOrderConstraint eoc* a timed automaton is generated as follows:

- Locations: $L = \{r_i\_EOC\_started, r_i\_EOC\_finished \mid 1 \leq i \leq n\} \cup \{init, error\}$,
- Broadcast Communication: $B^* = \{r\_EOC\_start, r\_EOC\_finished \mid i = 1, \ldots, n\}$, Handshake Communication: $B = \{\}$,
- Clocks: $X = \{\}$, Invariants: I is true for all locations,
- Urgency: $U(r_n\_EOC\_finished) = true$,
- $E = \{init, r_1\_start?, \emptyset, \emptyset, r_1\_EOC\_started\} \cup$
  $\{r_i\_EOC\_started, r_i\_finished?, \emptyset, \emptyset, r_i\_EOC\_finished \mid i = 1, \ldots, n\} \cup$
  $\{r_i\_EOC\_finished, r_{i+1}\_start?, \emptyset, \emptyset, r_{r+1}\_EOC\_started \mid i = 1, \ldots, n\} \cup$
  $\{r_n\_EOC\_finished, \tau, \emptyset, \emptyset, init\}$
- $I_{ini} = init$.

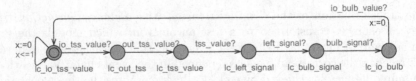

Fig. 5. Timed automaton of a latency timing constraint

Note that according to the definition of B^*, the generated signals are using broadcast communication. Furthermore, for every location $l \in L$, a TCTL-query $\varphi = AF(l)$ is generated. This property requires that on all paths of the system run every location is eventually visited eventually (i.e., the events are received in the specified order).

Requirements for Synchronized Execution of Events. A *Synchronization-TimingEvent* $sc = (scopeEvents, tolerance)$ consists of

- $scopeEvents \subseteq E$ describing the set of events, which have to occur only nearly simultaneously and
- $tolerance \in \mathbb{N}$ describing the maximum time which may occur between all $scopeEvents$, so that the execution can still be categorized as being simultaneous.

The requirement is fulfilled if $\forall e_i, e_j \in scopeEvents : |t_{e_i} - t_{e_j}| \leq tolerance$, where t_i is the time when event i occurs.

For every sc, a timed automaton is generated as follows:

- Locations: $L = \{sc\_init\}$, Signals: $B^* = \{e | e \in scopeEvents\} B = \{\}$,
- Clocks: $X = \{x\}$, Invariants: $I = \{\emptyset\}$, Urgency: U is false for all locations
- Edges: $E = \{sc\_init, e?, \emptyset, \emptyset, sc\_init\}$, $I_{ini} = \{sc\_init\}$.

Again, the generated signals are using broadcast communication. Furthermore, for the generated transitions functions are specified which are called each time the transition is taken. For each transition $e_i \in E$ the function e_i_receiving is called. In addition, local declarations are defined for each automaton as described in Listing 1.

```
Listing 1: Local declarations in UPPAAL

1  bool e_i_received = false;
2  void e_i_receiving ()
3  {isRunning(); e_i_received = true; isCompleted();}
4
5  clock x;
6  bool running = false;
7
8  void isRunning ()
9  { if (! running){x=0;running=true;}}
10
11 void isCompleted (){ if (e_1_received && ..e_n_received)
12 {e_i_received = false;
13 x=0; running=false;}}
```

Finally, a TCTL-query is generated as follows: $AG(running \implies x \leq tolerance)$. Figure 6 exemplifies the transformation of a Synchronization Timing Constraint which requires the runnables for the left and right actuator to be triggered synchronously. Analogously to the automaton the required local

Fig. 6. Example for a SynchronizationTimingConstraint synchronizing the bulb lights

declarations are generated, i.e., two flags *Bulb1_received* and *Bulb2_received*, two functions *Bulb1_receiving* and *Bulb2_receiving*.

For the verification of the AUTOSAR architecture all generated automata $A_i = (L_i, B_i, X_i, I_i, E_i, I_{i_{ini}})$ are connected to a network of timed automata $\mathcal{N} = (A_1 \parallel .. \parallel A_n)$. Then a *TimingConstraint* T is fulfilled by the model, iff $(\mathcal{N} \parallel T) \models \varphi$, that is the automaton for a single timing constraint is connected to the network of timed automata representing the software architecture and the network is checked according to the specified TCTL-formula.

5   Implementation and Evaluation

The transformations were implemented as an independent tool, which uses the automation feature of SystemDesk®to retrieve AUTOSAR model informations. It includes separated components for model conversion and export. The exporting module comprises functionalities to compile an XML file out of the timed automata model, which is compatible to the UPPAAL [13] model checker.

The efficiency of the approach was evaluated by transforming three scenarios while measuring the time for model transformation and model checking via UPPAAL. The measurements were performed on an Intel i7-4810MQ @ 2.8 GHz with 16 GB RAM and Windows 7 Professional. UPPAAL version 4.0.13 was used with BFS search order, conservative state space reduction and DBM state space representation.

Table 1 shows the model sizes and runtime measurements for three different AUTOSAR models, namely a tutorial project, a model of a fueling system and the already mentioned model for direction indication. For each demo project at least one constraint of each type was modeled and verified. In Fig. 7, the runtime results split into transformation and constraint checking time are visualized. The

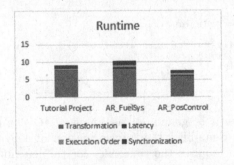

Fig. 7. Transformation and verification runtime

table given below gives exact numbers. Transformation and verification runtime is highest for the *AR_FuelSys* demo although it is not the biggest AUTOSAR model. The reason is that it contains more model elements for which timed automata have to be generated.

Table 1. Model size and runtime

Test system	Tut.Project	AR_FuelSys	AR_PosControl
AUTOSAR elements	748	723	503
Timed automata	26	38	23
Transformation time (s)	7.56	7.96	5.9
Latency constraint (s)	0.33	0.74	0.39
Execution order constraint (s)	0.4	0.53	0.5
Synchronization constraint (s)	0.95	1.13	0.94
Verification time $\sum$	9.24	10.36	7.73

The first results show that for these type of systems timing analysis is promising as the runtime is sufficiently low for real world use. Most of the time is spent in the transformation process. But as the transformation has polynomial runtime in the size of model elements, also larger models should be manageable.

6   Conclusion

In this work, an approach for the verification of timing requirements of AUTOSAR-based software architectures has been presented. Utilizing this method, timing requirements can be checked early and without access to source code. Only timing annotations (best case and worst case execution times) for runnable entites are required. They have to be introduced with the help of expert knowledge in a conservative fashion, or upper bounds for execution have to be figured out by static code analysis methods. For the verification of the AUTOSAR architecture existing tools for the verification of timed automata (like UPPAAL) can then be used.

By transforming AUTOSAR-architectures to timed automata a formal verification of timing requirements gets possible. The modeling of the AUTOSAR architecture and the required model elements for the analysis, however, have to be done manually. For example, timing requirements have to be specified. For this there is currently no tool available, which makes modeling time consuming and error prone. As future work, we will thus investigate how timing requirements can be precisely but easily (graphically) specified. Until now formal verification is only seldomly used in the software development process for automotive systems, because a successive application not only requires sound analysis methods, but also easy integration into existing development processes. Simplification of the formal specification and the quality analysis of timing requirements are thus crucial steps for the acceptance in industry.

References

1. AUTOSAR. http://www.autosar.org
2. Richter, K.: Compositional scheduling analysis using standard event models: the SymTA/S approach. Ph.D. thesis, Braunschweig (2005)
3. Feiertag, N., Richter, K., Nordlander, J., Jonsson, J.: A compositional framework for end-to-end path delay calculation of automotive systems under different path semantics. In: IEEE Real-Time Systems Symposium 2008, vol. 29 (2008)
4. Perathoner, S., Wandeler, E., Thiele, L., Hamann, A., Schliecker, S., Henia, R., Racu, R., Ernst, R., Harbour, M.G.: Influence of different system abstractions on the performance analysis of distributed real-time systems. J. Des. Autom. Embed. Syst. 13(1–2), 27–49 (2009)
5. Neumann, S., Kluge, N., Wätzoldt, S.: Automatic transformation of abstract autosar architectures to timed automata. In: Proceedings of the 5th International Workshop on Model Based Architecting and Construction of Embedded Systems, ACES-MB 2012, pp. 55–60. ACM, New York (2012)
6. Gehrke, M., Nawratil, P., Niggemann, O., Schäfer, W., Hirsch, M.: Scenario-based verification of automotive software systems. In: Giese, H., Rumpe, B., Schätz, B. (eds.) Dagstuhl-Workshop MBEES. Daghstuhl-Workshop MBEES, vol. 2, pp. 35–42. TU Braunschweig, Institut für Software Systems Engineering (2006)
7. Scheickl, O., Ainhauser, C., Gliwa, P.: Tool support for seamless system development based on autosar timing extensions. In: Embedded Real-Time Software and Systems 2012 (2012)
8. Heckmann, R., Ferdinand, C.: Worst-case execution time prediction by static program analysis. In: Jacquart, R. (ed.) Building the Information Society. IFIP Advances in Information and Communication Technology, vol. 156, pp. 377–383. Springer, Heidelberg (2004)
9. AUTOSAR: Layered software architecture (2013). http://www.autosar.org/fileadmin/files/releases/4-2/software-architecture/general/auxiliary/AUTOSAR_EXP_LayeredSoftwareArchitecture.pdf
10. Alur, R., Dill, D.: A theory of timed automata. Theor. Comput. Sci. 126, 183–235 (1994)
11. Olderog, E.R., Dierks, H.: Real-Time Systems: Formal Specification and Automatic Verification (2008)
12. Milner, R.R.: A Calculus of Communicating Systems. LNCS, vol. 92. Springer, Berlin (1980)
13. Behrmann, G., David, A., Larsen, K.G.: A tutorial on UPPAAL. In: Bernardo, M., Corradini, F. (eds.) SFM-RT 2004. LNCS, vol. 3185, pp. 200–236. Springer, Heidelberg (2004)
14. Baier, C., Katoen, J.P.: Principles of Model Checking. MIT Press, Cambridge (2008)
15. AUTOSAR: Autosar timing extensions template (2013). http://www.autosar.org/fileadmin/files/releases/4-2/methodology-and-templates/templates/standard/AUTOSAR_TPS_TimingExtensions.pdf

Verification by Way of Refinement: A Case Study in the Use of Coq and TLA in the Design of a Safety Critical System

Philip Johnson-Freyd[1]([⊠]), Geoffrey C. Hulette[2], and Zena M. Ariola[1]

[1] University of Oregon, Eugene, OR, USA
{philipjf,ariola}@cs.uoregon.edu
[2] Sandia National Laboratories, Livermore, CA, USA
ghulett@sandia.gov

Abstract. Sandia engineers use the Temporal Logic of Actions (TLA) early in the design process for digital systems where safety considerations are critical. TLA allows us to easily build models of interactive systems and prove (in the mathematical sense) that those models can never violate safety requirements, all in a single formal language. TLA models can also be *refined*, that is, extended by adding details in a carefully prescribed way, such that the additional details do not break the original model. Our experience suggests that engineers using refinement can build, maintain, and prove safety for designs that are significantly more complex than they otherwise could. We illustrate the way in which we have used TLA, including refinement, with a case study drawn from a real safety-critical system. This case exposes a need for refinement by composition, which is not currently provided by TLA. We have extended TLA to support this kind of refinement by building a specialized version of it in the Coq theorem prover. Taking advantage of Coq's features, our version of TLA exhibits other benefits over stock TLA: we can prove certain difficult kinds of safety properties using mathematical induction, and we can certify the correctness of our proofs.

1 Introduction

Sandia Laboratories builds extremely high consequence systems. Logical errors in these systems could incur enormous costs both financially and in loss of life. Sandia is therefore implementing new methodologies that incorporate formal methods early in development of high consequence systems. To complement this effort, specification languages are needed which comport with the way designers think about systems, and which are approachable for engineers who are not formal methods experts. At the same time, we need tools which make verification tractable at scale.

Towards this end, Sandia engineers have begun using the Temporal Logic of Actions (TLA) [7] to create formal specifications. TLA is a proven and effective formalism for describing the evolution of digital systems over time. However, TLA^+ and its tools impose certain limitations. TLA^+ comes with a model

M.H. ter Beek et al. (Eds.): FMICS-AVoCS 2016, LNCS 9933, pp. 205–213, 2016.
DOI: 10.1007/978-3-319-45943-1_14

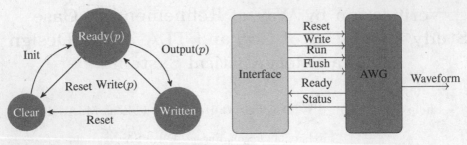

Fig. 1. Simplified AWG state machine   **Fig. 2.** AWG logical interface

checker [14] which is fully automated and useful for bug finding; it often fails to terminate, however, when attempting to prove complex properties. Furthermore, the model checker is a complicated program in its own right and so may contain bugs, and provides no certificate that would allow us to independently verify the proof.

To overcome these limitations we have designed TLA^{Coq}, a version of TLA embedded in the proof assistant Coq [6]. Coq is quite powerful, but this power comes at the expense of usability – its intended audience is primarily formal method experts. Therefore, the design of our embedding has been driven by the desire to leverage Coq's capabilities while retaining TLA's ease of use and relatively short learning curve.

As a demonstration of TLA^{Coq} we consider a component of a high conse-quence system produced at Sandia. We initially developed a formal model of this component, called the Arbitrary Waveform Generator (AWG), in TLA^{+}. After running into limitations with TLA^{+} we developed TLA^{Coq} and transitioned the AWG model to our embedding. Doing so allowed us to prove properties which we could otherwise only partially verify by way of model checking. It also enabled us to adopt a development approach where we composed orthogonal refinements to construct a complete model. The compositional approach is crucial: different refinements reveal different aspects of the system, we need to be able to work with refinements individually or in combination. We believe even larger gains will appear as we apply these techniques to bigger systems.

2   Application: Arbitrary Waveform Generator (AWG)

The Arbitrary Waveform Generator (AWG) is a component of a high conse-quence digital system being developed at Sandia. The AWG is used for storing "patterns" in memory which are later played out as timed waveforms. While relatively simple, the AWG component is a real circuit that is being incorpo-rated into silicon in production. Its specification was developed as a collaboration between formal methods experts and domain engineers with an eye towards more broadly introducing certain formal methods techniques at Sandia. This process of collaboration proved helpful early on in clarifying details of the AWG's orig-inal requirements document that otherwise might have been missed. And, the act of formalizing the resulting specification revealed weak spots and avenues to improve our formal method techniques.

The AWG needs to support two main operations. The first is to read in a pattern from its input and store that pattern in its memory. The second is to, upon receiving a special signal, begin playing out the value in its memory. At any time the AWG can also be "reset" by passing in a certain signal, clearing its memory. Thus, the AWG can be conceptually thought of as a state machine (see Fig. 1).

This description of the AWG is much more abstract than what would suffice to describe an implementation. For example, it does not include the intermediate states that will be encountered as the pattern is played out in a timed manner or while initiating the machine with a new pattern. We will therefore need to *refine* this specification. But, it is worth emphasizing that a formalization of the specification at this level of abstraction also is insufficiently detailed for those building components which interact with the AWG. The protocols a component uses to communicate with other components are very relevant to the design of those other components. Nonetheless, it is still important to have conceptual models, and we believe formal models as well, which operate at these higher levels of abstraction. We must refine protocols in addition to state machines.

Thus we will refine our model to clarify that the pattern is played out as a sequence, requiring an internal memory. Additionally we need to refine our model to describe the channels on which it communicates (See Fig. 2). These two refinements are largely orthogonal, but must both be incorporated into a full implementation.

3   Expressing the AWG in TLA$^+$

In order to formalize the AWG system we turned to the Temporal Logic of Actions (TLA). TLA has desirable properties for formulating a system like the AWG. Foremost, TLA specifications are not sensitive to the rate of the passage of time, i.e. it is stuttering invariant [3]. This enables the development of formal TLA specification using a process of refining more abstract specifications into more concrete ones in much the same way we approach designs like the AWG informally [5]. TLA takes a logic-centric view: specifications and theorems about specifications are both just logical formulae and the statement that one specification refines another is interpreted simply as that the more refined specification implies the more abstract one, perhaps along some "refinement mapping" of their underlying state spaces [1]. Stuttering invariance implies that refinements can in many instances *slow down time* through the addition of intermediate states in the refined specification which are not observable in the more abstract one.

We took a refinement based approach to formalizing the AWG in TLA$^+$[1]. Our initial specification, therefore, only modeled some very basic properties of

---

[1] The full code is available at https://github.com/philipjf/AWG-AVOCS-2016. Note that while we have typeset TLA$^+$ in this paper the original source are in ASCII format.

$$Next \triangleq Initialize$$
$$\lor Reset$$
$$\lor Flush$$
$$\lor \exists p \in Pattern.Write(p)$$
$$\lor Run$$

$$Reset \triangleq ready' = FALSE$$
$$\land status' \in MemStatus$$
$$\land memory' \in Pattern$$
$$\land output' = NilPattern$$

$$Fairness \triangleq WF_{vars}(Initialize)$$

$$Spec \triangleq PowerOn \land \Box[Next]_{vars} \land Fairness$$

$$vars \triangleq << ready, status, memory, output >>$$

Fig. 3. Excerpt of basic model in TLA$^+$

$$THEOREM\ Spec \Rightarrow \Box TypeInvariant$$
$$CommandsEnabled \triangleq ENABLED\ Run$$
$$\land ENABLED\ Flush$$
$$\land \forall p \in Pattern.ENABLED\ Write(p)$$

$$THEOREM\ Spec \Rightarrow \Box CommandsEnabled$$
$$THEOREM\ Spec \Rightarrow \Box(ENABLED\ Reset)$$
$$THEOREM\ Spec \Rightarrow (ready = FALSE$$
$$\rightsquigarrow ready = TRUE)$$

Fig. 4. Properties of basic model in TLA$^+$

the AWG system. The model (Fig. 3) is parameterized by a set called **Pattern** which serves to abstract away the details of the patterns stored in memory. The specification is then described in the TLA style in terms of "events" which relate successive states of the system. Some desired properties of this specification are shown in Fig. 4.

One of the areas of missing details is in the handling of commands. In the basic model, Run, Flush, and Write(p) are treated as events. However, we know that they are actually commands which come as input to the system and might take multiple steps to handle. Therefore, our first refinement is to incorporate the more detailed notion of commands by adding additional variables to track the command being processed and additional events for processing the current command and receiving a new one.

In addition to the more detailed theory of commands, we must refine the playing of patterns. The AWG should not play patterns to the output all at once, but rather play them slowly. In order to handle this we can modify our original basic specification via a second refinement to store the memory not as a single element of the abstract set **Pattern** but rather as a finite sequence of elements from such an abstract set. Accordingly, we must add additional variables and events to perform mult-step playback.

3.1 Limitations of the TLA$^+$ Framework

At this point we have described a family of TLA$^+$ models, each describing a different aspect of the AWG. We have extended the Basic model in two different ways incorporating different aspects of the full system we care about. We have also stated, and model checked, a number of properties. We would therefore like

Section Model.

Variables hr hr' : Z.

Definition Init :=
    1 <= hr <= 12.

Definition Next :=
    hr' = hr mod 12 + 1.

End Model.

Definition Spec :=
    'Init '/\ [][Next].

Fig. 5. A model of a clock in TLA^{Coq}

Theorem hour_inv :
    valid (Spec '=> [] 'Init).
Proof.
    unfold Spec, Init, Next.
    apply tla_inv.
    (* Base case *)
    intuition.
    (* Inductive case *)
    intros.
    assert (0 <= x mod 12 < 12)
        by (apply Z.mod_pos_bound;
            intuition).
    intuition.
Qed.

Fig. 6. Proof of type invariant for the clock

to complete the picture by combining all the various aspects of the three models into a single complete model. We would also like to verify the various correctness theorems we have stated.

However, we encounter challenges in both these goals. Both the Command model and the Memory model were developed by extending the Basic model, but in doing so we had to restate essentially the entire model. It would be undesirable indeed to have to fully write out yet another model. Instead, we would like to simply be able to assert that our full specification is exactly the refinement of the Basic model which extends the Basic model in the way the Command model does and the way Memory model does.

We are able to use the TLA$^+$ model checker to check the theorems we have stated, but only by first instantiating the abstract set pattern with a concrete, finite, set. The model checker tells us that our theorems are true, but only for this concrete set. How can we be sure they hold for *any* instantiation of Pattern? Moreover, the model checker will claim that the properties hold, but it does not provide any sort of witness or reason as to why this is true. Instead, we gain confidence in correctness only relative to our confidence in the correctness of the model checker. While a TLA$^+$ proof system (TLAPS) [4] which might help rectify some of these issues has been partially developed it is incomplete and does not currently support temporal reasoning.

4   Expressing the AWG in TLA^{Coq}

We want to be able to prove properties about our models using inductive reasoning. Moreover, we want to support parametric reasoning — it should be possible for us to consider some aspects of a model as abstract parameters and still be able to prove properties about that model independent of their instantiation. Further, we want proof witnesses and a small trusted base so we do not have to depend on the correctness of complex pieces of machinery like model checkers. Moreover, we would like a framework which also has good support for "programming in the large" and building abstractions.

Interactive theorem provers based on type theory excel at precisely this point. By using a small core logic they separate the problems of finding proofs and interacting with the system with the problem of checking a proof already found. Systems like Coq and Isabelle [13] come equipped with powerful automated methods as well as tools for developing new domain specific automation, but kept segregated from the logic kernel.

However, unlike what we see with TLA$^+$, Coq's logic is not geared specifically toward expressing systems which evolve over time. While TLA is well suited to describing systems like the AWG, vanilla Coq is not.

TLA^{Coq} is an embedding of TLA into Coq. It allows us to take advantage of Coq's features which make scalable verification tractable while presenting an interface similar to TLA. Moreover, while Coq is a highly advanced tool requiring a great deal of time to master, one of our goals on the AWG project has been to support collaboration between subject matter experts and system designers with formal methods experts. As such, we have aimed to make the embedding relatively straightforward to use even for non-experts. For example, we can use our embedding to formalize a model of a simple clock akin to that considered by Lamport [8,9].

The Coq code in Fig. 5 provides a complete specification of the clock using our library. The `Init` and `Next` definitions inside the `Model` section describe the initial configuration and evolution of the state of the clock which we encode as a single integer `hr`. `Init` requires this variable have a value between one and twelve. `Next` relates the variable `hr` to the variable `hr'` (representing the next time) whenever `hr'` is equal to one plus the value of `hr` modded out by twelve. These definitions are simply predicates in Coq and so involve no temporal operators. However, the definition of `Spec` below them occurs within the embedded TLA. While exceedingly simple, the clock already demonstrates the main features we need to specify the AWG. In particular, we can prove properties in addition to stating them. For example, an important property we can prove about the clock is that the value of `hr` will always be between one and twelve. The proof in Fig. 6 of this property demonstrates a standard style of proofs in our system, where TLA specific reasoning is used to handle the temporal backbone of formulae but standard Coq tactics are used for the non-temporal leaves. The availability of such general mathematical theorems is one of the benefits of working with Coq.

Using TLA^{Coq} we formulated the specification of the AWG module much along the lines of the clock above. Following the original version in TLA we approached this through a series of modules corresponding to the Basic, Command, and Memory refinements. As in the original specification we took the set of patterns to be abstract. To do so, we constructed each specification as a module functor. The Basic module is parameterized by a module which provides a representation of patterns. Mostly the translation is direct, however a typed encoding of the state means that some invariants now hold automatically and do not require proofs. Further, we can state and prove the other properties from the TLA$^+$ version of the specification.

The Command module was constructed in much the same way. Using Coq's inductive type system made it easy to express the type of the control variable as well as the type of commands. The last module translated was the Memory module. A parameter stores the maximal length of the vector of patterns in memory. We then instantiate the Basic module with a representation in which Basic patterns correspond to sequences of patterns in the Memory module and show refinement with respect to this instantiation.

Now, we have constructed two modules in Coq which each refine our original Basic specification. We want a specification which incorporates the details from each. We would like to be able to do this in a general way: we should not have to fully describe the combined refinement at the same level of detail as the others, but rather simply declare it as the combination of the memory and command refinements.

One option, available to us from TLA$^+$, is to take the models' conjunction [2]. However, a complexity arises in that the two models have different types to represent their states and we need to be explicit about what states we are using. Using the product of the two state spaces would lead to a model, but not the one we intend. Specifically, we would have, for example, two separate variables encoding the status. Instead we construct the combined specification as the conjunction of the two refinements restricted to the case where they map to the same thing in Basic. This "pull-back" definition is relatively simple in TLA^{Coq} and is highly appealing from a scalability perspective.

5   Implementing TLA^{Coq}

There are a number of ways to use a meta-logic as rich as Coq to host another logic or language. Often when considering embedded languages we contrast so-called "shallow" and "deep" embeddings [11]. In a shallow embedding each construct of the target language is directly mapped to a construct of the meta-language. By contrast, in a deep embedding the target language constructs are considered as data representing syntax. Existing work includes examples of both deep and shallow embeddings of TLA into Coq. In [12] a shallow embedding of TLA in Coq was constructed to prove a meta result that all TLA specifications of a certain form are "machine closed." As such, TLA formulae are interpreted as predicates on infinite sequences of states.

```
Theorem tla_inv_gen :
    forall (A : Type) (Init : Predicate A) (Next : Action A)
    (F P : Expr A), (valid ('Init '/\ [][Next] '/\ F '=> P)) ->
        (forall s, eval P s -> Next (s 0) (s 1) -> eval P (s @ 1))
        -> valid ('Init '/\ [][Next] '/\ F '=> [] P).
```

Fig. 7. Induction rule

A deep approach to embedding a TLA like logic in Coq was used more recently as part of the VeriDrone project [10]. VeriDrone combines discrete digital components with continuous physical ones in a hybrid cyber-physical system, and so their logic combines continuous time with the discrete transition semantics of TLA. Following Lamport, they use a two step approach where their logical syntax corresponds to a full set of "RTLA" formulae of which the stuttering invariant TLA formulae are a subset.

We take a mostly deep embedding approach to the handling of TLA formulae in Coq. TLA expressions are encoded as an inductive datatype parameterized by the type of states. However, our design yields simpler proofs for safety properties by ensuring that all formulae are stuttering invariant by construction. Safety properties are demonstrated via the induction rule in Fig. 7 without having to think about stuttering steps. We then use Coq's notation feature to present convenient TLA syntax.

Following Lamport [7], TLA^{Coq} formulae are interpreted as predicates over infinite sequences of states called behaviors. Our implementation "compiles" formulae to Coq functions from behaviors to Coq's Prop type. From there, proofs are done in Coq as per usual, and in particular may use Coq's standard automation facilities.

6   Conclusions

Our use of Coq to embed a TLA-like language yielded several practical benefits. Using refinement for composition, we were able to construct a model of a critical system component in stages, adding detail as we went. The use of Coq allowed us to construct proofs of correctness properties interactively, combining automation where possible with human insight where necessary. Unlike approaches based on bespoke model checkers, Coq also lends a very high level of confidence to our proofs.

The designers and engineers involved in the specification and verification of the AWG component found the effort to be worthwhile. Using a TLA-style specification forced us to consider details about how the high-level design worked early on. Without it, we probably would not have considered those details until they were encountered by programmers or revealed in testing, making them harder to correct.

The use of interactively-developed proofs rather than automated model checking comes at a cost in terms of development time and required expertise. Improved automation within Coq would be helpful and we are planning future work in this area. One obvious path is to replicate the capabilities of the TLA$^+$ model checker within Coq. We might even be able to prove the correctness of the model checker within Coq itself.

Further work could involve connecting TLA^{Coq} with other Coq based verification approaches, with the goal of "full stack verification," where low level implementations are proven to correspond to our high level models. One can imagine a world in which design, development, and specification happen in tandem, such that implementations are fully verified and correct by construction.

Formalizing the high level descriptions of systems as we have done with TLA^{Coq} is an essential step in this effort.

Acknowledgement. Sandia National Laboratories is a multi-program laboratory managed and operated by Sandia Corporation, a wholly owned subsidiary of Lockheed Martin Corporation, for the U.S. Department of Energy's National Nuclear Security Administration (NNSA) under contract DE-AC04-94AL85000. This work was funded by NNSA's Advanced Simulation and Computing (ASC) Program.

References

1. Abadi, M., Lamport, L.: The existence of refinement mappings. Theoret. Comput. Sci. **82**(2), 253–284 (1991)
2. Abadi, M., Lamport, L.: Conjoining specifications. ACM Trans. Program. Lang. Syst. **17**(3), 507–535 (1995)
3. Abadi, M., Merz, S.: On TLA as a logic. In: Proceedings of the NATO Advanced Study Institute on Deductive Program Design, pp. 235–271 (1996)
4. Chaudhuri, K., Doligez, D., Lamport, L., Merz, S.: The TLA$^+$ proof system: building a heterogeneous verification platform. In: Cavalcanti, A., Deharbe, D., Gaudel, M.-C., Woodcock, J. (eds.) ICTAC 2010. LNCS, vol. 6255, pp. 44–44. Springer, Heidelberg (2010)
5. Cohen, E., Lamport, L.: Reduction in TLA. In: Sangiorgi, D., de Simone, R. (eds.) CONCUR 1998. LNCS, vol. 1466, pp. 317–331. Springer, Heidelberg (1998)
6. The Coq Development Team: The Coq proof assistant reference manual. LogiCal Project, Version 8.0 (2004)
7. Lamport, L.: The temporal logic of actions. ACM Trans. Program. Lang. Syst. **16**(3), 872–923 (1994)
8. Lamport, L.: Refinement in state-based formalisms. Technical report, DEC Systems Research Center (1996)
9. Lamport, L.: Specifying Systems: The TLA+ Language and Tools for Hardware and Software Engineers. Addison-Wesley Longman Publishing Co. Inc., Boston (2002)
10. Ricketts, D., Malecha, G., Alvarez, M.M., Gowda, V., Lerner, S. Towards verification of hybrid systems in a foundational proof assistant. In: MEMOCODE 2015, pp. 248–257. IEEE (2015)
11. Svenningsson, J., Axelsson, E.: Combining deep and shallow embedding for EDSL. In: Loidl, H.-W., Peña, R. (eds.) TFP 2012. LNCS, vol. 7829, pp. 21–36. Springer, Heidelberg (2013)
12. Wan, H., He, A., You, Z., Zhao, X.: Formal proof of a machine closed theorem in Coq. J. Appl. Math. **2014**, 8 (2014). Article ID 892832, Hindawi Publishing Corporation, Cairo
13. Wenzel, M.: The Isabelle/Isar Reference Manual (2012)
14. Yu, Y., Manolios, P., Lamport, L.: Model checking TLA$^+$ specifications. In: Pierre, L., Kropf, T. (eds.) CHARME 1999. LNCS, vol. 1703, pp. 54–66. Springer, Heidelberg (1999)

Application of Coloured Petri Nets in Modelling and Simulating a Railway Signalling System

Somsak Vanit-Anunchai(✉)

School of Telecommunication Engineering, Institute of Engineering,
Suranaree University of Technology, Muang, Nakhon Ratchasima, Thailand
somsav@sut.ac.th

Abstract. Formal validation of railway signalling systems normally involves three processes: creating models; simulation; and verifying the models' dynamic behavior against the specified properties. It is well-known that the third process often encounters the problem of state explosion. To achieve fully automated formal validation, researchers usually abstract away details of operating procedures and concentrate on route interlocking that prevents train collision and derailment. Thus we encounter a dilemma between fully automated validation of an incomplete model or partial, semi-automated validation of a complete model. We argue that formally modelling the complete model will be more valuable for the on-going projects of the State Railway of Thailand because they provide insights and can be used to train new signal engineers. This paper focuses on the complete Coloured Petri Net (CPN) model of a typical Thai railway signalling system: a double-line station with one passing loop. The CPN model has included train movements that can be simulated and graphically visualized. In particular we illustrate how the CPN diagrams capture nine properties: Route interlocking, Flank protection, Approach signal release, Aspect sequence, Approach lock, Back lock, Alternative overlap, Sectional route release and Quick route release. Lessons learnt from using CPN Tools to model and validate the railway signalling systems are also discussed.

Keywords: Interlocking tables · Route-based interlocking · Approach lock · Back lock · Visualization extension

1 Introduction

During the last 30 years many research groups have been working on the application of formal methods to railway signalling systems. A comprehensive review of the research in this area can be found in [5,6]. Although most researchers focus on formal verification and validation, this paper places emphasis on formal specification instead for two reasons. First, the motivation for using formal

This work is supported by the National Science and Technology Development Agency and National Research Council of Thailand.

© Springer International Publishing AG 2016
M.H. ter Beek et al. (Eds.): FMICS-AVoCS 2016, LNCS 9933, pp. 214–230, 2016.
DOI: 10.1007/978-3-319-45943-1_15

methods is to reduce costs and increase productivity. To achieve this, the tools must be used by signal engineers. However, it is likely that signal engineers will be unable to comprehend theorem provers or model checking algorithms, so that formal validation and verification processes should be hidden. On the other hand, the signal engineers are more interested in developing the requirement specification and simulating the critical scenarios. Thus, they require modelling and simulation tools that are easy to use and have high expressive modelling power. Second, to alleviate the state explosion problem, researchers usually abstract away a lot of the details of operating procedures and concentrate only on the route interlocking[1] that prevents train collision. However, besides route interlocking there are other vital safety operating procedures to which failure to comply could potentially lead to danger. It seems a choice between either fully automated validation of an incomplete model or simulation of a complete model. We argue that formal specification and simulation of the complete model are more valuable for the on-going projects of the State Railway of Thailand.

Related Work. One of the good candidates for the modelling of railway signalling systems is Petri nets. There have been many researchers using Petri Nets for modelling railway signalling systems e.g. [1,8,16] but they transform the Petri Net models into other tools in order to conduct simulation or verification. For example, Sun [16] transformed Coloured Petri Net (CPN) model to a B-machine model. Hagalisletto et al. [8] also transformed their CPN model into Maude [3]. The verification and validation of the railway interlocking challenge drew a lot attention from model checking researchers. A comparison study of applicability bounds when using NuSMV and SPIN was conducted in [7]. Their result showed that the verification of medium and large interlockings were still out of reach. To push the applicability bounds further, several techniques have been proposed. Winter [20] pursued a significant improvement in run-time and memory usage by optimizing variable and transition orderings. A pioneering work by Haxthausen [10] systematically compared modelling and verification approaches developed by two different research groups: DTU/Bremen [9,11] and Surrey/Swansea [12,13]. Both approaches were able to detect all injected errors. Haxthausen et al. [9] proposed to apply bounded model checking combined with inductive reasoning for verification and validation of interlocking systems. James et al. [13] suggested that the nature of railway systems involved events (e.g. train movement) and state-based reasoning (the interlocking). To combine event-based with state-based modelling, James et al. proposed to use CSP||B for the modelling language. Incidentally, we point out that Petri Nets are a tool that already combines event-based and state-based modelling. In [13] James et al. also suggested three abstraction techniques. First, they reduced the verification problem for any number of trains to that of a two-train scenario. Second, they decomposed a large scheme plan into a set of smaller ones such that the safety of all smaller scheme plans implied the safety of the original scheme plan. Third, they abstracted a scheme plan such that checking the abstract scheme plan was

---

[1] No conflicted route can be used at the same time by multiple trains.

enough to ensure that the required safety properties hold for the concrete plan. Although James et al. [13] assumed that the train's length was shorter than a track segment, in [12] they pushed further by allowing trains to span any number of track segments. They also showed that considering only two trains was sufficient to analyse the safety properties.

Previous Work. In 2009 we [17] used CPNs [14] and CPN Tools [2] to model and analyse the signalling system of a single track railway station. To build the model we needed two pieces of data: the signalling layout and the interlocking tables. The CPN model was divided into two parts according to the data. First, a CPN model that mimics the signalling layout and simulates the train movements was created. Second, a generic model of the interlocking tables coded the content of the interlocking table into ML functions which are called on arc inscriptions or in guards. Modelling interlocking tables of other railway stations was simply done by changing the content of the ML functions. These ML functions were automatically generated from the interlocking table using Extensible Stylesheet Language Transformations (XSLT). By exhaustively searching for the states where trains collide, we formally verified this CPN model [17]. Nevertheless [17] had two problems. Firstly, where we had many signalling devices working together, the CPN diagram became too complex. Secondly, although the system was safe, the signalman could give sequences of route setting instructions that led the train traffic into a deadlock. Using state space generation, our CPN model generated a lot of safe terminal markings that had no train collision but in which the train traffic was in a deadlock. This was inconvenient when investigating terminal markings. To eliminate the first problem, we modeled in [18] the signalling layout by encoding the geographic information into *tokens*, data values that can have an arbitrarily complex (user defined) data structure. When the signaling layout is modified or rebuilt, we simply change the initial state of the model without having to modify the model structure itself. To avoid the traffic deadlocks in the second problem, [19] used the automatic route setting and automatic route canceling functions. Although these two procedures are not in the interlocking tables, both are standard operating procedures normally conducted by signalmen.

Contributions. Despite having solved the two problems of [17] in [18] and [19], there are still another two fundamental problems. Firstly, encoding the geographic information into *tokens* in [18] made the CPN model too difficult to read. Our counterparts, State Railway of Thailand (SRT) signal engineers, prefer the CPN model that mimics the signalling layout and simulates the train movements. To solve this problem, we use the visualization extension[2] of CPN Tools to display the status of signalling equipment representing train movements and signal aspects. Secondly, because of abstraction and assumptions, none of our previous CPN models has included all properties in the interlocking table.

---

[2] Visualization Extension v.0.9 Developed By M. Westergaard and M. Assiri.

Thus we rebuild a complete model of a double-line station with one passing loop, named Don Si Non. Our new model has included all properties in the interlocking table.

The rest of this paper is organised as follows. Section 2 briefly explains the railway signalling principle and desired properties. Section 3 describes the interlocking table along with the CPN model. Section 4 discusses lesson learnt and perspective. Section 5 presents conclusions and outlines suggested future work.

2   Introduction to the Railway Signalling Principle and Desired Properties

2.1   Railway Signalling Principle

To avoid collision the railway is operated by dividing the railway lines into *sections* in which only one train is allowed at a time. A train is not allowed to enter the section if there are objects blocking the passage of the train. The State Railway of Thailand's regulation divides the *section* into two categories: between two stations called *block sections* and within the station area. The railway signalling layout comprises a collection of railway tracks and signalling equipment. The three important signalling devices are track circuits, points and signals. A track circuit is used to detect the presence of a train. A point (or switch or turnout) is a mechanical installation used to guide a train from one track to another. Signals are classified into two types: main signals (e.g. warner, home and starter signals) and auxiliary signals (e.g. call-on, shunting, junction indicators). The main signal displays *red* when the train is forbidden to enter the section. When it displays *yellow*, the driver has authority to move the train entering the section and prepare to stop at the next signal. The *green* display gives the driver authority to move the train into the section. For more detailed descriptions of each signalling devices see [19].

After specifying track layouts, the signalling apparatus shall be arranged such that conflicting train movements are not allowed. This arrangement is called "interlocking". A collection of track circuits along the reserved *section* is called a *"route"*. The interlocking table is a collection of the *"routes"* in a tabular form specifying the states and actions of all related signalling apparatus. We divide the interlocking tables into 4 parts: Route setting; Signal clearing; Approach locking; and Route locked and Approach locked releasing. The tables are ambiguous and difficult to understand because the railway signalling is a concurrent system with a lot of exceptional conditions. Nevertheless the interlocking tables have been the main document for designing the railway signalling systems for many years.

More details of the interlocking table will be discussed when we discuss the CPN model of the associated properties.

2.2   Desired Properties

According to SRT's requirements, the desired properties of the signalling systems are classified into nine categories:

Property (1) Route Interlocking. The entry signal shall not display a proceed aspect (green or yellow) unless the reserved route is proven safe. Hence there is no train collision or derailment.

Property (2) Flank Protection. This is an important class of fail safe requirement. The equipment within the surrounding area of the reserved route that may cause an accident shall be in the safe position even if no train is expected to pass such a signal or such points. Points should lay in such positions that they do not give immediate access to the route. Even though those flank points and derailers are not located on the required route, when the route is set, they shall be locked in the safe position until the route is released.

Property (3) Approach Signal Release. When the train diverges to the loop line, the turnout speed must be significantly less than the mainline speed otherwise the train may derail. The speed restriction is enforced by keeping the entry signal red until the train occupies the track in front of the entry signal for 60 s.

Property (4) Approach Lock. After a route is set, the points are locked, and the entry signal is cleared. If the track circuit in front of (approaching) the entry signal is occupied, then the signalman cannot cancel the route by the normal procedure. Approach locking prevents the train driver from the sudden change of signal aspect from green or yellow to red.

Property (5) Backlock. When two consecutive setting routes are "nonstraight through route", the exit route cannot be canceled if the entry route is not released.

Property (6) Aspect Sequence. The driver must see a yellow aspect before a red one otherwise he cannot stop the train at the red signal.

Property (7) Alternative Overlap. Overlap is a section beyond a stop signal that must be clear and points must be locked before the reserved route is set. It is possible that a route may have more than one possible overlap depending on the previous route locked with its point lying positions.

Property (8) Sectional Route Release. The route locking property enforces that all points along the route cannot be used by another train's movement until the train clears the last point. This is inconvenient for a large yard with more concurrent train movements. A relaxation called "Sectional Route Release (SRR)" is adopted. While the train passes each section, it releases the locking affecting that section so that the points cleared by the train can be reused by other train movements.

Property (9) Quick Route Release. For shunting or track work, the train may leave the platform track into the block and then return to the station. Before the incoming route can be set, the outgoing route has to be canceled. The cancelation usually involves a long delay which is inconvenient and inefficient. Instead of canceling, the outgoing route can be released earlier when the signalman attempts to set the return route.

3   The Coloured Petri Net Model

Formal methods are techniques based on mathematically defined syntax and semantics for the specification, development and verification of software and hardware systems. They remove ambiguities and are indispensable for checking correctness of high-integrity systems. Coloured Petri Net (CPN) [14, 15] is a formal method which is widely used to model and analyse complex concurrent and distributed systems. An important advantage of CPNs is its graphical notation with the abstract data types providing conciseness with a high level of expressive modelling power. Our CPN model has been created and maintained using CPN Tools [2], a software package for the creation, editing, simulation and state space/reachability analysis of CPNs. It supports the hierarchical construction of CPN models [15], using constructs called *substitution transitions*. These transitions hide the details of subnets and allow further nesting of substitution transitions. This allows a complex specification to be managed as a series of hierarchically related pages which are visualized in a hierarchy page, automatically generated.

Our railway signalling model comprises 19 pages, 46 places and 53 transitions. The station yard comprises 4 point machines, 16 main signals, 6 call-on signals, 25 track circuits and 34 routes. We assume that the train's length is shorter than a track segment and a train may span either one or two track segments. Our previous work [17–19] did not include the following properties: Approach signal release; Back lock; Alternative overlap; Sectional route release; and Quick route release. On the other hand, this paper includes all nine desired properties listed in Sect. 2.2. The railway signalling model comprises nine substitution transitions (represented by double-line rectangles in Fig. 1) arranged according to the typical operating sequence of a route, e.g. `ReleaseRoutes`; `SetRoutes`; `ClearSignals`; `MovingTrain`; `ApproachLocked`; `BackLock`; `ApproachLockReleased`; `RestoreSignals` and `CancelRoutes`. Due to the space limitation we choose to discuss only `SetRoutes`; `ClearSignals`; `ApproachLocked`; `BackLock`; and `ReleaseRoutes`. These in fact cover all necessary information in the interlocking table.

3.1   Global Declarations and Route's State

Figure 2 shows the Global Declarations that define the data structures associated with the model. The status of signalling apparatus is captured by four places (represented as ellipses): `Track` typed by `TIDxPOS`; `Signal` typed by `SIDxGYR`; `POINT` typed by `NRxPIDxLU`; and `Block` typed by `BIDxCNG`. The data types of signalling apparatus are a product of device identification and its status (lines 1–15 of Fig. 2).

State transitions (line 18 of Fig. 2) are defined according to the route's life cycle. After the signalman initiates a route command and the required points are lying and locked in the correct positions, the interlocking attempts to clear the signal. The `SigClearing` state is created. After the signal is cleared, the route's state changes to `SigCleared`. When the approach lock condition is

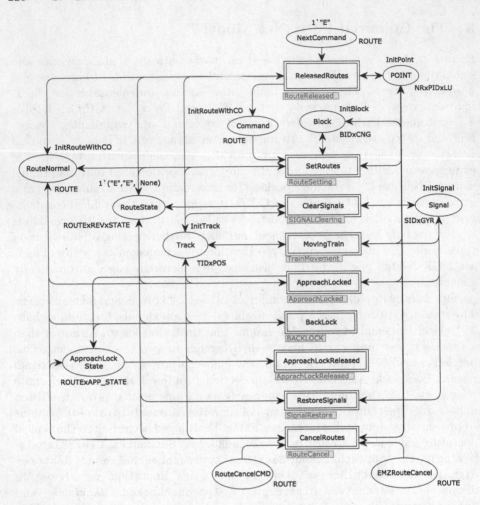

Fig. 1. The TOP_LEVEL page.

fulfilled, the route's state changes to SigLocked and puts a token into Place ApproachLockState in order to inhibit the cancel command. After the train passes the entry signal, the interlocking begins the route's normalization process (Normalizing state) and starts the sectional route release (SRR) process. When the normalization process ends, the state changes to RouteReleasing and waits for the last condition before releasing the route completely. Because the alternative overlap depends on another route that is currently used, we use a three-tuple (ROUTExREVxSTATE) to represent the route's state. "REV" stands for the reverse route. When there is no previous route set, we use "E" as dummy.

```
 1: (*————Point——————-*)-
 2: colset NR = with Normal | Reverse;
 3: colset PID = int with 99..115;
 4: colset LU = with LOCK | UNLOCK;
 5: colset NRxPIDxLU = product NR * PID * LU;
 6: (*————Track Circuits————-*)-
 7: colset TD = with noTrain | TrainCallOn | TrainUP | TrainDOWN
 8:                 | TrainSTOP | TrackFailed;
 9: colset TIDxPOS = product  STRING * TD;
10: (*————Signal——————*)-
11: colset GYR = with G | Y | R | CCC;
12: colset SIDxGYR = product STRING * GYR ;
13: (*————Block————-*)-
14: colset CNG = with COMING | NORMAL| GOING;
15: colset BIDxCNG = product STRING * CNG ;
16: (*————Route's State————*)-
17: colset ROUTE = STRING;
18: colset STATE = with SigClearing | SigCleared | SigLocked
19:      | BACKLOCKED | Normalizing | RouteReleasing | None;
20: colset APP_STATE = with APP_LOCKED | APP_LOCK_Releasing;
21: colset ROUTExREVxSTATE=  product ROUTE * ROUTE * STATE;
22: colset ROUTExAPP_STATE=  product ROUTE * APP_STATE;
```

Fig. 2. Global declarations.

3.2   Setting Routes

Substitution transition SetRoutes in Fig. 1 is linked to the second level CPN page named RouteSetting which plays the central role of route interlocking. As an example, Fig. 3(a) shows the station yard when routes 31(2) and 3-5(1M) are set consecutively. The content in the interlocking tables for route setting with its associated CPN diagram, RouteSetting, are shown in Fig. 3(b).

Column "DETECTS POINTS" shows that setting route 3-5(1M) to signal 31 requires the points 101 111 112 lying in the reverse position. If any points (101,111,112) are locked in normal position, the route 3-5(1M) cannot be set. If points 102 are locked in reverse position without route 31(2) being used, the route 3-5(1M) cannot be set. These conditions are specified in the guard function to prevent route 3-5(1M) from being set.

Column "Require Track Circuits" shows that the route 3-5(1M) requires track circuits 101AT, 101BT, 61T, 102AT to be cleared. In addition, for alternative overlap when points 102 are in reverse, it also requires track circuit 102BT to be cleared.

The symbol "=" in the interlocking table (Fig. 3(b)) means flank protection. The symbol "*U" means the train is going in the upward direction. For flank protection, route 3-5(1M) requires track circuits 2-72T, 2-4T to be cleared or occupied by the train going in the upward direction. In addition, in the case of alternative overlap, it requires track circuits 4-72T, 4-4T to be cleared or

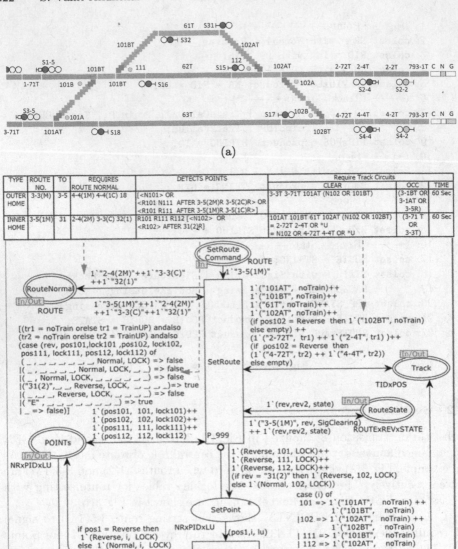

(a)

(b)

Fig. 3. (a) The station yard when routes 31(2) and 3-5(1M) are set consecutively. (b) The content in the interlocking tables for route setting with its associated CPN page named **RouteSetting**. (Color figure online)

occupied by the train moving in the upward direction. The track circuit requirements are modelled by the arc inscription connected to the place **Track** shown in Fig. 3(b).

Column "REQUIRES ROUTE NORMAL" lists the opposing routes that must not be currently in used (Normal). These opposing routes require the same lie of point positions and track circuits as 3-5(1M) does. The other conflicting routes are not listed in this column because they are already protected by the different setting of point positions. Place `RouteNormal` contains all normal routes. When 3-5(1M) is set, a token "3-5(1M)" is taken out from this place. This requirement is modelled by the arc inscription connected to the place `RouteNormal` shown in Fig. 3(b).

Transition `SetPOINTLock` sets and locks the associated points in the correct positions. In our previous CPN model [17–19], we moved and locked the points before checking all route setting conditions. We found that there were a lot of states in which the required points were locked in the conflict position because they were already used by other routes. For the purpose of formal verification, in order to alleviate the state explosion, we suggest that Transition `SetRoute` checks all conditions of route setting before moving and locking the points.

3.3   Clearing Signals

Substitution transition `ClearSignals` in Fig. 1 is linked to the second level CPN page named `SIGNALClearing`. As an example, Fig. 4 demonstrates the clearing of outer home signal 3-3 and warner 3-1 when the route's state is `SigClearing`. The warner 3-1 is simply a repeater of home 3-3. When 3-3 is red, 3-1 must be yellow. When 3-3 is yellow or green, 3-1 must be green. This properties are captured by Transitions `ChW_HY` and `ChW_HG`. To clear the outer home 3-3 from red to yellow there are two possible conditions. Firstly, "Approach signal release" is when the train occupies the berth track[3] for 60 s, modelled by

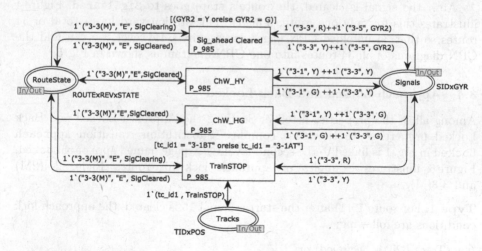

Fig. 4. An example of the CPN page: `SIGNALClearing` for route 3-3(M).

---

[3] The track circuit in front of the (approaching) home or starter signal.

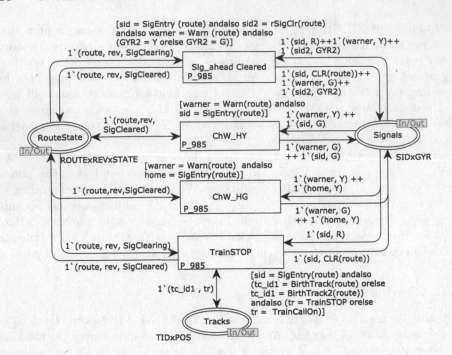

Fig. 5. The folded CPN page: `SIGNALClearing` for every route.

Transition `TrainSTOP`. Or secondly, the next inner home signal 3-5 is cleared (either yellow of green). These two conditions are listed in Column "Occ" and "Time" of Fig. 3(b).

After the signal is cleared, the route's state goes to `SigCleared`. Figure 4 illustrates this for only one route, 3-3(M). This station yard has a total of 34 routes so that 34 unfolded CPN pages are required. However, we can fold the CPN diagrams of all 34 routes into one CPN diagram as shown in Fig. 5.

3.4   Approach Locked and Back Locked

Among all of the properties listed in Sect. 2.2 the Approach Locked and Back Locked properties are the most complex. Substitution transition `Approach Locked` in Fig. 1 is linked to the second level CPN page named `ApproachLocked`. Figure 6 illustrates examples of approach lock for routes 15(1), 2-4(2M) and 3-3(M).

Type 1. For route 15(1) after the starter signal 15 is cleared, the approach lock conditions are following:

(1) (Track 62T is occupied) or;
(2) (Track 101BT is occupied) and (Point 111 is normal) or;
(3) (Track 1-71T is occupied) and (Point 111 and 101 are normal) and (Signal 1-5 is cleared) or;

(4) (Track 101AT is occupied) and (Point 111 is normal) and (Point 101 is reverse) or;

(5) (Track 3-71T is occupied) and (Point 111 is normal) and (Point 101 is reverse) and (Signal 3-5 is cleared)

These five conditions are captured by Transition Exit_SignalMainLine in Fig. 6.

Type 2. For route 2-4(2M) the approach lock occurs when the home signal 2-4 is cleared. Because this route diverges the train into 61T, the property "Approach signal release" is applied.

Type 3 and Type 4. For route 3-3(M) after the signal 3-3 is cleared, the approach lock conditions are following:

(1) Track 3-1AT or 3-1BT is occupied for 60 s (Type 3) or
(2) (Track 3-1AT or 3-1BT or 718-7T is occupied) and (the inner home 3-5 is cleared) (Type 4).

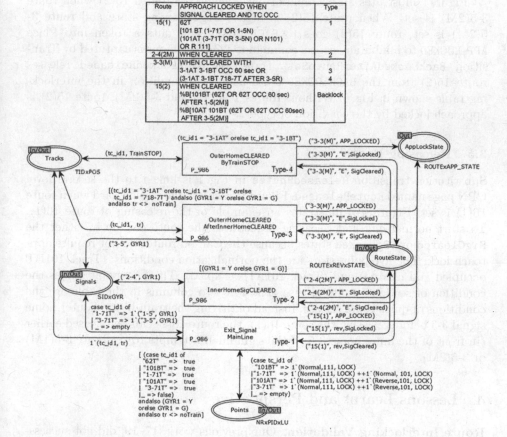

Route	APPROACH LOCKED WHEN SIGNAL CLEARED AND TC OCC	Type
15(1)	62T [101 BT (1-71T OR 1-5N) (101AT (3-71T OR 3-5N) OR N101] OR R 111]	1
2-4(2M)	WHEN CLEARED	2
3-3(M)	WHEN CLEARED WITH 3-1AT 3-1BT OCC 60 sec OR (3-1AT 3-1BT 718-7T AFTER 3-5R)	3 4
15(2)	WHEN CLEARED %B[101BT (62T OR 62T OCC 60 sec) AFTER 1-5(2M)] %B[10AT 101BT (62T OR 62T OCC 60sec) AFTER 3-5(2M)]	Backlock

Fig. 6. An examples of the CPN page: ApproachLocked for routes 15(1), 2-4(2M) and 3-3(M) and their associated contents from the interlocking table.

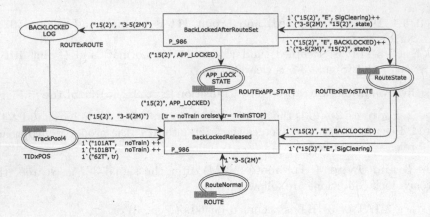

Fig. 7. The BACKLOCK page: route 15(2) is backlocked after route 3-5(2M) is set.

Figure 7 illustrates an example of backlocking for routes 15(2) when route 3-5(2M) is set. When route 15(2) is in the SigClearing state and route 3-5(2M) is set, route 15(2) goes to BACKLOCKED and puts a token into Place APP_LOCKED to inhibit any cancel command. This behaviour is captured by Transition BackLockedAfterRouteSet. Transition BackLockedReleased releases route 15(2) from the BACKLOCKED state using the condition in the interlocking table shown in Fig. 6. Without routes 1-5(2M) and 3-5(2M), route 15(2) is approach locked by the condition of type 2.

3.5 Releasing Route

Substitution transition ReleasedRoutes in Fig. 1 is linked to the second level CPN page named RouteReleased. Figure 8(a) shows the station yard when route 16(1) is set. Figure 8(b) illustrates an example of the releasing of route 16(1). To start normalizing and releasing procedures the route can be in either the SigCleared or SigLocked states because the Call-on routes do not require approach lock. The five-point stars are the normalization conditions: (Track 101BT occupied and cleared) and (Track 101AT occupied). The four-point star is the condition of sectional route release. The last two columns in the table are the conditions of quick route release. Instead of driving the train beyond outer home signal 3-3 before releasing the route 16(1), the route 16(1) can be released earlier (in front of the inner home 3-5) if the signalman attempts to set route 3-5(1M) or 3-5(2M).

4   Lessons Learnt and Perspective

Route Interlocking Validation. Our previous work [17–19] did not successfully validate the "Route Interlocking" property because we try to set any combination of non-conflicting routes at the same time. Of course, this leads to state

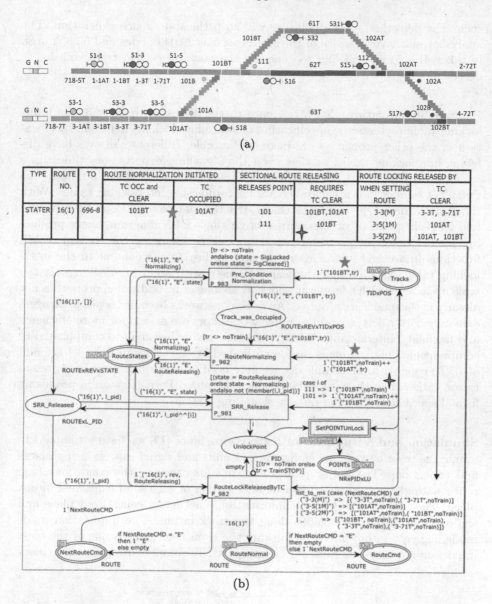

Fig. 8. (a) The station yard when route 16(1) is set. (b) An example of CPN model: RouteReleased for route 16(1) and its associated interlocking table.

explosion. However [4] suggested that to prove "global no-collision" properties it is enough to prove only "no two-train collision".

Thus we test the route interlocking by adding the CPN model of Fig. 9 in the TOP_LEVEL CPN page and adding an ML function call to conduct automatic route setting [19]. The stop option in the state space tool in CPN Tools is set such that detecting a train collision will stop the state space generation. The analysis result gives the size of the state space as 29,049 nodes and 53,853 arcs. It takes 41 h 5 min and 58 s to generate the state space. No train collision is detected.

Formal Specification. With reference to the discussion in Sect. 3, the interlocking table presents the specification of route interlocking well, but specification of the other properties are incomprehensible. Different railways have different interlocking tables so that even the signalling experts sometimes have trouble with the tables. With pattern matching and a graphical notation, the Petri Net formalism is a natural choice for formalising interlocking tables. With the abstract data type and hierarchical structure of Coloured Petri Nets, we can fold CPN diagrams of various routes into a single CPN diagram, hence producing a much more compact and generic model. By changing the content of ML functions in arc and guard inscriptions according to the content in the interlocking table, our CPN diagram can be reused with other interlockings. It can scale up to reuse with a larger interlocking so long as no additional properties not already in the model are required. As railway networks become larger; passengers demand shorter delays; and the railway operators are asking for more efficiency and flexibility, interlocking tables have progressively become too complicated to comprehend. This argument can be witnessed by the tables of Figs. 3(b), 6 and 8(b). To cope with the complexity we may need other formal forms of representation rather than the interlocking tables. Coloured Petri Nets are a promising formal specification for the railway signalling systems.

Simulation and Visualization Extension. Since [17] we have attempted to mimic the train movements along track circuits and signal aspects using places and transitions. The major problem is that for checking the conditions (e.g. route setting) we need all apparatus information of each kind contained in one place. Thus we have duplicated information: one in the centralized place and the other in distributed places along the track layout. The duplication made modelling very inconvenient. Mimicking the train movement is one of the most important requirements from our counterparts. To comply with this requirement

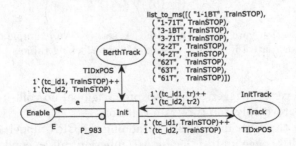

Fig. 9. Additional CPN diagram to the TOP_LEVEL page.

we adopt the recently developed Visualization Extension (VE). The VE code itself is written in JAVA but we call VE via ML functions in the Code Segments of transitions. This graphical visualization is useful when we conduct simulation for testing desired properties.

Modelling with Prioritized Transitions. Normally the interlocking controller works faster than train movements. To make the model compact we assign train movements a lower priority than interlocking controllers using prioritized transitions, hence avoiding much additional net structure required to implement the prioritization otherwise. Moreover we also adjust the order of precedence of each transition to make the model compact and work properly. It seems to be very useful but we discovered two drawbacks. Firstly, a slightly different order of precedence causes the model to behave differently. Secondly, the prioritized transitions cause a lower speed of state space generation (and simulation). Thus this feature should be used with care or should be avoided if possible.

5   Conclusion and Suggested Work

This paper presents the complete CPN model of a typical railway station of Thai railways. We illustrate how well our CPN diagrams capture all nine desired properties from the interlocking table. Route locking and flank protection properties are formally validated using state space analysis. Other properties have been simulated and visualised using a visualization extension. For illustrative purposes the paper focuses on the unfolded version of the model. Our counterparts use the folded version as the template applied to other stations in order to gain insights and train new engineers. In future we wish to investigate the formal modelling and analysis of the signalling systems for high speed trains.

Acknowledgments. This work is supported by Research Grant from the National Science and Technology Development Agency and National Research Council of Thailand. The author is thankful to anonymous reviewers and Dr. Guy E. Gallasch. Their constructive feedback has helped the author improve the quality of this paper. The author is also grateful to his colleagues from the State Railway of Thailand, Patama Sridaranop, Anan Phonimdang, Sommart Klinsukol, Ittipon Kansiri, Kittisak Siripen, Surapol eiamsaart and Navaporn Rittisuk.

References

1. Basten, T., Bol, R., Voorhoeve, M.: Simulating and analyzing railway interlockings in ExSpec. IEEE Parallel Distrib. Technol. Syst. Appl. **3**(3), 50–62 (1995)
2. CPN Tools. http://cpntools.org
3. Clavel, M., et al.: Maude Manual. http://maude.cs.uiuc.edu/
4. Fantechi, A.: Distributing the challenge of model checking interlocking control tables. In: Margaria, T., Steffen, B. (eds.) ISoLA 2012, Part II. LNCS, vol. 7610, pp. 276–289. Springer, Heidelberg (2012)

5. Fantechi, A.: Twenty-five years of formal methods and railways: what next? In: Counsell, S., Núñez, M. (eds.) SEFM 2013. LNCS, vol. 8368, pp. 167–183. Springer, Heidelberg (2014)
6. Fantechi, A., Fokkink, W., Morzenti, A.: Some trends in formal methods applications to railway signaling. In: Formal Methods for Industrial Critical Systems: A Survey of Applications, pp. 61–84 (2012)
7. Ferrari, A., Magnani, G., Grasso, D., Fantechi, A.: Model checking interlocking control tables. In: Schnieder, E., Tarnai, G. (eds.) FORMS/FORMAT - Formal Methods for Automation and Safety in Railway and Automotive Systems, pp. 107–115. Springer, Heidelberg (2010)
8. Hagalisletto, A.M., Bjørk, J., Yu, I.C., Enger, P.: Constructing and refining large-scale railway models represented by Petri nets. IEEE Trans. Syst. Man Cybern. Part C 37(4), 444–460 (2007)
9. Haxthausen, A.E., Peleska, J., Pinger, R.: Applied bounded model checking for interlocking system designs. In: Counsell, S., Núñez, M. (eds.) SEFM 2013. LNCS, vol. 8368, pp. 205–220. Springer, Heidelberg (2014)
10. Haxthausen, A.E., Nguyen, H.N., Roggenbach, M.: Comparing formal verification approaches of interlocking systems. In: Lecomte, T., Pinger, R., Romanovsky, A. (eds.) RSSRail 2016. LNCS, vol. 9707, pp. 160–177. Springer, Heidelberg (2016). doi:10.1007/978-3-319-33951-1_12
11. Hong, L.V., Haxthausen, A.E., Peleska, J.: Formal modeling and verification of interlocking systems featuring sequential release. In: Artho, C., Olveczky, P.C. (eds.) FTSCS 2014. Communications in Computer and Information Science, vol. 476, pp. 223–238. Springer, Heidelberg (2014)
12. James, P., Moller, F., Nguyen, H.N., Roggenbach, M., Schneider, S.A., Treharne, H.: On modelling and verifying railway interlockings: tracking train lengths. Sci. Comput. Program. 96, 315–336 (2014)
13. James, P., Moller, F., Nguyen, H.N., Roggenbach, M., Schneider, S.A., Treharne, H.: Techniques for modelling and verifying railway interlockings. STTT 16(6), 685–711 (2014)
14. Jensen, K., Kristensen, L.M.: Colored Petri nets: a graphical language for formal modeling and validation of concurrent systems. Commun. ACM 58(6), 61–70 (2015)
15. Jensen, K., Kristensen, L.M.: Coloured Petri Nets: Modelling and Validation of Concurrent Systems. Springer, Heidelberg (2009)
16. Sun, P.: Model based system engineering for safety of railway critical systems. Ph.D. thesis, Université Lille Nord de France, France, July 2015
17. Vanit-Anunchai, S.: Verification of railway interlocking tables using coloured Petri nets. In: The Tenth Workshop and Tutorial on Practical Use of Coloured Petri Nets and the CPN Tools, DAIMI PB 590, pp. 139–158. Department of Computer Science, University of Aarhus (2009)
18. Vanit-Anunchai, S.: Modelling railway interlocking tables using coloured Petri nets. In: Clarke, D., Agha, G. (eds.) COORDINATION 2010. LNCS, vol. 6116, pp. 137–151. Springer, Heidelberg (2010)
19. Vanit-Anunchai, S.: Experience using coloured Petri nets to model railway interlocking tables. In: Proceedings 2nd French Singaporean Workshop on Formal Methods and Applications, FSFMA 2014, Singapore, 13 May 2014, pp. 17–28 (2014)
20. Winter, K.: Optimising ordering strategies for symbolic model checking of railway interlockings. In: Margaria, T., Steffen, B. (eds.) ISoLA 2012, Part II. LNCS, vol. 7610, pp. 246–260. Springer, Heidelberg (2012)

Formal Techniques for a Data-Driven Certification of Advanced Railway Signalling Systems

Alessandro Fantechi[1,2](✉)

[1] DTU Compute, Lyngby, Denmark
alessandro.fantechi@unifi.it
[2] University of Florence - DINFO, Florence, Italy

Abstract. The technological evolution of railway signalling equipment promises significant increases in transport capacity, in operation regularity, in quality and safety of the service offered.

This evolution is based on the massive use of computer control units on board trains and on the ground, that aims at improving the performance of rail transport and maintaining high safety figures.

A brief review of possible innovation trends of signalling systems shows that they will be more and more based on the exchange of accurate and secure complex information, in order to ensure safe operation.

For this reason we want to advocate the adoption of a novel, data-driven safety certification approach, based on formal verification techniques, focusing on the desired attributes of the exchanged information. A discussion on this issue is presented, based on some initial observations of the needed concepts.

1 Introduction

The railway signalling sector has historically been reluctant to technological innovation compared to other markets, especially for those functions that have significant impacts on the safety of the railway.

The conservativeness of the domain and the strict safety requirements have indeed favoured, more than in other domains such as the automotive and avionic ones, the adoption of formal methods in the certification of software safety, when introducing computer-based control equipment. This because only formal methods can, in principle, promise the development of zero-defect software. This trend is witnessed by several success stories, too many to be exhaustively cited here, in both the main classes of railway signalling systems:

- *ATP/ATC (Automatic Train Protection/Control)* systems guarantee safe speed and braking control for trains, along the line, where the main safety criterion is to guarantee that two trains travelling at speed in the same direction stay a safe distance apart. The basic concept in ATP/ATC is the *braking curve*: safety is guaranteed if the speed is always below the line of the braking curve; should the speed be above the line, emergency braking is enforced.

© Springer International Publishing AG 2016
M.H. ter Beek et al. (Eds.): FMICS-AVoCS 2016, LNCS 9933, pp. 231–245, 2016.
DOI: 10.1007/978-3-319-45943-1_16

These systems accommodate both train distancing and protection of singular points of the line: for this purpose a line is divided in sections of which appropriate sensors detect occupancy by a train. Distancing is obtained by ensuring that at any moment the speed of the train is such that the train can be brought to a halt before entering in an occupied section, that is, the braking curve is at zero at the entrance of the occupied section; the value of allowed speed given by the braking cure depend on the number of free sections in front of the train. Protection of singular points of the line (e.g., an open level crossing) is obtained by setting the braking curve at zero at the protected point.   .

ATP/ATC systems are constituted by on-board components that receive information from wayside components. In the early computer-based systems of this kind, this communication is rather simple and occurs at specific points of the line. As a consequence, the safety enforcing algorithms were not excessively complex and were directly amenable to formal specification [22].

- *Interlocking systems* establish safe routes through the intricate layout of tracks and points. Interlocking systems have immediately called for a direct application of model checking, since their safety properties are quite directly expressed in temporal logic, and their specifications by means of control tables can be directly formalized [5,16,19,20]. Typical of these verification tasks is the combinatorial state space explosion problem, due to the high number of boolean variables involved: the first applications of model checking have therefore addressed portions of an interlocking system [2,13]; but even recent works [12,32] show that routine verification of interlocking designs for quite large stations is still a challenge for model checkers.

The conservativeness of the railway signalling sector has been recently broken by the latest technological evolution, which promises significant improvement on transport capacity, on the regularity of the service, on the very quality and safety of the offered service. Such evolution is increasingly based on the presence, on board trains and at ground, of processors that deal with more and more complex real-time information. This poses big challenges to the consolidated safety certification processes, and even make questionable, especially on the basis of the relatively high levels of density of faults (so-called *bugs*) experienced in software components [14], whether the necessary complexity of the software development of such systems, as well as of countermeasures put in place to make it safe, in the end could lead to the practical impossibility of getting these benefits.

In this work we will first do a brief review of some very innovative proposals that have been imagined and designed, involving both safe control of the movement of trains, and stations control equipments, that is, innovative ways to improve efficiency of rail transport. We show how they are based more and more, in order to ensure the safety of operation, on the availability and distribution of accurate and safe complex (*vital*) information, while the purely functional aspects maintain the traditional basic principles that are ultimately related to the physics of train movement.

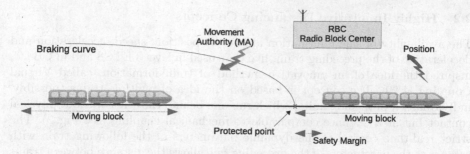

Fig. 1. Communication based moving block principle

Based on the observations made on the considered designs, we will try to draw some elements on how to systematically address the issue of safety certification of such complex systems, pointing where formal specification and verification techniques can be used at an advantage.

2 Innovation in Signalling Systems

2.1 "Communication Based" Distancing Systems

Emblematic of signalling systems innovation is the success of ERTMS/ETCS, which has assumed the role of a de facto standard for high-speed lines and for interoperability also outside Europe.

The widest form of adoption of this standard implements the level 2, which introduces radio communication between train and ground, but is based on the traditional *fixed block*, i.e. a segmentation of the track in sections, each of which sections containing at most one train; in this case the distance between successive trains, variable with speed, is measured as the number of free blocks that exist between two trains. The level 3 instead introduces the socalled *moving block*, in which trains are continuously monitored and maintained at braking distance between them, via a radio link to the control center. The moving block makes it possible to increase the line capacity and improves the flow of traffic and therefore energy efficiency.

The same concept – the moving block – underlies the most modern CBTC (Communication Based Train Control) systems, that offer the capacity of automatic driving in the subways, again controlling trains via a radio communication.

In these innovative distancing systems, the traditional, simple and easily observable binary consensus information exchanged between old days electro-mechanical devices is replaced by more complex information (e.g. Movement Authority - MA) continuously exchanged through advanced, mostly wireless, means of communication (see Fig. 1). In such systems, safety is guaranteed not only by the proper functioning of the equipment on the ground and on board the train, but also by the accuracy and integrity of information exchanged between the ground and on board, for example speed and position information produced on board the train and Movement Authority sent to the following train.

2.2   Highly Innovative Distancing Concepts

The availability of safe information about the position, speed, acceleration and deceleration of the preceding train, like that used in level 3 ETCS and in CBTC, inspired the idea of an innovative method of train formation, called Virtual Coupling [4,29]. The concept is based on the idea of multiple trains (possibly, individual self propelling units) which run one behind the other without physical contact but at a distance comparable to mechanical coupling (see Fig. 2). The strict real-time control of the dynamic parameters of the following train with respect to the parameters of the preceding one allows the distance between trains to be minimized, therefore allowing high flexibility, for example in the forwarding of different segments of a train to different destinations through the composition and decomposition during the run.

Although it still looks like a concept far from being implemented in reality, largely for the radical innovations needed in terms of safety rules, the concept inherits some of the principles of car platooning [1], that is being experimented in the automotive domain, and is already the object of an industrial patent [24]. Virtual Coupling is one of the challenges addressed in the Shift2Rail Joint Undertaking Initiative, and well represents the limits to which the technologies upon which ETCS is based can be pushed in a next future.

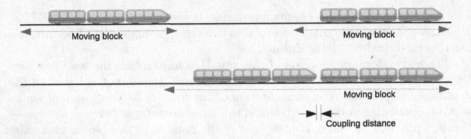

Fig. 2. The Virtual Coupling concept

2.3   Distributed Interlocking Systems

Current computer-based interlocking systems usually have a centralized design, with all logic residing in a single computer. Larger stations are sometimes partitioned in (still quite-large) areas, each governed by a subsystem of the whole interlocking. On the other end, a general trend in the different application domains of the so-called Cyber-Physical Systems is instead to attack complexity by means of distributed intelligence, that is, a plurality of computational elements each dedicated to a specific portion of the physical system to be monitored, controlled and commanded.

Following this trend, a fine-grained distribution of the interlocking logic over all processors deployed at the sensors and actuators along the track layout, i.e. within the track circuits, point machines, signals, etc. has been proposed [10,11, 15,17]. There are a number of advantages that such a fine-grained distributed can produce, such as (a) easier deployment and maintenance, (b) copper-free communication if wireless links are adopted, (c) vendor lock-in avoidance by means of an open, standard interlocking protocol stack. However, a shift to such fine-grained, distributed interlocking will probably not be implemented in practice in the next 10 years, although one industrial patent already has appeared for a similar concept [23], and another patent [31] even shifts the distribution of the interlocking logic in a CBTC system to on-board computers and direct train-to-train communication.

In a system like this every physical track element is equipped with a tiny computer, who knows the routes that interest the associated element, and receives and interprets route booking, release, and cancellation requests, dialoguing with the computer of adjacent elements. The overall safety of a plant of this kind can only be achieved by ensuring that the information on the routes reserved for incoming trains are properly shared in a consistent way by all distributed processors associated to the concerned elements.

2.4   Safety Paradigm Shift

The trend that is common to the signalling systems sketched in the previous sections is that trains are allowed to move within a *safety envelope* that is dynamically moving as well in front of the train. In the case of ATP/ATC systems the envelope is mainly related to the distance from the preceding trains; in the case of interlocking system the envelope is related to the reservation of a *route* for the train and therefore to the occupancy of tracks and to the position of points in front of the track. Capacity (intended as the number of trains that can use the same track one after the other in a given time interval) is higher the smaller is the safety envelope; the need for increasing track capacity asks for a reduction of the size of the envelope, but the minimal safe size of the envelope depends critically on speed (and hence also maximal capacity depends on speed) or on route reservation information.

In the quest for capacity, the concept of dynamic safety envelope can be pushed to make dynamic all the static safety constraints that are traditional in railways. For example, the concept of route that must be set free in front of a train and gives its movement envelope: routes are currently predetermined in terms of a sequence of track elements that need to be free, and points that need to be correctly positioned in order to reserve the route for a train. But routes could be dynamically generated in front of the train depending on the status of next track sections and points, allowing for last minute choice according to optimization strategies. Even, local (on board) choices based on the knowledge on the position and time of the next scheduled stop and on the position and speed of possibly conflicting trains may be envisaged, introducing the need of a correct balance between autonomy of choice and safety, on one side, and global optimization, on the other.

Moreover, the signalling systems sketched in the previous sections are clear examples of *systems of systems*, that is, are composed by subsystems of different technology, of different deployment (board/ground) - and hence belonging to different stakeholders - communicating through different media and protocols. In this situation, certification of the overall safety is really a complex task, for which novel paradigms need to be adopted in order to maintain certification costs under acceptable limits without mining safety.

Usually, safety assessment, according to CENELEC guidelines[1], is done by apportioning the safety requirements to the subsystems, following a hierarchical decomposition. One of the main instruments used in this apportionment is the definition of Safety Integrity Level (SIL), that assigns the maximal SIL to the components (be them hardware or software) whose malfunctioning directly affects the overall safety. The idea is that the certification efforts are concentrated on the highest SIL components, in order to contain costs. This process is however difficult, since most components are somehow involved in critical functions, hence it comes out that most, if not all, the components are assigned the highest SIL, with consequent increase in development and certification costs.

From the description of the signalling systems sketched in the previous section, it is evident that their operational reliability and safety is based on the availability of correct critical (often called *vital*) information describing the safety envelope parameters, to be exchanged between, or to be processed by, the processing units. We advocate therefore the adoption of a *data-driven* certification process, which focuses on the flow of the vital information among and inside (hardware and software) components.

Let us look at Fig. 1: the only safety requirement that we have to satisfy is that the MA transmitted to the second train correctly depends on the actual position of the preceding train (let us for the moment forget that MA is processed by the second train's onboard computer to enforce the braking if needed, and hence also this processing may contribute to unsafety). Hence, this is the only goal that the safety certification should have: Movement Authority depends in a certified way on the position of the preceding train. This simple statement implies however a huge amount of work on the components of the system, and is our belief that the most cost-effective way is to concentrate this effort on the flow of information exchanges and processing.

A similar approach is the one reported in [8] to address security issues by focusing on the critical data flow in complex systems: the example given in that paper is the detailed data flow of MA determination in a CBTC system. That approach is focused however only on security violations brought by possible attackers. It is our belief that such approach extends to other possible safety violations.

3   Integrity and Consistency of Vital Information

In reference to Fig. 1, let us detail the different aspects that are required by the example requirement that the MA correctly depends on the actual position of the preceding train.

---

[1] CENELEC EN 50126, 50128, 50129, 50159 is a series of documents regarding the safety of railway control and protection systems.

First, the measure of position and speed of a train has to be accurate, that is, precise.

A value of a measure of a physical quantity (either sensed or computed) can be said *accurate* if it remains within an admitted interval w.r.t. the actual value of the measured quantity, notwithstanding sensors and computing algorithms introduce systematic and random errors.

The accuracy of a measurement can be ensured by a number of widely consolidated techniques, starting from the quality itself of the sensors, to the replication of the sensors with appropriate voting algorithms, or to the composition of data from different sensors via data fusion algorithms, filtering and estimation. For example, in ERTMS level 2, there are independent ways of capturing the position of a train: track circuits that give a coarse grain position information, balises give exact position information in specific points of the line, on board odometry gives information, possibly subject to drift, on distance travelled, GPS receivers give also position information for trains outside tunnels. Data fusion algorithms are needed to get the best possible accuracy out of this information.

Numerical Analysis techniques are used to study the formation and accumulation of errors in processing.

We are not addressing accuracy in this context anymore, although it is a complex problem deserving a great deal of attention, and that introduces a further complexity dimension in the deployed software. We therefore are assuming that suitable accuracy is formally guaranteed to be achieved from every sensor reading and in every further numerical processing.

Second, the transmission of position and speed of a train to the RBC, its processing to deduce the Movement Authority, as well as the transmission of the latter to the following train, have not to violate the *integrity* of such information, that is, shall not corrupt it.

Third, the value of the position of a train stored in the on-board computer and that stored in the RBC have to coincide, that is, *consistency* should be guaranteed.

These attributes, to be obtained by techniques discussed in the next sections, can be defined more precisely:

- *Integrity* of a piece of information is satisfied if the information has not been corrupted by (hardware or software) faults occurred to the system that produces or stores it, or to the communication system that transmits it.

  Note that this integrity notion is closely linked to the levels of integrity known as SIL, which rather refer to the characteristics of robustness required for the processing systems: a component with a higher SIL is capable of producing information of higher (in the probabilistic sense) integrity.

- *Consistency* of a piece of information replicated in more storing elements is satisfied when the replicas have the same value (or values within given accuracy bounds) at the same time in all the storing elements. Notice that this definition includes the notion of *timeliness* of replicated information, that is the absence of cases in which at a given time two stored replicas of the same information (e.g. the status - free or reserved - of a route) refer actually to different time instants due to delays in the system.

4 Demonstrating Safety

As mentioned above, demonstrating the safety of a system requires to prove integrity and consistency of any vital information. Where this is not the case, countermeasures should be taken for the system to restore the integrity and consistency in a time compatible with the safety requirements established for the system, or to bring the system into a fail-safe state in case of detection of any violation. In fact, as usual, safety is composed by two distinct contributions: the ability of the system to work as intended, hence respecting the safety margins, and its ability to detect possible violations in time to bring the system to a fail state, which in the case of railways, means bringing trains to halt.

4.1 Data-Driven Safety Design Techniques

A number of consolidated fault-tolerance and fault-avoidance techniques and measures can be exploited to ensure the integrity and consistency of vital information: in the following we give a list (by no means exhaustive) of the main ones, taking care to distinguish the design techniques aiming at improving integrity or consistency, from those aimed at detecting their violations (to bring the system in a fail-safe state).

Data integrity can be threatened by different causes that can be classified as:

- random, typically hardware, failures;
- systematic hardware failures;
- communication failures;
- systematic software failures (software bugs);
- intentional attacks by intruders or saboteurs, especially when the data is communicated through an open transmission medium.

Consolidated techniques can be used to protect from hardware failures: in the case of hardware random failures, the usual fault tolerance techniques based on redundancy, also in the form of information coding, can be adopted for the consolidation of the integrity of the concerned vital information.

Analogously, redundancy or information coding can be adopted for detecting errors for fail safety.

Commonly used techniques for qualitative and quantitative assessment of reliability and safety, such as Fault Tree Analysis, FMEA, Markovian methods, etc.) can be used for the assessment of integrity of each information.

Systematic hardware failures can usually be traced to poor design or unanticipated operational conditions; using best practices and thorough testing under real operational conditions can reduce considerably the emergence of such a category of failures. Note that we tend to consider those failures due to problems in the design of complex programmable hardware components (such as FPGAs) as belonging to the class of software failures.

Each of the mentioned techniques increases the design costs; an appropriate combination (as indicated by EN50126 and 50129 guidelines) should be applied to all hardware components on which vital information depends, or in which it is stored, processed or through which it flows, but not necessarily to those that provably have no impact on the vital information flow.

One other typical example of random failures are communication failures due to noise and interference: safe transmission is typically obtained in this case by sophisticated error detection information coding, and retry in case of error detection: consecutive unsuccessful retries over a certain number force a fail-safe permanent failure detection. This basic technique has been exploited in a more elaborate fashion in the *Safety Layer* of the ERTMS Euroradio protocol [9]. Similar protocols based on a safety layer (according to the CENELEC standard EN50159) should be used for the exchanged vital information.

4.2 Software Faults

Among the fault categories cited above, software faults are of an increasing concern due to the exponential increase of the size and complexity of software embedded in signalling equipments [14].

In the railway sector, for what concerns software faults (which are deterministic and not random ones), reference has to be made to the CENELEC EN50128: 2011 guidelines that mandates the techniques to be used depending on the required SIL. For example, the application of model-based design techniques and formal methods are considered among the most effective measures to design (hopefully) zero-defect software, while software diversity is also considered to protect against software failures. Defensive programming, where redundant checks are seeded in the code to detect anomalous control flow, data flow or data values at run-time, is adopted to bring the system in a fail-safe state in the case of a detected failure.

These techniques are mandated by the guidelines for the software components of the highest SIL levels. In our view, integrity is an attribute of the data, rather than of the software components, hence it will be important to focus on the vital data processing.

If we look back to the safety envelope concept in the envisaged advanced signalling systems, we can note that at any time, the vital information that give the safety information parameters is distributed and/or replicated over a number of components, both on board trains and wayside. If we look in detail to the functionality of such components, we can see that the processing of vital information is carried by quite simple algorithms (e.g. calculation of the distance to the preceding train, or reservation of a route on the basis of a mutual exclusion algorithm). That is, the safety-related functions implemented in each components may quite easily undergo a formal verification. More precisely, we can summarize the steps of the needed safety verification process as follows:

– For each software component, focus on the vital information, by conducting an analysis of the steps that the data undergoes during its preparation, using a *data-flow analysis* [21] of the code responsible for handling such data. This analysis has the role of confining the most expensive techniques (such as formal verification) to those parts of the software that effectively affect vital information integrity. The application of these techniques can define the effective integrity level of a software component, although referring to only those data paths through which vital data flows.

- Code verification (by static analysis or formal verification) can use *program slicing* techniques [30] to focus on the essential properties to be verified. We can assume that, for the observations previously done, the relevant data paths can be fully formally verified not to violate integrity.
- When considering instead the flow between different software objects, we can resort to integrity policies [3, 28] that have been proposed in the past as a systematic approach to avoid that high integrity data flows through lower integrity components, either by statically checking the data flow, or by runtime checking of interactions between software objects.
- The consistency of replicated information in the distributed components, possibly subject to failures, has been the object of study of specific fault tolerant distributed algorithms, such as Distributed Consensus [7] or Byzantine Agreement [18] algorithms.

  These algorithms are designed to ensure consistency, defined as the combination of the two aspects of *validity* (in each not faulty distributed item the information is valid, that is, not corrupted, during the execution of the algorithm) and *agreement* (all replicas of the information on non faulty items coincide - or are all in the same accuracy range).

  One critical aspect of distribution is that clocks on separate processor may drift, so that the timeliness of information is at stake. The distributed consistency algorithms usually take care of this: since they require at least a round of coordination between the distributed items, at the round termination they are synchronized on the exchanged value and its global timestamp, possibly by recurring to specific clock synchronization algorithms.

  Typically these algorithms can be formally proved to ensure consistency properties on the basis of assumptions on the maximum number of admitted faulty items, and on specific properties of the communication media.

  These algorithms actually constitute a *consistency layer* on top of the *safety layer* discussed in Sect. 4.1.
- Each distributed component must be formally proved to comply to the distributed consistency algorithm when receiving/transmitting the local values of vital information.

A further challenging aspect related to the integrity of exchanged vital data is *security*, that is the absence of intrusion by a third party to infringe the privacy of the information or fraudulently take control of the functions of a system. This becomes increasingly important as the communication is based on open protocols at some level (internet, wireless, ...): since there is the trend to keep communication costs to an acceptable level by recurring at open protocols and media, it is believed that this aspect is by far the greatest concern for the deployment of the signalling systems whose safety is based on communication, in which security has a direct impact on the integrity of vital information.

The CENELEC standard EN50159, as well as recent developments in security and encryption techniques, attempt to mitigate this concern: the so called *cyber-physical security* research area, addressing other domains both in transportation and in other pervasive computing applications, has produced also results for the railway signalling domain; for example the security of the ERTMS train to trackside protocols has been formally analysed using the ProVerif tool in [25].

5 Quantitative Dependability Assessment

We can note that the notions of accuracy, integrity and consistency can be given also in probabilistic terms, that is, we can attempt to estimate the probability that at a given time a vital information is accurate, has not been corrupted, and its replicas are consistent.

To turn this in an overall probabilistic assessment of the safety of the system, the data-driven approach imposes that a suitable combined application of those techniques can produce for each component interested to the flow of vital information an evaluation of how the said attributes propagate through the component itself.

That is, such a process should provide certified components coming with accuracy, integrity and consistency figures for the produced information, expressed as a function of expected attributes of vital input information, if any. According to the data flow among components, the attributes of interest are then obtained by functional composition of all those given figures.

For example, fully formally verified software components typically propagate identically such probabilities from the input parameters to the output information due to the fact that they do not introduce any other violation. A communication protocol that introduces a non null probability of integrity violation that reduces of 5 % the integrity of the input data, and exchanges a vital datum of integrity probability 1 produces a vital datum of integrity 0.95.

In the considered systems, we can however notice how the emphasis on the safety of operation is increasingly counterbalanced by the need to ensure transport service availability and transport capacity.

Quantitative safety assessment is able to provide both the probability with which the system correctly works (that is, the reliability) and the probability that due to any problem the system has gone in a fail-safe state. A fail-safe state in the railway signalling domain typically ends up in non providing the service, since it correspond to some halted train, e.g. through the application of emergency braking or setting all signals to red, impacting therefore availability and capacity of the transport system.

The large number of critical computing components in a modern complex signalling system increases the number of cases in which the failure of one component can bring to a fail-safe halt of a system, causing the partial or full unavailability of transport service.

This effect is worsened by the number of communication links employed in these systems: typically, the safety layers of the communication protocols adopted in these systems exploit the principle of *positive* control to allow movement of trains: the train cannot move if no explicit Movement Authority has been received. Any serious transmission error (that is, persistent over a given period of time) eventually leads to a fail-safe state.

A more subtle phenomenon observed in radio-based train control, such as CBTC systems, is the indeterminate delay time in message transmission experienced when multiple trains require movement authorities and the available bandwith of the communication link is not sufficient to guarantee correct end-to-end transmission in due time. Retries tend to clog even more the link, with the fail-safe halt as ultimate consequence.

A careful evaluation of safety characteristics of a modern, complex, signalling system cannot therefore ignore an adequate analysis of availability attributes, in order to ensure an appropriate transport capacity, with the related operation cost effectiveness, through techniques of quantitative evaluation of these attributes [27]. Quantitative modelling of the adopted algorithms and protocols is therefore an important issue. As an example, we can refer to the experiences aimed at the quantitative evaluation of the ERTMS Euroradio protocol by means of a Petri Net model (see, e.g., [6,33]).

With regard to security, it is not simple to give a probabilistic measure of the contribution of security issues to the integrity of vital data: such a measure should be obtained on the basis of assumptions on the frequency of intrusion by third parties, as well as on the basis of the capacity of the security mechanisms to counter them. Sanders in [26] discusses some possible tools and methods for quantitative predictive assessment of security for large-scale systems.

Another area of difficult quantitative evaluation is the area of human interaction errors, which again can disrupt service through enforcement of a fail safe state by the control equipment. Statistical evidence of such problems should be collected in the operation of these advanced systems in order to include such evaluation in an overall quantitative evaluation of dependability.

6   Conclusions

In this paper we have outlined the basic principles that have to be considered when determining the safety of a complex signalling system in which the correct processing and transmission of vital information plays a vital role. In this regard, we have advocated the adoption of a data-driven certification approach, that takes into account the flow of vital information in the system, focusing the application of formal verification techniques on those parts of the system that have a major influence on the integrity and consistency of vital information.

It is our belief that such a shift will help to focus certification efforts on the actual threats to safety, lowering the certification costs, which form nowadays a major contribution to the cost of actual implementation of advanced signalling systems, if not even an effective barrier preventing their adoption.

We plan then to shape the basic principles sketched in this paper in a fully operational certification process, able to merge all the mentioned techniques in a single data-driven effort suitable to address the challenges of signalling systems of the next future.

Acknowledgements. This work is based on an invited presentation made at a workshop funded by the PART project of DTU Compute (Department of Applied Mathematics and Computer Science, Technical University of Denmark), and has been conducted while on leave from University of Florence, thanks to a grant of the Villum Foundation.

References

1. Bergenhem, C., Pettersson, H., Coelingh, E., Englund, C., Shladover, S., Tsugawa, S.: Overview of platooning systems. In: ITS World Congress, Vienna, 22–26 October 2012
2. Bernardeschi, C., Fantechi, A., Gnesi, S., Larosa, S., Mongardi, G., Romano, D.: A formal verification environment for railway signaling system design. Formal Methods Syst. Des. **12**(2), 139–161 (1998)
3. Biba, K.: Integrity Considerations for Secure Computer Systems. MITRE Co, Bedford (1977)
4. Bock, U., Bikker, G.: Design, development of a future freight train concept- "virtually coupled train formations". In: Schnieder, E., Becker, U. (eds.): 9th IFAC Symposium Control in Transportation Systems, 13–15 June, S. 410–415, Braunschweig (2000)
5. Bonacchi, A., Fantechi, A., Bacherini, S., Tempestini, M., Cipriani, L.: Validation of railway interlocking systems by formal verification, a case study. In: Counsell, S., Núñez, M. (eds.) SEFM 2013. LNCS, vol. 8368, pp. 237–252. Springer, Heidelberg (2014)
6. Carnevali, L., Flammini, F., Paolieri, M., Vicario, E.: Non-markovian performability evaluation of ERTMS ETCS level 3. In: Beltrán, M., Knottenbelt, W., Bradley, J. (eds.) EPEW 2015. LNCS, vol. 9272, pp. 47–62. Springer, Heidelberg (2015)
7. Chandra, T.D., Toueg, S.: Unreliable failure detectors for reliable distributed systems. J. ACM **43**(2), 225–267 (1996)
8. Chen, B., Schmittner, C., Ma, Z., Temple, W.G., Dong, X., Jones, D.L., Sanders, W.H.: Security analysis of urban railway systems: the need for a cyber-physical perspective. In: Koornneef, F., van Gulijk, C. (eds.) SAFECOMP Workshopps 2015. LNCS, vol. 9338, pp. 277–290. Springer, Heidelberg (2015)
9. Esposito, R., Lazzaro, A., Marmo, P., Sanseviero, A.: Formal verification of ERTMS Euroradio safety critical protocol. In: Proceedings 4th Symposium on Formal Methods for Railway Operation and Control Systems (FORMS 2003). L'Harmattan Hongrie, Budapest (2003)
10. Fantechi, A.: Distributing the challenge of model checking interlocking control tables. In: Margaria, T., Steffen, B. (eds.) ISoLA 2012, Part II. LNCS, vol. 7610, pp. 276–289. Springer, Heidelberg (2012)
11. Fantechi, A., Gnesi, S., Haxthausen, A., van de Pol, J., Roveri, M., Treharne, H.: SaRDIn - a safe reconfigurable distributed interlocking. In: WCRR 2016, Milano, May 2016
12. Ferrari, A., Magnani, G., Grasso, D., Fantechi, A.: Model checking interlocking control tables. In: Schnieder, E., Tarnai, G. (eds.) FORMS/FORMAT 2010, pp. 107–115. Springer, Heidelberg (2010)

13. Groote, J.F., van Vlijmen, S., Koorn, J.: The safety guaranteeing system at station Hoorn-Kersenboogerd. In: Logic Group Preprint Series 121. Utrecht University (1995)

14. Hase, K.R.: Open proof for railway safety software - a potential way-out of vendor lock-in advancing to standardization, transparency, and software security. In: 8th Symposium on Formal Methods for Automation and Safety in Railway and Automotive Systems (FORMS/FORMAT 2010), 2–3 December 2010, Braunschweig, Germany (2010)

15. Haxthausen, A., Peleska, J.: Formal development and verification of a distributed railway control system. IEEE Trans. Software Eng. **26**(8), 687–701 (2000)

16. Haxthausen, A.E., Peleska, J., Pinger, R.: Applied bounded model checking for interlocking system designs. In: Counsell, S., Núñez, M. (eds.) SEFM 2013. LNCS, vol. 8368, pp. 205–220. Springer, Heidelberg (2014)

17. Hei, X., Ma, W., Gao, J., Xie, G.: A concurrent scheduling model of distributed train control system. In: IEEE International Conference on Service Operations, Logistics, and Informatics (SOLI), pp. 478–483 (2011)

18. Lamport, L., Shostak, R., Pease, M.: The Byzantine general problem. ACM Trans. Program. Lang. Syst. **4**(3), 382–401 (1982)

19. James, P., Lawrence, A., Moller, F., Roggenbach, M., Seisenberger, M., Setzer, A., Kanso, K., Chadwick, S.: Verification of solid state interlocking programs. In: Counsell, S., Núñez, M. (eds.) SEFM 2013. LNCS, vol. 8368, pp. 253–268. Springer, Heidelberg (2014)

20. James, P., Moller, F., Nguyen, H.N., Roggenbach, M., Schneider, S., Treharne, H., Trumble, M., Williams, D.: Verification of scheme plans using CSP∥B. In: Counsell, S., Núñez, M. (eds.) SEFM 2013. LNCS, vol. 8368, pp. 189–204. Springer, Heidelberg (2014)

21. Kildall, G.A.: A unified approach to global program optimization. In: ACM SIGPLAN Symposium on Principles of Programming Languages (POPL), pp. 194–206 (1973)

22. DaSilva, C., Dehbonei, B., Mejia, F.: Formal specification in the development of industrial applications: subway speed control system. In: Proceedings 5th IFIP Conference on Formal Description Techniques for Distributed Systems and Communication Protocols (FORTE 1992), Perros-Guirec, pp. 199–213, North-Holland (1993)

23. Michaut, P.: Method for managing the circulation of vehicles on a railway network and related system. US patent 8820685 B2 (2014)

24. Ohmstede, H.: Method for reducing data in railway operation. US patent 7578485 (2009)

25. de Ruiter, J., Thomas, R.J., Chothia, T.: A formal security analysis of the ERTMS train to trackside protocols. In: Lecomte, T., Pinger, R., Romanovsky, A. (eds.) RSSRail 2016. LNCS, vol. 9707, pp. 53–68. Springer, Heidelberg (2016)

26. Sanders, W.H.: Quantitative security metrics: unattainable holy grail or a vital breakthrough within our reach? IEEE Secur. Priv. **12**(2), 67–69 (2014)

27. Schulz, O., Peleska, J.: Reliability analysis of safety-related communication architectures. In: Schoitsch, E. (ed.) SAFECOMP 2010. LNCS, vol. 6351, pp. 1–14. Springer, Heidelberg (2010)

28. Totel, E., Blanquart, J.-P., Deswarte, Y., Powell, D.: Supporting multiple levels of criticality, digest of papers. In: FTCS-28, The Twenty Eigth Annual International Symposium on Fault-Tolerant Computing, Munich, Germany, 23–25 June 1998, pp. 70–79. IEEE Computer Society (1998)

29. UIC: Virtually coupled trains. http://www.railway-energy.org/static/Virtually_coupled_trains_86.php
30. Weiser, M.: Program slicing. IEEE Trans. Software Eng. **10**(4), 352–357 (1984)
31. Whitwam, F., Kanner, A.: Control of automatic guided vehicles without wayside interlocking. US patent 20120323411 A1 (2012)
32. Winter, K., Robinson, N.J.: Modelling large railway interlockings and model checking small ones. In: Twenty-Sixth Australasian Computer Science Conference (ACSC 2003), pp. 309–316 (2003)
33. Zimmermann, A., Hommel, G.: Towards modeling and evaluation of ETCS real-time communication and operation. J. Syst. Softw. **77**(1), 47–54 (2005)

Author Index

Printed in the United States
By Bookmasters